Tax-efficient
Will Drafting

Tax-efficient Will Drafting

First Edition

LexisNexis®
Tolley

Members of the LexisNexis Group worldwide

United Kingdom	LexisNexis Butterworths, a Division of Reed Elsevier (UK) Ltd, Halsbury House, 35 Chancery Lane, London, WC2A 1EL, and London House, 20–22 East London Street, Edinburgh EH7 4BQ
Argentina	LexisNexis Argentina, Buenos Aires
Australia	LexisNexis Butterworths, Chatswood, New South Wales
Austria	LexisNexis Verlag ARD Orac GmbH & Co KG, Vienna
Benelux	LexisNexis Benelux, Amsterdam
Canada	LexisNexis Canada, Markham, Ontario
Chile	LexisNexis Chile Ltda, Santiago
China	LexisNexis China, Beijing and Shanghai
France	LexisNexis SA, Paris
Germany	LexisNexis Deutschland GmbH, Munster
Hong Kong	LexisNexis Hong Kong, Hong Kong
India	LexisNexis India, New Delhi
Italy	Giuffrè Editore, Milan
Japan	LexisNexis Japan, Tokyo
Malaysia	Malayan Law Journal Sdn Bhd, Kuala Lumpur
Mexico	LexisNexis Mexico, Mexico
New Zealand	LexisNexis NZ Ltd, Wellington
Poland	Wydawnictwo Prawnicze LexisNexis Sp, Warsaw
Singapore	LexisNexis Singapore, Singapore
South Africa	LexisNexis Butterworths, Durban
USA	LexisNexis, Dayton, Ohio

First published in 2007
© Reed Elsevier (UK) Ltd 2007
Published by LexisNexis Butterworths

A CIP Catalogue record for this book is available from the British Library.

ISBN for this volume
ISBN 978 0 7545 33061

Typeset by Columns Design Ltd, Reading, England
Printed in the United Kingdom by Polestar Wheatons Ltd
Visit LexisNexis Butterworths at www.lexisnexis.co.uk

About the authors

Stephen Arthur

Stephen Arthur, Barrister, LLB, CTA, TEP qualified as a solicitor in England in 1974, before joining the Chartered Institute of Taxation in 1975. From 1980 until 1998, he was lead tax partner with major London law firms and was then managing director of a Swiss trust company subsidiary of a major international bank. Stephen was called to the Bar in November 2002.

Stephen Arthur's practice encompasses UK and international taxation, trusts and offshore structures, private estate and corporate fiscal planning. He is an editor of the STEP Journal and was for 10 years, chairman of the European Branch of the Chartered Institute of Taxation.

Chris Jarman

Chris Jarman, TEP, was called to the Bar in 1976, and returned to practise at the Bar in June 2006 from Thirteen Old Square, Lincoln's Inn, after 20 years as a partner in one of London's leading solicitors' private client departments. In 28 years on the solicitors' side of the legal profession, Chris acquired wide-ranging expertise in both trust/succession law and tax law affecting private clients. His book, IHT Trusts 'Alignment': A Guide to the New Regime (Tolley 2006) was short-listed for the STEP Private Client Book of the Year Award 2007.

John Thurston

John Thurston, LL.B, TEP, solicitor is particularly interested in the law relating to wills, trusts, taxation, powers of attorney and elderly clients, and lectures on these topics frequently. He is the author of several titles,

including: "A Practitioner's Guide to Powers of Attorney"; "A Practition-
er's Guide to Trusts"; "A Practitioner's Guide to Inheritance Claims"; "A
Practitioner's Guide to Executorship and Administration" and "Estate
Planning for the Middle Income Client", all published by Tottel Publish-
ing. He is also a contributor to "Tolley's Administration of Trusts" and
"Tolley's Administration of Estates".

While every care has been taken to ensure the accuracy of this work, no responsibility for loss or damage occasioned to any person acting or refraining from action as a result of any statement in it can be accepted by the authors, editors or publishers.

Contents

Part A: Commentary

1   Introduction
Stephen Arthur

2   Will Planning
Stephen Arthur

Contents

3   Post-death reallocation of property devolving on death
Chris Jarman

Chapter 4.1 Trusts

John Thurston

Part B: Precedents

1   Will planning and testamentary trusts

Contents

2   Post-death reallocation of property devolving on death   329

Part C: Appendices

Preface

Stephen Arthur

When LexisNexis Butterworths first approached us in the early 2007 with the germ of an idea for this book, it did not take long for us to agree on the general format and content, and the division of labour between ourselves.

This book is written for the non-specialist professional, who is called upon to advise clients on the contents of Wills, and how to deal with the content of Wills after they become operative. If expert and specialist advisers can gain some crumbs of comfort from the contents of this book, we will only be pleased and pleasantly surprised. Hopefully, the level of detail included is sufficient to answer most questions, or at the very least, to show how problems can be approached, and where more specialist advice might be prudent.

In the interests of homogeneity, we have attempted to blend our disparate drafting styles so as to produce a coherent work. If we have failed to be wholly elegant in this respect, we hope that readers will look beyond that to the content alone.

The focus of the present Government, clearly indicated by the majority of stated targets noted in the HMRC Annual Report, and ignoring for the moment the Pre-Budget Statement of 9 October 2007, is to prevent tax avoidance and the 'unfair' use of the tax system (by those who can afford expensive advisers). With the exception of the 1970s, when the highest rate of income tax was 98% (or even, in one memorable year, in excess of 100% for some taxpayers), it has perhaps never been so true as now that governments of one particular colour invariably generate increased work for tax advisers. The complexity of the tax system in the UK seems always to increase, never to decrease. It will be interesting to see if the recently-announced proposals for the 'simplification' of CGT will survive Finance Bill 2008 in their present form. The (typically inadequately considered) proposed flat rate seems to be substantially off-target and to cause enormous 'collateral damage' if the intention was to close loopholes to stop perceived private equity fat cats from increasing their girth.

Our aim has been to try to cut through the maze of complex and confusing legislation and to present straightforward suggestions for solutions to many common fact permutations. We make no claims for particular erudition. This book is intended to be of practical use to advisers who need to give clients immediate practical and effective advice.

We accept full responsibility for any errors in the text.

Glossary

Publications

CG	=	HMRC's published Capital Gains Manual (so "CG12345" is paragraph 12345 in that manual)
IHTM	=	HMRC's published Inheritance Tax Manual (so "IHTM12345" is paragraph 12345 in that manual)
Law Society/ HMRC IHT correspondence	=	consolidated correspondence between the Law Society's Tax Law Committee and HMRC entitled "IHT and Trusts: Questions and Anomalies", available (published 3 October 2007) at http://www.lawsociety.org.uk/influencinglaw/ policyinresponse/ view=article.law?DOCUMENTID=363073
STEP/ HMRC children's trusts guidance	=	guidance dated 29 June 2007, agreed by HMRC entitled "Guidance on S71A, S71D and Accumulation and Maintenance Trusts", available (published 2 July 2007) at http://www.step.org/showarticle.pl?id=1893
STEP/ HMRC original IHT correspondence	=	consolidated correspondence between STEP/CIoT and HMRC entitled "Questions by STEP/CIoT and answers from HMRC to [sic] Schedule 20 Finance Act 2006 (revised April 2007)", available (published 10 May 2007; original version released November 2006) at http://www.step.org/showarticle.pl?id=1853
STEP/ HMRC pre-Budget IIPs correspondence	=	consolidated correspondence between STEP/CIoT and HMRC entitled "Finance Act 2006 Schedule 20: pre-existing interests in possession and related matters", available (published 11 June 2007) at http://www.step.org/showarticle.pl?id=1883

Statutes

AEA 1925	=	Administration of Estates Act 1925
FA	=	Finance Act
FOIA 2000	=	Freedom of Information Act 2000
I(PFD)A 1975	=	Inheritance (Provision for Family and Dependants) Act 1975
IHTA 1984	=	Inheritance Tax Act 1984
ITA 2007	=	Income Tax Act 2007
ITTOIA 2005	=	Income Tax (Trading and Other Income) Act 2005
TCGA 1992	=	Taxation of Chargeable Gains Act 1992

TLATA 1996	=	Trusts of Land and Appointment of Trustees Act 1996
TMA 1970	=	Taxes Management Act 1970

Terminology

A&M	=	Accumulation and maintenance
APR	=	Agricultural Property Relief
AIM	=	Alternative Investment Market
BMT	=	Bereaved Minor's Trust
BPR	=	Business Property Relief
CGT	=	Capital Gains Tax
CTT	=	Capital Transfer Tax
DPI	=	Disabled Person's Interest
GROB, GWR	=	Gift with reservation of benefit
HMRC	=	Her Majesty's Revenue and Customs
IHT	=	Inheritance Tax
IIP	=	Interest in Possession
IoV	=	Instrument of Variation (term used in HMRC Manuals)
IPDI	=	Immediate Post-death Interest
IVA	=	Individual Voluntary Arrangement
NRB	=	Nil-rate Band
Model will	=	The model draft will discussed in Chapter 3.2 (Precedent 1)
PET	=	Potentially Exempt Transfer
POA code	=	the POA legislation in FA 2004, Sch 15 as amended and statutory instruments made under it notably the Charge to Income Tax by Reference to Enjoyment of Property Previously Owned Regulations 2005 (SI 2005/724)
POA	=	Pre-owned Assets
SDLT	=	Stamp Duty Land Tax
TSI	=	Transitional Serial Interest

Part A

Commentary

Chapter 1.1

Inheritance tax in perspective

1.1.1   Capital transfer tax (CTT) (the precursor of inheritance tax (IHT)) was announced as effective from Budget Day 26 March 1974. No draft legislation was published until 15 November 1974. Estate planning advice simply could not be given during that eight month period until draft legislation was published. Even then, the proposals did not become law until the enactment of Finance Act 1975 (FA 1975). In the intervening period from 26 March 1974, from which time estate duty had been abolished, it was difficult, to say the least, to deal with payment of tax when obtaining probate.

1.1.2   At the time the UK was going through perhaps its first extensive bout of inflation, which has come to be reflected in what economic commentators call "boom and bust". For the first time for many years, property values were suddenly escalating, as were interest rates and inflation. The miners' strike had restricted the national economic output as a result of "the three-day week" imposed for all but essential workers in the autumn and winter of 1973. The importance of sterling in the global economy was being shaken for the first time due to rapid reduction in its purchasing power. A Labour Government had taken power and were promoting ideas about the imposition of a wealth tax, a new tax on development profits from land, and the imposition of a lifetime gifts tax. It was about that time that the then Chancellor of the Exchequer, Denis Healey, spoke, in the context of financially comfortable members of society, that he wanted to "squeeze the pips until they squeak". A limit on the purchase of foreign currency was imposed so that Britons holidaying outside the UK could take with them only the equivalent of £50 in foreign currency or travellers' cheques. Even allowing for the fact that £50 in 1974 could probably purchase 250 pints of beer, the limit was fairly Draconian.

1.1.3   When estate duty was abolished on 26 March 1974 the "exempt limit" was £15,000—a limit, which was replicated in the FA 1975 CTT legislation, as what is now known as the nil-rate band (NRB). At the time, a limit of £15,000 was sufficient to exempt from the charge to CTT perhaps 90% or more of residential properties in the UK. By way of example, a property in one particularly desirable residential street in London (known as The Boltons) would have sold in March 1974 for perhaps £45,000. The value today, in 2007, of that same property, is probably £7–8 million. That perhaps more than anything else demonstrates the tax creep imposed by the erosion of tax-exempt bands, which has given rise to the anguish of Middle England about payment of IHT. With newspaper articles claiming that the price of an average house in the UK is not far short of £200,000, the tax creep imposed by the erosion of the value of exempt tax bands puts the £300,000 NRB limit in stark perspective when compared with 1974.

1.1.4 Another provision which was carried over from estate duty into CTT was the fact that the top rate of tax was fixed at 75% on the "highest slice" of an estate.

1.1.5 An innovation introduced by FA 1975, which has now become an accepted part of professional life, and which indeed forms a substantial part of this book, was the introduction of post-death deeds of family arrangement. Nothing like this had ever existed prior to 1975 in terms of retrospective tax saving in relation to death duties.

1.1.6 Because of the spouse exemption available under CTT (which had not existed under the old estate duty, although an election could be made, when the surviving spouse inherited a life interest, to pay tax on the death of the first spouse rather than wait until the second death when asset values might be increased) it was to be expected that there would be a 10 to 15 year period before CTT started to contribute to the Treasury coffers to the same extent as estate duty. Just as that net contribution was starting to be felt in a positive way by the Treasury, there was a change of Government. That resulted in an complete reworking of the taxation of discretionary trusts in 1982, and the effective emasculation of the bite of CTT by FA 1986. That legislation rechristened CTT as IHT, as we know it today. Tax on lifetime gifts was effectively abandoned unless gifts were made within 10 years preceding death. PETs were invented. The generous reliefs available for business and agricultural property were also introduced, substantially extending the limited reliefs which had been available since the mid-1970s.

1.1.7 FA 1986 also introduced the principles of IHT in relation to gifts with a reservation of benefit. That legislation almost replicated the old estate duty provisions. Even today, the provisions dealing with gifts with reservation fit most uncomfortably within the general concepts and principles of IHT legislation. The pre-owned asset code introduced by FA 2004, effective from the following year, grafts further difficulties and complications on to the stock of legislation dealing with lifetime giving. In keeping with the introduction of CTT in 1974, the POA code was somewhat incoherent when first announced. Draft legislation was produced for consultation purposes, and was eventually substantially amended before implementation. Most iniquitous of all is the fact that the POA code has retrospective effect in relation to transactions which took place as long as 20 years before the imposition of the legislation. It was claimed that the POA legislation was introduced in order to deal with one specific anti-avoidance scheme (the debt scheme charged on a family home). In keeping with much other anti-avoidance legislation, it operates much more as a blunderbuss than a rapier, and has far wider consequences than perhaps even the legislators originally intended. The October 2007 Pre-Budget Review announcement of the proposal to allow transferable NRBs between spouses and civil partners is arguably a much simpler and more effective way of reducing the need for the home-loan scheme – but there is, of course, no suggestion that the POA legislation will now be repealed.

1.1.8   It is instructive to see that several other developed nations have, in recent years, completely abandoned taxes which impose death duties. To some individuals, it has always felt at least slightly immoral that hard earned savings from after tax income should suffer tax when asset ownership passes from an elder to a younger generation. To others, the substantial wealth of a few who had managed to accumulate capital over more than 100 years was held up as a "bad model" when compared with the general move towards equality and freedom in society in the 1960s. The imposition of CTT was one of the tax tools used to try to create greater equality within society.

1.1.9   Despite the erosion of effective exemptions and rate bands, for those who can afford expensive advisers in the field of estate planning, IHT is now regarded as being similar to the old estate duty, because, with good advice, payment of the tax can almost become optional. Is it ironic or simply coherent and consistent accident that the most tax-efficient and favoured will is to leave residue on trust for a surviving spouse-exactly the same estate planning advice which was given more than 30 years ago by estate duty practitioners? The difficulty always is, of course, that mortals are not in control of the timing of death. Substantial IHT liabilities can arise even in the best planned and advised families if deaths do not occur in the "right order".

1.1.10   The successive attacks by various Governments on trusts has, to some extent, been an antidote to the "optional" nature of IHT. The substantial restrictions to the tax savings possible with trusts for IHT and other tax purposes introduced by FA 2006 is at least the third substantial reworking of the taxation of trusts since 1974, without even taking account of the several attempts made in the same period to restrict tax benefits available from non-UK trusts. The benefit of giving estate planning advice, so that trust structures can be as flexible as possible, has never been more important, even if flexibility comes with a (usually small) tax cost. The thrust of the 2006 legislation, that young people should inherit assets between the ages of 18 and 25 if tax is to be saved, seems to many people to be at least one gesture too many and too far towards "yoof culture".

1.1.11   Despite the concerns of the newly rich and "middle England", whose families are facing IHT liabilities on death, IHT collectively seems to be a fairly small part of the annual contribution to Treasury coffers. It is difficult to find any specific reference to IHT in the HMRC annual report for 2005–06. Although the cost of collection is clearly falling (to just over 1% of total IHT collected – the cost is claimed to be 1·01p per £ collected) it is only income tax which is more expensive to collect, with a claimed collection cost of 1·27p per £ collected. However, income tax contributes £135 billion out of a total annual tax collected of £405 billion, ie almost exactly 33% of the total tax take. No figures are given for the precise contribution made to Treasury coffers by IHT. The figure is lost somewhere within the "other taxes and duties" amounting to £17 billion, ie IHT is some proportion of 4% of the total annual tax take. With stamp taxes contributing an identified £11 billion to the Treasury coffers at a claimed collection cost of barely one-fifth of the collection cost of IHT (stamp taxes collection costs were 0·2p for each £1 of tax collected) the comparative costs and collection yield of IHT should surely soon be brought under review in an economically sane society. However, only an optimist (or a depressed overworked adviser) would hope for a total abolition or radical simplification of IHT.

1.1.12 One of the most important methods of providing for effective estate planning advice across generations is to ensure that wills are drafted in a manner which is effective to minimise not only immediate liabilities to IHT, but also the occasions when IHT can arise within the family unit in the future. Although wills can be varied retrospectively by deeds of variation, for income tax and capital gains tax purposes often greater advantage could be obtained had the will been more tax-efficiently drafted in the first place. The purpose of this book is to show how that can best be done.

Chapter 2.1

Introduction to will drafting

Introduction

2.1.1   As this is essentially intended to be a practical book, some of the points made in this Chapter are entirely of practical, rather than of legal import.

2.1.2   Now that post-death variations of wills are commonly accepted, there is a school of thought which argues that the contents of a will are of less importance than used to be the case. However precise drafting is still absolutely necessary in order to avoid ambiguity. What is crucially important in order to obtain best advantage from the possibilities of making a post-death variation is that every taxpayer should have a valid will. If there is to be any post-death variation, the rules of intestacy which apply in the absence of any valid will made by the deceased will always be more restrictive and less flexible than is the case where there is a will, however simple the will may be.

2.1.3   It is important also not to forget that a will becomes a publicly available document, so that anyone who is interested in discovering details of family financial affairs may be able to obtain a copy of any will which has been proved for probate purposes. There may be occasions when this fact could be relevant to maintain family decorum. After all, that was one of the reasons why the doctrine of secret trusts came into being.

2.1.4   Finally, any professional who is consulted to draft a will and advise on estate and tax planning must get as many relevant facts as possible from the individuals who are about to make a will. This obvious point has to be made. The fact-finding mission should establish a complete list of all family assets and expectations, and the following should not be overlooked—

— the existence of life policies and whether they are written in trust

— any death in service benefit payable under or in connection with pension schemes

— the extent to which the surviving partner will 'need' capital assets, or whether they have or will have sufficient personal income from their own assets or pension income

— the nationality and domicile status of both partners

— the terms of any existing family trusts, and the extent to which the partners may already have reversionary interests in such trusts

— (if possible) the likelihood of either partner receiving a substantial inheritance from parents of in-laws or other relations, and whether it is possible to discuss such things with the elder generation in order to achieve the 'best' overall estate planning for the family.

Choice of executors

2.1.5 A testator usually has only three choices. These are—

— appointing exclusively family and friends;

— appointing exclusively professionals (such as lawyers and accountants);

— appointing a mixture of professionals and family and friends.

Each option has its advantages and disadvantages.

2.1.6 Where family and friends are appointed, a well drafted will should specifically give the executors power to employ whatever professionals they feel they need in order to help them do their job properly. It can often be a false economy for family and friends without administrative or professional training to try to deal with probate in the administration of an estate without professional help. However, friends and family will, by definition, be much closer to the needs and feelings of the immediate family of heirs. They may be able to deal much more flexibly than could professionals with questions of valuation and division of treasured collections, jewellery and house contents.

2.1.7 Where professionals are appointed as executors, either to act alone or in conjunction with family members, there will necessarily be greater formality. Professionals cannot afford to lose their reputations and put their careers at risk by taking short cuts for any one client. Professionals can sometimes be seen by family members as being aloof and unconnected with the immediate family of the deceased. The other side of this coin is that any professional appointed to act as an executor is likely to be wholly impartial. If there is any discord within the family, the professional will be at pains to try to deal with matters as quickly and efficiently as possible, simply in the interests of good business management. Generally speaking fees for probate work cannot be charged until work has been done and assets are available for distribution within an estate. The professional will therefore have a vested interest in dealing with matters quickly and efficiently because the sooner the work is done, the sooner his fee will be paid.

2.1.8 Another advantage of employing professionals, or appointing them to act as executors, is that professional advisers are usually alert to tax planning opportunities. They will have a network of contacts who may be required to draw up accounts or produce valuations which will be acceptable to HMRC. Ensuring that winding up an estate is dealt with promptly and efficiently is part of the grieving process for the surviving family.

2.1.9   Unless there are good reasons for appointing exclusively family and friends as executors, appointing a professional to act with members of the family can often provide a long term advantage, particularly where trusts are involved. Trusts are increasingly common as inflation far outstrips tax-exempt bands. It is prudent to appoint an informed professional as one of the trustees, in order to ensure that trust administration is properly dealt with. How many individuals without legal training are aware of the investment obligations imposed upon trustees by Trustee Act 2000, and the longer term, equitable obligations to maintain a fair balance between income and capital beneficiaries, where successive generations need to be catered for, under the terms of any trust?

Use of plain English

2.1.10   Wills must be drafted in plain English, so that no misunderstandings or ambiguities can arise. Tradition has it that this requires that wills be drafted without punctuation, in order to avoid possible arguments as to whether a comma means "but" or "and". There are a variety of different drafting techniques. Legal case history requires that some technical issues should ideally be addressed as part of will drafting. For example, what happens to estate income during the time it takes for probate to be obtained, and assets gathered under the control of the executors? Can the executors simply give the antique dining furniture to a legatee instead of paying a £20,000 cash legacy? What powers of investment will trustees have under the will? These technical matters can be set out in detail in the will, by way of "legal boiler-plate" clauses, or simply incorporated into a will by reference. STEP has produced and endorsed some standard terms and clauses which can usefully be incorporated into a will by reference. A copy of those current standard terms are set out in Appendix 1.

2.1.11   It is perfectly possible for a testator to purchase what are generally described as "will forms" from national stationers. The trouble with these latter forms is that individuals often complete the forms in a manner which is not entirely clear. It is well known apocryphally that weddings and funerals always bring out the best and worst traits in people's characters. Home drafted wills can give rein to individual's worst characteristics. Resolving the resultant family disputes and arguments from "amateur" wills has, over the years, provided many a lawyer with a comfortable fee income. Family disputes often seem to be based on a "dog in the manger" approach, where disappointed heirs may prefer to see the estate swallowed in legal fees rather than let other family members enjoy the benefit of family assets.

2.1.12 Another matter for consideration is whether executors appointed to deal with the probate of the will should also act as will trustees, where trusts are established, or whether there should be a separate body of trustees. Family circumstances and relationships will often dictate the answer.

2.1.13 Without wishing to oversell the legal profession, it is often the case that lay clients often underestimate the administration and effort required to deal with probate applications. What sometimes appears to be done with consummate ease by professionals is rather like watching a swan gliding across a pond: underneath the water webbed feet are, unseen, paddling furiously. By way of analogy, it is perfectly possible that anybody who is prepared to put in time and effort can safely service his own car. However, there comes a time when the effort involved in getting covered in oil and grease and lying on one's back on a cold concrete floor palls in favour of driving the car round to the nearest dealer and paying them money to complete the service. The dealer has all the appropriate tools and facilities and can complete the job in less than half the time. In the same way lawyers offices have "trained mechanics" who can deal quickly and efficiently with probate-related administrative correspondence.

Bequests to charity

2.1.14 Many testators choose to leave part of their assets for charitable purposes. It has become apparent in recent years that many charities have become somewhat aggressive in ensuring that they obtain their full and correct entitlement. By way of example, where a testator leaves specific legacies to family and friends, and then leaves all or part the residue of his estate to one or more named charity, it is not uncommon for the charity beneficiaries to challenge the level of executors' fees and expenses, in the hope that their challenge will result in a reduction in fees charged, and a corresponding increase in the amount available to the charity. If such challenges are to be avoided, testators should be advised to limit their charitable generosity to a fixed legacy, rather than a variable share in residue.

Jewellery and works of art

2.1.15 It is often prudent for testators not to list specific bequests of jewellery and works of art in a will, but to deal with such bequests in other ways. This is particularly the case if a testator is a collector or changes his assets on a regular basis, or if he is inclined to make lifetime gifts from his assets. Any lifetime changes in the ownership of such assets will require a new will or codicil to be made, if disappointments and uncertainties of description are to be avoided. In an ideal world, testators can use modern digital technology, available on every mobile telephone, to avoid difficulties of description. The simple expedient of taking photographs of appropriate items should often avoid dispute over descriptions.

2.1.16   The two most common ways in which such items are dealt with is for a testator to—

— leave a letter of wishes (not legally binding) addressed to his executors, giving requests/directions as to how the executors should dispose of treasured jewellery and works of art etc, or

— (in close and trusting families) to ensure in advance that beneficiaries are fully aware of the testator's wishes as to who will take which items.

Foreign assets

2.1.17   It is increasingly common for testators to own "second homes" in other jurisdictions. The laws which govern the freedom of disposition of estates may often be more restrictive in respect of non-UK real estate assets (land). The laws which govern the disposition of real property will almost invariably be the laws of the jurisdiction in which the property is situated. The majority of civil law jurisdictions, such as France, Spain, Portugal and Italy, where "second homes" are most often located, limit the freedom to bequeath assets by requiring that certain close family members shall be entitled to fixed shares in any inheritance of land.

2.1.18   Prudent advice to testators who own foreign real estate is that they should consider making more than one valid will: one dealing with all assets other than land owned in the named jurisdiction, and a second will, valid in the named jurisdiction where the "second home" is situated, dealing only with the devolution of that asset, in accordance with the relevant testamentary laws of that jurisdiction.

2.1.19   'Foreign' aspects of drafting wills are dealt with in more detail in CHAPTER 2.10.

Chapter 2.2

Ideal inheritance tax planning

Introduction

2.2.1 This Chapter deals mainly with inheritance tax (IHT) planning between spouses/civil partners. The reason for this is simple. In principle, transfers of value between spouses/civil partners are generally exempt from liability to IHT (except where the recipient is not domiciled in the UK for IHT purposes), see **CHAPTER 2.10** below; and any cross-generational asset transfers are liable to IHT. However despite the exemption available between legally recognised partners, it is not often best IHT planning simply to leave all assets by will to the surviving spouse/partner, even after the pre-Budget Review statement on 9 October 2007 which sets out proposals for some carry forward of any unused NRB to the survivor. It will be interesting to see whether the Government's recently announced initiative to extend the financial rights of "common-law spouses" in areas of family law will extend also to IHT. The burden of proof of establishing exactly when a couple begin or continue to "cohabit" is likely always to remain a difficult matter of evidence

2.2.2 In order to avoid duplication of options throughout the text, reference will be made generally to "partners" or "the surviving partner". This is to indicate the survivor of either a married couple or a civil partnership, ie any formal relationship between two individuals which qualifies for transfers of assets which are exempt from IHT without restriction within IHTA 1984 s 18.

2.2.3 Because the nil-rate band (NRB) is available only once to each individual, and is not transferable (subject to the implementation with effect from 5 April 2008 of the October 2007 pre-Budget Review proposals) it is important that the first partner to die should use his NRB, if assets are available of sufficient value, by leaving assets to anyone other than the surviving partner. At 40% tax, and with a NRB of currently £300,000, if this band is not properly utilised, the additional tax cost to a family unit is £120,000. The usual recommendation is to establish a trust for children and/or grandchildren, and sometimes also to include the surviving partner, in order to use this relief in the most flexible way possible. Some families may prefer to bequeath assets absolutely to children in order to use this NRB in a different way.

2.2.4 There is a discussion in paragraphs **2.7.16, 2.7.17** of how the new rules regarding transferable NRBs between partners may operate.

2.2.5 There is no ideal IHT planning for single individuals who own assets of significant value. For them, in general terms, only three alternatives are available—

— own as many assets as possible which qualify for special IHT treatment, such as business property or agricultural property;

— give away assets during lifetime and survive seven years, or write life insurance policies to cover payment of residual IHT;

— leave all assets to charity.

2.2.6 There is a short summary of assets which qualify for business property or agricultural property relief in paragraph 2.8.4.

Estate planning before will drafting

2.2.7 As has been made clear in the Introduction, much IHT planning during an individual's lifetime can amount to a calculated trade off between capital gains tax (CGT) and IHT. It is difficult to avoid both taxes by advance planning, so a choice may often have to be made between payment of the lesser of two evils, taking the timing of tax payment into account when making that choice.

2.2.8 Notwithstanding IHT planning, the first principle of effective estate planning is to ensure that individuals can jointly continue to enjoy a comfortable lifestyle in their retirement. They should not give away so many assets during their lifetime that they then feel financially uncomfortable. As we all get older, we generally start to feel, at some stage, financially insecure (almost regardless of the value of assets we own), and we wish to remain completely financially independent. For many families, the idea of parents becoming financially dependant on their children can be a difficult concept to accept. For others, with close-knit families, that may be an acceptable course of action to follow. However, despite the wishes of many parents to be generous to their children and give assets away to them, nowadays the risk of marriages ending in divorce, with consequent financial claims being made against "family assets", can create financial risks as a reward for generosity.

2.2.9 Giving assets away without reserving any personal benefit from the gifted assets, is now fraught with difficulties. These are largely occasioned by the combination of historic anti-avoidance legislation: referred to generally as "GROBs" (gifts with a reservation of benefit) and the pre-owned asset legislation introduced, with largely retrospective effect, by FA 2004. Gifts can be made, at seven-year intervals, to individuals or to trustees for the family. Gifts of assets other than cash may give rise to an immediate liability to CGT, although holdover relief can be available where the gift is made to trustees (TCGA 1992 s 260). If assets are retained until death, no CGT becomes payable, but IHT will be payable.

2.2.10   One fundamental fact which must never be lost sight of in the context of estate planning is that, except in the comparatively rare cases where one partner is suffering from a known fatal illness, there can never be any certain advance knowledge of when a death will occur. Deaths do not always occur in the "right" order. Road traffic or aircraft accidents, terrorist attacks or other circumstances may mean that prospective heirs often die before their parents. Any estate planning arrangements need to be flexible enough to accommodate necessary subsequent change.

2.2.11   Although this book is concerned with effective will drafting, much estate planning, before wills are drafted, involves discussing and making strategies which may often require trade-offs between payment of CGT or IHT. Payment of CGT is often the cheaper option, because although for many years the nominal rate of CGT has been 40% (the same as IHT), by the time that taper relief and other allowances are taken into account, the effective rate of CGT may be reduced to as little as 10% for business assets, or 24% for other assets. The impact of the pre-Budget Review proposals, set out on 9 October 2007, to apply a flat rate of 18% CGT across the board on all asset disposals, without taper or inflation relief, reinforces these arguments that CGT is usually the cheaper option. The pre-Budget proposals have been greeted with such opprobrious comment from many business sectors that it would not be surprising to see a different outcome from the claimed "simplification with one flat rate" approach when the detail of the draft legislation is published in due course. CGT also applies only to the profit or gain element in the value of an asset, over and above initial purchase costs, as calculated for tax purposes. IHT, on the other hand, is chargeable on 100% of the value of assets.

2.2.12   If estate planning strategy involves the creation of family trusts, during lifetime or by will, consideration has to be given as to who will act as trustee. There is some discussion of this in CHAPTER 2.1. During an individuals lifetime it is possible to give assets away to a trust, and yet still retain effective and practical control over the gifted assets by acting as a trustee. On death, when the terms of a will become effective, that trusteeship will come to an end. Who will act as successor trustee? Is it appropriate to draft both lifetime trusts and wills so that the testator/trustee can appoint a successor trustee by will? A trustee has onerous fiduciary duties always to act solely in the best interests of all the beneficiaries named or described in any trust instrument (and for this purpose, that will include a will). Trusts may be able to provide a (sometimes limited) shield against financial claims that may be made in divorce proceedings.

2.2.13   For IHT purposes, the best way of approaching estate planning is to ensure that spouses/civil partners are each able to use their NRB to the full. As noted in the introduction to this Chapter, this alone can, for some families, save up to £120,000 in IHT, assuming 2007–08 tax rates. Individuals should—

— try to create "additional" NRBs. If an individual makes a gift equal to the value of the NRB, and then survives the date of the gift by seven years, the individual will then become entitled to a further NRB. The value of the gift made falls wholly out of account for IHT purposes after seven years. There will be some IHT relief if a donor survives a gift for a minimum of four years, so that increasing proportions of the value of gifts made are ignored in the 5th, 6th and 7th years following the date of gift (IHTA 1984 s 7(4)). If a gift is made to an individual, for IHT purposes, the potential liability to that tax passes then to the recipient of the gift, because the asset will then belong to the recipient (IHTA 1984 s 200(1)(c)). In the usual course of events, arranging for a younger generation to own assets postpones the risk of payment of IHT. However, as already noted, the one uncertainty in estate planning is always that deaths do not always occur in the "right order". Life assurance is the only way to guard against this risk;

— try to pass ownership of assets which are most likely to increase in capital value (such as the field which one day might be available for planning permission to build a housing estate) to the next family generation as soon as possible, minimising the immediate tax cost of such ownership transfers;

— where appropriate, retain business assets for as long as possible, because they are often exempted from liability to IHT, as relief equal to 100% of the value of business assets may be available.

General strategic recommendations

2.2.14 It is often a good plan for assets to be owned in equal shares between spouses/civil partners. If there is inequality of asset ownership, at the very least, both partners need to own assets equivalent in value to the nil-rate band. The advantages of this are twofold. First it ensures that, whichever partner dies first, they can each comfortably afford to use their NRB. Second, provided that the wills contain a conditional survivorship clause (PRECEDENT 1 CLAUSE 8) it may reduce the effective rate of IHT payable within subsequent discretionary or 18–25 trusts, if both partners die within a short time of each other. The reason for this is that the NRB available to the discretionary trust created by each of the partners will be a greater proportion of the total trust assets whenever there is an occasion of IHT charge; either on making trust distribution or on successive decennial anniversaries of the creation of each trust. For example—

Trustees wish to make a £100,000 distribution from a trust created by W, at a time when no beneficiaries have yet reached the age of 25. Both parents died in the same car accident, and W being younger, is deemed to have survived H (See Precedent 3 clause 8 and Law of Property Act 1925 s 184).

If both parents owned assets with a value of £500,000, the two possibilities are—

(1) H left a NRB discretionary trust, with residue to W for life on an IPDI, remainder to the NRB trust, subject to a 30-day survivorship clause. IHT payable on the £100,000 distribution will be—

$$£\left(500,0\overline{0}0 - 300,000\right) \times 6\% = £\,12,000$$

$$\frac{12,000}{500,000} = 2\%$$

$$2\% \times £\,100,000 = £\,2,000 \text{ tax}$$

(2) As above, but without a 30 day-survivorship clause (ie W's estate inherits £200,000 from H so that her total estate is now £700,000). IHT payable on the £100,000 distribution will be—

$$£\left(700,0\overline{0}0 - 300,000\right) \times 6\% = £\,24,000$$

$$\frac{24,000}{900,000} = 2.6\%$$

$$2.6\% \times £\,100,000 = £\,2,600 \text{ tax}$$

2.2.15   Where investment assets are concerned, income tax advantages may also be obtained by ensuring that both spouses/partners have equal investment income. This can ensure that the lower rate bands of income tax applicable to the calculation of an individual's income tax liability can be fully utilised. The pre-Budget Review on 9 October 2007 made it clear that this whole area of tax planning is under review and that changes may soon be introduced, largely in response to the House of Lords' decision in *Jones v Garnett (Inspector of Taxes)* [2007] UKHL 35, referred to in more detail in paragraph **2.7.11**.

2.2.16   Where the family home is not owned on a joint basis, and when that home represents substantially the majority of the asset value owned by any couple, other problems may arise. Ownership of the family home in the context of using debt schemes to reduce IHT by utilising fully the NRB, is dealt with in some detail in CHAPTER **2.7**.

2.2.17   Wills should be drafted so as to provide—

— for assets equal to the NRB to be held for heirs on discretionary trusts;

— for the remainder of assets to be held on flexible trust for the surviving partner for his/her life; and

— for the trust assets thereafter to be held on discretionary trust for successive family generations when the second spouse dies.

2.2.18   Additional tax benefits can be obtained if non-resident will trustees are appointed. A summary of matters relevant to the appointment of non-resident trustees is included in CHAPTER **2.9**.

2.2.19 Wills drafted as summarised above provide an effective and flexible method of minimising IHT liabilities for the immediate next generation, while at the same time providing maximum flexibility to plan longer term to reduce income tax, IHT and CGT for successive generations. In this book the will precedent in PRECEDENT **1** reflects this model, and is referred to generally throughout as "the model will" by reference to which other alternatives and variations can be considered.

2.2.20 Technically this is not *the* most tax-efficient way of drafting a will. If a testator wishes to be as tax-efficient as is absolutely possible, he may prefer to substitute 18-to-25 for both the NRB discretionary trust, and the subsequent discretionary trust (or a further 18-to-25 trust) after the death of the surviving partner. As explained in CHAPTER **3.4**, using an 18-to-25 trust may marginally save some IHT compared with a discretionary trust. The practical disadvantage of using this structure is that trustees are left with no choice except to distribute assets absolutely to children or grandchildren beneficiaries when they reach the age of 25. This absolute distribution of trust assets will also trigger CGT liabilities (unless all trust assets are then invested in residential property occupied as a main residence by one of more beneficiaries: TCGA 1992 s 225) without generating cash to meet that CGT liability. Further, for many families, the idea of allowing young people to come into a substantial inheritance at the age of 25, with no option to defer payment of capital until a later date, is not attractive. There is no flexibility to deal with a young person who has fallen under the influence of unhealthy substances or is in the middle of a relationship breakdown. It is for this practical reason that the model will uses discretionary trusts, rather than 18-to-25 trusts. Not all advisers and estate planners will necessarily agree with this conclusion.

2.2.21 Use of the so called 18–25 "favoured trusts" allowed by FA 2006 (now incorporated into IHTA 1984 s 71 under the heading "accumulation and maintenance trusts") is not recommended, unless there are particular reasons why a testator wishes his children or grandchildren to become absolutely entitled to assets when they reach a specified age no older than 25. The biggest advantage of this type is trust is possibly due to an oversight in last-minute drafting by the Government in response to industry criticism of their original proposals. The tax charge on distributions is calculated by reference to the value of trust assets *immediately after the trust was made* – and that may have been as long as 30 years or more before the chargeable event. There is no difference in IHT treatment between this type of trust and a fully flexible discretionary trust; but an accumulation and maintenance trust has to be prescriptive as to when beneficiaries become absolutely entitled to assets. It is the better view, in general estate planning terms, to preserve flexibility so as to be able to adapt strategy to changing personal and family circumstances. There is some more detailed discussion in CHAPTER **3.4** of these trusts which now effectively replace accumulation and maintenance trusts for IHT planning purposes.

The structure explained

(1) Why use a trust for life for the surviving partner?

2.2.22   There are both practical and fiscal reasons for recommending the use of a flexible life interest trust.

2.2.23   The practical reasons are linked with age. If the surviving partner is advancing in years by the time s/he becomes "the surviving partner", some of the advantages of having family wealth controlled by trustees (of whom the surviving partner could, if desired, be one) include—

— trustees can act impartially in deciding what to do for the best in the light of the onset of mental or physical impairment;

— the fact that assets are owned in trust may have a bearing on the type and amount or local authority care provision which may become available to the surviving partner;

— trustees can be a useful barrier against importuning requests for money and inheritances from over-influential personal care providers or dominant children.

2.2.24   Where the surviving partner is much younger, trustees can provide useful family protection from the attentions of would-be new partners whose motives may perhaps be tainted by the lure of sharing in a substantial inheritance which is available to the surviving partner

2.2.25   The fiscal reasons include the provision of tax planning opportunities for the children of the testator. Those children may not come into their inheritance until they themselves are in their sixth or seventh decade of life. They will probably already have undertaken their own estate planning and have no direct "need" of personal ownership of substantial assets. A reversionary interest under a life interest trust is "excluded property" for IHT purposes and so can be dealt with in a completely tax neutral manner. An assignment of a reversionary interest into trust for children and grandchildren can be an extremely effective tax planning tool. Consider the following example—

> H dies leaving his residuary estate of £2,000,000 on trust for W for life with remainder equally to A, his son. W lives until she is 95, by which time the will trust fund is worth £3,500,000 and A has retired from his career as an investment banker, is 68 years old, and has three children and eight grandchildren. A's personal assets are worth £5,000,000. If A were to inherit the assets owned by his father's will trust, after payment of IHT on W's death, his own assets will increase in value by a net £2,100,000 (£3,500,000 x 60%). A's own potential liability to IHT will immediately increase by £840,000

(40% x £2,100,000). If A takes no action, it is likely that the £840,000 of IHT will become payable sometime within the next 20–25 years, when A dies.

If A simply assigns his reversionary interest to be held on discretionary trusts for his children and remoter issue, that transaction will be entirely tax neutral for A. (No CGT because A is the original owner of the reversionary interest: TCGA 1992 s 76; no IHT because the reversionary interest is "excluded property": IHTA 1984 s 48(1)). Even if IHT is payable at the full 6% on decennial anniversaries within A's trust, a most unlikely outcome (see Chapter 4.4), cumulative IHT of £840,000 will not be paid until 70 years after the creation of the trust. This will be the seventh decennial anniversary, ignoring any changes in the value of A's original trust fund of £2,100,000.

2.2.26 Trustees may also be able to make capital advances from the life interest trust, thereby using the surviving partner's NRB in the hope that the surviving partner may survive seven years and so become entitled to a further full NRB. It can sometimes be easier for trustees to take decisions of this nature than it can be for an individual surviving partner.

(2) Why use discretionary trusts?

2.2.27 Discretionary trusts are dealt with in detail in **CHAPTER 4.1**. Some limited explanation of the principal IHT and other fiscal benefits are given here.

2.2.28 The greatest advantage of a discretionary trust is the flexibility and ability to react to changing family and tax circumstances which is immediately available. There is no difference in immediate fiscal conse-quences to discretionary trustees of making a distribution from the trust to any generation of beneficiary – CGT age young IHT consequences for the trustees will be the same, regardless of the recipient beneficiary. The fiscal consequences for the recipient beneficiary will of course vary according the personal financial circumstances of that beneficiary in the tax year in which he receives a trust distribution.

2.2.29 An alternative method of drafting wills in order to preserve maximum possible flexibility is dealt with in **CHAPTER 2.5**. The most flexible will possible, which can be used to great tax planning advantage, is one which leaves all assets to trustees of a discretionary trust on the basis that trustees can use their powers of appointment within two years of the date of death in order to dispose of assets among heirs as they see fit, usually in the most tax-efficient way possible. Although this does provide the ideal opportunity to create future flexibility, many testators prefer to feel that they have had a direct input on how their assets will be dealt with for future generations, rather than leave matters to be dealt with by trustees after their death. In practice this ideal use of flexibility is more theoretical than common, but many wills are drafted in this way.

2.2.30 Although there is a ten-yearly charge to IHT on assets owned by a discretionary trust, for 50 years the aggregate IHT payable will often be substantially less than the 40% rate of IHT which will otherwise be charged on a death when asset ownership passes from one generation to the next. In addition—

— Each discretionary trust is entitled to its own nil-rate band s 48(1) (except where two or more trusts are created on the same day by the same settlor—examples of IHT calculations for discretionary and other "non-favoured" trusts are given in CHAPTER 4.4), so that if the value of assets owned by a discretionary trust in year of creation (YC) + 10 years, does not exceed the value of the NRB at that time (ie as annually adjusted upwards, supposedly in line with inflation), no IHT will become payable in YC+10.

— Even if tax does become payable in YC+10, IHT will be chargeable only on the excess of value over the then NRB. The maximum tax rate which will apply is 6%. Thus, for example, if the YC + 10 NRB is £500,000, and trust assets have a value of £550,000, IHT payable will be 6% x £50,000 = £3,000, or 0·54% of the total trust asset value. If the settlor had not created the trust, or otherwise given assets away, he would then be facing potential IHT liability on these assets of 40% x £550,000 = £220,000.

— If the family and the trustees wish to avoid any charge to tax on the tenth anniversary of the creation of the trust, they will have the flexibility to take action, before the tenth anniversary, to give assets from the trust to beneficiaries (children or grandchildren or others), or to vary the terms of the trust, so as totally to avoid that decennial tax liability. See CHAPTER 4.4 for examples.

2.2.31 There are also CGT advantages in using discretionary trusts. It has already been noted that much estate planning can require a trade off between payment of CGT or payment of IHT. There is some alleviation from double taxation in the way in which these two taxes interact. TCGA 1992 s 260 allows the general principle that wherever a transaction takes place which is chargeable (even at 0%) to IHT, it is always possible to make an election for CGT holdover. Making this election enables payment of the CGT, which would otherwise arise on that transaction to be deferred, so that the recipient of assets becomes responsible for payment of the CGT triggered by the disposal of assets. In general, holdover CGT does not become payable until the recipient of the assets gifted (from an individual or from trust) makes a CGT disposal of those relevant assets.

2.2.32 The interaction of TCGA 1992 s 262 with discretionary and accumulation and maintenance trusts is very helpful. On any occasion when assets are distributed from a discretionary or an accumulation and maintenance trust to beneficiaries, that is a chargeable event for IHT purposes. Even though the rate of charge of IHT may be minimal, or even 0%, it will be possible for the trustees and the recipient beneficiary jointly to make an election to hold over payment of CGT. This is an important and wide ranging planning opportunity. One of the most common problems which arises in terms of CGT planning is how to deal with the payment of tax if a chargeable occasion arises which does not generate cash from which tax can be paid. The relief provided by s 260 obviates the need for this consideration to be taken into account.

2.2.33 The application of CGT taper relief should not be overlooked. Once an asset is transferred from trustees to a beneficiary, a new period commences for the purpose of calculating taper relief on any subsequent asset disposal of the asset by the beneficiary (see generally TCGA 1992 Sch A1 para 2). These concerns may be relegated to a footnote in fiscal history after 5 April 2008 if the 9 October 2007 pre-Budget Review statement proposals to introduce a single flat rate of CGT of 18% are implemented in the manner presently proposed.

2.2.34 A precedent for the model will which is constructed on the basis recommended above is included in PRECEDENT 6.

Business property and agricultural property reliefs

2.2.35 The purpose of this book is to focus on tax effective will drafting. Some knowledge of the major points to take into consideration with regard to business property and agricultural property reliefs is essential in this context. Nevertheless, in a book of this nature space does not permit a full discussion of all relevant points in detail. CHAPTER 2.8 contains some explanations, comment, and will drafting and estate planning possibilities and examples, but the reader is referred to more specialist publications relating to IHT for a completely detailed explanation of this topic.

Chapter 2.3

Providing for the surviving partner

Introduction

2.3.1   As noted in CHAPTER 2.2, the paramount consideration of a tax-efficient will is nothing to do with saving IHT or other taxes, but to ensure that the surviving partner will be able to continue to enjoy a comfortable lifestyle after one partner has died. Wills should not be so restrictively drafted that the surviving partner feels that they are lacking in financial independence and comfort. Advancing years often bring (unwarranted) feelings of financial insecurity, and these psychological effects of advancing years should not be ignored in the interests of saving an extra few pounds of IHT.

2.3.2   To some partners, the idea that they would not be in total control of family assets after the death of the other partner, but that assets would be under the control of trustees, even if the surviving partner is one of them, is not a comfortable prospect. Setting out the fiscal and practical benefits, and gently persuasive advice, may not be able to overcome this practical resistance of character. If that is so, it would probably not be prudent to proceed with a completely tax-efficient will. This book is however concerned with tax-efficient will drafting. In this Chapter the detail of the proposed life interest flexible trust for the surviving partner is explained.

Should the surviving partner be a trustee?

2.3.3   If the surviving partner is a beneficiary under will trusts there is an immediate conflict between self interest and fiduciary duties to other beneficiaries if the surviving partner acts as a trustee. In order to avoid possible litigation concerning self dealing (acquiring assets directly from the trust, see *Sargeant v National Westminster Bank* (1990) 61 P & CR 518; *Edge v Pensions Ombudsman* [2000] Ch 602 at 621–622 and 632–633) it is preferable to insert specific wording and authority in the terms of the will trust. Examples of appropriate clauses are included in PRECEDENT 16.

2.3.4   Apart from the need to draft Will trusts appropriately so as to avoid difficulties of trust law, practical problems may also rise. What happens where one of a number of trustees starts to lose mental or physical capacity? Unless there is a specific provision in the terms of the trust which allows trustees to act by a majority decision, it has been long established that all trustee decisions must be unanimous (*Luke v South Kensington Hotel Co* (1879) 11 Ch D 121). As is the case with company directors, the courts make no distinction between executive and non-executive, or acting and passive, trustees. If one trustee is incapable of taking an effective business decision, the affairs of any will trust will technically become paralysed until such time as the ineffective trustee retires or has been removed. Trustee Act 1925 s 36(1) allows for the person named in any trust instrument as having the power to appoint a new trustee to use that power where (among other things) a trustee becomes incapable of acting or unfit to act. This alone may not be satisfactory because it is often the surviving partner who is named as the person who has the power to appoint new trustees. TLATA 1996 s 21 entitles the collectively absolutely entitled adult beneficiaries to give a direction in writing that a replacement trustee should be appointed if a trustee is incapable of acting by reason of mental disorder, but this too may be somewhat impractical.

2.3.5   There is no perfect alternative solution to this latter problem. For examples of compromise and workable clauses dealing with the mental and/or physical incapacity of a named trustee, or the person named as the Appointor with power to remove and appoint trustees, see PRECEDENT 15.

2.3.6   Both testators and surviving partners who wish to retain some effective control over assets held in will trust are often unwilling for the will trust to contain wording which allows trustees to act by a majority. The other absolutely necessary provisions where the surviving partner is a trustee and a beneficiary, as noted above are—

— the power to take benefit from the trust while acting as a trustee, provided that there are at that time at least two acting trustees (PRECEDENT 16); and

— the power to acquire assets from the trust on arm's length commercial terms (PRECEDENT 17).

2.3.7   There may be trustee investment decisions to take into account in the light of particular family circumstances. Where an interest in the family home is owned by trustees, and the surviving partner as a trustee (this is not appropriate if the trust is to take part in a debt scheme, see CHAPTER 2.7) expects to continue living in that property, appropriate clauses need to be included within the terms of the will trust. The trustees should be able to allow a beneficiary to occupy any trust property on whatever terms they think fit, including free of charge (PRECEDENT 14).

2.3.8   Consideration should also be given to the drafting as to whether it is necessary for the trustees to obtain the consent of any beneficiary who is entitled to occupy any trust property before that property can be sold, see

TLATA 1996 s 11. A clause which dispenses with the need for trustees to obtain the consent is included within PRECEDENT 10.

2.3.9 If shares in the family trading company are held in will trust, and the surviving partner is actively involved in the business, there may be additional provisions necessary to reduce the trustees' investment obligations required by Trustee Act 2000 or, more generally, to hold a balanced and diversified investment portfolio as is required by general principles of trust law. It is fairly standard modern drafting to allow the trustees to avoid having to diversify an investment portfolio. If continued family shareholding in a particular business is regarded as important, it is possible to include provisions which require a specific consent or formality to be followed before "specified shares" can be sold. An example of such provisions is included within PRECEDENT 11.

The flexible life interest trust

2.3.10 Elsewhere in this book the proposed life interest trust for the surviving partner has been described as a "flexible life interest trust". What exactly is meant by "flexible"?

2.3.11 In this context the flexibility required to be given to trustees is the freedom to appoint trust capital in as many ways as possible, without restriction. Trustees of such a will trust need to have the flexibility to advance capital directly to a surviving partner during his lifetime. They also need to be able to advance capital to other beneficiaries. Trustee Act 1925 s 32 requires that before a capital advance of this nature is made, the consent of the lifetime beneficiary needs first to be obtained. Is it appropriate to include a clause in the will trust which obviates the need to obtain any such consent? A clause which does exactly that is contained within PRECEDENT 9.

2.3.12 Other provisions often included within modern trusts are clauses which enable trustees to guarantee debt obligations of any beneficiary or of any company in which the beneficiary may has an interest (see PRECEDENT 13), or to make loans to beneficiaries on any terms which the trustees think fit. Without such a provision, the obligation on trustees to make "investments" of trust assets will prohibit them from making unsecured loans. Traditionally a loan is not regarded as an investment made by trustee unless it is made at a commercial rate of interest and made only on a secured basis. To lend money otherwise would amount to a breach of trust in the absence of specific trust wording. Trustee Act 2000 s 3 authorises trustees to "make any kind of investment that [they] could make if they were absolutely entitled to the assets of the trust". That alone should be regarded as sufficient, but some draftsmen may prefer to use alternative wording such as that included within PRECEDENT 14.

2.3.13   Where liquid assets are not available between partners in order to utilise fully the proposed NRB discretionary trust, there have been several variations on a theme in recent years involving the use of a debt secured on the family home, or simply promised by way of IOU from the surviving partner. The arrangements usually require the use of trusts. A full discussion of the possibilities available, in light of the most recent case decisions made public before this book went to print, is included within CHAPTER 2.7.

Variations in will drafting for testators with potential personal liability claims

2.3.14   The will structure recommended above is not always suitable for individuals who are partners in professional practices, such as lawyers, accountants and architects. Despite the fact that nowadays many professional firms are structured as limited liability partnerships, many partners are often concerned that one day their firm may face a claim resulting in substantial personal liability for professional negligence. The Enron-related demise of one of the world's largest accountancy practices (Arthur Andersen) was a salutary lesson.

2.3.15   Traditionally, individuals who were about to embark upon a hazardous business enterprise have structured their family affairs so that their spouse or partner would be the owner of the majority of family assets. Alternatively, some family assets could be owned by appropriate trusts. If all of such arrangements are to be effective, the individual directly concerned must remain solvent after transferring assets out of his own name, in order to ensure, so far as possible, that the provisions of all relevant insolvency and bankruptcy legislation could not be used to set aside gifts and transactions at below market value. For a full discussion of circumstances where gifts at and transactions at undervalue can be set aside the reader is referred to more detailed and specialist publications.

2.3.16   On the assumption that the individual professional partner has managed validly to structure the ownership of family assets so that his or her partner owns the bulk of those assets, how best should the will of the asset owning partner be structured? All the meticulous planning and structuring of asset ownership would be negated completely if the asset owning partner is the first to die, and leaves assets absolutely or on fixed interest trusts for the professional partner. In those circumstances all the family assets would become available to satisfy creditor claims in the event of the insolvency or bankruptcy of the professional partner.

2.3.17   The use of an old fashioned protective trust may be completely appropriate to deal with these circumstances. Trustee Act 1925 s 33 contains the relevant provisions detailing how a protective trust can operate in accordance with statute. It is of course open to any draftsman to vary (within limits) the statutory provisions in appropriate circumstances.

The professional partner can draw his will as recommended above (ie using the preferred flexible will model), leaving the usual fully flexible life interest trust for his surviving partner.

2.3.18 The will structure recommended for the partner who is not engaged in a "hazardous business" is as follows—

— assets equal to the NRB should be left for heirs (including the surviving partner) on discretionary trusts;

— the remainder of assets should be held on protective trusts for the surviving partner for his/her life; and

— thereafter assets should be held on discretionary trust for successive family generations when the second partner dies.

How do protective trusts work?

2.3.19 A protective trust is exactly what the name suggests. It is designed legally to protect family assets against claims from creditors. The standard statutory terms of a protective trust are that—

— the surviving partner will have a fixed but determinable life interest in trust assets;

— the fixed life interest will come to an end if the surviving partner life tenant does any of the following—

  • becomes bankrupt;
  • enters into a composition with creditors (an insolvent voluntary arrangement);
  • attempts to sell his interest under the trust;
  • takes any action the result of which would be to deprive him of the right to receive trust income;

— thereafter, the trust will become discretionary in nature and the surviving partner will, during his lifetime, be regarded as the principal beneficiary;

— after the death of the surviving partner, the trust should be drafted to remain discretionary in nature for the benefit generally of all family heirs.

2.3.20 The importance of the protective trust is that because the surviving partner's trust interest automatically becomes a discretionary interest on the occasion of any of the "trigger events", his interest is immediately deprived of any realisable value as far as creditors are concerned. In the absence of the protective trust mechanism, if the surviving spouse had a fixed life interest in the trust fund, and any of the trigger events occurs, the trustees would thereafter be obliged to pay trust income to the supervisor of an IVA, or to the surviving partner's trustee in bankruptcy.

2.3.21 The IHT legislation recognises the effect of protective trusts by preventing any charge to IHT arising on the occasion when the trust interest switches from being a fixed interest trust (prior to FA 2006 this would have been referred to as an interest in possession trust) to being a discretionary trust. See generally IHTA 1984 s 88, the effect of which is that the principal beneficiary is treated for IHT purposes as if his fixed interest had not come to an end, so that on the death of the principal beneficiary, an IHT liability will arise on the same basis as is the case for any other beneficiary who is treated as having a fixed interest in possession trust property (ie a pre-22 March 2006 interest in possession, or a post-22 March 2006 IPDI: IHTA 1984 s 49.

2.3.22 IHTA 1984 s 88 technically applies not only to protective trusts falling precisely within Trustee Act 1925 s 33, but also to "trusts to the like effect as that specified in s 33". The extent to which s 33 can be varied so that relief as a protective trust can still apply is somewhat unclear. HMRC's (slightly unhelpful) view was published in *The Law Society Gazette*, see APPENDIX 2. The trigger for that statement was that the provisions of IHTA 1984 s 88 as originally drafted had been used by a taxpayer to try to obtain a substantial tax advantage. When trustees of a protective trust used their discretionary trust powers to make fixed appointments of capital assets to remaindermen, it was subsequently claimed that the provisions of s 88 should continue to apply, so that the capital appointments should effectively be disregarded for IHT purposes. The courts did not agree – see *Cholmondeley v IRC* [1986] STC 384.

2.3.23 An example of an appropriate will precedent is included in PRECEDENT 3.

2.3.24 A protective trust could equally be used for children in appropriate circumstances, possibly after the death of a surviving partner who had an IPDI.

Further variations

2.3.25 Some testators are concerned that their surviving partner may enter into another marriage or civil partnership with the result that the family assets may ultimately be shared with the surviving partner's new partner's family. The recommended Will structure initially proposed in this Chapter does deal with this indirectly, through the use of a fully flexible life interest trust. If the surviving partner is not a trustee, as is recommended, it would probably not be difficult for the trustees to decide not to exercise their powers to appoint capital to the surviving partner if s/he has entered into a permanent relationship with a new partner. If the surviving partner is a trustee, matters could become more difficult.

2.3.26   An alternative method of dealing with this problem could be to use a protective trust structure, but to add an additional "trigger event" so that a fixed life interest will terminate, and a discretionary trust come into place, in the event that the surviving partner remarries or enters into a new civil partnership. Although not beyond doubt, it is thought likely that HMRC would accept that this condition is similar enough to Trustee Act 1925 s 33, as being a trust "to the like effect" as therein set out, in order to comply with IHTA 1984 s 88. It is emphasised that this is a view expressed (not entirely unanimously) by the authors, and has not been confirmed by HMRC. An appropriate clause is included within PREC-EDENT 3.

2.3.27   A similar suggestion which often comes up in practice is that any fixed or life interest should also terminate in the event that the surviving partner starts to cohabit with another partner. This is a provision which prudent trustees should regard as being practically unworkable. How exactly are trustees supposed to police the behaviour of the surviving spouse? At what point do occasional overnight visits become cohabitation? Even with the widest possible discretionary decision making powers given to trustees, it is the authors' view that such a provision is unwelcome and could not be sensibly operated in practice.

The non-domiciled partner

2.3.28   Where one partner is not domiciled in the UK tax-efficient will drafting becomes much more difficult. The normal limitless exemption for assets which are transferred to a surviving partner is replaced by a very restrictive limit of £55,000 of value as the maximum amount of exempt transfer to a non-domiciled surviving partner (IHTA 1984 s 18(2)). Unlike the NRB, this limit has not increased in line with inflation but has remained fixed since 1982.

2.3.29   In an ideal world, partners will try to ensure that the non-domiciled partner owns the majority of "jointly-owned" assets in order to maximise the possibility of holding "excluded property" which is wholly exempt from liability to IHT. The £55,000 limit applies equally to lifetime transfers as to transfers on death, so this ideally planned world is not always easy to achieve.

2.3.30   There is no magic tax-efficient solution to this problem. Once the NRB and the £55,000 non-domiciled partner exemption have been exhausted, any assets passing on death of a UK domiciled partner will attract IHT. In those circumstances it is advisable to leave assets absolutely to the surviving non-domiciled partner, rather than in trust. If the assets are held in trust, they will forever remain within the IHT net, because the testator will be domiciled in the UK at his date of death. Assets left absolutely to a non-domiciled partner can subsequently be settled into trust on terms that they can remain outside the IHT net as "excluded property", provided that the surviving partner has appropriate IHT domicile status at that time.

2.3.31 Further details on this topic, including the application of double tax treaties to this problem, are in CHAPTER 2.10.

Where both partners are not domiciled in the UK

2.3.32 As far as assets liable to IHT are concerned, the usual exempt provisions apply on transfers of assets between partners.

2.3.33 Where partners live mainly outside the UK, but one of them may spend considerable amounts of time in the UK over a period of years, the "deemed domicile" rules may come into play (IHTA 1984 s 267). This can be an awkward tax trap where deemed domicile status may arise after wills have been drafted but before one of the partners dies. For example—

> Mr and Mrs W live in Hong Kong but their three children and six grandchildren live in the UK. Mrs W retires and spends several months a year visiting her family in the UK. If Mrs W spends more than 3 months a year on average in the UK on a consistent basis, she will be regarded as UK resident for income tax purposes (see generally HMRC booklet IR20: Residents and non-residents—liability to tax in the United Kingdom). After 17 years (or possibly after 15 years and 1 month), even if she spends less than 6 months a year in the UK in any of those years, she will be regarded as deemed domiciled in the UK. Any assets which she owns and bequeaths to her husband in excess of a value equal to the NRB plus £55,000 will be chargeable to IHT.

2.3.34 IHTA 1984 s 267 operates in respect of any year of assessment "in which" an individual is resident in the UK. This is how it is possible for an individual to be deemed domiciled in the UK after a period. Only a little over 15 years, rather than the full 17 years, which is often assumed. For example—

> Mrs W first comes the UK in January 2000 and stays until the end of June that year. She spends between 3 and 4 months in the UK each year until May 2015 when she dies, having been in the UK since 5 April 2015.

> In a period of 15 years and 5 months, she will have been resident "in" the UK for 17 years and will therefore be deemed domiciled in the UK at the date of her death.

Chapter 2.4

Providing for children

Introduction

2.4.1 There are usually only two types of children with whom testators are concerned: adult and minor. Special considerations apply where there are minor or disabled children, particularly where the testator wishes to make provision for the unforeseen, fatal accident to both himself and spouse. In that event there are both technical and practical matters to take into account.

2.4.2 For adult children there may be concerns that marriage or other permanent relationship may encounter difficulties and provision needs to be made to try to protect as many family assets as possible so that they can be used directly for children or for grandchildren.

2.4.3 Although the recommended preferred version will dealt with in CHAPTER 2.2 uses discretionary trusts for the benefit of children, this Chapter is the most appropriate place to consider (if only to dismiss as largely irrelevant) the various trust options which are "favoured trusts" within the inheritance tax (IHT) regime as a result of a substantial changes made by FA 2006.

Minor children – practical points

2.4.4 Where a testator wishes to make provision to deal with the situation where both he and his partner may suffer a fatal accident, leaving minor children to survive them both, the most practical point to consider is who will be responsible for housing and looking after those minor children. It is fairly common practice to appoint a guardian in a will. The appointment will normally be regarded as effective for practical purposes, notwithstanding the formal requirement of Children's Act 1989 s 5(2) which provides that no appointment of a guardian for an infant will be valid unless made with the approval of the court.

2.4.5 Having decided upon the identity of any guardians for children, consideration then needs to be given as to how the nominated guardians will be able to accept the testator's minor children into their home. Will they need to build an extension? Do they have an adequate number of bedrooms? Will they need to move house? Will they need to acquire a bigger or additional estate car? In the most general terms, there are three ways in which these problems can be addressed. Either—

— a monetary legacy can be left to the nominated guardians with a (non-binding) request that they consider using the legacy to enhance living accommodation; or

— guardians can be included as beneficiaries under Will trusts, and the testator can leave a letter of wishes addressed to the trustees of that trust, indicating in what circumstances, and what amounts, the testator considers it appropriate that trust distributions should be made to or for the benefit of guardians. It may be that a testator would wish only that trustees might invest in residential accommodation, either jointly with guardians, or on terms that the guardians would be permitted to occupy the property on terms agreed with the trustees. Alternatively, trustees could make a loan (possibly on soft terms) to guardians to enable them to provide appropriate accommodation for minor children of the testator; or

— a separate trust fund could be established, giving the guardians a fixed interest in the trust fund until the youngest child of the testator finishes education or reaches a specified age, at which point the trust fund can be divided between the testator's children. It may be necessary to allow for the trustees of this fund to make capital advances to the guardians in order to provide maximum flexibility, while they are carrying out their obligations.

2.4.6 There is no immediate tax advantage in favour of or against any of the above methods of dealing with the situation. In the event of the death of both the testator and his partner, IHT will become payable, because there will be a cross-generational transfer of family assets. There is no difference in the amount of IHT levied, whether children inherit absolutely, everything is left to trustees, or part of the assets are left to children in trust and part left absolutely or in trust of guardians. Personal preferences of the testator and his partner, and their relationship with the potential guardians, are likely to govern the will drafting detail. The only relevant point for IHT purposes is that if grandparents (or financially comfortable other guardians) are appointed as guardians of minor children, their own IHT circumstances may be relevant in deciding whether it is fiscally prudent to leave pecuniary legacies to those guardians, rather than to make them beneficiaries under a fully discretionary will trust.

2.4.7 Another practical point that arises it is the choice of trustees where there are guardians. Often, the testator's first choice of guardian in the absence of his surviving partner is likely to be the same as his first choice of trustees. That immediately creates a potential conflict of interest, if guardians are also beneficiaries under Will trusts. Is it appropriate in the circumstances that one or more guardians should also act as trustee? If so, the usual provisions discussed in CHAPTER 2.2 should be included when the will trust is drafted. It may be appropriate to consider the appointment of a trust protector, if guardians are also to act as trustees. The obligations and duties of trust protectors are discussed in CHAPTER 4.1.

2.4.8 Appropriate clauses appointing guardians and leaving them a pecuniary legacy are included within PRECEDENT 8.

Trust possibilities for minor children

2.4.9 The range of trust possibilities available for minor children are—

— a bare trust;

— an interest in possession trust, qualifying as an IPDI within IHTA 1984 s 49A;

— a trust for bereaved minors (IHTA 1984 s 71A);

— an age 18-to-25 trust (IHTA 1984 s 71D);

— a discretionary trust.

Trusts for disabled persons

2.4.10 The IHT legislation also allows for favoured treatment for trusts for the disabled. Where it is necessary for a family to make provision for a disabled child (not necessarily a minor), it may be possible to obtain other tax advantages. IHTA 1984 s 89 provides that if at least one half of any monies applied from a trust *must* be applied for the benefit of a specified disabled person during his lifetime, even if the trust allows for 49% of the trust distributions to be paid away to other individuals, the disabled person will be treated as if he has an interest in possession on the trust property. The effect of this can broadly be summarised as being the following—

— the ten yearly charge to IHT will not apply to this trust, even though nearly half of the trust fund can be applied as if the trust were a discretionary trust; and

— IHT will not be charged on distributions from the trust fund to beneficiaries who are not the specified disabled person, but that disabled person will be treated as making a PET. Generally speaking a PET does not attract liability to IHT unless the individual making the PET dies within seven years of the transfer.

2.4.11 A "disabled person" for IHT purposes must—

— be suffering from mental disorder within the meaning of the Mental Health Act 1983 such that he is incapable of managing his own affairs (ie a formal notice has been given that the individual has been "sectioned"); or

— be in receipt of an attendance allowance under Social Security Contributions and Benefits Act 1992 s 64 (or the equivalent Northern Ireland legislation); or

— be in receipt of the disability living allowance, under Social Security Contributions and Benefits Act 1992 s 71 (or the equivalent Northern Ireland legislation) by requiring a certain degree of nursing care.

2.4.12

The precise details of these conditions are set out in IHTA 1984 s 89(4), and further details are also included in CHAPTER 4.5.

2.4.13 If there is more than one disabled child in a family, it is preferable to use a separate trust fund for each child. There are two reasons for this. First, for IHT purposes, the s 89 provisions require that, on the death of the "disabled beneficiary" that beneficiary is treated as having an interest in possession in the trust fund; with the consequence that the trust fund is aggregated with any personal assets owned by that beneficiary. The legislation does not precisely cater for more than one "disabled beneficiary", so splitting the assets into separate trust funds avoids argument with HMRC at a later date on the death of one of the disabled children, as to what proportion of the trust fund should be regarded as forming part of the estate of the deceased child. There could also be arguments, if the funds are not split, as to how or whether each child had enjoyed more than one half of applied trust benefits. Although common sense would demand that s 89 be read appropriately to allow for more than one disabled person, it is prudent to draft so as to avoid points of possible contention with HMRC where tax is at stake.

2.4.14 Secondly, for CGT purposes, if the separate trust funds can be regarded as separate trusts, each trust could be entitled to an annual CGT allowance which is equal to that available to an individual. Where disability benefits are means tested, there is a further advantage in using s 89 trusts. The trustees may be able to juggle CGT advantages against possible loss of disability benefits by prudent investment strategy, ie keeping trust income to a minimum when appropriate. The CGT rules do not precisely match the IHT provisions, see TCGA 1992 Sch 1 para 1.

2.4.15 Although it may be regarded by some as distasteful to consider tax planning advantages while making provision for disabled children, often such children sadly do not enjoy "normal" life expectancy, and the value of family assets available may be disproportionate to the financial needs of the disabled child, particularly where the State is paying for or providing primary health and nursing care. By way of example—

W, a widow, draws her will so that all the net residue of her estate (£5,000,000) is held on trusts whereunder her son John, who is a "disabled person", must receive not less than 50% of any trust distributions made during his lifetime, and her remaining 3 children and 10 grandchildren are also named as beneficiaries.

The trustees can pay the grandchildren's school fees, provided that John receives slightly more in each year than they receive in aggregate.

Hardly any income tax will be payable in respect of the school fees, because the income tax rules follow the trust distributions, rather than the deemed beneficial ownership imputed for IHT purposes by IHTA 1984 s 89.

Provided that not less than £500,001 is applied by the trustees for John's benefit (not necessarily immediately, but during his lifetime), the trustees would be able to purchase a house for £500,000 for W's daughter D, without incurring any IHT on distributing the £500,000 from the trust, provided that John survives the house purchase by seven years. John will be treated as having made a PET of £500,000.

2.4.16   For IHT purposes in the above example, John will be treated as if he is the beneficial owner of all the trust assets (IHTA 1984 s 49(1A)(b)). For CGT purposes, there will not be any liability on the trustees in respect of any deemed disposal and re-acquisition market value in the event of John's death because he is not the person entitled to an interest in possession in part of the settled property for the purposes of TCGA 1992 s 72(1), (1B).

For an example of an appropriate clause, which satisfies the provisions of IHTA 1984 s 89, see PRECEDENT 4.

2.4.17   In the example above it is assumed that there will not be any changes to the taxation of trusts, so that beneficiaries will continue to be able to obtain a refund of the tax credit available in respect of the 40% income tax already paid by the trustees. If the trustees are resident outside the UK, this 40% tax liability will not have to be paid. One of the proposals under consideration in the long awaited review of the taxation of trusts is that beneficiaries should not be able to obtain a tax repayment in respect of income tax paid by trustees (See CHAPTER 2.9).

Bare trusts

2.4.18   A bare trust is no trust at all for tax purposes, and does not merit further discussion here.

An IPDI (interest in possession) trust

2.4.19   The IHT advantage of this type of trust is that it is one of the "favoured trusts" under the regime introduced by FA 2006. Minor children who have a fixed interest in possession in trust income and capital will be regarded, for IHT purposes, as the absolute beneficial owner of the trust assets (IHTA 1984 s 52). The ten yearly charge to IHT, which applies to the majority of other trusts, will not here apply.

2.4.20 Whether it is appropriate to leave assets on IPDI trusts for minor children will depend to a large extent on the amount of assets available. It would hardly be prudent to leave substantial assets on fixed interest trusts, where minor children simply cannot prudently use or benefit from annual income which may be far in excess of their needs and requirements.

Trusts for bereaved minors

2.4.21 These trusts are the statutory trusts which arise on intestacy, or will trusts which are drafted in terms which match the statutory intestacy trusts. What many people see as the principal disadvantage of these trusts is that in order to avoid an IHT charge when trust distributions are made absolutely to minor children, those children *must* become absolutely entitled to all the trust assets when they reach the age of 18. This is seen by many people as being far too young an age for children to inherit substantial wealth.

If assets are substantial, again the same point arises with regard to an appropriate level of trust income which must be distributed to or applied for the benefit of minor children, see above.

18-to-25 trusts

2.4.22 These trusts were "invented" as part of the FA 2006 IHT reforms. They replace what used to be known as accumulation and maintenance trusts which had "favoured trusts" treatment under the IHT regime prior to 22 March 2006. 18-to-25 trusts, in reality have little "favoured trusts" status. They are taxed in exactly the same way as are discretionary trusts. The only fiscal advantage in having an 18-to-25 year trust as opposed to a discretionary trust is that the capital value of the trust fund when children are 18 years old is ignored when calculating the IHT charge which arises when beneficiaries become absolutely entitled at age 25. As demonstrated elsewhere in this book the effective tax cost of electing for the 18-to-25 regime as opposed to a fully blown discretionary trust regime is likely in most cases to be negligibly minimal. In trust terms, children beneficiaries *must* become absolutely entitled to trust assets no later than the age of 25. There are arguments both financial and prudent for and against the wisdom of this requirement.

Discretionary trusts

2.4.23 As by now has been made abundantly clear, at least one of the authors generally prefers the use of discretionary trusts wherever possible, because of the low effective charges to IHT which arise, and the maximum possible long term flexibility which is available where discretionary trusts are used. Although this preference admittedly does not extend to extremes the "tax-efficient" part of the title to this book, the view taken is that any minimal short term tax cost is usually far outweighed by long term future flexibility across generations. That flexibility will enable trustees to adapt quickly and, hopefully without tax penalty, to changing family circumstances over periods of many years.

2.4.24 Although judges in the family law courts in the UK seem currently to take a fairly broad brush approach where there are family trusts at a time when there is a relationship breakdown, the mere fact that beneficiaries have only discretionary rights, rather than any fixed and absolute right to receive trust income and/or capital, may perhaps on occasion, provide opportunities for greater retention of family assets for the children for whom the assets were intended, rather than having to share those assets with children's disaffected partners.

2.4.25 For a full discussion of the advantages and disadvantages of discretionary trusts, see CHAPTER 4.1.

Chapter 2.5

Flexible wills

2.5.1   As will be discussed in detail in CHAPTER 3.1 onwards, post-death variations are not limited to being made by deed between all consenting beneficiaries and executors. IHTA 1984 s 144(1) allows that any variation of a will made in writing and within two years of the death can be acceptable.

2.5.2   An example of a typical deed of appointment by trustees of a discretionary will trust are in. PRECEDENTS 19–20 It is the drafting, and estate planning strategy, behind that discretionary will trust, which will be discussed in this Chapter.

Drafting a flexible will

2.5.3   The idea behind a will which, on the face of it, leaves 100% of the testator's net assets to trustees of a discretionary will trust is simply that the testator abdicates all responsibility for taking personal decisions with regard to the disposition of his assets between his heirs. The testator simply leaves everything to be dealt with by his professional advisers in consultation with his heirs. A will of this nature is probably appropriate only for very financially sophisticated testators who own substantial assets, where tax and estate planning advisers have for many years already been accustomed to earning regular income from the testator and his family. The tax planning theory behind such wills is logically perfect. Human nature often gets in the way to thwart the ideal flexibility best advised by tax and estate planners. As a practical matter there are few testators who are receptive to a recommendation that they should leave their estate in this way. Generally speaking, testators need to be of a disposition such that they are inclined to take any legally possible action whatsoever, in order to reduce tax charges imposed by the government of the day. By far the majority of testators wish to retain at least some personal direction in their wills.

2.5.4   The terms of the fully flexible will include provision that the trustees of the discretionary will trust *shall* make an appointment in writing within two years of the date of death. The intent behind this drafting is twofold. First, it satisfies the requirements of IHTA 1984 s 144(1); and secondly it imposes a strict duty on the trustees to deal with matters before the second anniversary of the death.

2.5.5   An example of appropriate clauses to include in a fully flexible will is in PRECEDENT 6.

Advantages of the fully flexible will trust

2.5.6   The main advantage of adopting this drafting for a will is that the will trustees have complete discretion and freedom as to how they will distribute or hold assets which formed part of the testator's estate. They will not be concerned with having to obtain the consent of recalcitrant or difficult beneficiary heirs (as would be the case if a deed of variation were required in order to gain tax advantages for the family), nor should they become concerned with questions of whether or not any beneficiary has given consideration in order to acquire a greater benefit under the testator's estate. Given that all the heirs start off with nothing better than a hope of receiving a distribution from a discretionary trust, it is improbable that awkward questions relating to "consideration" will become relevant. The importance of there being no "consideration" in relation to any post-death variation within IHTA 1984 s 144 is dealt with extensively in CHAPTER 3.3. Everything will be dealt with, in the full discretion of the trustees, in accordance with the usual flexible discretionary clauses in the will trust. For an example see in particular, the trustee powers in the Schedule to the Model will in PRECEDENT 1.

The disadvantages of the fully flexible will trust

2.5.7   The main disadvantage of drafting a will so that all assets are held on a fully flexible discretionary will trust is that IHT has to be paid before probate of the will can be obtained (Administration of Estates Act 1925 s 25 and IHTA 1984 ss 211, 216). If an estate comprises valuable assets which are not held in trust, it is often not always practical to defer applying for probate until the will trustees decide how they will exercise their discretionary power to make an appointment. This can particularly be the case where there is a surviving partner who does not have adequate personal assets to finance necessary expenses pending grant of probate. Even where the estate comprises substantial interests in land and unquoted shares so that it is possible to defer payment of IHT by making an appropriate election (within IHTA 1984 s 227–229), cash flow for the executors may not be easy to manage.

2.5.8   The strategy behind the implementation of the fully flexible discretionary will trust is that any IHT which has to be paid (on the full value of the estate) in order to obtain probate will be repaid, together with some interest, once the will trustees have used their discretionary powers to create an IPDI which qualifies for IHT exemption. As that tends to be the usual outcome where there is a surviving partner whenever a fully flexible will is used, one has to question whether the drafting is worth the effort in the majority of cases. It may be that using the preferred Model will (see PRECEDENT 1) would be more simple and straightforward.

2.5.9   Money may have to be borrowed to finance payment of IHT. If and when an IHT repayment is made, interest will be paid at a lower rate than has been suffered by the executors. In addition, the executors will not be in control of the timing of when HMRC decide to make repayment.

2.5.10   The alternate strategy is simply to delay obtaining probate for as long as possible, so that the application for probate can be submitted at the same time as the trustees' deed of appointment is executed, in order to avoid payment of IHT. As already noted, unless the surviving partner owns personal assets which provide adequate cash flow, the practical aspects of financing living expenses in the period until probate is obtained cannot be ignored.

2.5.11   There is always the possibility that IHTA 1984 s 142 and/or s 144 may be substantially amended or repealed between the date when the will is signed and the death of the testator. Were that event to occur, the consequences of having a fully flexible will could be extremely expensive in IHT terms.

When should the fully flexible will trust be used?

2.5.12   The assets owned by the testator, and the particular circumstances of his family and heirs will almost certainly be the only relevant considerations. Examples where this strategy may be particularly appropriate include—

— where the surviving partner is uncertain of the "best" tax planned financial requirements of children/heirs;

— the possibility of obtaining planning permission for development land when the timing of planning permission is uncertain at the time when the will is drafted;

— if the testator's partner is likely to engage in a hazardous business venture at the time when the will is drafted, a fully flexible will may be a protective measure at a time when leaving assets on fully protective trusts within Trustee Act 1925 s 33 would not be completely appropriate (see paragraphs **2.2.19**, **2.2.20**);

— if there are no children or other heirs whom the testator would wish to take benefit from a nil-rate band (NRB) discretionary trust at the time when the will is drafted (there could be many reasons for this, such as the influence of drugs or in-laws, an irresponsible attitude to money which may have triggered a family argument, or many other circumstances), a fully flexible will can allow the benefit of the NRB to be retained in due course if circumstances change by the time of the testator's death, so that the discretionary will trustees could make an appointment to use the NRB.

Chapter 2.6

Dealing with the family home

Introduction

2.6.1 This Chapter focuses on the family home, on the assumption that the family home is the principal private residence which qualifies for exemption for capital gains tax (CGT) purposes (TCGA 1992 s 222). Esoteric CGT planning, and making elections between more than one residence, is not the focus of this book, so for that topic the reader should consult other specialist publications which deal with CGT planning in greater detail.

2.6.2 As a matter of preference, most tax lawyers have historically tried to dissuade clients from using the family home for tax mitigation purposes. Until the pre-owned asset (POA) legislation was introduced by FA 2004, the only effective way (other than expensive Eversden-type schemes) of mitigating IHT on the family home was—

— to borrow against it, and give away the borrowed money;

— to sell it and give away part of the cash proceeds; or

— to give away all or part of the house, retaining no personal benefit.

2.6.3 The tragic story of King Lear shows what can happen to generous parents who retain no home for themselves as they become old and feeble. That story has oft been held out to clients as a salutary warning. Also, it is a fact of life that, as we all become older, we become less confident of our financial and physical well being. The psychological strength afforded by owning and being in control of one's own home, as age advances, cannot often be understated.

2.6.4 However, where clients are insistent, and there is no other asset choice available for estate planning purposes, on occasion the family home has to be included within the tax planner's menu of assets for estate planning. In this context, estate planning has to be examined from two different perspectives: what can be done prospectively, during lifetime, to mitigate the IHT which will one day become payable in respect of the family home?; and how best can the family home be used to mitigate prospective inheritance tax (IHT) following the death of one partner, leaving a surviving partner who is likely to wish to continue living in the family home? Perhaps surprisingly the POA legislation may provide some help in the area of life time estate planning.

2.6.5 As had been said so often in this book, successful IHT planning during lifetime almost invariably requires a choice to be made between paying CGT and IHT. Assets owned by a deceased taxpayer are treated as having a CGT-free step-up in base value to market value at date of death (TCGA 1992 s 62(1)). Equally invariably, if a deceased taxpayer owns assets with a value in excess of the nil-rate band (NRB), paying CGT (on some profit element only of any asset) is the cheaper option, rather than paying 40% IHT on the full market value of assets owned. The problem is exacerbated when dealing with the family home, because any increase in value of the family home, if realised during lifetime, is usually exempt from liability to CGT, as the "principal private residence" exemption (TCGA 1992 s 222–226) should be available. This basic background fact underlies all else which follows in this Chapter. The tax rules are such that, with very limited exceptions, it is simply not possible to save both IHT and CGT on the same part of the family home. IHT planning may require that (at least part of) the family home is not comprised within an "estate" when an individual dies. To achieve this objective, if part of the family home is held in trust, or owned by other family members, the "prospective deceased" individual (a descriptive phrase used for many years by HMRC in the office currently known as HMRC Inheritance Tax (formerly Capital Taxes Office and before that Estate Duty Office, when they open files, on a pending basis, for individuals who have a life interest in settled property) must not be treated as the beneficial owner of all or part of the property, nor must he have previously owned all or part of the property. Perhaps unintentionally the amendments to the IHT trust regime made by FA 2006 may have provided some alleviation of tax planning difficulties in this area; for example where part of the family home is held in a NRB discretionary trust under which the surviving partner is able to continue living in family home.

2.6.6 The only alternative method of getting (part of) the value of the family home into trust, or owned by heirs, is to use a variation of "the loan scheme", dealt with in CHAPTER 2.7.

2.6.7 In keeping with the general thrust of this book, the focus in this Chapter is on wills, rather than lifetime IHT planning.

2.6.8 After the decision in the *Eversden* case ([2003] EWCA Civ 668; [2003] STC 822, CA) and prior to the introduction of the pre-owned assets legislation by FA 2004, there was little or no effective lifetime planning which could be undertaken to mitigate the prospective impact of IHT on the value of the family home. This was felt most keenly by home owning middle class southern England. Property inflation over the last 25 years has far outstripped the value of the NRB, so that many families find themselves facing substantial IHT liabilities, when their main asset of value is the main residence.

Basic planning

2.6.9   The main objectives of effective IHT planning in relation to the family home are usually—

— finding an IHT-free method of moving value from the estate of an older, to a younger, generation;

— not depriving the older generation (whether surviving spouse or otherwise) of the financial and psychological comfort of having a home to live in;

— maintaining maximum available CGT exemption in respect of value increase in the family home.

2.6.10

On first review, obtaining those apparently contradictory three objectives often seems to require the ingenuity of the alchemist in turning base metal into gold – perhaps not too remote an analogy in this context.

2.6.11   As described in CHAPTER 2.2, it makes sense to ensure that the NRB is fully utilised when one partner dies, leaving a survivor. Where the family home is the principal or only asset of value owned by a couple, it is usually good tax planning to arrange for approximate equality of asset ownership between them. This requires that, as soon as possible, the family home is owned as tenants in common, rather than as joint tenants. The recent case of *Phizackerley v HM* Revenue & Customs Comrs (2007) SpC 591 (STC (SCD) 328) which is particularly germane to this issue is discussed in full in CHAPTER 2.7.

2.6.12   Where the family home represents the most substantial asset of value owned by a couple, the driving reason for arranging ownership of the family home between them, rather than by one of them alone, is that, except in unusual and unfortunate circumstances, it is not often possible to predict with any certainty which partner will be the first to die. If the timing of death could be predicted with any certainty, estate planning would become much easier. It would always be possible then to plan for the best possible use of the NRB. Even where one partner has been diagnosed as having a fatal and incurable illness, there can be no certainty that the stress of hospital visiting, and coping with the bad news, may not precipitate the untimely death of the "healthy" partner.

Wills where main residence is owned as tenants in common

2.6.13 Since 22 March 2006 the IHT treatment of discretionary trusts and life interest trusts other than IPDIs is identical. The risk envisaged by trading IHT saving for payment of CGT on that part of the family home owned by a NRB trust has now disappeared. As mentioned in CHAPTER 2.7, the effect of HMRC Statement of Practice SP 10/79 (see APPENDIX 2) is no longer of relevance for IHT purposes. This means that CGT exemption can continue to be claimed under TCGA 1992 s 225 (private residence occupied under terms of settlement) in respect of the interest in the main residence, which is held by the NRB trustees. The important proviso is that the surviving partner must not have so much control over the NRB trust that s/he could be regarded as having a power of appointment over the interest in the main residence. IHT should not then be chargeable on that property interest on the death of the surviving partner, and CGT exemption under TCGA 1992 s 225, should continue to be available.

2.6.14 This arrangement is less complicated, and perhaps also less risky in terms of security of tenure for the surviving partner than the alternative that an interest in part of the main residence be left absolutely to adult children who could then settle that interest in favour of the surviving partner (thereby avoiding creation of an IPDI), on terms whereby the reverter to settlor exemption under IHTA 1984 s 72 will be available, notwithstanding restrictions to that relief made by FA 2006.

Has the surviving partner previously owned the main residence personally?

2.6.15 If at any time the main residence family home was owned exclusively by the surviving partner (for example, following divorce, before remarriage and subsequent transfer of the property into joint names with new spouse) the POA legislation may apply to impose an annual income tax charge in respect of the occupation, by the surviving partner, of the house which once upon a time belonged to him/her (FA 2004 Sch 15, subject to the exceptions in FA 2004 Sch 15 para 10 for transactions concerning a spouse or civil partner). There are only four solutions to this problem (in ascending order of cost, ie the cheapest option, subject to life expectancy of the surviving partner, is listed first)—

— it may be that the annual "benefit" for POA legislation purposes will be below the annual exemption, currently £5,000 (FA 2004 Sch 15 para 13);

— the surviving partner pays the annual income tax liability;

— the surviving partner pays market rent for use of (part of) the property;

— (assuming the Model will is being considered) the NRB trust could be converted to an IPDI so that the property forms part of the estate of the surviving partner for IHT purposes.

Can the surviving partner occupy the main residence under the NRB trust?

2.6.16   Unless deliberately intended, as is the case in paragraph above, the surviving partner's continued occupation of the main residence family home under the trust should be on terms such that s/he does not have an "interest in possession" under the trust. This usually requires, at the bare minimum, that the surviving partner undertakes to be responsible for the maintenance and proper upkeep in good condition of the whole of the family home. This should include payment of local taxes such as council tax. Now that there is no difference in IHT treatment between discretionary and life interest trusts, the effects of SP 10/79 (see APPENDIX 2) are significantly less important than they were before 22 March 2006. However it remains to be seen whether HMRC will use SP 10/79 arguments in the context of a NRB discretionary trust compared with an IPDI. They may choose to argue that there is in fact an IPDI so that IHT becomes payable on the full value of the family home on the death of the surviving partner.

2.6.17   If part of the main family residence is owned in trust, under which the surviving partner may not have an interest in possession, that may be helpful in reducing asset values for means testing purposes, should that become necessary in the context of local authority care provision. Although each local authority may take a different approach, legislation often requires that trust interests be ignored or substantially discounted.

Who should be trustees of the NRB trust which owns the main residence?

2.6.18   Where all of part of the family main residence is owned by trustees of the NRB trust, particular care needs to be given to the selection of trustees for that trust. There may be technical arguments which militate against the surviving partner being a trustee, or having rights to remove and appoint trustees. There may also be trust investment reasons why a professional adviser might decline to act as trustee.

Surviving partner as trustee of the NRB discretionary trust

2.6.19   The surviving partner may often wish to be the first named trustee, with power to remove and appoint new trustees, simply as a matter of being able to continue to control his or her future destiny relating to the family home. This is particularly the case where client families are not used to the idea of trusts. If, as is usually the case, the trustees have wide and flexible powers of appointment in respect of the assets in the trust, it could be argued that the surviving partner retains sufficient control over the family home that s/he should be regarded as if there were an IPDI in place, and not the desired discretionary trust. This will result in the value of the trust interest in the family home being treated as part of the estate of the surviving partner for IHT purposes, notwithstanding IHTA 1984 s 5(2) which specifically ignores any general power of appointment insofar as that power relates to settled property.

2.6.20 There is a far more detailed discussion of the position of the surviving spouse as trustee of the NRB trust in CHAPTER 2.3.

Chapter 2.7

Debt schemes and the family home

Introduction

2.7.1   During the late 1980s and 1990s as property values far out-stripped the rate of increase in the nil-rate band (NRB) for inheritance tax (IHT) purposes, "Middle England" families increasingly faced substantial liabilities to IHT, occasioned almost exclusively by the increase in value of their family home. Many retired teachers, doctors, dentists and others found themselves in receipt of a comfortable retirement pension, with perhaps £50,000–£100,000 of quoted investments in their personal ownership, and a family home with a value far in excess of £500,000. Even allowing for the use of two full nil-rate bands for IHT purposes, on the death of the surviving partner the family could often be facing IHT liability on perhaps £250,000: a tax bill for the family of £100,000.

2.7.2   Schemes were widely promoted, with a generic description as being "home loan arrangements". The purpose of these arrangements was to ensure that the full value of the NRB could be used on the death of the first partner, without adversely affecting the continued lifestyle of the surviving partner. Often two trusts were used as part of the arrangements. In the simplest arrangement, the first step involved partners selling their family home to a trust under which they retained an interest in possession (Trust 1). The market value purchase price was left outstanding by way of debt due to be paid by the trustees. The terms of the debt in some more complicated arrangements could be index-linked or equity-linked to the underlying value of the property. This was largely a tax neutral trans-action for IHT purposes because of the interest in possession IHT provisions as they were prior to 22 March 2006, and because of the principal private residence exemption for CGT purposes. Stamp duty could also be avoided prior to the increase in the rates of stamp duty from 1% to 4%, and the advent of Stamp Duty Land Tax (SDLT), with the consequence that SDLT liabilities could no longer be avoided or deferred by leaving property sales to rest on contract. This alone was a substantial deterrent to implementing the scheme because of the increased and unavoidable transaction costs.

2.7.3   The second step involved the partners assigning their right to repayment of the debt due from the trustees of Trust 1 to the trustees of a second (usually discretionary) trust (Trust 2) for the benefit, generally of children and issue, but from which the two partners were excluded. The assignment of debt was a PET, and in due course the amount of the assigned debt would, it was hoped, be a deductible charge against the value of the property in which the partners, or the survivor of them, continued to live.

2.7.4 Many similar arrangements have also been implemented by post-death deed of variation, as demonstrated in CHAPTERS **3.1** onwards. See also PRECEDENT **1** CLAUSE **7**.

2.7.5 The first attempt by the government to nullify the effect of these lifetime arrangements was the introduction of FA 1986 s 103, which (in the broadest terms) disallows debts as a deduction from the testator's estate if the amount or value of the debt in some way derives from the value of assets which originated from the testator. That by itself was not regarded as the conclusive nail in the coffin of the scheme, and it continued to be widely promoted, with the careful drafting of lifetime trusts, despite the SDLT costs involved.

2.7.6 Much more drastic legislation introduced to kill the scheme is contained in FA 2004 s 84 and Sch 15, known generally as the "pre-owned asset (POA) legislation". In broad terms, this legislation imposes an annual income tax liability on any taxpayer who continues to enjoy an asset, for a consideration which is less than full market value, if he has previously attempted to give away that asset. The POA legislation has dramatic effect and is largely retrospective in the way it imposes current income tax liabilities by reference to transactions which took place as long as 20 years previously.

2.7.7 In consequence, the use of lifetime home loan schemes has substantially reduced. However many testators whose family asset value is principally locked into the family home may still wish to try to use part of the value of the family home in order to satisfy an NRB legacy when one partner dies. If the value of the family home can be so used, the family can achieve a tax saving of at least £120,000 now that the NRB is set currently at £300,000.

2.7.8 The way in which this can be done is by drafting a will which specifically authorises executors to give, and the trustees of the proposed NRB discretionary trust to accept, an IOU or other "promise to pay" which can be charged on the family home, and in which the surviving partner continues to live. That IOU will be treated as satisfying the legacy to the NRB discretionary trust. Detailed consideration needs to be given to the terms upon which any surviving partner will continue to occupy the family home, and to the ownership history of the family home between the two partners, in order to ensure that the amount of any debt or IOU will, in due course, be properly allowed as a deduction against the value of the estate of the surviving partner. As was previously the case, a more advanced version of the scheme includes provisions which allow the value of the IOU to increase in line with indexed price inflation or property values. For an example see PRECEDENT 1 CLAUSE 7.

Another problem

2.7.9   The case of *Phizackerley v HM Revenue & Customs Comrs* (2007) SpC 591 (STC (SCD) 328) reinforced the dangers of implementing the home loan schemes, where the family home had not been purchased by an equal financial contribution by husband and wife. As is a fairly common arrangement, the family home was purchased in joint names, but appears to have been financed exclusively by the husband. The husband worked throughout the marriage, and the wife provided a full and hard-working contribution to the marriage, but never had any gainful employment. On advice, the joint tenancy was severed several years before the wife died, so that husband and wife owned the family home as tenants in common at the time of her death. When she died the total value of her assets did not exceed the NRB. By her will she left a NRB legacy to a discretionary trust, with the residue of her estate being left to her husband absolutely. In order to constitute the NRB discretionary trust, the husband, as sole executor of his wife's estate, promised to pay £150,000 (index-linked) to the trustees of the NRB discretionary trust.

2.7.10   HMRC challenged the arrangements on the basis that the debt was not a deductible expense in the estate of the husband because of the provisions of FA 1986 s 103. The tribunal upheld HMRC arguments, and did not accept arguments that the wife had fully contributed to the marriage, had equitable rights to marital assets, and therefore had effectively provided full "consideration" for her interest in the family home. Counsel for the taxpayer argued unsuccessfully that had there been any petition for divorce, almost certainly the wife would have been entitled to claim at least 50% of the family assets. The tribunal narrowly construed the provisions of s 103 by treating the tenancy in common interest in the family home held by the wife at her death as being an asset which was derived from her husband and in consequence denied the deductibility of the debt from the husband's estate when he died.

2.7.11   Many commentators and practitioners find the logic of the judgement of the Special Commissioner hard to follow and accept. This is so particularly in light of the House of Lords decision in the case of *Jones v Garnett (Inspector of Taxes)* ([2007] UKHL 35). This case is referred to more generally as *Arctic Systems*, the name of the family company germane to the decision of the case—where, in the context of income tax legislation involving settlements, the House of Lords specifically recognised that a non-working spouse had an equitable claim to some part of the value of family assets, so that a gift of shares in a family company from husband to wife, and the addition of value to those gifted shares as a result of the earnings of the husband, was not regarded as a gift sufficient to create a settlement in favour of the wife.

2.7.12   It is unfortunate that it seems unlikely that *Phizackerley* will be appealed. The amount of tax at stake compares unfavourably with the costs of litigation, and the vagaries of pursuing litigation, with the possible consequent risks of having legal costs awarded against party who is unsuccessful on appeal, are such that it is understood that the decision will rest unchallenged for the time being.

The future?

2.7.13   There are some very helpful comments on the impact of *Phiza-ckerley* (published before the decision regarding *Arctic Systems*) on the STEP website (www.STEP.org), available to STEP members and non-members alike. A copy of those comments is included in **APPENDIX 8**.

2.7.14   As a general rule, it may still be possible to use the home loan scheme successfully as part of tax-efficient will drafting by ensuring that the surviving partner is not left an absolute interest in residue, but is left in IPDI in those assets, with remainder to the next generation in due course. It is then clearly arguable that any deduction in respect of the IOU is not made from the estate of the surviving partner directly, but that it reduces the value of the trust assets (the residue of the estate), which need to be aggregated with the personal estate of the surviving partner by reason of the IPDI. The alternative method of the executors creating a charge over the relevant residential property is also considered still to be effective.

2.7.15   The Model will contained in **PRECEDENT 1** adequately deals with this point, see in particular clause 7 of that will.

2.7.16   The substantial changes made to IHT by FA 2006 with effect from 22 March 2006 have actually helped immensely with estate planning for the family home, so that the effect of *Phizackerley* will in any event be limited. Now that interest in possession (or life interest) trusts (other than the "favoured trusts" detailed in **CHAPTER 2.5** are taxed in the same way as discretionary trusts (falling into what is generally referred to as "the relevant property regime") for IHT purposes, it is quite easy now to obtain both IHT and CGT advantages by use of a NRB trust holding part of the family home, under which the surviving partner can be a beneficiary. The trustees can permit the surviving partner to occupy the family home, and CGT exemption will continue to be available under TCGA 1992 s 225 because the terms of SP10/79 (**APPENDIX 2**) regarding when HMRC will regard an "interest in possession" arising are largely now irrelevant. The only danger to avoid is that the surviving partner's interest under that NRB trust should not be regarded as an IPDI.

2.7.17   Finally, the introduction of the transferable NRB between part-ners, introduced in the Pre-Budget Review by the Chancellor of the Exchequer on 9 October 2007, has reduced the importance of this type of tax planning using the NRB to own some of the value of the family home. The published draft clauses for inclusion in the 2008 Finance Bill are set out in full in APPENDIX 7, and have the effect that a surviving partner's own NRB on death can be increased, if an appropriate election is made, up to a maximum of the amount of the NRB at the death of the surviving spouse. The draft legislation contains a complicated formulaic calculation of the maximum amount of transferable NRB. The formula is required, and limitations set, to deal with the occasions (possibly seldom to be encountered in practice) where a surviving partner is the survivor of two or more deceased partners who had not used their own personal NRBs to the full.

2.7.18   There are four obvious drawbacks to the immediate adoption by estate planners of the Government's new proposals regarding the transfer of unused NRBs between recognised partners, even though those proposals will not take effect for death before 5 April 2008. Those drawbacks are—

— if assets (such as the family home) may increase in value at a rate quicker than the NRB increases in amount, lower rates of IHT will be payable in future if those assets are owned by a NRB trust created by the first partner to die, rather than by using the transferable NRB on the surviving partner's death; and

— the limits of the NRB are known until 2009/2010 (respectively £312,000 for 2008/09 and £325,000 for 2009/10-FA 2006 s 155) – but thereafter it is not clear the extent to which the "old" legislation (IHTA 1984 s 8) linking the NRB to inflation as measured by the Retail Prices Index will continue to apply; and

— if all residue is left on discretionary trusts on the death of the second partner, the effect of the transferable NRB will not be taken into account when charging IHT within that trust on 10-yearly anniversaries – only one NRB will be taken into account for tax calculation purposes; and

— in view of the present Government's reversals of tax policy during the debates about FA 2006 which introduced substantial changes to the IHT treatment of trusts, there can at present be no guarantee that the draft legislation will be enacted in its present form.

Chapter 2.8

Business property relief and agricultural property relief

Introduction

2.8.1 In the context of tax-efficient will drafting, retirement is not usually an option for the testator. It is usually better for the owner of a business to run it until he drops, unless he is prepared to make a lifetime gift. If he does not, at the date of death, own the relevant property which might qualify for business property relief (BPR) or agricultural property relief (APR), no relief will be available. The same point arises in relation to lifetime planning where the owner of a business is negotiating a sale; for so long as the business is owned, 100% BPR may be available, so lifetime planning involving gifts should be made immediately prior to, rather than after, any sale. The disadvantage of making lifetime gifts is that, even if capital gains tax (CGT) holdover of relief can be claimed on making a lifetime gift, long term CGT liabilities will not be avoided because the tax free step up in base value available on death will no longer be available.

2.8.2 The reliefs are generous when they are available. At best 100% of the value of any relevant business property which has been owned by a testator for a minimum period of two years can be exempted from liability to IHT. This relief alone can allow for limitless cross-generational transfers of value to take place without any effective charge to IHT being imposed.

2.8.3 The way these reliefs operate is to reduce in value for IHT purposes property which qualifies for the relief. The reduction in value is either 100% or 50%.

2.8.4 Relief at 100% is available in respect of—

— any business or interest in a business;

— securities in a company which are unquoted and which give the transferor control of the company, either alone or in conjunction with other securities and unquoted shares which he may own;

— any unquoted shares, and this includes shares which are listed on

AIM, provided the company in which shares are owned is itself carrying on a business, which is not within the "naughty businesses" listed in paragraph **2.8.8** below.

2.8.5 In general terms, the principles behind the legislation seem to be that business assets which comprise all or part of a family business, or which are likely to be illiquid, will qualify for IHT relief.

2.8.6 The limited relief at 50% reduction in value is available in respect of—

— quoted shares or securities which immediately before the transfer gave the transferor control of the company (either by themselves or together with other such shares or securities owned by him);

— land, buildings, plant or machinery which are used wholly or mainly for the purposes of a business carried on by a company controlled by the transferor or a partnership of which he is a member;

— land, buildings, plant or machinery used wholly or mainly for the purpose of a business carried on by the transferor which is settled property in which he is beneficially entitled to an interest in possession.

A business or an interest in a business

2.8.7 Individual assets used in the business, eg a small part of the site of a garden nursery, do not qualify for relief.

2.8.8 A business which consists of dealing wholly or mainly in securities, stocks or shares, land or buildings, or for making or holding of investments will never qualify for BPR (IHTA 1984 s 105(3)): "the naughty trades".

2.8.9 An interest in a business includes the interest of a partner in the partnership business. It also includes a sum deposited at Lloyds by an underwriter so long as it is not excessive in relation to the risks covered. This contrasts with sizeable cash balances in other businesses. There may be negotiation with HMRC as to whether the cash in the business account at the relevant day was really required for the purposes of the business.

2.8.10 A loan to a business is not an interest in it, see *Beckman v IRC* (2000) SpC 226 (STC (SCD) 59).

AIM quoted shares

2.8.11 For BPR purposes, any shares which are not quoted on a recognised stock exchange can qualify as business property in respect of which full IHT relief is available. Shares quoted on any other EU junior market, or NASDAQ Europe (but not NASDAQ itself) are regarded as "unquoted" for this purpose so that BPR is available, provided that the relevant minimum period of share ownership is observed – usually a minimum of two years (IHTA 1984 s 106).

2.8.12   The only further restriction on the availability of relief is that shares in companies which carry on any of the "naughty trades" (investing or trading in property or quoted securities etc (IHTA 1984 s 105(3)) do not quality for BPR relief.

2.8.13   There is of course the practical commercial disadvantage in investing in shares quoted on AIM or other similar stock exchange. Any significant investment does really equate to a strategic investment decision, which is somewhat removed from direct tax planning considerations. It is a fundamental principle of effective tax planning that saving tax should never be regarded as a guiding principle which takes precedence over commercial investment decisions. Tax saving should never wag the commercial dog.

2.8.14   The practical difficulty with investing in shares listed on AIM in order to obtain business property relief is the danger that concerns about tax relief may outweigh a sensible investment strategy. Shares which are traded on AIM tend to be largely illiquid, and/or are subject to some volatility. There is also the concern that the two year minimum ownership requirement may be a long time in some market sectors where consolidation is taking place. It is not uncommon for aim listed companies to be taken over by fully listed companies, in which case business property relief will no longer be available. Although the investment might be sound, BPR will be lost due to matters beyond the taxpayer's direct control.

2.8.15   Some investment houses are promoting dedicated AIM listed portfolios in order to attract investment from individuals who seek to benefit from BPR.

What is a "business"?

2.8.16   Legislation is not particularly helpful as to what precisely qualifies as a "business" for the purposes of BPR. IHTA 1984 s 103(3) refers only to the fact that—

> "... 'business' includes a business carried on in the exercise of a profession or vocation, but does not include a business carried on otherwise than for gain."

2.8.17   Although some guidance as to what constitutes a "business" can be taken from VAT case law, it must be remembered that the majority of VAT law is based on the European concept of what constitutes an "economic activity".

2.8.18 HMRC seem to give some credibility to the arguments put forward by the counsel for the Crown in *Customs & Excise Comrs v Lord Fisher* ([1981] STC 238) where the following tests were formulated—

— is the enterprise "a serious undertaking earnestly pursued" or "a serious occupation not necessarily confined to commercial profit making undertakings"?

— is the enterprise "an occupational function actively pursued with reasonable or recognisable continuity"?

— does the enterprise have "a certain measure of substance as measured by the quarterly or annual value of the supplies made"?

— is the enterprise "conducted in a regular manner and unsound and recognize business principles"?

— is the enterprise "predominantly concerned with the making of supplies to customers with [for] consideration"?

— are the supplies made "of a kind which, subject to differences in detail, are commonly made by those who seek to profit by them"?

2.8.19 Although the above tests have not been accepted as being definitive, nevertheless, it seems clear that HMRC does pay important regard to those formulations. Where a company is incorporated to make profits for shareholders, it seems that any gainful use to which assets are put will normally be regarded as the carrying on of a "business" (see *American Leaf Co v The Director-General* [1979] AC 676).

2.8.20 Apart from the "naughty trades" referred to above, in accordance with common sense, BPR does not apply where a company is in course of liquidation, or a business is subject to a contract for sale. It is worthy of note that a business which is subject to an option for purchase will still qualify for full BPR. The option is not regarded as a contract until it is exercised.

2.8.21 Many of the reported cases in relation to BPR are concerned with the borderline between the "business" and "the holding of investments". In a number of cases, the facts have turned on the nature of the use to which a farmhouse is put after some of the agricultural buildings have become redundant for agricultural purposes. For this purposes, APR and BPR can form the basis of alternative claims by taxpayers. At the end of the day, difficult factual issues will be determined by the particular facts and circumstances of individual cases. It is clear that one of the most important factors to take into account is the amount of time and energy which the taxpayer contributes to making economic activity successful. The underlying (unspoken) principle seems to be that the holding of investments is largely a passive activity as far as the holder of investments is concerned.

2.8.22   Since income tax legislation was amended so as to treat the letting of land in a very similar manner to other commercial trading activities, there have been a number of cases concerned with BPR in relation to the letting of land. In very broad terms, it seems that activities relating to the letting of land in the simplest form are more likely to be treated as the holding of investments, whereas the managing of caravan pitches and sites, or the provision of bed and breakfast or hotel accommodation, may very well, on occasion, be regarded as the operation of a business, dependent on the particular facts and circumstances of individual cases.

2.8.23   As a practical point, even where the activities carried on are clearly "a business" qualifying for BPR, anti-avoidance legislation may prevent all assets within the business qualifying for relief in certain circumstances. IHTA 1984 s 112 lists several categories of "excepted assets" which do not qualify for relief. In practice, most arguments about excepted assets focus on cash balances within any business, and the extent to which the cash balances are excessive or required for the purposes of carrying on the business in future.

2.8.24   Unless fully commercial and current business need can be demonstrated for retaining cash balances, HMRC will almost invariably challenge the availability of BPR in respect of those cash balances retained in any business on the occasion when any chargeable transfer occurs for IHT purposes. In the context of businesses with seasonal cash flows (eg private schools where substantial fee balances are always held on account at the beginning of each academic term), clearly demonstrated historical trading patterns will need to be shown if BPR is to be allowed.

Agricultural property

2.8.25   Relief is available in respect of the agricultural value of any property on the basis that the relevant property is subject to a perpetual covenant prohibiting its use for anything other than as agricultural property (IHTA 1984 s 115).

2.8.26   The relief is similar to BPR, in that relief is given by a 100% deduction of the value of the agricultural property from the chargeable estate.

2.8.27   Until 1981, and previously under the estate duty regime which was in place until 1974, there was no condition regarding any minimum period of ownership, so deathbed planning was possible, simply by purchasing woodlands or other property qualifying for the relevant agricultural property relief. The law was amended in order to target the relief on working (and retired) farmers, rather than "non-farming investors".

What is agricultural property?

2.8.28 The legislation is not helpful. There is no clearly defined statutory definition although IHTA 1984 s 115(2) allegedly helps. Technical analysis is much like designing the committee's camel – known with certainty only when seen. The initial definition is, like some alleged divorce customs, thrice circular—

> "... agricultural land or pasture and any woodland or pasture ...used in the intensive rearing of livestock ...if the woodland or building is occupied with agricultural land or pasture and the occupation is ancillary to that of the agricultural land or pasture, and also includes such cottages, farm buildings and farmhouses, together with the land occupied with them, as are of a character appropriate to the property" (IHTA 1984 s 115(2)).

2.8.29 Breeding and rearing horses on a stud farm is specifically mentioned. It was decided, in *Hemens v Whitsbury Farm & Stud Ltd* (1988 2 WLR 72) that stud farming was not "agriculture" at general law. This was presumably because the draftsman recognised that stud farms might not qualify as sufficiently "intensive" rearing, particularly as nominated mares do not often stay for long at the stud.

2.8.30 As a matter of practice HMRC seem to follow, without specific statutory authority, the definition of "agriculture" in the Agricultural Tenancies Act 1995, which includes—

> "horticulture, fruit growing, seed growing, dairy farming and livestock breeding and keeping, the use of land as grazing land, meadow land, osier land, market gardens and nursery grounds, and the use of land for woodlands where that use is ancillary to the farming of land for other agricultural purposes" (Agricultural Tenancies Act 1995 s 38(1)).

2.8.31 In order to qualify for the relief the taxpayer must either—

— have occupied the relevant land for the purposes of agriculture for at least two years; or

— have owned the relevant land for only seven years before the relevant IHT transfer during which period it has been occupied (by him or another, including a company controlled by the taxpayer) for the purposes of agriculture (IHTA 1984 s 117).

2.8.32 As is the case with business property, relief is not available, if the agricultural property is subject to a contract of sale.

The farmhouse

2.8.33   There is no direct statutory cross reference to the CGT legislation which governs CGT exemption for a principal private residence and "the permitted area", which is either grounds up to a maximum of 0·5 hectare, or—

> "such area, larger than 0·5 of a hectare, as the Commissioners concerned may determine if satisfied that, regard being had to the size and character of the dwelling-house, that larger area is required for the reasonable enjoyment of it (or of the part in question) as a residence." (TCGA 1992 s 222).

2.8.34   HMRC originally took the view that they would deny relief if it seemed to them that the house was not a working farmhouse, but a desirable residence surrounded and enhanced by farmland? If the latter, even if APR is not denied, HMRC have been known to argue that only the agricultural value of such a residence should qualify for APR, ie any premium market value as a result of potential seekers of desirable homes being in the market, should be chargeable, rather than relieved. It is a fact of contemporary life that farmhouses often attract a substantial premium to their (agricultural) value-particularly where they are Queen Anne houses within 25 miles of central London. The Special Commissioners have not always seen eye to eye with HMRC when these arguments have been advanced (see the article on this topic in *Taxation*, October 2003).

2.8.35   There has been much litigation in recent years, concerning the valuations of "farmhouses". Large houses surrounded by agricultural land can command a substantial premium in the contemporary marketplace, but it is clear that not all houses which were originally constructed to be farmhouses will qualify as agricultural property. Another pitfall to avoid is the purchase of sporting estates. Where land is used for rough grazing, but the main economic value derives from shooting rights, the sporting value of the land does not form part of agricultural property valuation purposes (*Earl of Normanton v Giles* [1980] 1 WLR 28).

2.8.36   In order to qualify for relief any dwellinghouse must—

— be a farmhouse (or farm cottage);

— have been occupied for the purposes of agriculture for the appropriate period;

— be connected with other agricultural property;

— be of a character appropriate to agricultural property (ie a stately home or substantial mansion in the middle of a farm may not be 'appropriate' for agricultural purposes).

2.8.37   Whether or not a farmhouse qualifies as such depends on whether farming activities are or can be carried on from that property. In

Rosser v IRC ([2003] STC (STD) 311) the deceased taxpayer had given away 39 out of the 41 acres of land which had originally belonged to him. His house was used principally for the purpose of providing refreshments and meals for those who worked on the land which he had given away. HMRC took the view (with which the court agreed) that the farmhouse had ceased to be a working farmhouse and had simply become a retirement home for the deceased taxpayer prior to his death.

2.8.38 Adventurous taxpayers living in what is essentially a private home have also not had any success in claiming APR. In *Dixon v IRC* ([2002] STC (SCD) 53) a three bedroom cottage on a plot of 0·6 of an acre was denied relief notwithstanding that the taxpayer claimed that 0·5 of an acre constituted an orchard.

2.8.39 The reported case which is likely to be regarded as the (current) last word in bringing together all relevant cases is probably *Lloyds TSB (Executors of Antrobus) v IRC* ([2002] STC (SCD) 468), where the judgement of the Special Commissioner, at page 480, included the following—

> "… the principles which have been established for deciding whether a farm-house is of a character appropriate to the property may be summarised as: first, one should consider whether the house is appropriate by reference to its size, content and layout, with the farm buildings in a particular area of farmland being farmed; secondly, one should consider whether the house is proportionate in size and nature to the requirements of the farming activities conducted on the agricultural land or pasture in question; thirdly that although one cannot describe a farmhouse which satisfies the 'character appropriate' test one knows one when one sees it; fourthly, one should ask whether the educated rural layman would regard the property as a house with land or a farm; and finally, one should consider the historical dimension and ask how long the house in question has been associated with the agricultural property and whether there has been a history of agricultural production."

2.8.40 Any appeal from a decision of HMRC on such matters (areas and values) lies to the Lands Tribunal.

Will drafting pitfalls

2.8.41 The most common pitfalls come from the interaction of IHT exemptions and the reliefs for BPR and APR. Many practitioners have seen or heard the phrase "gifts of partially exempt residue", made a mental flag to look at the detail one day if forced to, but otherwise to avoid the problem until it occurs, because this is a problem area. It can often be the operation of BPR and APR which causes the problem, not just gifts from residue to charities.

2.8.42 Will drafting and planning needs to resolve the conflicts between—

— leaving assets to a surviving partner in order to enable him/her to maintain a comfortable lifestyle; and

— maximising exemptions and reliefs for IHT purposes;

— providing a mechanism for future flexibility if circumstances change from what is expected – always the key to successful tax planning.

2.8.43   IHTA 1984 s 39A makes clear that the benefit of a specific gift of property which qualifies for BPR or APR goes to the specific legatee. This can be demonstrated by a simple example—

> T has used his Nil-rate Band (NRB), and the remainder of his estate comprises business assets qualifying for 100% relief valued at £500,000 and an investment portfolio of the same value.
>
> *Option 1*: business property to partner, investment portfolio to children. IHT payable = £200,000 on the investment portfolio.
>
> *Option 2*: business property to children (absolutely or on trust), investment portfolio to partner. IHT payable = £Nil.

2.8.44   This is strictly interpreted by HMRC. For Option 2 above to operate, there must be a *specific gift* of the business property to the children. Appropriation of business property in satisfaction of a pecuniary legacy will not satisfy the provisions, nor will the payment of a legacy "out of" assets which qualify for relief.

Planning to obtain Option 2 results – a real option?

2.8.45   Perhaps it simply is not appropriate for the children to inherit the business assets, but the price of the tax payment is such that some planning is required.

2.8.46   Advance planning might draft the will such that the BPR assets are specifically gifted to the children (or to trustees for their benefit), but another provision in the will (or in a separate lifetime disposition) could grant to the partner an option to purchase the BPR assets. The option could be for a nominal price (say, £100) or for full value. Provided that the option is just that, and not a binding contract, Option 2 tax saving will result. There will also be a further tax-free CGT re-basing on the death of the second partner, assuming that the assets qualifying for relief are then still in the ownership of the surviving partner.

2.8.47   The full value option price allows of two further planning alternatives: either the parties are placed in the Option 1 position without IHT liabilities; or the price can be left outstanding, secured as a debt on (non-business?) assets retained by the surviving partner.

Temporary discretionary trust?

2.8.48 The fully flexible two year discretionary trust will (see CHAPTER 2.5) can be used for the totality of the estate, and the trustees can make an appropriate appointment within two years of the death, claiming relief under IHTA 1984 s 144.

2.8.49 At risk of duplication of some of the points made in CHAPTER 2.5, some of the perceived disadvantages of this approach may be—

— the testator's wish to "do things personally" from the grave;

— initial payment of IHT must be made to obtain probate, and a subsequent repayment claim will need to be submitted;

— assets must be "settled property" (ie not still forming part of an estate in administration) at the time the trustees make their appointment; IHTA 1984 s 144 relief will otherwise not be available;

— what if s 144 is repealed or amended after the testator's death but before the trustees make the appointment?

Property attracting relief not specifically bequeathed

2.8.50 The examples used in this section were originally published by Professor Lesley King in an article in *Trusts and Estates Tax Journal*. The examples demonstrate how BPR can be fickle in its application if the will draftsman does not take all relevant factors into account.

2.8.51 Completion of appropriate HMRC forms, and calculation of tax liability, will not be straightforward where there are assets of this nature. Perhaps an unexpected tax saving may result from leaving assets to be dealt with as all or part of estate residue.

2.8.52 In the absence of a specific bequest, the relief is apportioned between all estate assets, using a formula fraction, set out in IHTA 1984 s 39A(4). For example—

> T leaves pecuniary legacies of £200,000 to A and to B and the residue of the estate (which includes property eligible for BPR) to C. The benefit of the BPR is apportioned through the estate so that both the pecuniary legatees and the residuary legatee benefit.

> The formula—

$$\frac{R}{U}$$

has to be used to work out how the relief is apportioned between all the estate assets. R is the value of the estate as reduced by agricultural and business relief (less the value of any specific gifts qualifying for relief); and U is the unreduced value of the estate (less the value of any specific gifts qualifying for relief), as demonstrated below.

T, who has exhausted his NRB, dies leaving to his daughter a farm worth £600,000, qualifying for 100% relief. The rest of his estate is worth £2,000,000 and includes property attracting BPR of £800,000. He leaves a pecuniary legacy of £600,000 to his son, residue to his partner. The gift of the farm attracts 100% relief and the daughter alone gets the benefit of the relief. The BPR of £800,000 must be apportioned between the son and the partner.

The formula operates as follows—

— R is £2,000, 000 less £800,000 = £1,200,000;

— U is £2,000, 000.

$$£600,000 \text{ x } \frac{1,200,000 \text{ (R)}}{2,000,000 \text{ (U)}} = £360,000$$

To find the value attributed to the son's legacy, multiply by R/U—

The value attributed to the residue is—

$$£1,400,000 \text{x } \frac{1,200,000 \text{ (R)}}{2,000,000 \text{ (U)}} = £840,000$$

The effect is that the son takes a legacy of £600,000, but IHT is calculated on a value of only £360,000. If the property eligible for BPR been left specifically to the son, there would have been no IHT payable at all.

Had the legacy been given tax-free, and the residue to an exempt beneficiary, it would have been necessary to gross up the tax-free legacy.

Making best use of business property and agricultural property relief

2.8.53 If the testator owns assets which qualify for 100% BPR or APR, it is axiomatic that he should not "waste" that relief by leaving those assets to his partner. Any transfer of assets to a partner will in any event be exempt from liability to IHT. The better course of action is clearly to ensure that assets qualifying for 100% relief from charge to IHT should be bequeathed to heirs, other than a surviving partner. A discretionary or fixed interest IPDI trust would seem to be the most logical and flexible long term ideal solution.

2.8.54 PRECEDENT 2 contains a clause which shows how property qualifying for relief can be clearly directed to be part of NRB discretionary trust recommended as part of the model will.

2.8.55 Where there are the assets of sufficient value available within the family, it may be possible to obtain a tax advantage by "double dipping" the relevant relief. Consider the following example—

H owns a controlling shareholding in W Ltd, the company which manufactures widgets. H's shareholding has a market value of £2,000,000. H's other assets have a value of £3,000,000.

By the terms of his will H directs that—

— assets equivalent in value to the NRB left on discretionary trust for his children, grandchildren and surviving partner;

— his shares in W Ltd are also left to the trustees of that same discretionary trust;

— the remainder of this assets are left to his surviving partner on flexible life interest trust.

No IHT is payable on H's death, because no chargeable assets have been the subject of any chargeable transfer.

Once the administration of H's estate is complete, the trustees of the discretionary trust can agree to sell the shares in W Ltd to the surviving partner for a cash payment of £2,000,000. The transaction will be free of CGT, because the shares in W Ltd will have the same value as the probate purposes. If there is any argument about valuation, provided the sale takes place within one year of the death, an election can always be made to substitute the sale value for probate value (IHTA 1984 ss 179, 181).

If the surviving partner holds the shares in W Ltd two years, 100% business property relief will again be available if a further gift is made of those shares, or if the surviving partner holds the shares until death

The consequence is that there is a transfer of £4,000,000 from one generation to the next without payment of the £1,600,000 IHT which would otherwise be chargeable.

Chapter 2.9

Non-resident will trustees

Introduction

2.9.1   There is much complex UK legislation with regard to the taxation of benefits and distributions provided by offshore trustees to UK resident trust beneficiaries. Over the last 25 years there have been successive attempts by governments in the UK to impose penal taxation so as to make the use of offshore trusts substantially less attractive to UK resident beneficiaries. However fiscal advantages do remain in some circumstances, and it seems likely that the number of circumstances where non-resident trustees may provide domestic UK tax saving opportunities will increase, particularly if the Government does introduce fixed 40% taxation on UK trusts, with no refundable tax credit available in respect of the income tax suffered by trustees. This is one of the main proposals put forward in a Government consultation paper (*Modernising the Tax System for Trusts:* August 2004) shortly prior to FA 2005, but not all of which have yet been implemented. The stated intention of introducing flat rate trust taxation at 40% was introduced by FA 2006, but the restriction of availability of beneficiary tax repayments in respect of tax credits for income tax paid by trustees has not yet been introduced, not least because of the difficulties in dealing with the accumulated tax credits held by many trustees, usually including the 15% "additional rate income tax for trusts" which was imposed on discretionary and accumulation and maintenance trusts after 1973.

Fiscal advantages of non-resident will trustees

2.9.2   A non-resident will trust can operate almost as a tax-exempt roll-up fund, similar to a UK pension fund. No UK income tax need be suffered within the trust, apart from any withholding taxes suffered on interest or dividend investment income. If/when the proposal is introduced to disallow beneficiaries to claim income tax repayment in respect of income tax paid by trustees, non-resident trusts will be at a significant advantage.

2.9.3   If the will trust is discretionary in nature, no income tax will become payable unless/until income distributions are paid to a UK resident beneficiary who is liable to pay UK income tax.

2.9.4   Any individual UK resident beneficiary will be entitled to his or her own tax allowances and reliefs in calculating what, if any, income tax should be paid on the receipt of a trust distribution.

2.9.5   No UK capital gains tax (CGT) will be suffered unless/until capital distributions are paid to a UK resident beneficiary who is liable to pay CGT.

2.9.6   Any individual UK resident beneficiary will be entitled to his or her own tax allowances and reliefs in calculating what, if any, CGT should be paid on the receipt of a trust distribution.

2.9.7   Although it is possible for effective rates of CGT payable to be increased by a penalty if realised capital gains are not distributed shortly after the tax year in which the gains are realised, the level of penalty is controlled by the effective rate of CGT payable by a UK resident beneficiary in the year in which a capital distribution, liable to CGT, is received. Often matters can be arranged so that the effective rate of CGT suffered is minimal.

2.9.8   For UK fiscal purposes, irrespective of trust law or the manner in which trust accounts are maintained, no distributions can be made from realised capital gains until such time as amounts equal to *all* realised trust income have first been distributed. This fundamental rule of UK taxation concerning offshore trusts results from substantial changes to UK tax law introduced in 1981, at a time when the highest rate of income tax was reduced from 75% to 60%, and tax on realised capital gains was "only" 30%.

2.9.9   If realised capital gains are retained by offshore trustees for a period of six years prior to any distribution of those realised gains (TCGA 1992 s 87 refers to such realised undistributed gains as being "stockpiled gains" in the hands of the trustees), as a technical matter it is possible, under current law, that the "headline" rate of CGT payable may be increased to up to 64% (or possibly only 28.8% with effect from 5 April 2008). This is explained in more detail below.

2.9.10   As already noted above, it is most unlikely that this "64% headline rate" of possible CGT liability will ever become payable. Discretionary trustees should have so much flexibility under the terms of any will trust that they should be able to arrange affairs so that trust assets can be made available to potential beneficiaries in such a way as to avoid liability to CGT at penal rates.

2.9.11   A clause appointing non-resident will trustees is in the model will in PRECEDENT 1.

UK tax treatment of distributions and benefits from non-resident trusts

2.9.12 The fundamental UK rule is that the effective rate of taxation payable on trust distributions/benefit provided will be dictated entirely and exclusively by the personal fiscal circumstances of the UK resident beneficiary who receives a distribution or enjoys any particular benefit. The UK tax treatment of trust distributions received by any UK resident beneficiary can be summarised as follows—

— distributions will first be taken as absorbing all realised trust income (ICTA 1988 s 740). For this purpose any reference to trust income or gains includes income or gains which have arisen to any underlying entities (such as offshore companies) owned by trustees;

— in so far as there is a shortfall of realised income to finance distributions, trustees will be treated as making distributions of realised capital gains (TCGA 1992 s 87); and

— in so far as distributions are made out of trust capital, they will be treated for UK tax purposes as advance payments of capital gains as yet unrealised, so that when future capital gains are realised within the trust structure, CGT liabilities will arise by reference to the prior capital distributions already received (TCGA 1992 s 89);

— if a "benefit" is provided (such as an interest-free loan or rent-free occupation of a holiday home) the way in which tax is charged is similar to that which applies to "benefits in kind" provided to employees by their employers. By way of example a beneficiary who borrows £100,000 interest-free from the Trustees will be treated as if he has a "trust benefit" equivalent to the official HMRC official rate of interest (see FA 1989 s 178 and the Taxes (Interest Rate) Regulations, SI 1989/1297 as amended). The HMRC official rate of interest approximates to the base rate for lending of the major clearing banks. If the HMRC official rate is 6%, for each year that the loan is outstanding, £6,000 will be added to the beneficiary's taxable income, and tax will be payable on that amount. There may be scope for argument as to whether the annual notional interest should be liable to income tax or CGT. If CGT is relevant, the effective rate of tax payable will depend on the individual beneficiary's marginal top rate of income tax and/or whether the beneficiary has used his or her annual exempt amount for CGT purposes.

2.9.13 If non-resident trustees make distributions for the benefit of young beneficiaries by way of payment of school fees, it is perfectly possible that the actual amount of annual taxation payable will be almost insignificant. A trust distribution of just over £16,600, made from realised capital gains, to a UK beneficiary with no other income or gains, would give rise to UK tax liability of slightly over £200, as shown below, using rates and allowances and exemptions current for 2007–08. The Government announced at the time of the spring Budget in 2007 that the 10% income tax band shown is to be abolished, and the basic rate of income tax will be reduced to 20% from 5 April 2008, but this has not yet been included in legislation. For example—

	£
Annual CGT exemption	9,200
Single person's allowance	5,225
	14,425
10% income tax band	2,230
Gross distribution	16,655
Tax payable (10% x £2,150)	(223)
Net distribution after tax	16,432

2.9.14

The net distribution figure to each of three grandchildren makes a substantial contribution towards financing payment of school fees.

2.9.15   If the trustees were to make further distribution payments to infant children who have no other source of income or realised personal capital gains, they would enable parents to be relieved from their most expensive outgoings. If an additional £32,370 (the maximum income tax band liable to tax at 22%) were to be distributed, aggregate additional tax liability would be £7,121. So, a total gross distribution of £49,025 (£16,655, the gross distribution shown in the calculation, plus the £32,370 as above) would give rise to an effective rate of tax of approximately 14% for each beneficiary, leaving each beneficiary with a net £41,904 after payment of all taxes. This calculation ignores the effect of any CGT surcharge. If the surcharge is payable, the effective rate of surcharge would be 1·4% (10% of the effective rate of tax suffered) for each year (up to a maximum of six) that the realised gains remain offshore, undistributed, after the end of the year of assessment following that in which the gain was realised (TCGA 1992 s 91). If distributions were restricted to £16,432 (the net distribution shown in the calculation), the effective rate of surcharge would be 10% x 0·0134%, ie 0·00134%, for each year since the gain was realised; a negligible amount, falling a long way short of the headline 64% maximum tax rate possible.

2.9.16   As noted in paragraph 2.9.9 above, it is likely that the rate of CGT will be standardised at 18% with effect from 5 April 2007. If that change takes place and applies equally to the surcharge arrangements for delayed capital distributions from non-resident trusts, the maximum effective rate of CGT on such distribution will reduce from the current 64% to a more modest 28.8% (ie 18% + (6 x 10% x 18%) = 28.8%. It will probably not be long before taxpayers come to regard that as an unacceptably high rate of tax – but it does increase the attractions of non-resident trusts, when capital gains, taxed at the highest possible rate of liability, will still suffer tax at rates lower than the higher rate of income tax – a partial return to the tax regime as it was prior to 1981.

2.9.17   Any parent who pays income tax at 40% and wishes to pay school fees or spend £16,432 on any child during the course of a year (whether simply purchasing clothes, paying for holidays etc) would have to have a gross income of £27,387 (£27,387 x 60% = £16,432). The difference between that gross income and the income required to be distributed by the Trust in order to obtain the same net advantage for each child is £10,995.

2.9.18   There are many other possibilities of using non-resident trusts to maximum advantage in order to minimise UK taxation payable by UK resident beneficiaries. The detail of those possibilities is beyond the scope of this book.

Chapter 2.10

Non-domiciled partners and overseas aspects

Introduction

2.10.1   The overseas aspects of tax-efficient will drafting involve two broad categories of assets and individuals—

— UK resident and domiciled individuals who own non-UK assets which may be subject to "forced heirship" rules for inheritance, with consequent considerations for IHT planning, and the need to analyse potential conflicts of laws; and

— individuals who are not domiciled in England and Wales as a matter of general law, who own UK assets and/or non-UK assets, and who may be treated as deemed domiciled in the UK for IHT purposes (IHTA 1984 s 267).

2.10.2   For non-domiciled individuals, substantial tax savings can be achieved by focusing on property which is described in the IHT legislation as "excluded property". Generally speaking, non-UK situate assets which are owned directly or indirectly by a non-domiciled individual. "Forced heirship" rules (the English speaking catch-all phrase used as a shorthand description of the civil law rules regarding devolution of assets on death) and possible conflicts of laws also need to be taken into account for these individuals.

2.10.3   UK domiciled individuals may also be entitled to "excluded property", and this is something that should be checked before embarking on will drafting. This is often particularly relevant where one of the testator's parents has already died, leaving the surviving partner with an IPDI or an IIP under a will trust. It is most likely that the testator will then be entitled to inherit all or part of the capital assets within the deceased parent's will trust. That reversionary interest will be "excluded property" unless the will trust is treated as an offshore trust for UK tax purposes (IHTA 1984 s 48). Similarly if the testator's family has a history of family trusts, there may very well be one or more reversionary interests to which the testator is entitled. Usually it is not possible to deal with reversionary interests under a will, but as part of drafting the will, advice could be given as to how best the excluded property reversionary interests could be dealt with in order to achieve tax savings within a family. An example of how this can be dealt with is in CHAPTER 2.2.

2.10.4 Where partners have different domicile status, the interaction of the IHT deemed domicile rules and some of the detailed provisions of double taxation treaties dealing with death duties, may have to be taken into account, see below.

Situs of assets

2.10.5 In order to analyse the extent of potential exposure to IHT for a non-domiciled individual, it is necessary to have some understanding of the rules regarding the situs of assets. Space does not permit a detailed discussion of this concept and reference should be made to more specialist reference works for detailed analysis. Suffice to say that the rules set out below provide a set of generally reliable working assumptions, unless there are special circumstances surrounding the nature of particular assets—

— bank accounts are situated in the jurisdiction where the relevant branch or account is maintained;

— quoted stocks and shares are situated in the jurisdiction where they are quoted and traded;

— unquoted shares in an incorporated company are situated in the jurisdiction where the company is incorporated;

— real estate (land) is situated in the jurisdiction where the land is; and

— loans secured on real estate will probably be treated as being situated in the jurisdiction where the land is.

Domicile

2.10.6 Before looking at will drafting strategies in relation to foreign domicile, it is imperative to have an understanding of the general law of domicile, and the particular IHT rules which may treat a non-domiciled individual as being domiciled in the UK.

2.10.7 Domicile is a concept peculiar to the common law. It is contrasted with fiscal residence. Fiscal residence can be determined solely as a matter of fact, by counting the number of days when an individual may be physically present in a particular jurisdiction. In some jurisdictions, such as the UK and the USA, the "counting of days" may need to extend over a period of several years. Domicile is a far larger concept than residence. It is determined by a mixture of law, fact and intention. Often an individual's intentions for the future can only be analysed with the benefit of hindsight.

2.10.8 For IHT purposes, "domicile" has a special meaning because the legislation requires that the concept of "deemed domicile" be addressed.

Domicile at common law

2.10.9   HMRC make clear in their instruction manuals to Inspectors that domicile is a matter of law and is not specifically a tax matter (see IM1635). The HMRC instruction manuals actively dissuade HMRC officials from becoming involved in discussion and/or correspondence regarding the domicile status of individual taxpayers, unless a substantial amount of tax turns on the conclusion. Even then the standing rubric is that individual officers should refer questions regarding domicile to specialist units within HMRC (the Centre for Non Residents in Bootle – see Residence Guide RG3 and EIM42804 and SE41050 in the Manuals Section of HMRC website).

2.10.10   Apart from specialist legal publications, one of the best short summaries of the law regarding domicile is in the HMRC publication known as IR20: Residents and non-residents—liability to tax in the United Kingdom. This booklet, available on HMRC website and also from most HMRC offices, contains a succinct and useful summary of the law of domicile.

2.10.11   The place of an individual's domicile is usually determined by the place where the individual habitually lives, as a matter of his choice. The individual's—

— nationality; and

— intentions for the future regarding his desires to establish permanent physical residence

will also be relevant considerations in establishing where an individual has his "roots".

2.10.12   Against that background, a simple outline of the law of domicile can be summarised by the following general rules—

— every individual always has a "domicile". An individual can never have more than one domicile status at any time; it can never be "dual", as is sometimes the case with nationality;

— a *domicile of origin* is acquired at birth;

— a child's domicile of origin will be the same as the child's father's domicile status at the child's date of birth;

— until a child becomes adult, the child's domicile status will change if the father's domicile status changes. Because a child's domicile of origin, and domicile during childhood, is wholly dependant on the domicile status of the child's father, it is known as a *domicile of dependence*;

— an adult can abandon his/her domicile of origin or dependence by making a positive choice to acquire a different domicile status – a *domicile of choice* – by establishing a permanent home and "centre of vital interests" in a different jurisdiction. Case law in the UK shows that this may not be easy to achieve;

— as a matter of general common law, a woman is regarded as automatically acquiring a domicile of dependence on the occasion of her marriage. She is regarded as acquiring (if different from her own domicile of origin or choice) the same domicile status as her husband. In the application of UK law, that rule has been overridden by statute since 1 January 1974. For UK purposes a woman's domicile status now continues, after her marriage, to be analysed by reference to her own personal circumstances.

2.10.13 There have been a number of UK court decisions regarding domicile over the years. These cases demonstrate that, as a matter of common law, it is very difficult to shed ones domicile of origin and to acquire a new "domicile of choice". One example of a court decisions is the case of a Canadian who lived in the UK (with his English wife) for more than 40 years. When he became a widower he continued to hold the intention of returning one day to Canada, but when he died in the UK he had not by that time put that intention into practice. The Court of Appeal held that he was still domiciled in Canada as a matter of common law (*CIR v Bullock* [1976] STC 409).

Deemed domicile

2.10.14 For IHT purposes an individual will be treated as being domiciled in the UK if—

— "he was domiciled in the United Kingdom within the three years immediately preceding the relevant time; or

— he was resident in the United Kingdom in not less than seventeen of the twenty years of assessment ending with the year of assessment in which the relevant time falls" (IHTA 1984 s 267(1)).

2.10.15 In estate planning parlance, this treatment is usually referred to as deemed domicile.

2.10.16 Unlike common law, therefore, for inheritance tax (IHT) purposes an individual can be treated as domiciled in the UK (deemed domiciled) solely based on an analysis of factual matters – for how many years has an individual been physically resident in the UK? As a matter of general law the individual may well continue to be treated as domiciled elsewhere.

2.10.17 The description of deemed domicile can, on the face of it, be misleading. IHTA 1984 s 267 set out above requires careful reading. The test is not simply 17 complete years of physical residence in any 20 year period. The test is whether an individual has been resident *in* the UK at any time in (ie during) any year of assessment. The point can be simply illustrated—

> T, a national of Ruritania who had never previously lived in the UK, arrived in the UK on the 30 March 1993. T's domicile status needs to be analysed on 6 April 2008. As a matter of fact T has been resident in the UK for 15 years and one week in the period from 30 March 1993 to 6 April 2008. For IHT purposes T will be treated as domiciled in the UK on 6 April 2008 because he has been resident *in* the UK *in* 17 years out of the 20 years of assessment ending 2008–09 as demonstrated below—

Year of assessment	Resident in UK
1992–93	6 days to 5 April 1993
1992–93 to 2007–08	15 years
2008–09	1 day

Excluded property

2.10.18 "Excluded property" is, as the description suggests, property which is ignored for IHT purposes. In the context of will drafting within the structure of the IHT legislation, which property is "excluded property"?

2.10.19 IHTA 1984 ss 6, 48 set out the relevant statutory rules. Those sections are not here set out in full, and the reader is advised to consult the relevant legislation if advising a non-domiciled testator.

2.10.20 The most commonly encountered overseas property regarded as excluded property are as follows—

— "Property situated outside the United Kingdom is excluded property if the person beneficially entitled to it is an individual domiciled outside the United Kingdom." (IHTA 1984 s 6(1)).

— "A holding in an authorised unit trust and a share in an open-ended investment company is excluded property if the person beneficiary entitled to it is an individual domiciled outside the United Kingdom." (IHTA 1984 s 6(1A)).

— "Where property comprised in a settlement is situated outside the United Kingdom—

   • the property (but not a reversionary interest in the property) is excluded property unless the settlor was domiciled in the United Kingdom at the time the settlement was made, and
   • s 6(1) above applies to a reversionary interest in the property but does not otherwise apply in relation to the property." (IHTA 1984 s 48(3)).

Partners with different domiciles

2.10.21 The most commonly encountered problem with regard to drafting wills is where spouses do not have the same domicile status. Where one spouse is domiciled in the UK (whether as a matter of common law or deemed domicile for IHT purposes) and the other spouse is not UK domiciled, great difficulties can be encountered in making transfers of assets from the domiciled to the non-domiciled spouse. The usual rule is that asset transfers between spouses are regarded as exempt transfers for IHT purposes (IHTA 1984 s 18(1)). That normal rule is displaced where the recipient spouse is not domiciled in the UK. The exempt limit is then restricted to £55,000. A limit of value which has remained constant since 1982 (IHTA 1984 s 18(2)).

2.10.22 The only domestic exception to this rule is where assets are transferred by a domiciled to a non-domiciled spouse pursuant to a Court Order consequent on divorce or judicial separation. Any such asset reallocation is specifically exempted from being a chargeable transfer of value for IHT purposes (IHTA 1984 s 11(1)). This extreme form of tax planning strategy perhaps gives meaning to the concept of an "amicable divorce".

Effect of double taxation treaties

2.10.23 The UK has concluded only ten double taxation treaties concerned with estate taxes. This compares with the 120 or more income tax, corporation tax and capital gains tax treaties. Of the ten treaties which deal with estate taxes, only six have been concluded since what is now IHT was invented in March 1974. These six treaties are with Ireland, the Netherlands, South Africa, Sweden, Switzerland and the USA. The other four current treaties are with France, India, Italy and Pakistan.

2.10.24 Double taxation treaties become relevant where estate taxes are payable in two separate jurisdictions in respect of the same asset. A double tax treaty never imposes a liability – it will determine which of two states have taxing rights in respect of particular assets, in order to prevent a dual charge to tax on the same asset. For example—

T, a banker from New York and a US citizen has worked for 17 years for an investment bank based in London. He owns a house in London which is worth £2,000, 000 when he unexpectedly dies of a heart attack on his way to a meeting.

The house is liable to IHT in the UK because it is UK situated real estate. It is also liable to estate taxes in the US (which are higher than IHT in the UK) because T is a citizen of the USA and is domiciled in New York. T is also treated as domiciled in the UK (the 17 years' residence in the last 20 years) so UK IHT applies to his worldwide assets.

The terms of the UK/USA Treaty will determine which jurisdiction has the prior claim to tax the assets in T's estate.

2.10.25   In order to achieve a solution to the different tax claims which arise in the above example, most double taxation treaties usually contain two broad categories of provisions which set particular rules—

— regarding the situs of assets; and

— for determining domicile status, where fiscal domicile is usually the basis upon which estate taxes are levied.

2.10.26   As noted above, when the deemed domiciled provisions were first introduced into UK legislation on 26 March 1974, the original proposal for a deemed domicile test was 7 years residence in any 10 year period. There was such an outcry against that proposal that by the time legislation was finally available (in November 2005) the original proposal had been changed to that which is contained in current legislation ie 17 years fiscal residence in any 20 year period. Without exception, all the double taxation treaties relating to estate taxes/IHT which have been negotiated since 1974 contain provisions which may allow domicile status to be decided by reference to a test based on seven years out of ten residence test, where the Treaty needs to be invoked to determine in which of two states an individual is to be treated as domiciled.

2.10.27   When double taxation treaties are used to determine in which jurisdiction an individual will be treated as domiciled, the relevant tests are usually a combination of habitual residence, nationality and local legislation. Where the law of domicile itself is relevant (as can be the case with the Treaty with Italy), practical difficulties may arise because civil law does not have the same concept of "domicile" as does common law. In civil jurisdictions, an individual may often be treated as "domiciled" in the village in which he was born and where he is entitled to vote in general elections. That is a far cry from the tests required under common law with regard to fact and intention. Practical difficulties can occur if HMRC in the UK, before accepting a non-domiciled claim, require a legal opinion from a civil lawyer that the deceased individual was domiciled in the civil law jurisdiction. It is vitally important to ensure that the civil lawyer whose opinion is sought understands the common law rules with regard to domicile before he writes his opinion.

2.10.28   Although there is not space within this book to provide detailed examples of how double taxation treaties can affect IHT payable as a result of wills drawn for UK resident individuals, a few examples are appropriate—

— The Treaty with Pakistan (Double Taxation Relief (Estate Duty) Order (Pakistan), SI 1957/1522), which predates the introduction of IHT by nearly 20 years, effectively disapplies the IHT rules regarding deemed domicile. The result is that the common law rules regarding domicile would continue to apply. Even though a non-domiciled partner may have been resident in the UK for more than 20 years.

— The Treaty with Sweden (SI 1981/840) has particular rules with regard to real estate and nationality rather than residence. Surprisingly, this treaty is still operational notwithstanding the fact that Sweden has abolished death duties.

— The Treaty with the US (which is very similar to that with South Africa), concluded after the introduction of IHT (SI 1979/1454), effectively allows for a testator to leave a US-domiciled partner an IPDI interest, without reference to the £55,000 limit of tax exemption which would otherwise apply by reason of IHTA 1984 s 18(2). Ultimately IHT will be payable in the UK on the death of the surviving partner because there are provisions in the Treaty which prevent capital appointments being made on tax-free basis by will trustees to the US-domiciled surviving partner.

2.10.29   From the above examples, it is clear that expert advice needs to be taken where issues arise with regard to different domicile and nationality status between partners who wish to draw wills.

Chapter 3.1

Disclaimers and deeds of variation

Introduction – what is happening in the real world?

3.1.1 Before looking at the statutory rules dealing with variations and disclaimers, which introduce a degree of counter factual treatment for certain purposes provided the relevant conditions are fulfilled, it is instructive to consider the underlying nature of what is taking place as a matter of property law, for the reason stated in paragraph **3.1.27** below. Just as the special tax treatment afforded in 1975 to trusts for beneficiaries under age 25 (FA 1975 Sch 5 para 15) led to the "invention" of a species of trust never previously identified, accumulation and maintenance trusts, so the special tax treatment afforded to deeds of variation from 1978 (originally confined from 1975 to deeds of family arrangement) has resulted, in many cases in which that treatment is invoked, in dispositions taking an unnecessarily complex form that would not previously have been contemplated (see paragraph **3.1.212** below), and which is all too easily capable of obscuring exactly what it is that is entailed in the variation.

3.1.2 The majority of cases that seek to make use of these special tax rules involve variations. But, as will be seen later in this chapter, the rules extend equally to disclaimers, which will be dealt with first because they have a much longer history. For more detail in relation to disclaimers in the context of wills, reference can be made to *Halsbury's Laws of England* (4th Ed) Vol 50 (2005 Reissue): Wills, paras 441–444, 471, 472.

3.1.3 In this chapter the term "original beneficiary" will be used to connote the beneficiary of the original disposition that is being varied or disclaimed, and "new beneficiary" or "new beneficiaries" for the person(s) in whose favour a variation is made. As will be seen (see paragraph **3.1.13** below), the identification of the beneficiary who takes the property in question after a disclaimer is not something which the original beneficiary can influence, so "new beneficiary" is not used in the context of disclaimers.

Disclaimers

Disclaimers generally at common law

3.1.4 At common law, neither a donor *inter vivos* nor a testator can compel an intended beneficiary to accept his bounty, whether or not the gift is onerous. As it was put so graphically by Ventris J over 300 years ago, in *Thompson v Leach* (1690), 2 Vent 198, a man "cannot have an estate put into him in spite of his teeth". Provided the original beneficiary has done nothing to accept any benefit from the gift, legacy or interest provided in his favour, and is of full capacity, he is entitled to disclaim it.

3.1.5 On a gift being disclaimed, the property or interest affected will then pass as though it had never been conferred on the original beneficiary (see paragraph **3.1.13** below); but this does not mean that the original beneficiary is treated for all purposes as though the gift or legacy had never been given (see paragraph **3.1.16** below). There is no rule that lapse of time bars a disclaimer; but the longer the time elapsed since a gift took apparent effect, the more persuasive must be the evidence that he has genuinely done nothing to accept the gift. Lack of knowledge of the gift may of course have a substantial bearing in that context.

3.1.6 In contrast to the particular requirements if special treatment for IHT purposes is required (see paragraph **3.1.51** below), there is no particular formal requirement for a disclaimer at common law. As the nature of the act is non-acceptance, as opposed to the disposition of an interest already vested, it can be made orally or, if the circumstances are clear enough, even by conduct (see for example *Cook v IRC* [2002] STC (SCD) 318). Even in relation to land, although a disclaimer is included in the definition of "conveyance" in the Law of Property Act 1925 (LPA 1925) s 105(1)(ii), an express exception is made for disclaimers from the basic rule in the LPA 1925 s 52(1) that a conveyance of land or of an interest in it must be by deed if it is to operate to convey a legal estate; by the LPA 1925 s 52(2)(b), that rule does not apply to disclaimers made under certain provisions of the Insolvency Act 1986 (which are made by service of notice) or to [any other] disclaimers that are not required to be evidenced in writing.

3.1.7 However, there is a presumption that a gift will be accepted, and so the evidence must be clear that permanent disclaimer of the gift as a whole was intended (it was not strong enough to this effect in *Cook v IRC*). Thus where a life tenant refused (without consideration) to accept income payments, and no-one had acted to their detriment in reliance on this, she was allowed to change her mind eight years later as to future income payments (*Re Young, Fraser v Young* [1913] 1 Ch 272). Similarly a refusal by a life tenant to take possession of an onerous leasehold property did not deprive him of entitlement to the income from the proceeds of sale (*Earl of Lonsdale v Countess Berchtoldt* (1857) 3 K & J

185). Because of this willingness of the courts to allow retraction of a disclaimer in certain circumstances where made for no consideration, as seen in the cases just cited, use of a deed is advisable in any case where a voluntary disclaimer is intended to be irrevocable; see generally *Halsbury's Laws of England* (4th Ed) Vol 50 (2005 Reissue): Wills, para 444.

3.1.8 A disclaimer of an interest under a will cannot be made until the will has taken effect through the death of the testator: *Re Smith, Smith v Smith* [2001] 3 All ER 552, [2001] 1 WLR 1937. This can be seen as a direct consequence of the analysis of a disclaimer as a refusal to accept the gift; something which is not yet available for acceptance cannot be refused.

Disclaimer after the beneficiary's death

3.1.9 Conversely, in stark contrast to the possibility of a variation in those circumstances (see paragraph **3.1.18** point (d) below), there is nothing to prevent the interest of an original beneficiary being disclaimed by the personal representatives of an original beneficiary who has died after the testator, provided—

(a) this course would still have been open to the original beneficiary himself had he survived, and

(b) the personal representatives themselves have also done nothing to accept the interest.

HMRC indicate in IHTM35164 that they consider such a disclaimer would need to be executed by both the personal representatives of the original beneficiary and the beneficiaries of the original beneficiary's estate, though this is not strictly the case. Plainly the personal representatives would disclaim at their peril if they did not act with the approval of the beneficiaries to whom they are accountable – after all, the disclaimer (especially where tax planning is involved) will usually involve a direct and deliberate loss of value to the estate they represent – and it is probably this which HMRC have in mind. However, the personal representatives would be adequately protected if they obtained the consent (or were given the directions) of the beneficiaries as a whole by other means (even, it would seem, orally, subject to the obvious evidential preference for writing); and of course if some of the beneficiaries were not of full capacity it would be necessary, for the personal representatives' protection, to obtain the approval of the court, which again would not be expected to be embodied in the disclaimer itself. All the same, where time and other constraints allow, it will clearly be preferable to adopt the procedure indicated by HMRC, simply to avoid having to argue the issue with them.

Partial disclaimer

3.1.10 A disclaimer at common law is an all or nothing matter. Acceptance of any part of the gift, to any degree, will preclude disclaimer of any of it: it is inconsistent with an intention to renounce or disclaim the gift. In *Re Joel, Rogerson v Joel* [1943] Ch 311, [1943] 2 All ER 263, CA, a bequest of a house "together with" its contents was held to be a single gift, so that one element could not be disclaimed while accepting the other. On the other hand, if on a true interpretation of the will there are two distinct gifts, there is nothing to prevent the legatee accepting one and disclaiming the other, unless the contrary can be inferred from the circumstances. If a particular gift is (apart from this rule) susceptible in principle of partial acceptance and partial rejection, and a testator wishes to facilitate the disclaimer of it in part, a clause can be included providing for this; although some draftsmen prefer a longer form of words which treats any cash legacy as a collection of legacies of £1 any number of which can be disclaimed while accepting the others, it is thought that an express power to disclaim in part while accepting as to the remainder would be upheld without that degree of artificiality.

Consideration for a disclaimer

3.1.11 At common law a disclaimer does not have to be gratuitous. It would be perfectly valid (provided no benefit had been accepted in respect of the gift itself that is being disclaimed) if the original beneficiary demanded and received a price from the subsequent beneficiary, thereby in a sense exploiting the gift from which he then declines to take any benefit: see Re *Wimperis, Wicken v Wilson* [1914] 1 Ch 502. (The presence of consideration in that case – the payment of a lump sum in return for the disclaimer of an annuity – was not raised as an issue affecting the validity of the disclaimer; merely the question whether the original beneficiary, being a married woman, was disqualified from disclaiming an interest that was subject to a restraint on anticipation.)

Disclaimer of joint interests

3.1.12 Joint beneficial interests under a will (as opposed to interests as tenants in common) are a rarity; but if property is left to persons jointly then a disclaimer by one is ineffective. If the bequest is to be declined, it must be declined by all of them, or the joint tenancy must be severed before the disclaimer. This was decided, in somewhat unusual circumstances, in *Re Schär, Midland Bank Executor and Trustee Co v Damer* [1951] Ch 280, [1950] 2 All ER 1069, though Vaisey J went on to construe the deed in question as a release of the interest in question to the other joint beneficiaries.

Destination of property disclaimed

3.1.13 It is important to remember that – following directly from the nature of a disclaimer as a refusal to accept a legacy, not a disposition of the property in question – an original beneficiary who disclaims his interest has no control over the destination of the property. That is exclusively a matter for the will, or, so far as the will does not extend, then for the law of intestacy. (If a lifetime gift is disclaimed the disposition fails; for a testamentary gift the principle is similar in that the property falls back into the estate and a substitute destination must be found.) Thus—

(a) a cash legacy to X, residue to Y; if X disclaims, the legacy fails and falls into residue;

(b) residue to X for life, remainder to X's daughter for life, remainder to X's grandchildren; if X disclaims, X's daughter's life interest takes immediate effect;

(c) residue to X, Y and Z in equal shares; if X disclaims, Y and Z take equally;

(d) ¼ of residue to X, ¼ to Y and ½ to Z; if X disclaims, there is a partial intestacy as to "his" ¼. If X is one of those entitled under the intestacy rules, the gift to him under the intestacy rules is clearly a separate gift, and it is not an inescapable conclusion that his disclaimer will have covered the intestacy entitlement as well; it depends on the proper interpretation of the disclaimer, so the drafting of a disclaimer needs to take account of such a possibility. Consider—

  (i) "I disclaim my entitlement under clause 6 of the will", as compared to

  (ii) "I disclaim any entitlement of mine in respect of the deceased's residuary estate".

3.1.14 The testator might of course anticipate the possibility of a disclaimer: there is no reason why he should not include a clause (generally) to the effect that if a beneficiary disclaims his entitlement then the interest disclaimed should go instead (for example) to any children of the original beneficiary living at the testator's death, or (alternatively) should devolve as though the original beneficiary had predeceased the testator. But without such a provision it is a fallacy that a disclaimer will trigger a substitution clause in the will in favour of the children of the original beneficiary. So it would make no difference to the result in example (c) of paragraph **3.1.13** above if the will had contained a proviso to the effect that if any of X, Y and Z failed to survive the testator the share he would have taken should go instead for his children's benefit. As indicated there, if X disclaims, it is Y and Z, not X's children, who become entitled to the share in question. X would need to enter into a variation, not a disclaimer, if he wishes his children to take in his place. The condition applicable to a typical substitution clause for children of the "front-line" beneficiaries is that the latter should have failed to survive the testator (or to reach a relevant contingency age, where applicable); unless the testator provides for the effect of a disclaimer as above, that condition is simply not fulfilled on a disclaimer, because the disclaiming beneficiary did in fact survive the testator, and the substitution clause cannot therefore take effect. Similarly, as pointed out in CG31470, if a will leaves a fund to A for life with remainder to such of A's children as survive A, a disclaimer by A will not vest the interests of A's children absolutely: their interests remain contingent on surviving A, as specified by the will, even though A no longer has any interest in the fund.

3.1.15 Disclaimers of interests under the intestacy rules call for particular care if unexpected consequences are to be avoided. Indeed, for clarity it must be recommended that, where an intestacy is concerned, a variation is used instead of a disclaimer every time. Suppose, for example, that the deceased died unmarried and intestate, survived by his mother and brother. In those circumstances his estate passes entirely to his mother under the AEA 1925 s 46(1)(iv). If she had failed to survive, it would have passed instead on the statutory trusts for his brother, under the first limb of AEA 1925 s 46(1)(v). However, if his mother disclaims, the estate will not go to his brother: AEA 1925 s 46(1)(v) as amended is prefaced with the words "If the intestate leaves no spouse or civil partner and no issue and no parent", and the mother's disclaimer does nothing to affect the operation of that condition. The intestate did indeed leave a parent. The deceased's estate would therefore, on the mother's disclaimer, pass to the Crown, the Duchy of Lancaster or the Duchy of Cornwall as appropriate, as *bona vacantia* under the AEA 1925 s 46(1)(vi).

Retrospection at common law

3.1.16 The person who becomes entitled on a disclaimer by the original beneficiary is entitled with effect from the death (subject to any interests taking priority over the one disclaimed). Thus if the disclaimed interest was in possession from the death, the fallback beneficiary is entitled retrospectively to the income accruing from the fund in question since the death, even if a significant amount of time has gone by since the death. The original beneficiary has no entitlement whatever in the light of his disclaimer. To this extent, in one sense, the disclaimer has some retrospective consequences. But it is not true to extrapolate from this a proposition that the original beneficiary who disclaims is to be treated as never having had any form of rights in respect of the gift disclaimed. Two decisions of the Court of Appeal in relation to estate duty held—

(a) that the original beneficiary was, before disclaiming, competent to dispose of the property disclaimed (*Re Parsons, Parsons v A-G*, [1942] 2 All ER 496); and

(b) that the disclaimer operated as an extinguishment of a right in respect of the disclaimed property, at the expense of the original beneficiary and (whether or not it was possible to make out an intention to this effect on the part of the disclaiming beneficiary) for the benefit of the person who takes in the light of the disclaimer (*Re Stratton's Deed of Disclaimer; Stratton and ors v IRC*, [1958] Ch 42, [1957] 2 All ER 594).

Variations

What is a variation?

3.1.17 Variations as such are of course in general designed to take advantage of legislative provisions which provide for certain retrospective effects or other exemption (see paragraphs **3.1.28**, **3.1.76**, **3.1.142**, **3.1.152** below). But although those provisions tend to be expressed in terms of varying dispositions, and many people speak of varying or rewriting a will, some aspects of the tax treatment of variations cannot be properly understood without appreciating exactly what is in fact happening as a matter of property law when such a variation is entered into. In a nutshell, whatever the terms in which the variation is expressed – and it is often drafted as the insertion or substitution of clauses into the deceased's will, further helping to obscure the true nature of the operation, see paragraphs **3.1.212** ff below – the original beneficiary is simply making a disposition to the new beneficiary of something which, in imprecise terms, "came to him from the deceased" (under the will, intestacy law or otherwise). (As HMRC put it in a recent update to CG31600, "Strictly speaking, the instrument of variation does not actually vary the will itself, but only the effects of the will".) That disposition is made at the date the variation takes effect, and on the terms decided by the original beneficiary; it could be by way of gift, exchange or (unusually) outright sale. If it is a disposition into trust, then the original beneficiary will be the person who made that trust, both in the sense of causing it to come into being and in the sense of contributing the value that enters it. The parties to the deed considered by the Special Commissioner in Personal Representatives of *Glowacki v HMRC* Spc631 (decision released 21 August 2007) did their utmost to confuse the issue by purporting to make "such variation of [the deceased's] disposition of [a house] as will have effect ... as if [the deceased] in her lifetime and immediately before the transfer deemed to have been made by her under [IHTA 1984 s 4] had transferred the House to [X] ... absolutely". However the Special Commissioner rightly held (at paragraph 34 of his decision) that what was contemplated in the statutory reference to a variation (in particular in IHTA 1984 s 142, see paragraphs **3.1.28** ff below) was "a change in the way in which property that the deceased beneficially owned immediately before his death devolves as compared with how it would otherwise devolve as a result of the person's death. That is 'the variation'." (The reference to beneficial ownership is to be read in the light of the Special Commissioner's reference in paragraph 32 of his decision to the definition of a person's estate in IHTA 1984 s 5 as the aggregate of all property to which he is beneficially entitled – this in turn is qualified for the purpose of the IHT relief as described in paragraph **3.1.30** below.)

Some common misunderstandings

3.1.18   It is on to that principle that the deeming rules of tax legislation, so far as they extend, are grafted and, where applicable, provide for different consequences for the purpose of the particular taxes concerned. Keeping this analysis in mind allows certain common misunderstandings to be avoided—

(a) That the personal law of a foreign domiciled testator must be consulted in order to establish whether his will can validly be varied at all, or whether a trust of the sort intended can validly be established by means of a variation. In truth, it is the personal law of the original beneficiary – determined, under English principles at least, by his domicile – that is relevant for these purposes. If he is capable of making a gift, then he is capable of redirecting to someone else assets that he has inherited from someone overseas (though he may need to take account of the law of the country where the assets are situated, for example if his intended new beneficiary is debarred from owning property there through enemy status); and if he is capable of forming a trust of the type proposed, then that trust will be valid irrespective of whether it was one which the deceased's personal law would have allowed him to incorporate in his will. (The comment in paragraph 36 of the Glowacki decision that "any variation must reflect a change in the actual disposition of a person's estate that could have occurred at the time of the deemed transfer of value under [IHTA 1984 s 4]" is not inconsistent with this proposition – the Special Commissioner was not concerned in that paragraph with foreign law issues affecting what the deceased could actually have done, merely that what must be varied "is the destination of the estate on its deemed transfer under [IHTA 1984 s 4]".)

(b) That the perpetuity period applicable to any trust formed by means of the variation will start on the death of the deceased. That is certainly true, in English law terms, if the deceased's will established a trust and the variation consists merely of an adjustment of the beneficial interests under it. But if the original beneficiary was absolutely entitled, then any trust coming into being as a result of the variation is, in property law terms, a disposition taking effect on the date the variation is entered into; and the perpetuity and accumulation rules apply on that basis. That said, there is in general no harm in expressing the perpetuity period to commence (or to be reckoned by reference to lives in being) at a date *earlier* than the date of the disposition, and this is often done (if perhaps without consideration of the alternative) in variations for which the "inserted clauses" drafting style is employed (see paragraph **3.1.212** below).

(c) That setting up a trust by way of variation of an estate somehow improves the asset protection status of the trust. In reality, in the event of an external attack of the sort mentioned below, its position is no different from what it would be if the trust had been established by some other means. Such attacks could involve a variety of statutory provisions, including—

(i) various provisions of the Insolvency Act 1986 under which transactions at an undervalue can be set aside at the instance of the original beneficiary's trustee in bankruptcy (or of a creditor of his without his necessarily having become insolvent);

(ii) various provisions of social security legislation which treat a claimant (to means tested state or local authority benefits, including for example income support or care home fees) as still possessing resources of which he has deliberately deprived himself;

(iii) the Matrimonial Causes Act 1973 s 37, under which a reviewable disposition (as defined) can be set aside if shown to have been made with the intention of defeating a claim to financial relief under that Act (or, if made within three years beforehand, if not proved to have been made without such intention); and

(iv) the I(PFD)A 1975 s 10 (see paragraph **3.3.6** below, point (f)), under which the person to whom a disposition was made within six years before the death of the disposer, and otherwise than for full valuable consideration, can be ordered to provide property as specified by the court for the purpose of making financial provision under that Act, if it is shown that the disposition was made with the intention of defeating a claim under that Act.

(d) That a will can be varied to eliminate or redirect a life interest given to a person who has already died by the date the variation takes effect. As pointed out by the Special Commissioner in *Soutter's Executry v IRC* [2002] STC (SCD) 385 (and substituting English terminology), the personal representatives of the deceased life tenant have by that time no item of property which they can surrender or assign: they "could not have continued to receive the [life interest] so they had nothing to give up or vary ... a purported [assignment] of an expired [life interest] has no reality". If of course neither the life tenant during his lifetime, nor his personal representatives since his death, have in fact received any benefit in respect of the life interest, or done anything that signifies definite acceptance of it, the personal representatives – with suitable authority/consent from the beneficiaries of the life tenant's estate – can still disclaim the benefit of the life interest (see paragraph **3.1.9** above): that is simply a refusal to accept the benefit that the life interest would have conferred, and indeed HMRC's instruction in IHTM35042 points out to examiners that, although they must reject a variation of this type, they should nevertheless inform the parties "that if it is possible for the life tenant's personal representatives to disclaim the life interest as a matter of general law, then you may accept the IoV as a disclaimer of a life interest". (It would seem, incidentally, that nothing should turn in this context on whether the fund in which the life interest subsisted was or was not producing income, or even capable of doing so.) But a variation is a different matter, and it is too late to redirect the interest once it has come to an end.

Disclaimers and variations by residuary beneficiaries

3.1.19 The nature and subject matter of the original beneficiary's disposal call for somewhat closer analysis in a case where the variation is entered into by a residuary beneficiary in that capacity and his share of the estate has not yet been distributed to him (or at least not yet in its entirety – distributions on account are commonplace, but for present purposes it is assumed that the variation is made before any distribution). The same analysis, in its most straightforward form, would also hold good where an interest in residue is disclaimed, at any rate to the extent that the disclaimer might fall to be treated for any purpose as a disposal.

3.1.20 While the estate remains in course of administration, a residuary beneficiary has no equitable or other proprietary interest in respect of any of the assets held for the time being by the personal representatives. All he has is a *chose in action* (what might be called a legal intangible right, using the word "legal" in the lay sense and not in intended contradistinction to "equitable"), comprising the right to compel the due administration of the estate by the personal representatives: *Sudeley v A-G* [1897] 1 AC 11, *Barnardo's Homes v Special Commissioners of Income Tax* [1921] 2 AC 1, *Commissioner of Stamp Duties v Livingston* [1965] 1 AC 694. (The right to compel due administration of course includes the right to compel distribution of the residuary estate, when ascertained, to the beneficiaries entitled to receive such distribution; it is a different way of expressing what in more modern times would probably be referred to as a right to hold the personal representatives accountable for their acts and omissions in the administration.) That right is exercisable only personally against the personal representatives; a proprietary right to the assets in the hands of the personal representatives, good as against the whole world, does not arise until the personal representatives have (expressly or impliedly) assented to the vesting of property in the beneficiary, or appropriated it to him, on completion of the administration or earlier release of particular assets from the personal representatives' rights to resort to those assets for administration purposes.

Analysis of residuary beneficiary's variation

3.1.21 There is no logical reason why this chose in action, like most other legal intangible rights (including rights of action against third parties), cannot be assigned, in whole or in part, to an assignee chosen by the original beneficiary; and certainly no authority that the authors are aware of to prevent such assignment. (The reason for making this point is explained in paragraphs **3.1.23–3.1.26** below.) An assignment of the full share of a single original residuary beneficiary is the simplest scenario to follow; the new beneficiary becomes, in place of the original beneficiary, the person who is entitled to compel due administration and receive the residuary estate when ascertained. If the variation relates to a fractional part of the original beneficiary's entitlement, each of them has a parallel right to compel due administration, which as above would include compelling the distribution of residue, when ascertained, to the original beneficiary and the new beneficiary in the shares resulting from the variation.

3.1.22   The analysis is less clear-cut if an original residuary beneficiary makes a variation which provides for the new beneficiary not to have a share of residue but rather a fixed sum. Inevitably, that sum would fall to be paid out of the original beneficiary's share of residue, not out of the estate before ascertainment of residue, though in practice if the original beneficiary were the sole residuary beneficiary and the estate was suffi-cient it might look as though there were no difference between those concepts. (Many would probably speak of this, and indeed draft it, as the provision of an additional legacy; but it would not be a legacy in the same sense as any other pecuniary legacies left by the will, since if one were to suppose that the estate, net of debts, testamentary expenses and adminis-tration costs, was at the end of the day insufficient to meet the original legacies plus the fixed sum specified by the variation, the original legacies would take priority under the normal order for application of assets; it would therefore be residue – and so the fixed sum provided by partial assignment of it – which would be reduced. The other legacies would not abate rateably with the fixed sum unless the original legatees had all joined in the variation to provide for this.) The authors are not aware of any authority either way, but because of the near impossibility of expressing any consequent partial assignment of the original beneficiary's *chose in action* in percentage terms (the percentage would vary as the value of the assets under administration changed), it is thought that a variation of this type might potentially be analysed as a charge of the fixed sum on the original beneficiary's share, rather than a partial assignment as such. However, for the reason explained in paragraph **3.1.96** below it is felt that it would be fruitless to attempt to reach a definitive conclusion on this issue.

HMRC's competing analysis

3.1.23   The authors of the section of HMRC's CGT Manual dealing with variations and disclaimers put forward a completely different prop-erty law analysis of a variation by a residuary beneficiary where the administration is still continuing. Their approach may lead to arguably more practical consequences for CGT purposes than the analysis set out above (see paragraph **3.1.98** below); but the authors are unable to see any legal justification for the HMRC analysis as a matter of law. The HMRC view is recorded in paragraph **3.1.25** below; the CGT consequences said to flow from it (which in a number of respects produce a more lenient result than the analysis explored above) are noted in paragraph **3.1.97** below.

3.1.24   Normally it will be possible – and strongly advisable – to avoid the issue as to the precise legal analysis, by ensuring that the CGT backdating provisions apply (see paragraphs **3.1.76** ff below). But if that is not, or cannot be, done, and the treatment proposed in the CGT Manual proves for any reason *less* favourable in a particular case than that which would apply based on what the authors consider to be the correct analysis above, there would seem to be grounds for contesting the HMRC approach.

3.1.25   Perhaps misled by a description of the residuary beneficiary's *chose in action* as a personal right – which of course would have been intended, in the context, to distinguish it from a proprietary right (see paragraph **3.1.20** above), not to connote that it is personal to the person possessing it – HMRC assert that—

(a)   "This *chose in action* is personal to the [original beneficiary] and is not disposed of if the devolution of the estate is varied. The variation therefore only disposes of the future proceeds of this *chose in action*. The proceeds of an existing *chose in action* which will arise in the future are themselves a *chose in action*. At the date the variation is effected this second *chose in action*, which may be described as a future *chose in action*, is acquired by the [new beneficiary] under the variation." (CG31950)

(b)   "On a disposal of a future *chose in action* for valuable consideration the [original beneficiary] should be treated as having made a disposal for capital gains tax purposes on the date that the … variation was effected. The [original beneficiary] is contracting to deliver to the [new beneficiary] the assets he or she will eventually receive from the estate." (CG31961)

(c)   "If the non-retrospective variation is made for valuable consideration then the [new beneficiary] acquires a *chose in action* at the date of the assignment, being a right to the future expectation of assets vesting from the estate." (CG31972)

(d)   "An agreement to assign a future *chose in action* … is only a good assignment when it is made for valuable consideration. When there is no valuable consideration the assignment can only take effect once there are specific assets that the [original beneficiary] can assign. This position is only reached when assets vest from the estate to the [original beneficiary], normally when the residue is ascertained." (CG32001)

(e)   "Because the original *chose in action* is personal to the [original beneficiary] and is not disposed of despite the variations that have occurred, the transfers of assets that are made by the personal representatives when the assets vest are transfers to the [original beneficiary as] legatee." (CG32030)

3.1.26 Doubtless a lengthy debate could develop as between the HMRC view and the authors' view outlined above. This book is not the context for such a debate, though one criticism of HMRC's starting point is made in paragraph **3.1.95** below. Suffice it to say that one factor which might be pertinent to a decision between the two, if the matter were to come before a court, is to consider what would be the position if a voluntary variation, made when the original beneficiary was demonstrably solvent, provided for the whole of the original beneficiary's residuary share to pass to the new beneficiary; but if, by the end of an unavoidably lengthy administration period (eg because the personal representatives had to defend third party litigation against the estate), either

(a) the original beneficiary had become bankrupt. If HMRC were right in treating such a variation as not constituting an effective assignment until residue had been ascertained, the assignment would fail and the original beneficiary's share would pass to his trustee in bankruptcy; but if, as the authors consider, the variation took effect as an immediate assignment of the original beneficiary's chose in action, the trustee in bankruptcy could only take anything if he could succeed in setting aside the gift (which is unlikely to be possible on the premise that there could be shown to have been no doubt over the solvency of the original beneficiary at the time); or

(b) the original beneficiary had died. Again, if there were no effective assignment of the chose in action during the lifetime of the original beneficiary, the chose in action would form part of the original beneficiary's estate at his death, and (assuming as would almost certainly be the case that it was not executed in a manner satisfying the requirements of the Wills Act 1837, s 9) the variation could not be resuscitated in some way thereafter when the executors of the original deceased were able to complete the administration of his estate.

It is thought that a court would strain against the implications of the HMRC analysis in both these examples.

Relevance of property law analysis

3.1.27 The property law analysis of a disclaimer or variation, as described above, will be applicable for tax purposes as well, except to the extent that a different treatment (particularly backdated effect for IHT and to a degree CGT) is prescribed by statute. Different provisions are relevant for the different taxes that have to be considered in a typical case, and these will be considered in turn.

IHT treatment

Property comprised in the deceased's estate

IHT effects where relevant conditions are met

3.1.28 For IHT purposes a complete backdating of the effects of a disclaimer or variation is available under IHTA 1984 s 142, provided a number of conditions are met (see paragraphs **3.1.51** ff below). Where this is applicable, IHTA 1984 s 142(1) provides that the IHTA 1984 is to apply as if the variation had been effected by the deceased or, as the case may be, the disclaimed benefit had never been conferred. Additionally, by IHTA 1984 s 17(a), a variation or disclaimer to which IHTA 1984 s 142(1) applies is not a transfer of value.

Dispositions that can be varied within the IHT relief

3.1.29 This treatment is available, under IHTA 1984 s 142(1), where the variation relates to (or the disclaimer is of the benefit of) any of the dispositions of the property comprised in the deceased's estate immediately before his death, whether those dispositions were effected—

— by will,

— under the law relating to intestacy,

— or otherwise.

The law relating to intestacy need not necessarily be that of any part of the UK. As regards the "or otherwise" words, the most common situation in which this category is invoked in practice is property of which the deceased was one of two or more beneficial joint tenants, so that his severable share devolved at his death automatically on the survivor(s); but it would also include property passing under foreign law "forced heirship" provisions that override a will, by nomination (eg National Savings investments if dealt with in this way), or even a disposition by way of secret trust. HMRC will also accept as within IHTA 1984 s 142 a variation which redirects the deceased's interest in a partnership where that interest accrues automatically to the other partners, without payment, under the terms of the partnership agreement; but they will generally resist attempts to use that section to backdate a variation of the contractual destination of his partnership share in cases where value falls to be given for it: see IHTM35073.

3.1.30 However, IHTA 1984 s 146(5) modifies for this purpose the general rule of IHTA 1984 s 5 as to what is comprised in the deceased's estate: for the purpose of IHTA 1984 s 142(1) that expression—

(a) includes excluded property; but

(b) excludes property to which the deceased was treated as beneficially entitled by virtue of the gifts with reservation rule in FA 1986 s 102; and

(c) excludes settled property to which the deceased was treated as beneficially entitled by virtue of an estate IIP under IHTA 1984 s 49 as amended (though HMRC will accept as part of the free estate property in which the deceased had an estate IIP but *also* had a general power of appointment which he exercised by will – see IHTM35072, and see also paragraph **3.1.74** below).

Multiple variations

3.1.31 It was argued in *Russell and anor v IRC* [1988] STC 195, [1988] 2 All ER 405 that the dispositions resulting from a variation to which FA 1978, s 68 (the pre-consolidation equivalent of IHTA 1984 s 142) applied could themselves be further varied by a second variation under that section, on the ground that the effect of the statutory backdating was to render the dispositions resulting from the first variation "dispositions (whether effected by will … or otherwise) of property comprised in the deceased's estate immediately before his death". The "or otherwise" category was dismissed on the ground that these words "must be construed in the light of the *ejusdem generis* rule as limited to dispositions, whether by acts of parties or operation of law, which take effect on the death of the deceased' ([1988] STC 195 at 204). As regards the "by will" category, Knox J held that it was not legitimate to stretch the statutory fiction (that the dispositions resulting from the first variation were to be treated as having been made by the deceased) so far as to treat those dispositions as capable of further variation within the scope of the section. This "involves taking the hypothesis further than is necessary. No authority was cited to me of a statutory hypothesis being applied to the very provision which enacts the hypothesis. Such a tortuous process would merit a specific reference in the enactment to itself" ([1988] STC 195 at 205).

3.1.32 The *Russell* case established, therefore (as formulated in IHTM35081) that "an instrument will not fall within IHTA 1984 s 142 if it further redirects any item or any part of an item that has already been redirected under an earlier instrument". However, this is not to say that multiple variations are not permissible; as is acknowledged in IHTM35083, "in any particular estate, there can be as many instruments of variation as there are items of property … The only prohibition is on purporting to *redirect the same item, or part of it, more than once*" (emphasis in original). Indeed, in *Russell* itself, there had been not one but four successive instruments of variation before the one which was ruled outside the scope of the then equivalent of IHTA 1984 s 142; and the variations made by those successive instruments were cumulative to each other, effectively adding additional cash sum provision for each of four different individuals while in each case otherwise repeating the same provisions substituted in the will. Knox J held that, to the extent that the substituted clause in each case spelt out provisions other than the additional cash sums, each of these four deeds comprised a repetition of, not a substitution for, the dispositions in the will, and therefore not a variation of those dispositions, so each successive further variation was admissible for backdated effect. Nevertheless, that drafting style of substituting everything that has gone before is not to be recommended, and indeed if a real world, rather than make believe, drafting style had been employed (see paragraphs **3.1.212** ff below) the objective of the disallowed variation in *Russell* could have been achieved by means of an incremental, as opposed to completely substitutional, drafting approach.

Variation of a disposition

3.1.33 The *Glowacki* decision (see paragraph **3.1.17** above) disposed of the (novel, but hopelessly over-optimistic) argument that IHTA 1984 s 142 could "operate to remove property from a person's estate so that it is no longer part of the estate subject to the deemed transfer of value on death" (see paragraph 36 of the decision). It is sometimes suggested, more plausibly, that these variation provisions can be used simply to supply administrative powers and provisions not included in the will which are thought to be helpful. Whilst there is no doubt that the beneficiaries of a will, acting collectively, can authorise the personal representatives or trustees to do administrative acts which are not otherwise within their powers, the better view is that this does not constitute the variation of any *dispositions* of the will. That is consistent with the Special Commissioner's formulation in *Glowcaki* (at paragraph 36) that "What [IHTA 1984 s 142] must vary is the *destination* of the estate on its deemed transfer under [IHTA 1984 s 4]" (emphasis supplied); and it is certainly the view taken by HMRC: IHTM35011 records that—

> "In our view the word 'disposition' as used in IHTA 1984 s 142(1) refers—
>
> — not to the content of the provision appearing in the will (or other relevant dispositive instrument or statute), but
>
> — to the result of applying that provision
>
> so that the focus is on the post-death beneficial interest.
>
> Accordingly the IoV must purport to change the destination of property in the estate from that prescribed by the disposition (however effected) which originally applied on the death to the property."

3.1.34 This last statement in IHTM35011 is however too sweeping, in that the introduction of, for example, a power of appointment, enabling the trustees or some other party to change otherwise fixed beneficial interests, would operate to change the beneficial interests (making them defeasible when before they were not, or less so). There seems no reason why modifications to dispositive powers should not also be seen as variations affecting the "post-death beneficial interest": for example, the introduction (by consent of the remaindermen or default beneficiaries, not by means of a power already contained in the will) of additional members of the class of objects of a power of appointment, or the extension (by similar consent) of the statutory power of advancement in Trustee Act 1925 s 32 to the whole of a beneficiary's vested or presumptive share of the fund. (In this context it is thought that the statutory power of advancement should be seen as having a dispositive character even though, in a different but still IHT-related context, it was seen by the Court of Appeal as more in the nature of an administrative provision in *Lord Inglewood and anor v IRC* [1983] STC 133.) Provided there are changes to the beneficial dispositions in the sense outlined above, there is in the authors' view no reason why a variation should be denied IHT effect just because, in addition, consequential or ancillary changes are made to the administrative provisions of the will.

Variations after distribution

3.1.35 Backdating treatment for IHT is available, subject to the various conditions applicable, whether or not the administration of the deceased's estate has been completed or the property has been distributed in accordance with the original dispositions: IHTA 1984 s 142(6). Thus there are plenty of situations in which, as a matter of property law, dispositions can be varied or disclaimed without the deceased's personal representatives being involved or even knowing about the matter at all – apart from one specific requirement for IHTA 1984 s 142 to apply (see paragraph **3.1.65** below), they would only need to be notified (let alone to be signatories to the variation) if the variation affected property that was still in their hands as personal representatives or trustees of the estate. Where it had already been distributed to the original beneficiary, or the variation related to property that had devolved by survivorship, the original beneficiary can obviously dispose of it as he chooses without any involvement, or further involvement, of the personal representatives.

The impact of sales and other post-death changes

3.1.36 To be capable of backdating treatment for IHT, the subject-matter of a variation must, as stated, be a disposition "of the property comprised in [the deceased's] estate immediately before his death". This does not, however, mean that the particular assets which are redistributed by a variation – after or before vesting in the original beneficiary – must be assets which were held as such by the deceased at his death. It is the gift, not the property, that is being redirected. This is recognised by HMRC in IHTM35025, which notes that—

> "as IHT does not have and in general does not require any expansive statutory definition of 'property', there may be an apparent disparity between the subject-matter of the property in fact comprised in the estate immediately before the death and that of the purported redirection attempted by the IoV".

3.1.37   The point can be appreciated most obviously in relation to the redirection of a residuary gift in the deceased's will. Suppose that by far the greatest part of the value of the deceased's estate at his death comprised a house, and that it was obvious from the outset that the personal representatives would have to sell the house in order to have sufficient funds to settle the deceased's debts and funeral expenses and pay the inheritance tax, cash legacies and administration costs. It would be absurd if a variation were precluded just because the assets remaining available for distribution to the original beneficiary – or for that matter already distributed to him – comprised the balance of the proceeds of that sale, rather than the house itself; and nothing published by HMRC or decided by the courts leads one anywhere close to such an absurd conclusion in the IHT context. But it is no different in the IHT context (in possible contrast to CGT, see paragraphs **3.1.84** ff below) if the sale was made by the original beneficiary after the original asset had vested in him. To understand the issue clearly, it is necessary to focus on the (original) disposition that is being varied (as emphasised in IHTM35011, quoted in paragraph **3.1.33** above). The requirement is that that (original) disposition must have been of property that was comprised in the deceased's estate immediately before his death, as that expression applies for the purposes of IHTA 1984 s 142 (see paragraph **3.1.30** above); but it does not follow in any way from this that the specific items of property comprised in the estate at death must still be held (by the personal representatives or the original beneficiary) at the date of the variation. In summary, this somewhat flexible approach to the word "property" within IHTA 1984 s 142 is no different to the accepted interpretation of "settled property" in the IHT legislation more generally, in effect to connote a fund as distinct from the items of property from time to time comprised in it.

3.1.38   In fact, it is submitted that the principle extends further than just the immediate proceeds of sale of an asset that was held by the deceased at his death, and that the key requirement is to be able to demonstrate that what is being passed on does clearly represent what came to, or is due to, the original beneficiary as a result of the disposition that is being varied. Having said that, however, it is clear from IHTM35026 that, despite recognising implicitly that changes in the assets derived from the disposition in the will should not of themselves take a variation outside IHTA 1984 s 142, HMRC nevertheless wish to check carefully all cases that fall within that category. Where clear tracing cannot be shown, therefore, it can be expected that they may seek to deny backdated treatment (though the variation would of course take effect in accordance with its terms in other respects, with tax consequences accordingly). Example 2 in IHTM35026 reads—

> "It is possible that the subject matter of the redirection is property which cannot be identified as forming part of the estate immediately before the death. For example, shares which may have been acquired by way of exchange or capital reorganisation of the company. Where this applies, you should ask the

taxpayer for an explanation of the discrepancy and, on receipt of their replies refer the case to [IHT Technical Group]".

3.1.39 Sales of the "original" item of property should in general not cause problems, even where carried out by the original beneficiary following distribution rather than by the personal representatives, so long as the sale proceeds have been kept separate from other assets not derived from the estate and the variation takes effect in relation to those sale proceeds. Experience shows however that clients do sometimes act first and seek advice afterwards. The two main areas of difficulty are likely to comprise the blending of cash, and reinvestment. Where relevant, it is recommended that a detailed statement be prepared before a variation is proceeded with, showing the tracing process – and showing any danger areas such as the introduction of funds from other sources – in order to assess (with suitable advice) the extent of any risk that the variation might be rejected from the backdating point of view. If the proposal involves formation of a settlement, the prospect of an immediately chargeable transfer if IHTA 1984 s 142 does not apply may be a disincentive to proceeding where tracing is not entirely clear. If on the other hand what is proposed is merely the redirection of assets to another individual absolutely, it may be that the risk tolerance could be quite high as the resultant transfer of value, if backdating is disallowed, would be a PET and full exemption would be achieved on survival for seven years in the usual way. However, in either case the risk assessment must take account of any potential GROB implications of failing to attract IHTA 1984 s 142 treatment, and also of the implications as regards other taxes (see below) to the extent that advantage is intended to be taken of special tax treatment for variations under those respective taxes.

3.1.40 This tracing issue will not arise in relation to disclaimers. By definition the original beneficiary must have received no benefit at all from the testamentary gift, or he will be unable to disclaim the benefit of it. Therefore it will be entirely clear that a disclaimer relates to the disposition in the will, which was plainly of property comprised in the estate at death, whatever the personal representatives have done in the meantime with the estate or the asset bequeathed

Particular consequences of IHT backdating

3.1.41 Thus, for property that passes under the deceased's will, the IHT effects are indeed as though the will had been rewritten by the deceased (with full capacity!) immediately before he died. In consequence, subject to one important and sometimes confusing qualification dealt with in paragraphs **3.1.43** ff below—

(a) exemptions and reliefs will be applied to the varied provisions;

(b) HMRC accept that the GROB rules are inapplicable if the original beneficiary retains or resumes some benefit in respect of the property redirected: they take the view that IHTA 1984 s 142(1) has the effect that the deceased (and so not the original beneficiary) is treated as the donor, see IHTM35151, though it would not be impossible for them to construct arguments to the contrary if so minded; and

(c) where the variation results in property being settled property, even where the original beneficiary had been absolutely entitled—

   (i) the settlor of the settlement for IHT purposes will be the deceased, not the original beneficiary;
  (ii) at least where the variation relates to property that devolved as part of the deceased's free estate under his will or intestacy (see paragraph **3.1.42** below), the settlement will be regarded as one which was effected by will or under the law relating to intestacy (condition 1 for IPDI status of an IIP, under IHTA 1984 s 49A(2)) and its trusts as having been established under the will of the deceased (so as to be capable of giving rise to a BMT or an age 18-to-25 trust, under IHTA 1984 s 71A or s 71D, if the deceased was the parent of a beneficiary, subject to the terms of those trusts meeting the relevant conditions for those sections to apply);
 (iii) a first IIP under any resultant trust will meet condition 2 for IPDI status, under IHTA 1984 s 49A(3), as its beneficiary will be treated for all IHT purposes as having become entitled to it immediately after the death;
 (iv) if the deceased died before 22 March 2006, the beneficiary of a first IIP under any resultant trust will, in addition, be treated as having been entitled to that IIP immediately before Budget Day 2006 (nothing in the definition of an IPDI requires that this expression is confined to deaths on or after 22 March 2006), so that a further IIP taking effect on its termination is capable of being a TSI if the other conditions in IHTA 1984 s 49C or s 49D are fulfilled (see the reply to Question 3 in the Law Society/ HMRC IHT correspondence (**APPENDIX 6**), and to Question 40 in the STEP/HMRC original IHT correspondence (**APPENDIX 3**)); and
  (v) also if the deceased died before 22 March 2006, a trust created by the variation which meets the conditions for A&M trust status in the pre-2006 version of IHTA 1984 s 71 will attract that status with effect from the death, and thus through the remainder of the transitional period allowed for such trusts by the FA 2006 changes. Although, from 6 April 2008, that trust will have to provide for absolute vesting by age 18 if it is to retain A&M trust status—
    – its beneficiaries need not necessarily be children of the deceased, nor even grandchildren of a common grandparent,
    – the class of beneficiaries may remain open pending the first interest actually vesting,
    – power can be retained to vary the shares in which members of

the class are to take or indeed to exclude individual members of the class from benefit altogether, and

– power can be conferred for the trustees to apply income of one beneficiary's share for the benefit of any member or members of the class who are for the time being living and under age 18.

The last two points appear now to have been conceded by HMRC in respect of BMTs as well, despite the stark contrast of drafting approach between "one or more beneficiaries" in the amended IHTA 1984 s 71 and the singular "the bereaved minor" in IHTA 1984 s 71A; but the ability to keep the class open, and the non-restriction to children of the deceased, may yet prove attractive in variations made prior to 22 March 2008.

3.1.42   The consequences set out at point (c) in paragraph **3.1.41** above, except for point (c)(v) which was not raised as such, were confirmed by HMRC, in less detailed terms, in their replies to questions 40 to 42 in the STEP/HMRC original IHT correspondence (**APPENDIX 3**). It is however dangerous to read the reply in relation to IHTA 1984 ss 49A(2), 71A, 71D(b)(ii) as extending beyond the terms of Example 12 in paragraph 38 of the STEP/HMRC original IHT correspondence (**APPENDIX 3**), which was specifically in the context of the variation of a will. If instead the disposition being varied fell into the "or otherwise" category (see paragraph **3.1.29** above) – ie was not itself made by will or under the law relating to intestacy – it is hard to argue that the statutory fiction, that the variation is treated as having been made by the deceased, should be stretched so far as to treat the property in question as having been settled (where a trust results) *by the deceased's will*. HMRC take the view that it does not, see their reply to questions 1 and 2 in the Law Society/HMRC IHT correspondence in **APPENDIX 6** (and see also paragraph **3.3.16** below). Accordingly, if a trust is formed by what is commonly referred to as retrospective severance of a joint tenancy—

(a) if it is an IIP trust, the IIP beneficiary will certainly be treated as having had that IIP since the deceased's death; but it would seem that the IIP is incapable of being an IPDI because the trust cannot be shown to have been established by the deceased's will or the intestacy law; and

(b) if the deceased was a parent of the beneficiary (within the extended meaning of "parent" in IHTA 1984 s 71H) and the trust provides for the beneficiary to become absolutely entitled by age 18 or at least by age 25, it would seem that it would nevertheless be incapable of being a BMT or an age 18-to-25 trust under IHTA 1984 s 71A or s 71D, because the trusts were not established under the deceased parent's will (nor, obviously, are they the statutory trusts for issue of an intestate).

Short term interests resulting from a variation

3.1.43 Even where the necessary conditions for backdating under IHTA 1984 s 142 are met, it is necessary to be aware of an important qualification to the backdating effect. This applies, by virtue of IHTA 1984 s 142(4), where a variation results in property being held in trust for a person for a period which ends not more than two years after the death. HMRC explain this distinctly obscure provision in IHTM35133 as meaning in their view that the short term nature of the interest must be a direct result of the variation itself, not in combination with other events, before IHTA 1984 s 142(4) applies. They spell out that if the interest created by the variation is not limited in terms to cease within the two year period, but in fact does come to an end within that time, for example as a result of the life tenant's death, then IHTA 1984 s 142(4) will be inapplicable and the usual consequences will follow.

3.1.44 The same should apply in principle if the interest is assigned, or divested by appointment, within that same period. However, care must be exercised in this regard, particularly if the interest was in favour of the testator's spouse such as to give rise to spouse relief on the death, since HMRC are known to be suspicious of arrangements which might lead to the property reverting to the original beneficiaries after spouse relief has been gained by means of a variation: see IHTM35093. Their suspicion even extends to cases where an IIP created by a variation is to last "slightly" longer than the two year period caught by IHTA 1984 s 142(4): see IHTM35095. (Both those paragraphs of the IHT Manual as published show that some text has been withheld in reliance on exemptions in the FOIA 2000 suggesting that the omitted text is considered important to revenue protection.)

3.1.45 If IHTA 1984 s 142(4) does apply, the short term interest is effectively disregarded, subject to a further qualification discussed in paragraphs **3.1.46–3.1.49** below. The IHTA 1984 is to be applied (and so, as IHTM35133 puts it with two useful examples, tax is to be charged on the testator's death) as if the disposition of the property that takes effect at the *end* of the period had had effect from the *beginning* of the period. Thus if the short term interest was in favour of the surviving spouse, the fund in question does not qualify for spouse relief on the death. Conversely, if the settlor of the short term interest is the surviving spouse, then under HMRC's interpretation, confirmed in the rather improbable Example 2 in IHTM35133, spouse exemption will apply on the testator's death because the short term interest is disregarded for IHT, even though it takes full effect for trust law purposes and for the purposes of other relevant taxes. This may give rise to potential tax planning opportunities in appropriate circumstances, see paragraphs **3.1.176** ff below.

3.1.46 The closing half sentence of IHTA 1984 s 142(4) provides that "this subsection shall not affect the application of this Act in relation to any distribution or application of property occurring before that disposition takes effect". ("That disposition" refers back to the disposition that takes effect at the end of the period for which the short term interest is to subsist as a result of the variation; called here the reversionary disposition.) HMRC interpret this in IHTM35134 as meaning that "if there is an application or distribution of trust capital during the continuance of the short term interest, the trusts actually applying from the death govern the IHT treatment of that event". This reference to "the trusts actually applying from the death" is peculiar, and the example given immediately after that statement, reproduced below, makes clear that what is meant in fact is the trusts taking effect under the terms of the variation, ie deemed by IHTA 1984 s 142(1) to have had effect from the death. (The text of the example in IHTM35154 does not appear to have been updated to reflect the changes made by FA 2006 Sch 20, but this does not affect the principle.) It reads as follows (omitting cross-references)—

> "By Will, T leaves the whole estate equally to his children. By a valid IoV within IHTA 1984 s 142(1), the children settle £200,000 from the estate on trust for their mother for a period of 18 months from the date of death, with remainder to themselves. Twelve months after the death, the whole of the fund is appointed to the grandchildren.
>
> The IoV creates a short term interest which is ignored, so there is no spouse exemption and the estate remains chargeable on death. However, when the appointment to the grandchildren takes place, the real position is taken into account. So a charge to tax arises under IHTA 1984 s 52 as the widow's life interest has come to an end."

3.1.47   Essentially, what seems to be indicated is that, for the limited purpose of determining the IHT consequence of a distribution or application of trust property that is made before the reversionary disposition takes effect, but not for other IHT purposes, the usual backdating rule in IHTA 1984 s 142(1) is assumed to have taken effect (albeit without having operated in relation to the determination of exemptions or reliefs on the deceased's death). Of course, if the appointment in the HMRC example were to the grandchildren absolutely (or on bare trusts despite minority, see the eventual HMRC reply to question 33 in the STEP/HMRC original IHT correspondence, APPENDIX 3), an actual charge to tax would only arise if the widow then died within seven years after the appointment, as the deemed transfer of value would be a PET by virtue of IHTA 1984 s 3A(1A), (2).

3.1.48   What is left unclear, by reference to the facts of this example, is whether there is any further consequence for IHT of the fact that, as a result of IHTA 1984 s 142(4), the estate is treated as having been left to the testator's children as a result of the reversionary disposition to them. Because the closing words of that subsection are seen as giving rise to a deemed transfer of value on the part of the widow (whose IIP would have been an IPDI and so an estate IIP by virtue of IHTA 1984 s 142(1), but for

IHTA 1984 s 142(4)), it is assumed that HMRC would not look for additional IHT consequences in relation to the fact that the property was, before the appointment, comprised in the children's estates – whether on the making of the appointment or at the time the short term interest would have expired had it been allowed to run its course. The analysis, if HMRC's starting point is correct in the first place, is far from clear, and if the children's reversionary entitlement was absolute then it may be that the property – in their estates from the death, despite the variation, by virtue of IHTA 1984 s 142(4) – has left their estates without a disposition by them and so no transfer of value by them (nor any gift for the purpose of the GROB rules). However, if the nature of their reversionary interests was such that the property is to be regarded as settled property with effect from the testator's death, even disregarding the mother's IIP under IHTA 1984 s 142(4), then the children would have had IIPs in settled property which, because they are deemed by IHTA 1984 s 142(4) to have been effective from the death, would have been IPDIs. This could arguably give rise to a disastrous position: in addition to the mother's transfer of value in favour of the grandchildren, the children's (fictional) IPDIs would have come to an end as a result of the outright appointment to the next generation, seemingly giving rise to parallel transfers of value by them under IHTA 1984 s 52, which would also involve deemed gifts for the purpose of the GROB rules by virtue of FA 1986 s 102ZA. To avoid that result it would be necessary to construe the closing words of IHTA 1984 s 142(4) which give rise to the widow's transfer – "this subsection shall not affect the application of this Act in relation to any distribution or application of property occurring before that disposition takes effect" – as displacing totally the consequences of the IPDI that was, up to then, treated as existing by the opening part of the very same subsection – not merely as preserving the "real world" termination of the mother's IIP.

3.1.49 The arcane impact of IHTA 1984 s 142(4) can be explored further by marginally altering the facts in the HMRC example (see paragraph **3.1.46** above). Assume that, instead of an appointment being made to the grandchildren after 12 months, the children at that time assign their interests under the reversionary disposition to the grandchildren, who therefore become absolutely entitled at the date the widow's short term interest expires under the provisions of the variation itself. The closing words of IHTA 1984 s 142(4) do not therefore come into play – there is no distribution or application of property *before* the reversionary disposition takes effect. The mother's short term IIP has been allowed to run its full course. However, the assignment of the reversionary interests would constitute either the actual termination, or the deemed termination by virtue of assignment (IHTA 1984 s 51), of the children's IIPs (deemed IPDIs, as above). As the HMRC interpretation of IHTA 1984 s 142(4) is to ignore entirely the mother's IIP, it would seem to follow that the children at the date of the assignments make either PETs (if the grandchildren are immediately absolutely entitled subject to the mother's continuing actual IIP) or chargeable transfers (the trust entering the relevant property regime) if the children's interests are in any way contingent, for example on surviving the mother. (If they take IIPs and the assignment occurs before 6 April 2008 the children would take TSIs, again with PET treatment: IHTA 1984 s 49C.)

3.1.50 All in all, except so far as the rule for short term interests can be positively utilised for tax planning purposes (see paragraph **3.1.45** above), the conclusion must be that an IHT variation that involves creating an interest which will terminate within two years from the death should be avoided. At best it is likely to achieve nothing in IHT terms; at worst, if changes occur during the currency of the short term IIP, the precise application of IHTA 1984 s 142(4) is even more obscure than in the absence of such changes, and could give rise to unexpected tax charges, or at the very least lengthy debate with HMRC as to exactly how the provision should be applied.

The conditions to be satisfied for IHT backdating

3.1.51 IHTA 1984 s 142 lays down a number of conditions which must be met before the backdating effect described above will be applicable. The first three of these apply to both variations and disclaimers, the fourth only to variations. (As will be seen in the relevant sections below, some of them also apply in similar terms where special treatment is required in respect of other taxes.) The conditions, examined in more detail below, are as follows—

(a) The variation or disclaimer must be made within two years after the death of the deceased (IHTA 1984 s 142(1), opening words); see paragraph **3.1.52** below.

(b) The variation or disclaimer must be made by instrument in writing by the persons who benefit or would benefit under the original dispositions (IHTA 1984 s 142(1)): see paragraphs **3.1.53** ff below.

(c)The variation or disclaimer must not be made for consideration in money or money's worth, other than another such variation or disclaimer in respect of another disposition of property in the same estate and which also satisfies all the conditions for application of IHTA 1984 s 142(1): see paragraphs **3.1.57** ff below.

(d)In the case of a variation only, the instrument must contain a statement that IHTA 1984 s 142(1) is intended to apply to the variation, such statement to be made by all the parties making the instrument and additionally, in certain cases, by the deceased's personal representatives: see paragraphs **3.1.63** ff below. (Prior to 1 August 2002 a different condition applied in this regard, involving the making of an election by those parties, which could either be contained in the instrument itself or in a separate document, but which in either case had to be notified to the Inland Revenue (as they then were) within six months after the making of the variation, though with a discretion on their part to accept late notifications, as to which see IHTM35056, IHTM35057. As this provision is spent it is not explored further in this book.)

Two year time limit

3.1.52   The two year requirement is an absolute time limit: there is no provision for this deadline to be extended, by HMRC or otherwise. IHTM35013 spells out that HMRC officers must treat instruments of variation produced to them, or known by them to have been executed, with appropriate priority to enable a response to be sent (where at all possible) in time for the taxpayers to review their position before the time limit expires. This practice will have been more important, and potentially helpful, in the days when an election could be submitted separately (see point (d) of paragraph **3.1.51** above); because a "second bite at the cherry" is not possible for the same property (see paragraphs **3.1.31**, **3.1.32** above), and a variation will usually be effective as a matter of property law even if it fails to meet the conditions of IHTA 1984 s 142 (eg through not including the necessary statement of intent), it will not generally be possible to rescue a failed attempt at backdated IHT effect through a second document. Subject to the evidence supporting this, an application to the court for rectification would be needed in those circumstances – HMRC will generally not accept an informal "rectification" by deed, see IHTM35086. But if, as a matter of general law, a variation is wholly ineffective – or seemingly in some circumstances only partially ineffective – (for example through not all necessary parties having been joined to make the variation which the instrument purports to make), it appears from the second half of IHTM35045 that HMRC may be prepared to accept that the instrument is void *ab initio* provided the parties submit their written agreement that it is to be so regarded, thus opening the way for a second, correct, attempt so long as the two year period has not yet expired. In those circumstances a prompt indication of the HMRC view of the first attempt would undoubtedly be useful.

Parties to make the written instrument

3.1.53   Apart from the limited involvement of the deceased's personal representatives that is required in certain cases (see paragraph **3.1.65** below), the necessary parties to the instrument under IHTA 1984 s 142(1) – reflecting the "real world" transaction – are all those who benefit or would benefit under the original dispositions that are being varied; in other words, the original beneficiary(ies) whose interests are adversely affected by the changes made. (That is of course not limited to those who have actual equitable interests that are being given up or prejudiced; it will include all those who are objects of powers of appointment and the like, if the purported effect of the variation is to take priority over those powers to any degree.) The instructions in IHTM35044, IHTM35045, IHTM35047, IHTM35048 make clear that HMRC will examine this aspect carefully, especially where a variation is effected of more than the simplest of trusts in the will; they will look for contingent or potential future born beneficiaries who are not made parties, and will draw attention to any failure to deal fully with the beneficial interests affected by the purported outcome of the instrument. However, those instructions also recognise that the document may achieve a part of its objective even if not the whole of it, and that it can be effective as a variation to that extent – thus having some effect on the IHT position in the deceased's estate; see for instance Example 1 in IHTM35047.

3.1.54   Complications can obviously arise in this regard where it is identified that the interests of minor or unborn beneficiaries might be adversely affected by the desired solution. (That includes cases where they are objects of a power of appointment, not merely where they are given definite interests in the fund; but it may sometimes be feasible to use a power of appointment in such a case to bring about a situation where a variation can be effected without the participation of the minor or unborn beneficiaries, see paragraphs 3.2.37 ff below.) They are not in a position to execute the instrument themselves, and HMRC rightly take the view that it is not sufficient for a parent or guardian to purport to execute it on their behalf: see IHTM35045, where they note correctly that "An IoV which adversely affects the interests of minor or unborn beneficiaries can achieve total validity only by obtaining the approval of the Court (on an application under the Variation of Trusts Act 1958 or under the Court's inherent jurisdiction)." The court will obviously need to be satisfied that such an exercise is for the benefit of the party(ies) on whose behalf its approval is sought; so (bearing in mind the damaging implications of extraneous consideration) such variations will tend to involve an exchange of interests rather than a pure giving up of the rights of the minor or unborn beneficiary. In view of the statutory requirement that the instrument is "made by" the original beneficiaries, it is advisable that the form of court order should authorise a given person to execute the deed on behalf of those on whose behalf the court's approval is given.

3.1.55   Often it will be found that the new beneficiary(ies) are in practice made parties to the document as well. Making them named parties will put them in a stronger position to sue on any dispositive provisions of the instrument should need arise, though where a trust is declared they already have all necessary remedies available even without being made parties. However, even if they are named as parties, there is absolutely no necessity for them to *execute* the deed in that capacity – any more than a bank will execute a mortgage deed where land is mortgaged in its favour, even though it is always a party to it in order to take the benefit of its provisions. Only if the new beneficiaries are themselves varying some other disposition as original beneficiaries, or are asked to undertake some responsibility, such as acting as trustees of a fund settled by the variation, do they need to execute it. (Care should be of course taken with regard to the undertaking of responsibilities other than as trustees of the varied property, lest that constitute extraneous consideration which defeats the IHT backdating.)

3.1.56 Circumstances arise not infrequently where two people have died within a relatively short time of each other and a variation (or occasionally disclaimer) in relation to the estate of the first to die is advantageous. The likely circumstances for such an exercise are examined further in paragraphs **3.1.200** ff, **3.1.206** ff below. Where the estate of the second to die is being decreased by a variation of this sort (paragraphs **3.1.200** ff below), the statutory requirement seems to dictate that it is the personal representatives of that person who must make the variation, just as where that person's interest is being disclaimed. As noted in the discussion of disclaimers in paragraph **3.1.9** above, HMRC take the view that the beneficiaries of that person's estate are *also* necessary parties, and although that view may be open to question, for the reasons indicated there, it is prudent to adhere to it where possible. Exactly the same considerations will apply to variations as to disclaimers. Nevertheless, when it comes to variations, IHTM35042 appears to display a more accommodating stance than IHTM35164 dealing with disclaimers; see further paragraph **3.1.204** below.

No extraneous consideration

3.1.57 Many variations are made as essentially gratuitous gifts (often made for essentially tax planning reasons), but others involve much more of a bargain between those involved – in the nature of a "deed of family arrangement" as envisaged by the original capital transfer tax legislation before 1978 (see paragraph **3.1.1** above). Between those extremes are cases where, again for tax planning reasons, interests in the estate are being adjusted between beneficiaries, with the same individuals both giving up and receiving benefits. In the second and third groups, at least one if not all parties will have given consideration for what they give up. The rule in IHTA 1984 s 142(3) will deny backdating for the entirety of the transactions embodied in the instrument if there is any element of consideration – or more accurately, of consideration in money or money's worth – that comes from outside the death estate (in terms, consideration that does not consist of "the making, in respect of another of the dispositions, of a variation or disclaimer to which [IHTA 1984 s 142(1)] applies"). In IHTM35100 HMRC explain the primary purpose of the bar on extraneous consideration as being "to ensure that spouse, civil partner or charity exemption is not available for property given to non-exempt beneficiaries".

3.1.58 This is a wide ranging exclusion of which it is all too easy to fall foul, especially when the essential purpose of the variation is to resolve some dispute (albeit admittedly in as tax-efficient a manner as possible), rather than specifically to improve the IHT position *per se*. Matters such as an agreement by one party to pay another's legal costs of the negotiations, or the giving of an indemnity for potential future tax charges, or even the redirection of a pension scheme lump sum which became payable on the death (but was outside the deceased's IHT estate), have all been known to lead to backdating being refused. However, there are times when the point seems to be taken too far. The bar is on consideration *in money or money's worth*, and a request to pension trustees to exercise their discretion in favour of a given beneficiary seems to fall into neither of those categories (the decision remains for the trustees in exercise of a fiduciary power), even though it is undeniably consideration; yet that, too, has in the past been used as justification to refuse backdating.

3.1.59 It should be remembered that it is not necessary for consideration to be recorded in the instrument of variation for it to be capable of causing a problem. If the deed shows simply that A redirects a benefit to B, but B (or C) makes a payment to A and A would not have completed the deed but for that payment or the promise of it, then that payment is just as much consideration for A's variation as if the deed had actually recorded it as such. On the other hand, an unrelated gift from B to A – when A would have gone ahead (and perhaps did) irrespective of what might have been in B's mind, if A had known about it at all – does not fall into any ordinary understanding of "consideration" for which A's variation was made. It is thought that HMRC would have difficulty sustaining an attack if those latter facts were established. For this reason, Examples 1 and 3 in IHTM35100 could be read as putting forward a proposition that is simply wrong in law. Continuing the above scenario of a variation by A in favour of B, both examples speak of B (Example 1), or C (Example 2) making a payment to A "to compensate [A] for the loss of" what had originally been left to him; they both see the payment as consideration for the variation, yet that would only properly be so if it had been discussed and agreed and the variation would not have proceeded without an understanding that the payment (or, at the least, some payment) would be made.

3.1.60 Probably it is this consideration provision which (at least in part – cf "without there being a bona fide variation"), underlies the enquiries which examiners are instructed in IHTM35093 to make "where a chargeable beneficiary makes an IoV in favour of the deceased's spouse or civil partner", and to refer immediately to IHT Technical Group "where the answers ... indicate any possibility that the spouse or civil partner may not retain all the redirected benefits"—

"you should ask the taxpayers—

— whether there had been any discussion between the parties before the IoV was made about how the benefit redirected to the spouse or civil partner should be dealt with, and

— whether subsequent to the IoV the spouse or civil partner has made any transfers to the original chargeable beneficiaries, or is contemplating making any such transfers."

3.1.61   Where something is done in return for the giving up of a claim or potential claim in a court of law, the giving up of that claim is plainly consideration for what is done; and it is not straining language to regard it as being consideration in money or money's worth, as it plainly has a potential monetary value to the other party even if the claim would not be a marketable asset in its own right. From this point of view it is in analytical (as opposed to policy) terms a little surprising to read the following in IHTM35100—

> "A disclaimer or variation made to avoid or compromise a claim under the [I(PFD)A] 1975 is accepted as not caught by [IHTA 1984] s 142(3) unless the deceased dies domiciled outside the UK, in which case the matter should be referred to [IHT Technical Group]. The bar against consideration relates only to extraneous consideration and will not prevent a rearrangement of assets within the will."

3.1.62   Whatever the merits in policy terms of such an approach, it does seem to be stretching a point to regard the giving up of a claim under the I(PFD)A 1975 as constituting a variation or disclaimer, within IHTA 1984 s 142(1), in respect of another of the dispositions of the property comprised in the deceased's estate immediately before his death. Nevertheless, parties acting in reliance on this published practice should have nothing to fear from IHTA 1984 s 142(3) in practical terms. (The apparently different view taken where the deceased died domiciled outside the UK – which at first sight looks very hard to reconcile with the otherwise relaxed approach to the issue, as there can be no technical difference between the two cases – can be easily explained when it is remembered that a valid application under the I(PFD)A 1975 can only be made where the deceased died domiciled in England and Wales: I(PFD)A 1975 s 1(1). The assertion that a variation is made in consideration of such a claim being given up would thus be a clear justification for HMRC looking more closely at the claim, in the IHT context, that he was neither domiciled nor deemed domiciled in the UK.)

IHT statement of intent

3.1.63   In the case of a variation, backdated treatment for IHT purposes – even if the other three conditions already described are fulfilled – is optional, in the sense that, if the parties require it, the relevant persons (see paragraph **3.1.65** below) must include a statement of intent that the backdating provision should apply; but if they do not require it then they can omit that statement. For a disclaimer, however, this requirement does not apply, and if the disclaimer is valid as a matter of law (see paragraphs **3.1.4–3.1.12** above) then backdated treatment will apply for IHT purposes automatically. There is an equivalent provision in the CGT legislation (see point (a)(iv) in paragraph **3.1.76** below); but the inclusion of a statement of intent should always be considered separately for each of the two taxes: it should not be taken as a foregone conclusion that backdated treatment should be sought for both taxes or neither.

3.1.64   Such a statement of intent must be contained in the written instrument that effects the variation; the facility for rectifying an omission by submitting a separate document within a given time afterwards was removed by the 2002 change from an election to a statement of intent (see paragraph **3.1.51** ABOVE, point (d)). The recommended form of statement of intent, as set out in IHTM35028, is "The parties to this variation intend that the provisions of section 142(1) Inheritance Tax Act 1984 [and section 62(6) Taxation of Chargeable Gains Act 1992] shall apply". HMRC note that the statement must include the appropriate statutory references; but they go on to indicate that the use of the pre-August 2002 wording of "electing" for the relevant provisions to apply – presumably based on older precedents – will be regarded as a statement of the parties' intent. (It is likely that this would be upheld by a court if the parties subsequently sought to resile from backdated treatment and contend that the "election" wording failed to meet the requirement of IHTA 1984 s 142(2).)

3.1.65   Under IHTA 1984 s 142(2A), the relevant persons who must make the statement of intent are basically all those who make the instrument. However, if the result of the variation (if given backdated effect) would be that additional tax is payable, the statement will be invalid unless, in addition, the personal representatives join in making it, even if they would not otherwise need to be parties to the instrument. The same subsection goes on to provide, in a curious double negative, that "personal representatives may decline to make a statement under subsection (2) above only if no, or no sufficient, assets are held by them in that capacity for discharging the additional tax". In practice that must be taken as a positive obligation to join in making the statement if they do hold sufficient assets for the purpose (which must of course be tested taking into account other existing liabilities of theirs). It is suggested (though the question is not known to have arisen hitherto for decision by a court) that the "sufficiency" of assets held falls to be assessed by reference to their current realisable value, and that if assets are subject to a restriction on disposal where the personal representatives are unlikely to be able to obtain a necessary consent, or the market in the particular assets is at that time so depressed that a buyer at a price the personal representatives could justify to their beneficiaries could not realistically be found, then the personal representatives could legitimately maintain that the assets in question should be left out of account in deciding whether they hold sufficient assets to discharge the additional tax. Any question which might arise on this is between the personal representatives and the beneficiaries: HMRC would not be involved in any dispute.

3.1.66   Note that this requirement for the personal representatives to join in the IHT statement of intent applies even if the variation relates to a part of the estate which does not vest in the deceased's personal representatives in the first place, such as a severable share in joint property. This is because, under IHTA 1984 s 200(1)(a), the personal representatives are accountable for IHT in respect of the whole of the deceased's estate on death (in its IHT sense), other than property which was comprised in a settlement immediately before his death (or even then, to the extent that the settled property comprised land which vests in the personal representatives on death – in practice, where a settlement within the Settled Land Act 1925, of which the deceased was life tenant, comes to an end on his death). The fact that they may have a right to be reimbursed for that tax, under IHTA 1984 s 211(3), does not detract from their need for the funding to pay it in the first place.

3.1.67 Because a statement of intent is not required for a disclaimer to be given backdated effect, it follows that the personal representatives will never be necessary parties to a disclaimer, even if it results in an increased charge to IHT on the death. That is at first sight not unreasonable, because by definition the original beneficiary who enters into a disclaimer (typically the surviving spouse, if exemption is being lost as a result) cannot have accepted a distribution of the property in question, or the disclaimer would be invalid: see paragraph **3.1.4** above. By contrast, a variation could be made after the personal representatives had completed the administration and distributed all the assets. The property will therefore be under the control of the personal representatives, who will therefore in principle be in a position to realise the asset if they have no other means of raising the additional tax. However, even then, it is foreseeable that problems could arise if the assets in question are illiquid, or subject to restrictions on disposal.

IHT treatment if conditions are not all met

3.1.68 If a variation is made and any one of the necessary four conditions (paragraph **3.1.51** above) is not met, then the original beneficiary's disposition (see paragraph **3.1.17** above) will be a transfer of value, not protected from being such by IHTA 1984 s 17. The status of that transfer of value (chargeable, exempt or potentially exempt), and the value transferred by it, will be determined according to normal principles. Furthermore, where relevant for IHT purposes, the settlor of any trust established by the variation will be the original beneficiary. The one potential exception to this would be if and to the extent that a variation of the sort discussed in paragraph **3.1.22** above must be analysed as a charge, rather than partial assignment, of the original beneficiary's *chose in action* as residuary beneficiary. If that were correct, and the variation were made for no, or no adequate, consideration, then the charged amount would not be a deductible liability in valuing the original beneficiary's estate (IHTA 1984 s 5(5)), so there would be no transfer of value at the time of the variation – rather, when the "charged" sum was ultimately satisfied.

3.1.69 The same will apply if a disclaimer is made which is valid as such at common law, but which fails to meet all the three conditions that apply to it for IHT backdating (points (a)–(c) in paragraph **3.1.51** above). This seems to follow from the analysis in the estate duty cases noted in paragraph **3.1.16** above; although the IHT legislation is expressed very differently from that under which estate duty was charged, it is considered that the disclaimer would constitute a disposition, if not of the asset or right left to the original beneficiary then at least through his omission (indeed refusal) to exercise his right to accept the property left to him (see IHTA 1984 s 3(3)).

Property devolving under a pre-existing trust

Backdating available subject to conditions, for disclaimer only

3.1.70 Backdating treatment for IHT under IHTA 1984 s 142 is, as explained above, confined to property comprised in the estate of the deceased immediately before his death – in the modified sense explored in paragraph **3.1.30** above. By virtue of IHTA 1984 s 142(5) that excludes, inter alia, settled property in which the deceased had an estate IIP. However, although a variation as such of the ensuing interests under the trust (whether absolute or otherwise) cannot therefore have its effect backdated to the death for IHT purposes, a separate provision allows backdating for a disclaimer. IHTA 1984 s 93 provides—

> "Where a person becomes entitled to an interest in settled property but disclaims the interest, then, if the disclaimer is not made for a consideration in money or money's worth, this Act shall apply as if he had not become entitled to the interest."

3.1.71 A disclaimer within this provision can give rise to an increase in the tax chargeable on the termination of a preceding estate IIP without the agreement of the trustees of the settlement or of the former beneficiary or his personal representatives. That of course mirrors the position for disclaimers, as opposed to variations, under IHTA 1984 s 142 (see paragraph **3.1.67** above). However it will be noticed that IHTA 1984 s 93 displays several points of stark contrast to IHTA 1984 s 142—

(a) There is no statutory time limit within which a disclaimer can take effect under this rule; its validity as a disclaimer will be judged purely on common law principles (see in particular paragraph **3.1.5** above).

(b) There is no requirement even that the trust, or the interest disclaimed, should have any connection with the death of any person, let alone that the trust property should have been included in the deceased's estate.

(c) There is no requirement that the disclaimer be made in writing – though writing is of course advisable for evidential purposes (and a deed is advisable if the disclaimer is intended to be irrevocable, see paragraphs **3.1.6**, **3.1.7** above).

3.1.72 It is not clear from the wording of IHTA 1984 s 93 whether or not it is meant to be available to provide backdating treatment for the disclaimer of an interest in property that is settled by the will of a deceased person (whether or not that interest is in possession with effect from the death and is therefore an IPDI). The property so settled obviously becomes settled property, and the beneficiary becomes entitled to the interest – in many cases with effect from the death, if only with the assistance of the administration period provision in IHTA 1984 s 91. Ostensibly disclaimer of such an interest should be possible under this provision, therefore. If that were so, it would provide, in that particular situation, a slightly more flexible alternative to IHTA 1984 s 142 for backdating the effect of a disclaimer to the death – in particular, free of the two year time limit and of the requirement for an instrument in writing (though still subject to the common law rules as to non-receipt of benefit, see paragraphs **3.1.4**, **3.1.5** above).

3.1.73 However, subject to the rather "hard case" considerations examined in paragraph **3.1.172** below, point (b), it is thought that the better interpretation of IHTA 1984 s 93 is that the words "a person becomes entitled to an interest in settled property" connote that the property must already be settled property at the time the person becomes entitled, so that, where the entitlement arises on a death, the settlement must have existed from some time before the death. This interpretation avoids an anomalous overlap between the two provisions, with one imposing less stringent requirements than the other. Additionally, focusing on the status of the property as settled property immediately before, rather than immediately after, the person becomes entitled to an interest also avoids a possible conclusion that a beneficiary to whom an immediate absolute interest is appointed, but who wishes to disclaim that interest, is denied backdating treatment under this section.

3.1.74 Certainly the final paragraph of IHTM35165 suggests that HMRC regard the two sections as mutually exclusive—

"If the deceased had an interest in possession and they had, and had exercised by will, a general power of appointment over the property, we regard that property as part of the deceased's estate at death and *any disclaimer must meet the conditions of IHTA 1984 s 142 rather than IHTA 1984 s 93*" (emphasis supplied).

(Bear in mind that a standard residuary gift will operate to exercise any general power of appointment exercisable by the testator: Wills Act 1837 s 27.) This view evidently follows from the fact that the property does then pass under the deceased's will; but that does not alter the fact that it is only included in the deceased's estate for general IHT purposes by virtue of IHTA 1984 s 49(1) (after FA 2006 it is thought that this reference to an IIP must be read as referring to an estate IIP), which in principle will exclude the property from the scope of IHTA 1984 s 142 (see IHTA 1984 s 142(5)). HMRC cannot instead rely on IHTA 1984 s 5(2), which generally includes in a person's estate property over which they have a general power of appointment, because that does not apply where the property in question is settled property. Anyone seeking to vary within two years the devolution of the property provided for by the settlement in those circumstances will presumably be happy to take the benefit of the HMRC view just quoted. However, where the deceased made such an appointment by will and a beneficiary disclaims the appointed interest more than two years after the death, it would seem to remain open to the trustees of the settlement, and the deceased's executors, to argue that his disclaimer should attract the benefit of IHTA 1984 s 93 even though the interest disclaimed was conferred by the will.

If conditions for backdating not fulfilled

3.1.75   If the disclaimer of an interest under an existing settlement is made in circumstances that do not attract backdating treatment under IHTA 1984 s 93 – in essence, if it is made for consideration in money or money's worth – then it will be treated for IHT purposes like any other disposition of an interest in settled property. Thus—

(a) If it is an estate IIP, within IHTA 1984 s 49, then as the disclaimer brings the interest to an end—

   (i) The original beneficiary will be regarded as having made a transfer of value of the underlying trust capital under IHTA 1984 s 52, at the date of the disclaimer, subject to the exclusion of excluded property (IHTA 1984 s 53(1)) and to the value transferred being reduced by the amount of the consideration (IHTA 1984 s 52(2)). The status of that transfer of value as exempt, chargeable or potentially exempt will depend on the nature of the interests that take effect under the trust in the light of the disclaimer, and where relevant on the identity of the persons entitled, in the usual way.

   (ii) The original beneficiary will also be regarded as having made a gift of the underlying capital for the purpose of the GROB rules (FA 1986 s 102ZA), but that will only give rise to actual problems if he benefits in future from property then comprised in the settlement or has some other potential interest under the settlement that he has not similarly disclaimed. This deemed gift appears to arise even if the disclaimer involved no element of gratuitous disposition or intent at all, ie even if the consideration given in return for it was full consideration.

(b) If it is an IIP that is not an estate IIP, there is no actual or deemed transfer of value – neither the underlying trust capital nor even the IIP itself forms part of the beneficiary's estate (as to the latter see IHTA 1984 s 5(1)(a)(ii), (1A)), so even though the disclaimer will count as a disposition of the IIP (see paragraph **3.1.69** above) the original beneficiary's estate is not reduced by it. The immediate IHT consequences, if any, will be determined by the status of the trust immediately before and immediately after the disclaimer.

(c) If it is a reversionary (or future – IHTA 1984 s 47) interest, then its value will leave the estate of the original beneficiary as a result of the disposition constituted by the disclaimer. Whether that gives rise to a transfer of value will depend on whether the reversionary interest is prevented from being excluded property by any of paragraphs (a) to (c) of IHTA 1984, s 48(1). If it is, the resultant transfer of value would *prima facie* be a chargeable transfer, since the reversionary interest in question would be destroyed by the disclaimer and so cannot become comprised in the estate of another beneficiary such as to attract spouse exemption or PET treatment; the next beneficiary would take by virtue of the terms of the settlement, in other words in right of an interest that they already held. But it may be that the value of the next beneficiary's interest would have been increased as a result of the disclaimer; and, to the extent of that increase, spouse exemption or PET treatment would after all be applicable, according to the circumstances, by virtue of IHTA 1984 s 18(1) or s 3A(2)(b), as the case may be.

CGT treatment

Limited backdating effect – outline

3.1.76   The backdating treatment that is available for CGT purposes in the case of a variation or disclaimer is similar in many respects to that described above for IHT purposes, but fundamentally different in one important respect. The areas of similarity will not be discussed in this section – reference can be made back to the discussion of the particular requirement in the IHT context. In summary—

(a)   The points of similarity are—

> (i)The variation or disclaimer must be made within two years after the death: TCGA 1992 s 62(6).
> (ii)It must be made by an instrument in writing made by all the original beneficiaries (see paragraphs **3.1.53** ff above): TCGA 1992 s 62(6). HMRC accept that a Tomlin order compromising proceedings under the I(PFD)A 1975 is a variation to which TCGA 1992 s 62(6) is capable of applying if the other conditions are met: CG31820 (see paragraphs **3.3.37** FF below).
> (iii)Extraneous consideration will preclude the statutory backdating (see paragraphs **3.1.57** ff above, but see also paragraphs **3.1.79**, **3.1.80** below): TCGA 1992 s 62(8).
> (iv)For backdating to apply, the instrument effecting a variation (but again not a disclaimer) must contain a statement, by the parties making the instrument, of their intent that TCGA 1992 s 62(6) should apply: TCGA 1992 s 62(7). (Again before 1 August 2002 this requirement took the form of an election to be made within six months after the variation: see paragraph **3.1.51** above, point (d).) There is no requirement for CGT that the personal representatives should join in that statement.

(v) The dispositions to which the variation or disclaimer may apply are differently expressed, but amount for practical purposes to essentially the same range as for IHT backdating, subject to one technical issue of interpretation that appears not to have been taken by HMRC at any time (see paragraph **3.1.78** below, point (a)). For CGT they must be dispositions that relate to "property of which the deceased was competent to dispose" (TCGA 1992 s 62(6)); this expression is discussed further in paragraphs **3.1.77, 3.1.78** below.

(vi) It is immaterial whether or not the administration of the estate is complete or the assets have been distributed in accordance with the original dispositions: TCGA 1992 s 62(9).

(vii) Where the conditions are fulfilled, the variation or disclaimer does not constitute a disposal [of anything] for CGT purposes: TCGA 1992 s 62(6)(a).

(b) The key difference (discussed further in paragraphs **3.1.81** ff below) is that, although as with IHT the variation is treated as having been made by the deceased, or as the case may be the disclaimed benefit is treated as never having been conferred, this treatment in the CGT context is not for all CGT purposes, but *only* for the purpose of the application of the "death" rules in the earlier part of TCGA 1992 s 62. (In particular, backdated treatment does not extend to the issue of who is the settlor of any trust that results from the variation, see paragraphs **3.1.102** ff below.) Those "death" rules, so far as relevant for present purposes, comprise—

(i) The personal representatives, or other person on whom the assets devolve, are deemed to acquire the assets in question at the deceased's death, for their market value at that time, without a corresponding disposal by the deceased (TCGA 1992 s 62(1)).

(ii) On a person acquiring an asset as legatee, he takes over the personal representatives' base cost and acquisition date, and no chargeable gain accrues to the personal representatives (TCGA 1992 s 62(4)). Note that the latter provision is not to the effect that the personal representatives are not treated as disposing of the asset – merely that no chargeable gain (and therefore also no allowable loss – TCGA 1992 s 16(2)) accrues to them when they dispose of it to a legatee.

Property of which the deceased was competent to dispose

3.1.77   TCGA 1992 s 62(10) defines "assets of which a deceased person was competent to dispose" as being—

"assets of the deceased which (otherwise than in right of a power of appointment or of the testamentary power conferred by statute to dispose of entailed interests) he could, if of full age and capacity, have disposed of by his will, assuming that all the assets were situated in England and, if he was not domiciled in the United Kingdom, that he was domiciled in England, and include references to his severable share in any assets to which, immediately before his death, he was beneficially entitled as a joint tenant".

3.1.78 This definition broadly encompasses the entirety of the deceased's estate to which IHTA 1984 s 142 is capable of applying (see paragraph **3.1.30** above), but with the following differences or potential differences—

(a) In view of the definition of "assets" in TCGA 1992 s 21(1) (see particularly s 21(1)(b)) it does not include sterling currency, though it includes a debt expressed in sterling such as is constituted by a credit balance in a bank account. That is understandable in the context of the original function of the definition, for the purpose of the rule in TCGA 1992 s 62(1) as to acquisition of the deceased's assets by the personal representatives on his death; but if the same exclusion applied for the purposes of TCGA 1992 s 62(6) it could – in theory at least – create unexpected difficulties for a variation to the extent that it was made in consideration of another variation relating to sterling currency in the estate. In that event the consideration would be "extraneous", with the consequence of disapplying TCGA 1992 s 62(6) altogether. However, it is suggested that this anomalous result should not apply, because the dispositions that can be varied within TCGA 1992 s 62(6) are those of the *property* of which the deceased was competent to dispose. The use of the word "property" as opposed to "assets" – unusual though it is in the CGT legislation – seems to provide justification for avoiding the unexpected exclusion of sterling currency; although TCGA 1992 s 62(10) does not in terms provide a definition of the "property of which the deceased was competent to dispose", it is suggested that this expression would be construed by analogy.

(b) Property over which the deceased had a general power of appointment is within his estate for IHT unless it is settled property (IHTA 1984 s 5(2)); but on the face of it TCGA 1992 s 62(10) excludes property that the deceased can dispose of by will if he can only dispose of it in right of a power of appointment. (As regards the IHT treatment of settled property in which the deceased had an estate IIP but also exercised a general power of appointment in his will, see paragraph **3.1.74** above.) Both the statute and CG30363 fail to draw the distinction which might have been drawn between general and special powers of appointment, and it must be supposed that a variation relating to property over which the deceased had a general power of appointment (whether or not it was settled property) will be denied backdating treatment for CGT purposes even though, depending on the precise circumstances, it may attract it for IHT purposes.

(c) HMRC specifically state in CG30362 (consistently with the definition of assets of which the deceased was competent to dispose) that an interest in partnership assets which passes automatically to the surviving partners is excluded from that definition; contrast the practice for IHT in IHTM35073, referred to in paragraph **3.1.29** above.

Extraneous consideration

3.1.79   There is a hidden contrast between the CGT and IHT provisions that prohibit extraneous consideration where statutory backdating is required. Whereas under IHTA 1984 s 142(3) the "permissible" consideration for IHT purposes is confined to "the making, in respect of another of the dispositions, of a variation or disclaimer to which [IHTA 1984 s 142(1)] applies" (paragraphs **3.1.57** ff above) – ie in respect of which an IHT statement of intent is also made – for CGT purposes this is marginally extended in TCGA 1992 s 62(8) to "the making of a variation or disclaimer in respect of another of the dispositions".

3.1.80   Thus if dispositions A and B are varied by the respective original beneficiaries, each in return for the other, IHT backdating will be available for one only if it is opted for in relation to the other as well. By contrast, CGT backdating can apply to one even if it is not invoked for the other. This may be logical, in the sense that one of the gifts varied (after completion of the administration) may have been a cash legacy, and neither element of the CGT treatment available under TCGA 1992 s 62(6) would be relevant to the redirection of the cash already distributed to the legatee. But this feature opens up the possibility that a CGT statement of intent can be made in relation to one or some of the variations contained in a given instrument, but not to all of them, at any rate so long as they are clearly distinguished from each other in the instrument.

Application of the CGT death provisions

Where limited backdating applies

3.1.81   Where a variation attracts limited backdating under TCGA 1992 s 62(6), the new beneficiary is treated as the legatee in place of the original beneficiary. (The original beneficiary or the new beneficiary, or both, could be a body of trustees; but the change in this context must be brought about by a variation, not by the exercise of a power under the trust established by the original dispositions, compare paragraphs **3.2.31**, **3.2.32** below.) The consequences are summarised as follows in CG31630 (adapted to use the same terminology as in this chapter, see paragraph **3.1.3** above)—

"... the effects of the variation are treated as being retrospective to the date of death for most purposes of CGT.

—   If the assets are vested in personal representatives at the time the deed is executed, there will be no chargeable occasion for them either on the execution of the deed or when they vest assets in the [new beneficiary].

> — Whether or not the assets have already been vested in the [original beneficiary], there will be no chargeable occasion for the [original beneficiary] when the deed is executed.
>
> — If the assets have vested in the [original beneficiary] and the [original beneficiary] has disposed of the assets before the deed is executed, then the disposal is no longer treated as an occasion of charge for the [original beneficiary]. Instead it is treated as an occasion of charge for the [new beneficiary]."

For disclaimers, the first two points are stated in substantially identical terms in CG31480;the third point, if correct in itself, is of course inapplicable to disclaimers in any case, since a disclaimer is impossible in law where the legatee has accepted the benefit of the gift.

3.1.82   The third point quoted in paragraph **3.1.81** above is open to some doubt, and is called into question by a recent change to the CGT Manual only a few paragraphs before this: see generally the discussion in paragraphs **3.1.83** ff below. The precise wording of the legislation on the second point – no "chargeable occasion" for the original beneficiary – is "the variation or disclaimer shall not constitute a disposal for the purposes of this Act" (TCGA 1992 s 62(6)(a), and see point (a)(vii) in paragraph **3.1.76** above). Unlike the limited effects of the backdating under paragraph (b) of that same subsection, this "no disposal" treatment is therefore for all CGT purposes. The potential implications of this are explored further in paragraph **3.1.115** below.

The impact of sales and other post-death changes

3.1.83   The third point in CG31630 (see paragraph **3.1.81** above) is in any event potentially surprising; for some years after the precursor of TCGA 1992 s 62(6) was introduced by FA 1978, it was thought that the Inland Revenue (as they then were) took the view that, once the original beneficiary had disposed of an asset that he had received as legatee, he was no longer in a position to vary the disposition of assets of which the deceased was competent to dispose. That view seems perhaps to be re-emerging: amendments to the CGT Manual made since this chapter was first drafted introduce a qualification which seems to conflict with the third point quoted in paragraph **3.1.81** above from CG31630 (which remains unamended in this respect). CG31601 now reads as follows (again adapted for the terminology used in this chapter)—

> "An instrument of variation may be executed even if the assets involved have already vested in the [original beneficiary]. But if the assets have been sold by the [original beneficiary] before the instrument is executed, there would appear to be difficulties in accepting the instrument's validity as an instrument of variation, on the basis that in general law the instrument takes effect from the date of execution, and no one can make a gift of property which he or she does not have. So what the person executing the instrument can do is to make a gift of cash, not the asset which is no longer owned. See further the Special Commissioner's decision in *Soutter's Executry v CIR* [2002] STC(SCD)385, an IHT case."

3.1.84   The *Soutter* case was, as acknowledged in the above quotation, decided in the IHT context (see paragraph **3.1.18**, point (d), above), and in fact concerned the issue whether the interest left by the will still existed so as to be capable of being disposed of in the "real world" (in that case a life interest, after the death of the life tenant); thus, whether indeed the document truly effected any disposition at all, such as to be properly described as a variation of the original disposition. That is a different issue from the extent to which statutory backdating effect can be invoked for a disposition which clearly did validly take effect in relation to something presently owned by the original beneficiary – in HMRC's example, the proceeds of the earlier sale by him. This latter question, it is suggested, is susceptible of different answers for IHT purposes and CGT purposes respectively, resulting from the different nature of the two taxes, and the different results of backdating, if applicable, as between the two taxes—

(a)IHT is concerned with value, and transfers of it, rather than assets; and in this context, as discussed in paragraphs **3.1.36–3.1.39** above, what is relevant is whether the variation can be shown to be of "a disposition of property comprised in [the deceased's] estate immediately before his death". For the reasons given in that discussion, the all-important requirement is to be able to trace the present assets (the subject-matter of the disposition in fact made by the original beneficiary in his variation) clearly back to assets in the estate to which the original disposition in the will related.

(b)CGT on the other hand is concerned with disposals of assets, and the scope of the statutory backdating is much more limited than for IHT, being concerned merely with avoiding (in appropriate circumstances) a disposal by the original beneficiary, and applying the death provisions (both to the personal representatives and to the new beneficiary) as though the latter had taken under the will etc in place of the original beneficiary (see paragraph **3.1.76**, points (a)(vii) and (b) above). For CGT the variation must be of a disposition of "property of which the deceased was competent to dispose" (discussed at paragraphs **3.1.77**, **3.1.78** above), and as explained there (most particularly at paragraph **3.1.78** point (a) above) "property" should be accepted as meaning for this purpose little more than the general CGT concept of "assets" – not the more extended meaning that it has in IHTA 1984 s 142 (see paragraphs **3.1.36**, **3.1.37** above). Seen in that context, there is certainly some technical basis (even without having to rely on the Soutter case) for the HMRC view in CG31601 (quoted in paragraph **3.1.83** above, and contradicting CG 31630 quoted in paragraph **3.1.81** above) that CGT backdating should not extend to treating the new beneficiary, rather than the original beneficiary, as having made for CGT the disposal in fact made by the original beneficiary prior to the variation. That view would also avoid practical difficulties, in the form of reporting implications, as exposed in the following example.

3.1.85

Example

Assume that the deceased died in say February 2006, and the asset in question vested immediately in the original beneficiary (eg the deceased's severable share in joint property, explicitly included in the definition in TCGA 1992 s 62(10), or property overseas which devolves under local law direct to the beneficiary without the intervention of personal representatives – note the counterfactual assumptions used in that definition to encompass such assets). In such a case it is not impossible that the original beneficiary could have sold the asset before 6 April 2006; nor is it impossible (assuming that de deceased and the original beneficiary were not married or civil partners, such as to attract the related property valuation rule in IHTA 1984 s 161) that a gain for CGT purposes will have accrued even in that short space of time, at least in the case of erstwhile joint property, because of the valuation discount that is likely to apply to the deceased's half share. That disposal would have been reportable on the original beneficiary's self-assessment return due by 31 January 2007, and any tax due would have been payable by that date. Yet the time limit for a variation would not expire until over a year later, in February 2008, by which time it would be too late for the original beneficiary to amend his return under TMA 1970 s 9ZA. Similarly, if the variation were effected close to the two year time limit, the new beneficiary would under this interpretation be deemed to have realised a chargeable gain in a tax year for which he, too, was out of time to amend his return to include that disposal under the same provision. Although the CGT Manual contains lengthy instructions as to action in the tax districts dealing with the original and new beneficiaries where a variation does not attract backdating effect for CGT (see CG32040–32072), HMRC do not address how this degree of backdating is to be dealt with in practical terms if a variation were to qualify for it.

3.1.86   However, that is not to say that backdating should be, or is, denied where assets held by the deceased at his death have been disposed of by the personal representatives, rather than by the original beneficiary, as with the residuary estate example discussed in the IHT context in paragraph **3.1.37** above. One basis given by the House of Lords in *Marshall v Kerr* [1995] 1 AC 148 (see paragraphs **3.1.114, 3.1.115** below) for their decision (that the original beneficiary should be seen as the settlor of a settlement created by the variation) was that the statutory "no disposal" wording in TCGA 1992 s 62(6)(b) does not apply to the transfer of an asset (there a residuary beneficiary's *chose in action*, see paragraph **3.1.20** above) that was not property of which the deceased was competent to dispose immediately before his death. However, HMRC have accepted in countless cases that assets eventually vested in the new beneficiary by the personal representatives are, in consequence of TCGA 1992 s 62(6), acquired by him as legatee; and there has been no suggestion by them that the original beneficiary should, in reliance on that line of reasoning in

Marshall v Kerr, be taxed on a disposal of his chose in action (for which he probably has a nil base cost, see paragraph **3.1.91** below). It is thought that such a suggestion would be taking the *Marshall v Kerr* decision too far beyond its particular context.

Where backdating does not apply

Variation after vesting in original outright beneficiary

3.1.87   Where the original beneficiary is already absolutely entitled to the property in respect of which he makes the variation (including after an assent or appropriation made by the personal representatives), and backdating under TCGA 1992 s 62(6) is inapplicable for any reason, then the original beneficiary makes a disposal of any assets involved in the usual way, and the new beneficiary (whether trustees or an individual) makes a corresponding acquisition. This is so whether or not the variation is made for consideration. Normal CGT principles apply. (The same applies in the case of a disclaimer, though there will be fewer cases where beneficial vesting has taken place without acceptance of the legacy by the original beneficiary.)

3.1.88   Whatever the conclusion one reaches on the issue of whether the variation provisions of TCGA 1992 s 62(6) are capable of extending to cases where the original beneficiary has since disposed of the property he received from the estate (see the discussion of HMRC's apparently conflicting indications in paragraphs **3.1.83–3.1.86** above), HMRC note that, if for whatever reason the backdating provision does not apply in such a case, the proceeds of the original beneficiary's disposal pass to the new beneficiary (CG31920) and the original beneficiary remains chargeable on the actual disposal made by him (CG31920 and CG31932). This conclusion of course reflects precisely the "real world" analysis of what is in fact taking place with a "variation" in those circumstances, namely a gift by the original beneficiary to the new beneficiary of the property held by the original beneficiary at that time, which happened to derive from the testator's estate (see paragraph **3.1.17** above).

Variation before vesting in original outright beneficiary

3.1.89   If on the other hand the variation is made in respect of a share of the residuary estate which is left to a beneficiary outright, but has not yet been distributed or appropriated, and the administration of the estate is continuing, the correct analysis of a typical variation will, it is suggested, usually be that the original outright beneficiary will have assigned his rights as a residuary beneficiary (see paragraphs **3.1.21** ff above) to the new beneficiary, either in part or in whole. (If the original dispositions provided for property to be held in trust, see paragraphs **3.1.99** ff below.) Where those rights are assigned, and the CGT backdating provisions do not apply, it is necessary to examine separately the CGT position of the original beneficiary, the new beneficiary, and the personal representatives. The CGT consequences of HMRC's competing (and surprising) property law analysis, as set out in the CGT Manual (see paragraphs **3.1.23–3.1.26** above), will be examined and compared after that, see paragraphs **3.1.95–3.1.98** below.

The original beneficiary

3.1.90 The residuary beneficiary's *chose in action* (see paragraph **3.1.20** above) is itself an item of property, and so an asset for CGT purposes. Accordingly, where the variation involves an assignment of that *chose in action* (see paragraphs **3.1.21**, **3.1.22** above), that will constitute a disposal, or part disposal, of it by the original beneficiary. His disposal, and the acquisition of the *chose in action* by the new beneficiary (whether trustees or individual), will generally be deemed to take place at market value under TCGA 1992 s 17, and if it is a part disposal then the usual apportionment of base value will be needed (but see paragraph **3.1.91** below). The exception to this is where, exceptionally, the disposal was by way of a bargain made at arm's length and the original and new beneficiaries are not connected persons (c f TCGA 1992 s 18(2)), in which case the actual consideration given by the new beneficiary will be taken (at its value at the date of the variation). To the extent that a "charge" analysis is preferred over the partial assignment analysis in the circumstances discussed in paragraph **3.1.22** above, it is thought that this would be seen as being by way of security for the amount payable, and no CGT disposal would be entailed even if the charge were viewed as a transfer (TCGA 1992 s 26(1)).

3.1.91 Concern is sometimes expressed that the original beneficiary can have no allowable base value for the *chose in action*: he gave no consideration for it, and even if he is to be regarded as having acquired it on the death of the deceased there was plainly no corresponding disposal of it (the *chose in action* did not exist in the deceased's lifetime), so the market value rule is excluded in relation to his acquisition by virtue of TCGA 1992 s 17(2)(a). The authors are not aware of HMRC having taken this point in practice, sound though it seems in principle; and it is not foreshadowed in the paragraphs of the CGT Manual dealing with "non-retrospective" variations (CG31900–CG32100) – though a nil base cost is noted, in relation to the interest of an original beneficiary in *settled* property, in CG38001. But the reason for this may lie simply in the extraordinary analysis set out there (see paragraphs **3.1.23** ff above), which in the authors' opinion is not sustainable in law however well meaning the CGT results that it seems designed to achieve.

3.1.92 Both because of the nil base cost risk, and because of the obviously difficult valuation exercise which could be involved on a disposal of the original beneficiary's *chose in action*, other than relatively late in the course of the administration, the prudent advice has to be to ensure wherever possible that a variation where the underlying assets have not yet vested in the original beneficiary should be brought within the backdating treatment of TCGA 1992 s 62(6). As pointed out in paragraph **3.1.24** above, that also avoids having to grapple with the precise legal analysis as to the nature of the transaction that takes place on the variation, or to rely on what is thought to be purely concessionary treatment based on an unsustainable legal analysis.

The new beneficiary

3.1.93 To the extent that the new beneficiary acquires a *chose in action* – either the whole of the *chose* to which the original beneficiary was entitled, or a part of it – he will do so for the same consideration that accrues to the original beneficiary on the corresponding disposal (see paragraph **3.1.90** above). When he receives a distribution from the personal representatives in respect of that *chose in action*, the distribution is not received by him as legatee – that treatment can only arise if the variation was brought within the backdating provisions of TCGA 1992 s 62(6). Accordingly the receipt of the distribution constitutes a disposal *pro tanto* of the *chose in action*, in consideration of the distribution received (whether the latter is in cash or other assets), and the new beneficiary may realise a chargeable gain or an allowable loss as a result. Note that the new beneficiary might be an individual or the trustees of a trust to which property is directed as a result of the variation, so long as the property in question would not have become settled property apart from the variation.

The personal representatives

3.1.94 For the same reason, that the new beneficiary does not take as legatee, the personal representatives will make a disposal for CGT purposes of any assets they distribute to the new beneficiary. As this is not a disposal by way of bargain at arm's length, it will be for a market value consideration under TCGA 1992 s 17(1).

The analysis in the CGT Manual

3.1.95 It will be seen that the analysis which the authors consider correct does lead to some potentially onerous CGT results in a case where statutory backdating under TCGA 1992 s 62(6) is unavailable. HMRC's peculiar analysis of the property law position, as set out in the CGT Manual (see paragraphs **3.1.23–3.1.26** above), brings about in their view a different analysis for CGT purposes. Their views all appear to proceed from the initial premise that the original beneficiary's *chose in action* is non-assignable (see paragraph **3.1.25** above); that seems, frankly, inconsistent with the House of Lords' analysis in *Marshall v Kerr* ([1995] 1 AC 148 at 166 per Lord Browne-Wilkinson, with whom the other law lords agreed while for the most part adding further speeches of their own) that the original (residuary) beneficiary in that case had settled her *chose in action* by entering into the deed of family arrangement; that conclusion would of course be impossible if the *chose in action* were truly non-assignable.

3.1.96 Nevertheless, the HMRC approach, technically flawed though it may be, does lead to a generally less harsh CGT result than the authors' analysis in cases where statutory backdating has not been achieved for any reason. It is suggested that, while this remains their published approach, it can be taken to be more or less akin to a statement of practice or an extra-statutory concession, even though statements in the Manual do not have quite the same formal status. It is therefore appropriate to give an account of it here. When intending to rely on this practice, it would be wise to check that it is still set out in the CGT Manual at the relevant time; and see paragraph **3.1.98** below as to recording in a tax return the fact of reliance on it.

3.1.97 HMRC's analysis as set out in CG31940–CG32072 will be applied by them except (CG32080) where the original dispositions involved property becoming settled property subject to the completion of the administration, see paragraphs **3.1.99** ff below. (Note also CG31850 ff, dealing with sales of a residuary beneficiary's interest during administration, which refer forward to these same paragraphs.) It can be summarised as follows—

(a) If the variation was made for valuable consideration (including a straightforward sale of the original beneficiary's interest, or a compromise of a claim under the I(PFD)A 1975 by way of Tomlin order that does not contain a CGT statement of intent or is made outside the two year period from death)—

   (i) the original beneficiary does not make an assignment of his *chose in action* at the date of the variation, because that is ineffective; but the variation operates as a contract "to deliver to the [new beneficiary] the assets he will eventually receive from the estate" – with this contract placing the eventual disposal at the date of the variation by virtue of TCGA 1992 s 28 (CG31961);

   (ii) the assets which are the subject of that disposal cannot be known until vesting has actually taken place, so a definitive CGT computation is impossible until hindsight allows this after vesting has taken place. The chargeable assets that vest (in the original beneficiary, not the new beneficiary) are thus disposed of by the original beneficiary, with the disposal consideration being apportioned between the chargeable and non-chargeable assets (CG31962, CG31970);

   (iii) when the assets vest, the new beneficiary is regarded as disposing of a separate *chose in action* (his "contractual" rights against the original beneficiary arising from the variation, see CG31950) for the then value of the assets (both chargeable and non-chargeable) that vest from the estate and are "delivered to him by the [original beneficiary]". His acquisition cost for that *chose in action* equates to the (total, not apportioned) consideration received by the original beneficiary (CG31971–CG31973);

(iv) in the case of a variation that is "made in return for the [new beneficiary] giving up a right to take court action", the value of that consideration should be determined by reference to the amount that a suitably informed buyer would have been prepared to pay to acquire "such an interest" (CG31980). This, on examination, appears to describe a process of valuing the interest disposed of, rather than the consideration received for it (the claim or alleged claim given up); it might be open to challenge if relevant, for example where a wholly unmeritorious claim is compromised simply to secure a quiet life and to allow the administration of the estate to proceed.

(b) If the variation was made otherwise than for valuable consideration—

(i) the variation operates, at the date it takes effect, as neither an actual assignment nor a contract to assign. Instead, a disposal for CGT occurs only when assets actually vest from the estate. "At that time the [original beneficiary] is deemed to both acquire and immediately dispose of the assets to the [new beneficiary]"; (CG32001, CG32002);

(ii) the consideration for this (deferred) disposal by the original beneficiary is the market value of the chargeable assets comprised in that disposal; because his acquisition is as legatee, his acquisition cost is their value at death (or later acquisition by the personal representatives) by reference to TCGA 1992 s 62(4) (CG32002);

(iii) although CG32010 states that the new beneficiary only acquires chargeable assets at the date the assets vest, which is at least consistent with the rest of this approach, CG32031, CG32032 go on to cast doubt on this by repeating, *verbatim*, CG31972, CG31973 speaking of a disposal by the new beneficiary of his *chose in action*. Apart from the fact that he can only have a chose in action if he has some enforceable right – when on this HMRC analysis he has received neither an assignment of the original beneficiary's chose in action nor even the benefit of a contract to transfer anything (as to which see paragraph **3.1.26** above) – the two repeated paragraphs speak of consideration given by the new beneficiary for the chose in action he acquires, which is at variance with the context and the heading to each paragraph. It is thought that their inclusion is erroneous, not least by comparison with the action the new beneficiary's tax district is instructed to take in CG32072.

(c) In either case, it is the original beneficiary who acquires assets from the estate on distribution by the personal representatives, and he does so as legatee because, under the HMRC analysis, he could not validly part with his rights as residuary legatee – his *chose in action*. Accordingly the personal representatives do not realise a chargeable gain when the assets vest, whether the variation was made for valuable consideration or not (see CG32030 – though overtly only concerned with the case where no consideration passed).

3.1.98   For the reason indicated in paragraph **3.1.96**, where a variation (or other assignment of an interest in residue) has taken place in circumstances where backdating under TCGA 1992 s 62(6) is inapplicable, it is suggested that returns are submitted on the basis of the practice outlined in the CGT Manual (adding a note to that effect in the "white space" on the return, referring to the relevant passages, which should be checked at the time in case of any changes) unless the authors' preferred analysis produces a more favourable result in the particular circumstances. Facets of the authors' analysis which lead to a harsher CGT result than that described by HMRC are the following—

(a)   it involves difficult valuation issues (and potentially discrepancies between the assumptions at the disposal date and the actual net value eventually realised) in respect of the original beneficiary's *chose in action*, especially at a comparatively early stage in a complex administration (see paragraphs **3.1.90**, **3.1.92** above);

(b)   it involves the likelihood of nil base cost problems for the original beneficiary (see paragraph **3.1.91** above); and

(c)   it involves an element of potential double CGT charge as between the personal representatives on the one hand and the original and new beneficiaries on the other. The personal representatives will have made chargeable disposals of all chargeable assets in the estate, either on realising them in the course of administration or on distribution to the new beneficiary (see paragraph **3.1.94** above). At the same time, the price paid by the new beneficiary, or the market value of the original beneficiary's chose in action, as applicable, will reflect the estimated value of the entire share of residue being dealt with (with some uncertainty, no doubt, as to the extent to which allowance should be made in the process for CGT that would be incurred by the personal representatives in realising chargeable assets of the estate); and similarly, when the new beneficiary realises a gain on the assigned *chose in action* at the time he receives a distribution, the whole distribution will constitute consideration received. So CGT will have been charged, in effect, on the whole net value of the beneficial interests, whether the ultimate distribution is in the form of chargeable assets or cash. By contrast HMRC's artificial analysis—

   (i)   whether the variation was or was not made for valuable consideration—
      – secures that the personal representatives do not realise chargeable gains on assets distributed in kind, by treating the distribution as routed through the original beneficiary; and, further,

    – restricts the chargeable gain realised by the original benefici-
ary, both by taking account only of chargeable assets that are
ultimately distributed and "passed on" by him (apportioning
the actual disposal consideration, where relevant, between
those and the non-chargeable part of the distribution), and by
allowing him to inherit the personal representatives' base value
on the footing that, despite having parted with all interest
under the variation, he is still treated as taking as legatee;

but—

(ii) where the variation was made for valuable consideration,
acknowledges that the original beneficiary's chargeable gain
cannot be computed until the assets have vested. In a complex
estate this could be a number of years after the date of the
variation, and is thus hard to reconcile with the certainty
demanded by the self-assessment system.

Variation where property was to be held in trust under the original dispositions

3.1.99   In cases where the will provides for part or all of the residuary
estate to become settled property, HMRC rightly point out in CG32080
that the legatees for the purpose of the rule in TCGA 1992 s 62(4) are the
trustees of the settlement in question. They (and not the beneficiaries
under the trust) are also the persons with the *chose in action* discussed in
paragraph **3.1.20** above, viz the persons directly entitled to compel due
administration of the estate and receive distribution of the appropriate
share of residue when ascertained. (This point will of course be rather
blurred in the typical case where the will appoints the same persons as
executors and trustees, and the beneficiaries under the trust undoubtedly
have *locus standi* to take action against those persons should need arise. A
precise demarcation of the capacity in which they were sued would be
otiose in those circumstances.) This gives rise to the following consequences, one of which is discussed in the CGT Manual but the others not.

Trust removed by variation

3.1.100   If the variation (as opposed to an appointment out of trust, see
paragraphs **3.2.31**, **3.2.32** below) involves property no longer passing into
that trust, and backdating under TCGA 1992 s 62(6) does not apply,
then—

(a) To the extent that the variation takes effect after property has already
become vested in the trustees of the trust, the variation will fall to be
treated like any other termination of a trust by agreement. The
original beneficiaries giving up interests in any of the trust property
will dispose of those interests; but so long as they have not acquired
their interests for consideration in money or money's worth (other
than some other interest under the same settlement), and the trust has

never had non-resident or dual-resident trustees, the original beneficiaries will not realise any chargeable gain (or allowable loss) as a result: TCGA 1992 s 76. The trustees on the other hand will make a deemed disposal and reacquisition (the latter in the capacity as bare trustees for the new beneficiary) under TCGA 1992 s 71(1). The availability of holdover relief (subject to the new beneficiary being UK resident) will depend in the usual way on the nature of the assets held in the trust (TCGA 1992 s 165, Sch 7), or on the nature of the interests conferred by the trust and their IHT results (TCGA 1992 s 260); also on whether the original beneficiary, as settlor, or his spouse or civil partner is interested under the settlement (TCGA 1992 ss 169B–169G). Note however that if the variation qualifies for IHT backdating under IHTA 1984 s 142 then none of the circumstances for holdover relief under TCGA 1992 s 260 will be satisfied.

(b) Where property remains in the hands of the personal representatives, the result of the variation will be that, when the time comes for distribution, the distribution will fall to be made to the new beneficiary outright, not to the trustees. On the face of it the new beneficiary therefore does not take as legatee, and the personal representatives would therefore make a chargeable disposal of the assets they vest in him – realising a chargeable gain or a (potentially useless) allowable loss in doing so. However, in CG32081–CG32100 HMRC outline a slightly more favourable approach. Taking the simplest example of a trust for A for life remainder to B absolutely, with A's life interest being deleted by the non-backdated variation so that B receives residue absolutely when the administration is complete, they point out in CG32082 that B's right to the assets so received derives partly from the will and only part from the variation. It therefore appears that they are prepared to view B as a legatee in these circumstances to the extent of his actuarial interest (as a proportion of the combined actuarial values of A's and B's interests – they do not spell out whether these actuarial valuations are to be undertaken as at the date of death, the date of the variation or, notionally, the date of actual distribution, but probably the date of death is the most rational of the three). Accordingly, CG32082 and CG32090 indicate that any gain or loss of the personal representatives will be confined to a proportion of each asset equating to the proportion of beneficial interests not originally held by the new beneficiary; and the new beneficiary will have an acquisition cost for each asset made up of his "original" proportion of the probate value plus his "acquired" proportion of the asset's market value at the date of vesting. (Seemingly for taper relief purposes – no longer relevant from 6 April 2008, if the CGT proposals in the Pre-Budget Report of 9 October 2007 are enacted in the form announced – B's period of ownership as to the whole asset would therefore start from the date of death, by virtue of TCGA 1992 Sch A1 para 14; and similarly for private residence relief under TCGA 1992 s 222(7).) HMRC's basic approach that the trustees do not take as legatees, even for the purpose of "delivering" the assets to the new beneficiary, is of course not inconsistent with their more general, and more questionable, analysis described in paragraphs 3.1.23–3.1.26, 3.1.97 above, because by the time of the distribution the trustees would receive it as bare trustees for the new beneficiaries, a different capacity from that of the single deemed trustee under TCGA 1992 s 69(1). But the practice just described, which has a trust beneficiary as a "legatee" when apart from the variation it would have been the trustees alone who took as legatees, does have an air of concession about it on any view.

Trust continues after variation

3.1.101   If a variation deals only with adjustments to the beneficial interests within the trust created by the will/intestacy, and the trust remains in being at the time the personal representatives come to release assets from the administration, then "all went according to plan" so far as TCGA 1992 s 62(4) is concerned: the trustees are the legatees and take over the personal representatives' base cost and acquisition date in the usual way, irrespective of whether the variation has qualified for backdating treatment under TCGA 1992 s 62(6). However, so far as the parties to the variation are concerned, in the absence of backdating each party who gives up an interest will seemingly make a chargeable disposal of his inchoate right (a *chose in action* of some kind, albeit distinct from that of the trustees, see paragraph 3.1.99 above) as beneficiary of what would, after distribution, have been settled property. In contrast to the position if the variation had taken place after distribution to the trustees (see point (a) in paragraph 3.1.100 above), it is doubtful whether TCGA 1992 s 76(1) provides protection, applying as it does to disposals "of an interest created by or arising under a settlement". The legislation does not provide a definition of "settlement" as such, merely of "property comprised in a settlement" (see TCGA 1992 s 68, making that expression synonymous with "settled property" ie any property held in trust other than a bare trust within TCGA 1992 s 60); so it may be arguable that the original beneficiaries' interests should be seen as arising under a settlement even during the administration period, irrespective of the fact that there is no settled property until after distribution. That argument is perhaps fortified when "an interest created by or arising under a settlement" in TCGA 1992 s 76(1) is contrasted with "an interest in settled property" in TCGA 1992 ss 76(2), 85(1); though, against this, these contexts can be explained on the basis that the circumstances described in the latter provisions could not arise except to the extent that there was settled property as such, whereas TCGA 1992 s 76(1) is not of necessity so restricted. The section in the CGT Manual dealing with TCGA 1992 s 76 (CG38000–CG38041) does not address this issue, but it can be expected that HMRC will argue that the two expressions were intended to be interchangeable.

The settlor of any resultant trust

3.1.102 As mentioned above, the backdating effects of a variation or disclaimer for CGT purposes, even where all the conditions are met, does not extend beyond the death provisions in TCGA 1992 s 62. Apart from the express provision that "the variation or disclaimer shall not constitute a disposal for the purposes of this Act" (TCGA 1992, s 62(6)(a), see paragraph **3.1.76** above, point (a)(vii)), all other CGT consequences will follow the "real world" analysis of what takes place (see paragraphs **3.1.17** ff above). The "trust modernisation" legislation included in FA 2006, by which a number of principles and definitions were standardised as between income tax and CGT, included provisions identifying the settlor of a settlement. The CGT provisions are found in TCGA 1992 ss 68A–68C.

3.1.103 However, this "general" definition of "settlor" applies only "unless the context otherwise requires" (TCGA 1992 s 68A(1)). It must be noted that several important sets of provisions contain separate definitions as to when a person is a settlor and of what property. It is suggested that the provision of specific definitions of "settlor" for particular provisions should be seen as a context which requires one to disregard the general provisions and to apply the specific definition in their place. These separate definitions are in fact all very similar in effect to each other, and are examined in paragraphs **3.1.113** ff below; they comprise—

(a) both sets of provisions charging CGT on a settlor where he or certain others have an interest under the settlement—

    (i) TCGA 1992 s 77–79 for UK resident trusts, "the onshore settlor charge", see TCGA 1992 s 79(1)–(5A);

    (ii) TCGA 1992 s 86, Sch 5 for non-UK resident trusts, "the offshore settlor charge", see TCGA 1992 Sch 5 paras 7, 8);

(b) (until 1998 when the identity of the settlor ceased to have any significance in this context) the provisions charging CGT on beneficiaries of non-UK resident trusts, "the offshore beneficiary charge", see TCGA 1992 s 97(7) as originally enacted (and considered, in a pre-consolidation version, in *Marshall v Kerr* [1995] 1 AC 148, see paragraph **3.1.111** below); and

(c) the provisions preventing holdover relief where a settlor or his spouse or civil partner have an interest under the settlement: TCGA 1992 ss 169B–169G, "the holdover restrictions", see TCGA 1992 s 169E. These rules would however be relevant only where CGT backdating does not apply, because, as noted in paragraphs **3.1.81, 3.1.82** above, if it does apply there is no disposal by the original beneficiary on which a claim for holdover relief might have to be considered in the first place.

The "general" settlor definition

3.1.104 Areas in which the "general" provisions will apply will include—

(a) determining the residence status of the trustees (as a single deemed person under TCGA 1992 s 69(1)) in a case where the actual persons making up that single deemed person comprise at least one who is UK resident and at least one who is not UK resident (see TCGA 1992 s 69(2B)); and

(b) working out the extent of a trust's annual exemption (TCGA 1992 Sch 1 paras 1, 2).

3.1.105 The new TCGA 1992 s 68C contains some particular rules relevant in the context of variations, which are explained in the following paragraphs; but it must be appreciated that—

(a) these rules apply—

   (i) only to variations occurring on or after 6 April 2006 (irrespective of the date the deceased died) – see FA 2006 Sch 12 para 1(5); and
   (ii) then only where TCGA 1992 s 62(6) applies in respect of the variation;

   and

(b) seemingly, they apply only to variations, not to disclaimers. That is not stated explicitly, but it is thought that the reference to a disposition being varied, coupled with the condition that TCGA 1992 s 62(6) must apply "in respect of the variation", would lead to that conclusion. An example of a trust coming about as a result of the disclaimer might be a will that is drafted on a basis that the testator's surviving spouse is to take outright, but that if she predeceases *or disclaims* (see paragraphs **3.1.13, 3.1.14** above) then the property is to be held in trust for their children. (Curiously what must be varied is a disposition "following" a person's death – not "taking effect on" the death; but it is thought that the two expressions would in practice be regarded as synonymous in the context, and this is implicit in CG37888.) It would appear that HMRC may share the view that it is only variations to which TCGA 1992 s 68C applies, not disclaimers; certainly the passages in the CGT Manual covering the identity of the settlor, CG37886–CG37903, are geared to variations alone – see in particular CG37888.

Variations since 5 April 2006 attracting CGT backdating

Where the trust would not exist but for the variation

3.1.106   Where property becomes settled property as a result of the variation and would not have done so but for the variation, essentially the original beneficiary in respect of that property is treated as having made the settlement and as having provided the property for the purposes of the settlement (TCGA 1992 s 68C(2)), which in turn leads to his being a settlor within TCGA 1992 s 68A (also inserted by FA 2006). Both these provisions, while applicable for all CGT purposes, are qualified by "except where the context otherwise requires" (see TCGA 1992 s 68A(1), 68C(2)). It is possible for more than one person to be a settlor by this route, as where a variation is made by two or three beneficiaries who were absolutely entitled to the property in question jointly or in specified shares and who together direct that the property should be held as settled property; but under this provision only an original beneficiary who was absolutely entitled (in one of the four ways instanced in TCGA 1992 s 68C(3)) can be a settlor, since by definition if the original beneficiary had less than an absolute interest the property would already have been settled property under the original disposition.

Where the trust would exist anyway under the original dispositions

3.1.107   If under the original dispositions property would anyway have been settled property, and the terms of the trust in question are varied without giving rise to the property passing into a different trust, TCGA 1992 s 68C has nothing to say, and the inference is that the natural identification of the deceased as the settlor of that trust, under TCGA 1992 s 68A(2)(b), is unaffected by the variation (see paragraph **3.1.112** below). However where property does move from one trust to another as a result of a variation, the deceased will be regarded for "general" CGT purposes as having made the other settlement (and so as being a settlor of it). He will be treated as having made it immediately before his death, except in the case of a settlement which actually arose on his death (see TCGA 1992 s 68C(7), (8)).

3.1.108   TCGA 1992 s 68C(5), (6) deal with slightly different cases in this regard, with the same conclusion—

(a) TCGA 1992 s 68C(5) applies if the property "would have become comprised in a settlement" [sc, but for the variation] which arose on the deceased's death, or was in existence by then; the deceased will be the settlor of the separate settlement even if he was not a settlor of the trust into which the property would have passed. (This in practice reflects simply the fact that he would under general principles have become a settlor of that trust anyway, *pro tanto*, as and when property of which he was competent to dispose had in fact been released into that third party's settlement.)

(b) TCGA 1992 s 68C(6) applies where the property was already actually comprised in a settlement immediately before the variation, being a settlement of which the deceased is the settlor anyway; this provision confirms that the deceased is a settlor of the transferee settlement too.

Disclaimers, variations before 6 April 2006, and variations not attracting CGT backdating

3.1.109 If the specific rules in TCGA 1992 s 68C do not apply, by reference to points (a) or (b) in paragraph **3.1.105** above, then (still for "general" CGT purposes) one must fall back on the more general provision in TCGA 1992 s 68A whereby a person will be a settlor if—

(a) he has made or entered into the settlement directly or indirectly; or

(b) the settled property includes property of which he was competent to dispose immediately before his death and the settlement arose on his death; and particularly if

(c) he has provided, or undertaken to provide, funds directly or indirectly for the purpose of the settlement; or

(d) he has made a reciprocal arrangement with another person for the other person to make or enter into the settlement.

3.1.110 In order to judge the position under those tests, the position falls to be assessed by reference to what is taking place under the variation or disclaimer as a matter of property law: see paragraphs **3.1.1–3.1.27** above.

Where the trust is created as a result of the variation

3.1.111 Essentially, however, applying TCGA 1992 s 68A to the "real world" analysis (if one can use that expression despite the strictures of the Special Commissioner in *Soutter's Executry v IRC* [2002] STC (SCD) 385 at 388 that it risks "a diversion of thought") is unlikely to lead to any different a result from what is now spelt out more explicitly in TCGA 1992 s 68C. In *Marshall v Kerr* [1995] 1 AC 148 the House of Lords decided that a residuary beneficiary who had (otherwise than for full consideration) directed her share of residue into a trust was the settlor of that trust for the purpose of the CGT charge on beneficiaries of non-UK resident trusts (now TCGA 1992 ss 87 ff; prior to 1998 these provisions did not apply if the settlor of an offshore trust had no UK residence or domicile connection, which the deceased in that case did not but the original beneficiary did). In particular, the House of Lords accepted the Crown's argument (substituting current references) that one must identify what was the property settled by the [variation] – in the "real world" –

and then ask whether there is anything in [TCGA 1992 s 62(6)] which requires one to assume a state of facts inconsistent with the original beneficiary having been the settlor of the property so identified; their conclusion was that there is not. On the facts of that case, they held that the original beneficiary had settled her *chose in action* as residuary beneficiary (see paragraphs **3.1.19** ff above), and was therefore the settlor of the settlement for the purpose of the offshore beneficiary charge. CG37888 makes clear that HMRC will regard that decision as applicable equally in the context of the extent of the trustees' annual CGT exemption, and there seems no reason why it should not apply also to determine the residence of the trustees.

Where the trust existed (or would have existed) without the variation

3.1.112   In principle a variation which leaves property subject to the same trust as it was in (or would have entered, eg had the administration of the estate been completed by the date of the variation) would not affect the identity of the settlor of that trust. HMRC appear to accept that in general, though by analogy with their comments in relation to variations of trusts (as opposed to the variation of dispositions taking effect on death) one might infer that they would see one or more of the beneficiaries making the variation as settlors if the property passed from the existing trust to some new trust (cf CG37901–CG37903). CG37889 instances a relatively common form of variation where, primarily for IHT reasons (see paragraph **3.1.159**, point (a)(i), below), a life interest trust under the will for the testator's surviving spouse is varied in part to create a NRB discretionary trust. HMRC comment, a little gratuitously—

> "In such a case, where the spouse continues to be a beneficiary of the new discretionary trust, it would often be appropriate to regard this, except for the purposes of inheritance tax, as little more than a cosmetic arrangement, particularly if the broad intention is that the bulk of the income should be paid to the spouse. So this would be regarded for capital gains tax purposes as a variation of the original will trust, and not as giving rise to a new separate settlement. The deceased remains the settlor."

Special settlor definitions

3.1.113   The individual definitions of "settlor" noted in paragraph **3.1.103** above as applicable under TCGA 1992 ss 79, 169E, Sch 5 paras 7–8, and also TCGA 1992 s 97(7) in its form prior to 1998, are not expressed in identical terms (and TCGA 1992 s 97(7) in fact invoked the meaning given in the income tax settlor attribution provisions, see paragraph **3.1.129** below); but the substance of all four definitions is essentially the same, focusing – as indeed does the "general" definition in TCGA 1992 s 68A (see paragraph **3.1.109** above) – on a person's provision of property directly or indirectly, including by means of reciprocal arrangements with another person. (Detailed study of the wording of each set of provisions is of course advisable in a specific case where it might be contended that the facts fall outside their scope.) Since 1998, TCGA 1992 s 97(7) has defined (referentially) only "settlement" and not "settlor", because as mentioned in paragraph **3.1.103** above, point (b), the identity of the settlor is no longer relevant to the offshore beneficiary charge.

3.1.114 *Marshall v Kerr* [1995] 1 AC 148 was in terms concerned with the offshore beneficiary charge, and thus with the income tax definition of "settlor" that was invoked by the precursors of TCGA 1992 s 97(7). CG37888 confirms that HMRC regard the decision in as applying (anyway in relation to variations executed before 6 April 2006) also for the purpose of the onshore settlor charge and the offshore settlor charge; equally, it would not extend the decision in any way to see it as applying also for the purpose of the holdover restrictions. As seen in paragraph **3.1.111** above, that decision affirmed the approach taken in this chapter generally, namely to ascertain the nature of a variation in the "real world" and then see how far the "real world" analysis is displaced by clear statutory provisions. The residuary beneficiary's *chose in action* that was settled in that case was not among the assets of which the deceased was competent to dispose, so could not be the subject of "non-disposal treatment" under the (slightly differently worded) precursor of TCGA 1992 s 62(6)(a).

3.1.115 The *Marshall v Kerr* reasoning noted in paragraph **3.1.114** above leaves open the intriguing possibility that an original beneficiary might yet argue that he should avoid being treated as a settlor – on the basis that TCGA 1992 s 62(6)(a) resulted for CGT purposes generally in their not having made a disposal [into settlement] at all – if what was redirected by means of the variation comprised solely assets (preferably just chargeable assets, but see point (a) in paragraph **3.1.78** above) that were demonstrably comprised, in that form, in the deceased's estate immediately before and after death; assets of which, therefore, he *was* competent to dispose, unlike the residuary beneficiary's *chose in action*. This would clearly be possible to achieve in many cases, in view of the express provision that a variation can be recognised even after distribution has taken place in accordance with the original dispositions (TCGA 1992 s 62(9)). The argument would run that the statutory wording *would*, on those facts, displace the real world analysis, as indeed had been argued for the taxpayer in *Marshall v Kerr*, albeit unsuccessfully because the *chose in action* was not an asset of which the deceased had been competent to dispose. However, the authors do not consider it a foregone conclusion that a provision preventing a "disposal" – a term used throughout the CGT legislation as an occasion for computing a gain or loss, which might then be a chargeable gain or an allowable loss – can legitimately be stretched to force a conclusion that the original beneficiary should additionally not be seen as having provided property for the settlement that undoubtedly results from the variation. It should be noted additionally that in CG37888 HMRC suggest that the "general" definition of "settlor" in TCGA 1992 s 68C (read with TCGA 1992 s 68A) will apply where a variation is made on or after 6 April 2006 and the instrument contains a CGT statement of intent. (The actual reference is to notice being given under TCGA 1992 s 62(7) – a curious anachronism given that the passage was only added to the CGT Manual in autumn 2007.) This is questionable by reference to the fact that this "general" definition applies only where the context otherwise requires (see paragraphs **3.1.103**, **3.1.106** above, and note also the interpretation inherent in the rewritten version of the income tax rule that was originally identical in effect to TCGA 1992 s 68C, as referred to in paragraph **3.1.124** below).

3.1.116 The foregoing comments relate to a situation where a settlement has come into being as a result of the variation, but would not have done so otherwise. Where a trust existed in any case (or would have existed after the completion of the administration), then HMRC, in CG37887, identify their approach as being to establish (much as where backdating applied, see paragraph **3.1.112** above) whether a new separate settlement has come into being (with the affected property passing from the existing settlement into the new one), and if so who is the settlor of it. Instances are given of minor changes that would leave the property within the same settlement; beyond that, HMRC merely cross refer to paragraphs dealing with the variation of trusts by agreement (see CG37882, CG 37889, CG37900).

Income tax treatment

Generally

3.1.117 The income tax legislation contains no backdating provisions for deeds of variation, or for that matter for any other form of post-death restructuring (though see paragraphs **3.3.7**, **3.3.8** below in relation to orders under the I(PFD)A 1975 s 2). Accordingly, with one exception in connection with the POA charge, dealt with in paragraph **3.1.134** below, the income tax position of all parties will be ascertained according to the "real world" analysis of what is taking place behind the mask of a variation or disclaimer (see paragraphs **3.1.1–3.1.27** above).

Pre-variation income

3.1.118 Income accrued or received (as appropriate to the charging provision) in the hands of the original beneficiary, or treated as distributed to him in respect of an interest in residue (cf ITTOIA 2005 Pt 5 Ch 6 (ss 649–682)), will remain taxable in his hands despite the variation, wherever an income tax liability has arisen on it prior to the date of the variation. (This is not relevant to a disclaimer, since obviously if the original beneficiary has received income from or referable to the original disposition in that context he will no longer be in a position to disclaim the benefit of that disposition.)

3.1.119   For this reason it is common to find that a variation is expressed to leave unaltered the destination of any income (or payment taxable as income) received by the original beneficiary up to the date of the variation; many original beneficiaries would be concerned at finding that they had income tax to pay on amounts that they had in fact provided should be paid to the new beneficiary.

3.1.120   On the other hand, if the original beneficiary has adequate resources and wishes to divest himself of the maximum possible amount by means of the variation, he could perfectly well provide for pre-variation income to pass to the new beneficiary in addition to the underlying capital, on a basis either—

(a)   that he will settle the tax liability from his other resources, or

(b)   that what passes is the net amount after retaining the amount of any tax paid or payable by him on it.

3.1.121   The one thing to be clear on, if taking option (a) in particular, is to redirect only the amounts received after deduction of tax where applicable. This is because there must be a concern that any attempt to pass on an amount not actually received from the disposition being varied could lead to at least partial refusal of backdating treatment for IHT or CGT; or even full denial, to the extent that another variation was made in consideration of this one, since the resultant payment in respect of the tax deducted at source would risk being classed as extraneous consideration within paragraphs **3.1.57** ff above and point (a)(iii) of paragraph **3.1.76** above.

The settlor of any resultant trust

3.1.122   The main significance of a person being the settlor of a trust for income tax purposes will of course usually be for the purpose of the rules attributing to the settlor any income arising under the settlement (which is charged accordingly under ITTOIA 2005 s 619(1)) – what will be referred to here as the "settlor attribution rules". Such attribution occurs, subject to income arising or having arisen within the settlement, if—

(a)   the income arises from property in which the settlor has an interest within ITTOIA 2005 ss 624–628;

(b)   payments are made to or for the benefit of an unmarried minor child of the settlor within ITTOIA 2005 ss 629–632; or

(c)   a capital sum is paid directly or indirectly to the settlor, by the trustees or a body connected with the settlement, within ITTOIA 2005 ss 633–643.

3.1.123   As mentioned in paragraph **3.1.102** above, the "trust modernisation" legislation of FA 2006 sought to standardise a number of definitions and principles as between income tax and CGT. Accordingly it is no surprise that provisions to the same effect as described for CGT in paragraphs **3.1.105–3.1.108** above are to be found in the income tax legislation with effect in relation to variations occurring on or after 6 April 2006 (irrespective of the date the deceased died) – see FA 2006 Sch 13 para 1(3). These provisions were initially in ICTA 1988 s 685D, but following the enactment of the fourth Bill produced by the Tax Law Rewrite project they are to be found, from 6 April 2007, in ITA 2007 ss 472, 473. (This chapter will refer for convenience only to the post-rewrite provisions.)

3.1.124 However, it is expressly provided in ITA 2007 s 467(8) that those sections (among others) do *not* apply for the purpose of the settlor attribution rules. (Wording to this effect did not appear in the pre-Rewrite version of the trust modernisation legislation, and the new ITA 2007 s 467(8) is listed in the table of origins as "drafting". Given the implicitly different meaning of "settlement" in the two contexts – compare paragraph **3.1.126** with paragraphs **3.1.129, 3.1.130** below – this may well have been the correct interpretation of the wording initially inserted into ICTA 1988, and see also the discussion in paragraph **3.1.115** above in relation to the equivalent provisions for CGT; but the rewritten statute is clear beyond doubt on the issue.) Although the results are in fact likely to be similar in most cases, it is thus necessary to examine the position separately for the settlor attribution rules and for more general income tax purposes.

General income tax purposes

3.1.125 Aside from the settlor attribution rules (as to which see paragraph **3.1.129** below), the identification of the settlor will primarily be necessary in order to determine the residence (and so UK income tax liability) of the single deemed person comprising the trustees (ITA 2007 s 474) in cases where at least one trustee is UK resident and at least one is not UK resident: ITA 2007 ss 475, 476. Additionally, it will be necessary in order to ascertain whether the newly-extended basic rate band for trustees (ITA 2007 s 491) (one of the less helpful products of the trust modernisation project, since it was not accompanied by the income streaming that had been hoped for and is therefore likely in many cases to produce nothing more than increased complexity, with a tax saving incapable of exceeding £180) has to be curtailed under ITA 2007 s 492 on the basis that the settlor made at least one other settlement that is still current.

3.1.126 For these and any other general income tax purposes, there is (as for CGT, see paragraph **3.1.101** above) no definition of "settlement" as such, merely of "settled property" and "property comprised in a settlement": see ITA 2007 s 466, which (like its CGT counterpart, see paragraph **3.1.103** above) is applicable "for the purposes of the Income

Tax Acts, except so far as, in those Acts, the context otherwise requires" (and also, by virtue of ITA 2007 s 478, in any regulations made, at any time, under a provision of the Income Tax Acts). In effect that definition follows the CGT rule as it always was, applying to any property held in trust other than a bare trust. ITA 2007 ss 467–473 then deal with who is to be regarded as the settlor of any settled property within that definition, and as already noted ITA 2007 ss 472, 473 mirror the CGT provisions of TCGA 1992 s 69C. In particular, those provisions only apply where the variation is the subject of limited backdating for CGT purposes by virtue of TCGA 1992 s 62(6); it is slightly surprising that this should matter, particularly for income tax purposes, but it at least ensures consistency between the two taxes.

Variations since 5 April 2006 attracting CGT backdating

3.1.127   For a fuller explanation of the position where limited CGT backdating does apply to a variation (but seemingly not a disclaimer, see point (b) in paragraph **3.1.105** above) made on or after 6 April 2006, reference should be made to paragraphs **3.1.106–3.1.108** above: corresponding principles will apply for income tax as for CGT, given that both sets of provisions were designed and drafted to bring about the same results; but in brief—

(a)   where the variation is made by an original beneficiary who was absolutely entitled, and results in property becoming settled property, that original beneficiary will be the settlor;

(b)   where the trust would have existed even apart from the variation, the deceased is the settlor – under ITA 2007 s 473 if the property passes into a different settlement, or by virtue of the more general rule of ITA 2007 s 467(2)–(4) (the income tax equivalent of TCGA 1992 s 68A(2)(b)).

Disclaimers, variations before 6 April 2006, and variations not attracting CGT backdating

3.1.128   In these cases the rules in ITA 2007 ss 472, 473 do not apply, and in the same way as with the equivalent CGT provisions it is necessary to apply the more general definition in ITA 2007 s 467 in the light of the "real world" analysis of the variation or disclaimer. The question is whether the original beneficiary has "made" the settlement or "provided property" for it; see generally paragraphs **3.1.109–3.1.112** above. However for income tax purposes there will not be any scope for argument, on the lines put forward unsuccessfully in *Marshall v Kerr* but just possibly still open in slightly different circumstances (see paragraph **3.1.115** above), that the "real world" analysis might be displaced by some statutory fiction that precludes treatment of the original beneficiary as settlor: as already stated, there is no backdating provision that applies for income tax purposes.

The settlor attribution rules

3.1.129   For the purpose of the rules noted in paragraph **3.1.122**, "settlement" is given a notoriously wide meaning by ITTOIA 2005 s 620(1), as including "any disposition, trust, covenant, agreement, arrangement or transfer of assets (except that it does not include a charitable loan arrangement)". The same subsection goes on to define "settlor", in relation to a settlement, as the person by whom the settlement was made; ITTOIA 2005 s 620(2), (3) then go on to treat a person as having made a settlement if—

(a)   he has made or entered into the settlement directly or indirectly; and particularly if

(b)   he has provided, or undertaken to provide, funds directly or indirectly for the purpose of the settlement; or

(c)   he has made a reciprocal arrangement with another person for the other person to make or enter into the settlement.

3.1.130   The main limitation on the scope of the word "settlement" in this definition (in its earlier manifestation as TA 1970 s 454(3)) arises from the interpretation put on it by the majority of the *House of Lords in IRC v Plummer* [1980] AC 896, [1979] STC 793, and applied again by the *House of Lords in Jones v Garnett* [2007] 1 WLR 2031. In *Plummer* it was held that it applied only to transactions which included an element of bounty; the House of Lords rejected an Inland Revenue argument that it should catch all transactions that were not *bona fide* commercial transactions. (The annuity which had been bought from a charity in that case, as part of an acknowledged tax avoidance scheme, was nonetheless bought for full consideration, and involved no element of bounty.) Thus a variation which is entered into, for example, by way of hard-negotiated compromise of a claim under the I(PFD)A 1975, and as such is likely to involve demonstrably no element of bounty, would not involve the making of a settlement for the purposes of the settlor attribution rules (by anyone), even if it results in property becoming settled property within the general income tax rule in ITA 2007 s 466; as such the original beneficiary could retain an interest under the trust without the trust income thereby being attributed to him.

3.1.131   It will have been noticed that the definitions in ITTOIA 2005 s 620(2), (3) have more than a passing resemblance to the general definition in ITA 2007 s 467; the main distinctions being first that the special supplementary rules in ITA 2007 ss 470–473 do not apply in relation to the settlor attribution rules, and secondly that the definitions of "settlement" and "settled property", to which the "settlor" definitions are inextricably linked, are both wider (including arrangements, covenants etc) and narrower (excluding cases where there is no element of bounty) than the purely trust based definition applicable for general income tax purposes under ITA 2007 s 466. It is therefore to be expected that, as with

CGT (paragraphs **3.1.113–3.1.116** above) and general income tax purposes (paragraph **3.1.128** above), the identification of the settlor for the purpose of the settlor attribution rules must again be approached in the context of the effect of a variation or disclaimer in the real world.

Transfer of assets abroad

3.1.132   The settlor attribution rules noted in paragraph **3.1.122** above apply to overseas trusts as much as to UK-based trusts; but despite the wide meaning given to "settlement" they only catch income that arises at settlement level. If there is, for example, an underlying company structure, income at that level is left to be dealt with under normal income tax principles if the trust (owning such a company) is UK resident. However, if trust is not UK resident, then not only is the person who transferred assets into such a structure potentially taxable on all income arising within the structure if he has power to enjoy that income, but also beneficiaries who receive benefits provided out of assets available for the purpose in consequence of such a transfer are potentially taxable by reference to such income, so far as not actually taxed in the transferor's hands. These rules, newly bolstered by a tightening of the exemption for *bona fide* commercial transactions without any tax avoidance purpose, are now to be found in ITA 2007 ss 714–751 (previously ICTA 1988 ss 739–746).

3.1.133   These rules, of course, look to identify the "transferor", not the "settlor". However, in the context of trusts or other structures established by way of variation of dispositions on death, the two concepts will be for practical purposes synonymous. Just as with the settlor attribution rules, what will be relevant will be the analysis of the variation in terms of general property law principles – in the "real world", as there is no backdating rule that can create an alternative fictional statutory world for them.

The POA charge

3.1.134   This is not the context in which to explore the background to or workings of the POA charge, introduced in FA 2004 Sch 15 as a novel way of bolstering the IHT GROB rules. Suffice it to say that there are certain dispositions which expressly do not trigger the application of the POA rules. By virtue of FA 2004 Sch 15 para 16—

> "Any disposition made by a person ('the chargeable person') in relation to an interest in the estate of a deceased person is to be disregarded for the purposes of this Schedule if by virtue of section 17 of IHTA 1984 (changes in distribution of deceased's estate, etc) the disposition is not treated for the purposes of inheritance tax as a transfer of value by the chargeable person".

This exclusion goes beyond variations and disclaimers, since IHTA 1984 s 17 prevents a transfer of value in other cases of post-death rearrangements – transfers by a legatee in accordance with the deceased's wish, redemption of a surviving spouse or civil partner's life interest on an intestacy, and (in Scotland) renunciation of a claim to legitim (or equivalent statutory rights associated with civil partnership).

3.1.135   It is believed that the intention is that every case of a variation or disclaimer should be protected from triggering the POA charge regime. However, unfortunately, the drafting employed (which was the second attempt, replacing an earlier formulation during the passage of the Finance Bill) is not ideal for that purpose. There are two potential gaps, though it is not thought that HMRC should seek to rely on either (and indeed situation (a)(i) below is instanced in Appendix 1 to HMRC's official guidance on the POA charge legislation as one where the exclusion *will* apply)—

(a)   On its face, the exclusion can only apply if a disposition made by the original beneficiary in the course of a variation would have been a transfer of value (as a result of his estate being reduced) if it were not for the saving in IHTA 1984 s 17. Thus—

    (i) if an original beneficiary who was absolutely entitled under the original dispositions enters into a variation creating a trust under which he has an IIP – which is backdated under IHTA 1984 s 142 so as to be an IPDI – nothing has left his estate, and there is no transfer of value irrespective of IHTA 1984 s 17; or

    (ii) if a variation involves remaindermen under a trust in the will giving up their interests in favour of the life tenant or some third party, the interests given up will be excluded property for IHT purposes under IHTA 1984 s 48(1), and for the purpose of determining whether a transfer of value has taken place no account is taken of excluded property which leaves a person's estate – IHTA 1984 s 3(2). So again such a variation involves no transfer of value by the remaindermen, even without the assistance of IHTA 1984 s 17.

(b)   The exclusion only applies to a disposition "in relation to an interest in the estate of a deceased person". If a variation redirects property that has already been distributed to the original beneficiary, then obviously the disposition that takes place is not of an interest in the deceased's estate, but of the property itself. Although it may be a transfer of value apart from IHTA 1984 s 17, technically it too is not within the exclusion in FA 2004 Sch 15 para 16 (and so is not protected from POA charge consequences), unless an unusually (and it is thought unjustifiably) wide interpretation can be placed on the words "in relation to".

Stamp duty and SDLT treatment

Stamp duty

3.1.136 A number of draftsmen still appear to make a habit of including a certificate under category M (or sometimes category L) in the Schedule to the Stamp Duty (Exempt Instruments) Regulations 1987, SI 1987/1688 in every deed of variation they prepare. In nearly every case such certificates are now unnecessary as a matter of law. It may be that such inclusion is an unthinking continuation of pre-2003 practice; or it may be in some cases that it takes conscious account (as the path of least resistance) of the long out of date instructions in HMRC's IHT Manual referred to in paragraph **3.1.146** below.

3.1.137 Since 1 December 2003, stamp duty under FA 1999 Sch 13 (the modernised charging provisions in place of the Stamp Act 1891) is chargeable "only on instruments relating to stock or marketable securities": FA 2003 s 125. (This is subject to associated modifications to charge stamp duty on transfers of interests in a partnership, but only to the extent that the value of the partnership share is referable to stock or marketable securities: FA 2003 Sch 15, paras 31–37.) The heads of charge in FA 1999 Sch 13 that are potentially relevant to variations and disclaimers can be summarised as—

(a) transfer on sale (FA 1999 Sch 13 paras 1–9);

(b) transfer otherwise than on sale (FA 1999 Sch 13 para 16);

(c) declaration of trust, release or renunciation, and surrender, in each case unless the instrument constitutes a transfer on sale (FA 1999 Sch 13 paras 17, 22, 23).

3.1.138 Therefore stamp duty is only in point in the first place, so far as concerns an instrument effecting a variation or a disclaimer, if the instrument in question—

(a) operates as one of the types listed in points (a)–(c) in paragraph **3.1.137** above – which must be analysed according to the true effect of the document "in the real world"; and

(b) relates to stock or marketable securities. In this connection—

    (i) stock and marketable securities that are still vested in the deceased's personal representatives, and have not been the subject of an assent or appropriation, can in principle be ignored, as the instrument would then relate not to the underlying assets but to the original beneficiary's interest in them (or, in the case of a residuary beneficiary, to his right to compel due administration of the estate – paragraph **3.1.20** above); there are, though, some who would play safe and assume that the instrument "relates to" stock or marketable securities which are the subject of a specific bequest to the original beneficiary even if not yet released to him; and

(ii) even if already released by the personal representatives, an instrument will not relate to stock or marketable securities, but rather to a beneficial interest in them, if the stock or marketable securities form settled property and the instrument does not operate as a transfer of the entire beneficial interest of all persons interested in them.

Only if a variation or disclaimer is in principle within the now restricted charge to stamp duty, as explained above, need an exemption certificate be considered.

Disclaimers

3.1.139 The first point to appreciate, before considering the available exemption certificates, is that for stamp duty purposes a disclaimer is either a release or renunciation or a surrender (see point (c) in paragraph **3.1.137** above). The statutory wording relating to those types of instrument (FA 1999 Sch 13 paras 22, 23) does of course contemplate that some instruments in those categories are capable also of operating as transfers (and so, in appropriate circumstances, transfers on sale); so can a disclaimer do so as well? "Transfer", for the purpose of the charge on transfers otherwise than on sale, is defined as including "every instrument, and every decree or order of a court or commissioners, by which any property is transferred to or vested in any person" (FA 1999 Sch 13 para 16(2)); and equivalent words are found in the somewhat longer definition of "transfer on sale" in FA 1999 Sch 13 para 1(2). The key concept is that the property must be transferred to, or vested in, a person *by the instrument*; that does not describe a disclaimer in terms of its analysis under the general law: see paragraph **3.1.13** above.

Exemption certificates for voluntary dispositions: category L

3.1.140 Many instruments of variation serve to redirect property for no consideration in money or money's worth. As such, if they relate to stock or marketable securities as explained above (see point (b) in paragraph **3.1.138** above), they can be certified within category L without reference to whether they meet all of the conditions for IHT or CGT backdating. Category L comprises—

> "the conveyance or transfer of property operating as a voluntary disposition inter vivos for no consideration in money or money's worth nor any consideration referred to in Stamp Act 1891 s 57 (conveyance in consideration of a debt etc)".

3.1.141 Where the instrument falls within that description, and relates to stock or marketable securities, inclusion in it of a category L certificate (or its endorsement or attachment on or to the instrument, as specified in the Stamp Duty (Exempt Instruments) Regulations 1987 reg 3), provides exemption from the £5 fixed duty charge in FA 1999 Sch 13 para 16 (transfer otherwise than on sale). However, it will be seen that such a certificate is available only if the instrument operates as a conveyance or transfer in the first place. Seemingly that does not include a disclaimer (see paragraph **3.1.139** above), which therefore cannot in true analysis bear a category L certificate, but remains liable to a £5 fixed duty under FA 1999 Sch 13 para 22 or 23. (By the same reasoning, a disclaimer would also not have been liable to voluntary disposition duty under the Finance (1909–10) Act 1910 s 74, since that section too required that an instrument operate as a conveyance or transfer; so compulsory adjudication under FA 1985 s 82 would not be applicable.)

Exemption certificates for variations: category M

3.1.142   Where there is consideration of some variety for a variation that relates to stock or marketable securities, then a category M certificate should be included (or endorsed or attached) provided the instrument satisfies the conditions that apply for this, as set out in FA 1985 s 84(1)–(3). This requirement applies whether or not backdating treatment for IHT and/or CGT purposes is being invoked by the inclusion of the relevant statement of intent. Category M reads—

> "The conveyance or transfer of property by an instrument within FA 1985 s 84(1) (death: varying disposition)".

3.1.143   The conditions just referred to (and other features) mirror most of those applicable for CGT limited backdating, namely those listed in points (a)(i)–(iii), (v), (vi) in paragraph **3.1.76** above: two year time limit from death, instrument in writing, no extraneous consideration, dispositions of property of which the deceased was competent to dispose, and irrelevance of whether or not the administration has been completed. Interestingly there is no definition in FA 1985 s 84 of "property of which [the deceased] was competent to dispose"; although this is the same term used in TCGA 1992 s 62(6), that section contains a lengthy definition (see paragraph **3.1.77** above), which in some ways extends the meaning of the expression and in others cuts it down. It is perhaps a reasonable working assumption that HMRC would expect (and if the matter ever came under scrutiny might be persuaded) to apply the stamp duty provision consistently with the scope of the CGT variation provision, which in turn essentially matches in scope the IHT variation provision albeit with a few differences or potential differences (see paragraph **3.1.78** above).

3.1.144   In the same way as was seen in paragraph **3.1.141** above, by reference to the analysis in paragraph **3.1.139** above, a disclaimer in the true common law sense (paragraph **3.1.13** above) would not qualify for a category M exemption certificate because it does not operate as a conveyance or transfer, but as a release, renunciation or surrender. This is thought to be the reason why FA 1985 s 84(1) – which provides exemption for duty as a transfer on sale but imposes a £5 fixed duty subject to compulsory adjudication where a category M exemption certificate is not included, endorsed or attached – does not in terms include a disclaimer, merely a variation. But again, because a disclaimer is for that reason not within FA 1985 s 84, and charged simply as a release, renunciation or surrender, it is not subject to compulsory adjudication. It remains chargeable simply with a fixed duty of £5 under FA 1999 Sch 13, paras 22 or 23.

3.1.145 There is another consequence of the restriction of FA 1985 s 84 to variations and not disclaimers – this consequence being of potentially greater significance if the point is taken by HMRC. It relates to the bar on extraneous consideration if the favoured treatment of the section is to apply (FA 1985 s 84(2)), which in this respect is marginally more restrictive than for IHT or CGT: the only "permitted" consideration for this purpose is confined to the "variation" of another disposition of property of which the deceased was competent to dispose. Therefore, on the face of it, the disclaimer of disposition A in return for the variation of disposition B will deny the relief from transfer on sale duty in respect of the acquisition by the beneficiary of the variation of disposition B, even though both elements would be eligible for both IHT and CGT backdating. The subject matter (of the variation, at the date it is made) would still have to be stock or marketable securities for this to constitute a problem; and with foresight the problem can be avoided by ensuring that the original beneficiary of disposition A is expressed to make a variation of that disposition rather than a disclaimer of it. But it is thought that this is, in theory at least, a trap for the unwary, and an unintended one at that.

Outdated instructions in the IHT Manual

3.1.146 It is clear that the IHT Manual has not been revised to take account of the 2003 changes in stamp duty law. At the time of writing, the instructions to HMRC staff state that—

(a) it is a necessary feature of an instrument of variation that it "must contain a stamp duty exemption certificate" (IHTM35031);

(b) where the instrument is not duly stamped or does not contain the appropriate exemption certificate (IHTM35060)—

   (i) any communication [from HMRC Inheritance Tax] "must contain a caveat in such terms as 'provided the document is duly stamped and adjudicated, or the appropriate exemption certificate under the Stamp Duty (Exempt Instruments) Regulations 1987 is attached'"; and

   (ii) "if the parties are relying on the instrument to reduce the liability to inheritance tax, you must insist that the document is stamped, or the exemption certificate is attached, before giving effect to the terms of the instrument".

3.1.147   In any case where an instrument of variation or disclaimer does not relate to stock or marketable securities, and objection to the absence of a stamp duty exemption certificate is received from HMRC on the above lines, they should be referred to FA 2003 s 125, and advised that the legislation takes priority over their out of date internal instructions.

SDLT

Acquisition on death generally

3.1.148   When a chargeable interest in land in the UK (that is, most interests, equitable interests included) is transferred to a person, or vested in them by some other means, that person acquires it as the "purchaser" under a land transaction for SDLT purposes (FA 2003 s 43), whether or not there is any consideration given for the transaction by him or anyone else. (SDLT can also be relevant in certain cases involving contributions to or withdrawals from a partnership with land among its assets, see FA 2003 Sch 15 as amended.)

3.1.149   But for an exemption in FA 2003 Sch 3 para 3A as inserted by FA 2004 s 300(1), even an assent or appropriation by the personal representatives of a deceased person in favour of a legatee or other original beneficiary would attract a charge to SDLT. However, provided that person gives no consideration in such a case other than the assumption of "secured debt" – a money obligation that was secured on the property immediately after the death – his acquisition is exempt under that provision. (Note that this provision is distinct from the identically numbered paragraph 3A which was – in an unusual error – inserted into FA 2003 Sch 3 by the Tax and Civil Partnership Regulations 2005, SI 2005/3229 reg 174 (made under FA 2005 s 103), and mirrors for civil partnerships the exemption for transactions in connection with divorce and other matters involved in marriage breakdown.) If there is some other consideration so that the exemption does not apply as such, the amount of secured debt assumed is left out in ascertaining the chargeable consideration: FA 2003 Sch 4 para 8A(1).

3.1.150   Even the vesting of land in a deceased person's personal representatives, by virtue of the grant of probate or of letters of administration, will involve an acquisition by them. Although they undoubtedly give no actual consideration, it does seem arguable at first sight that any debt secured on the property might constitute chargeable consideration for their acquisition by virtue of FA 2003 Sch 4 para 8, since there is no exemption as such directed to this situation. However, this point has not been taken by HMRC (and it would undoubtedly cause widespread and justified outrage if it were, amounting as this would, for practical purposes, to a tax charge on the death of a property owner other than one who had afforded to buy without mortgage assistance or had cleared his mortgage); and it is possible to see that the personal representatives' obligation to pay the deceased's debts (secured or unsecured, subject only to the sufficiency of the estate assets) arises purely as a result of their accepting office as personal representatives, and is not linked, other than by coincidence of time, to the vesting in them of the deceased's interest in the land. Thus it is suggested that any change in the rights or liabilities of the personal representatives (the only "party" to the land transaction), which probably do change as a result of the grant, nevertheless do not change "as a result of or in connection with" the land transaction.

Disclaimers

3.1.151 No special treatment is laid down in the SDLT legislation for a disclaimer. This is unsurprising, since a disclaimer operates not as a disposition in its own right but as a refusal to accept the (testamentary or other) gift in question: see paragraphs **3.1.4**, **3.1.13** above; on disclaimer of an interest under a will or intestacy, the beneficiary who takes instead takes under the will or intestacy, not under the disclaimer. An assent or appropriation in his favour will then be eligible for the exemption described in paragraph **3.1.149** above.

Variations

3.1.152 As regards variations, by contrast, an exemption from SDLT is provided in FA 2003 Sch 3 para 4, subject to satisfaction of the relevant conditions. Those conditions, and the other features, of the exemption are essentially the same as the requirements for a stamp duty category M exemption certificate (see paragraph **3.1.142** above), except that (reflecting the fact that SDLT operates without reference to whether a document is used) there is no requirement that the variation should have taken place by means of an instrument in writing. Thus the variation must take place within two years from death (irrespective of whether or not the administration has been completed or the property distributed), it must relate to dispositions of property of which the deceased was competent to dispose, and there must be no extraneous consideration. (As with the stamp duty exemption certificate under category M, the expression "competent to dispose" is not defined for this purpose, and again one is dependent on a supposition of consistency with the scope of the CGT provision: see paragraph **3.1.143** above.)

3.1.153 In the same way as was seen in connection with category M exemption certificates for stamp duty purposes, the SDLT provision denying exemption if there is any extraneous consideration (FA 2003 Sch 3 para 4(2)(b)) is marginally more restrictive than for IHT or CGT. The only "permitted" consideration is, again, confined to the "variation" of another such disposition: see paragraph **3.1.145** above. Thus if a disposition on death (disposition B) is to be varied where the variation will involve a land transaction, and in return for it another disposition on the death (disposition A) is to be given up, it will be advisable to ensure that the form of the transaction involves a variation, not a disclaimer, of disposition A. That is so whether or not disposition A relates to land or an interest in land.

3.1.154 Where there is consideration for a variation of disposition B which includes not only a variation of disposition A, but additionally something extraneous, the exemption in terms will be unavailable. But it is provided by FA 2003 Sch 4 para 8A(2) that, in those circumstances, the consideration consisting of the variation of disposition A is left out in ascertaining the chargeable consideration for the acquisition by the beneficiary of the variation of disposition B.

3.1.155 If, after a variation, the deceased's personal representatives assent to land vesting in the new beneficiary, it is not clear that the exemption in FA 2003 Sch 3 para 3A (the first paragraph so numbered) (see paragraph **3.1.149** above) would be available. That relates only to a person's acquisition of property "in or towards satisfaction of his entitlement under or in relation to the will of a deceased person, or on the intestacy of a deceased person". There is no statutory backdating of entitlements for SDLT purposes, and so if any consideration is given – including in this instance the assumption of secured debt – then that would be chargeable consideration, leaving the new beneficiary's acquisition of the legal estate technically exposed to an SDLT charge even though (a) his acquisition of the beneficial interest, under the variation, was exempt and (b) the original beneficiary would have been entitled to exemption if the assent had been made in his favour.

3.1.156 In a case where the exemption in FA 2003 Sch 3 para 4 does apply, Form SDLT60 (a "self-certificate" that no land transaction return is required, see FA 2003 ss 77(3)(a), 79(3)(b), Sch 11)) must be completed accordingly, even if the variation itself does not give rise to a need for registration (typically that would arise on a land registry transfer following, or simultaneously with, the variation itself). The out of date instructions in the IHT Manual (IHTM35031, IHTM35060), as referred to in paragraph **3.1.146** above, could foreseeably lead to objection from HMRC Inheritance Tax that an instrument of variation relating to land lacks the (allegedly) necessary stamp duty exemption certificate. Without detracting from the suggested counter to this in paragraph **3.1.147** above, pointing out the limits of the charge to stamp duty since 2003, it is to be recommended, where an interest of land is involved, that a copy of the completed Form SDLT60 be supplied to HMRC—

— when forwarding to them a copy of an instrument of variation which gives rise to a land transaction, and

— certainly when responding to an objection of the sort just referred to, even though, in contrast to the stamp duty legislation, there is no bar on recognising the effect of a land transaction (as distinct from registering it, see FA 2003 s 79(1)) in the absence of a Revenue certificate or a self-certificate.

When to use the variation rules and when not

General principles

3.1.157 In this section it will be assumed that a variation (or disclaimer) is being effected, by all necessary parties, within two years after the deceased's death, by deed, and without extraneous consideration. That of itself – subject to the potential issue of a variation in exchange for a disclaimer, see paragraphs **3.1.145**, **3.1.153** above – will be enough to satisfy the requirements for a stamp duty category M exemption certificate (if the deed relates to stock or marketable securities) or the SDLT exemption (if it involves the acquisition of an interest in land in the UK). The issue, therefore, is whether a statement of intent should be included in relation to IHT, CGT or both (see paragraphs **3.1.63–3.1.67** and point (a)(iv) of paragraph **3.1.76** above).

IHT

3.1.158 If a deed of variation as such is being considered in the first place, it will generally have been mooted from the IHT point of view; otherwise the proposal would be likely to have been expressed in terms of a lifetime gift by the original beneficiary. In the large majority of cases it will be appropriate to include an IHT statement of intent, but not universally so.

3.1.159 The purposes for which it will often be advantageous to invoke the statutory treatment under IHTA 1984 s 142 include the following—

(a) Where residue has been left to the surviving spouse or civil partner of the deceased (outright or for an estate IIP)—

  (i) To ensure (if still desired following the introduction of a transferable NRB, see **APPENDIX 7**) that the NRB is fully used by chargeable transfers on the death of the first of a couple (married or civil partners) to die, by means of—
    – outright gifts to the next generation or to third parties; or
    – formation of a NRB trust, typically discretionary though not necessarily so – see paragraphs **2.2.16**, **2.2.17** above, and **PRECEDENT 1**.
  (ii) To improve the utilisation of APR or BPR available to the estate, by—
    – diverting relievable property to chargeable beneficiaries (which would include the trustees of a relevant property trust), in addition to other provision, or

- substituting specific legacies of relievable property for general, non-relievable legacies to chargeable beneficiaries so as to avoid the loss, or partial loss, of reliefs by the operation of IHTA 1984 s 39A.

(iii) To divert post death growth in the value of the estate to chargeable beneficiaries who received cash legacies under the will, without altering the IHT liability on the first death, by substituting a legacy of suitable amount to the spouse and residue to the chargeable beneficiaries.

(iv) To divert excluded property comprised in the estate in favour of chargeable beneficiaries.

(v) Seemingly, to utilise, where circumstances allow, the rule in IHTA 1984 s 142(4) regarding short term income interests created by deed of variation – see paragraphs **3.1.43**–**3.1.50** above and paragraphs **3.1.176** ff below.

(b) Where it is wished to increase the exempt portion of the estate—

(i) To divert property in favour of the deceased's surviving spouse or civil partner, whether absolutely or for an IIP (that will thus be an IPDI) – see paragraphs **3.1.169** ff below – but always remaining aware of the limitation of exemption in that respect to £55,000 of value, net of reliefs, if the surviving spouse or civil partner was not, but the deceased was, either domiciled in the UK or deemed domiciled here.

(ii) To provide for legacies for charitable or other public purposes (by public purposes meaning within one of the exemptions in IHTA 1984 ss 24, 24A or 25) – see paragraphs **3.1.180** ff below.

(iii) Exceptionally, to establish a heritage property maintenance fund within IHTA 1984 s 27 or an employee trust within IHTA 1984 s 28.

(c) Where two people (typically but not necessarily a married couple or civil partners) have died within two years of each other, to decrease, or for that matter increase, the estate of the survivor as in points (a)(i) or (b)(i) above – see paragraphs **3.1.200** ff, **3.1.206** ff below.

(d) Generally—

(i) To pass value down one or even two generations, where the original beneficiary is already adequately provided for – see paragraphs **3.1.164** ff below.

(ii) To provide for a beneficiary for whom it is thought that increased provision ought to be made, or to have been made by the deceased, without this involving a gift by the original beneficiary.

(iii) Where the deceased was neither domiciled nor deemed domiciled in the UK, to create a trust which will benefit from the excluded property rules in the future to the extent that trust assets are invested in non-UK situate property or in UK authorised unit trusts or open-ended investment companies.

(iv) To establish a (relevant property) trust under which the original beneficiary is interested, or indeed to pass property on to another individual outright, without the property forming part of the original beneficiary's prospective estate on death and without the original beneficiary being caught by the GROB rules or the POA charge rules in respect of benefits retained or subsequently enjoyed – see point (b) of paragraph **3.1.41**, and paragraphs **3.1.134, 3.1.135**, above.

3.1.160 Contraindications to an IHT statement of intent are relatively limited, but one example might be where a claim under the I(PFD)A 1975 is being compromised within the two year period from death by the provision of a life interest (eg in a residence) for the claimant's benefit. If the compromise is brought about by means of a Tomlin order, the effect for IHT – just as with a deed of variation containing an IHT statement of intent – will be to create an IPDI such that the property will form part of the new beneficiary's taxable estate on his or her eventual death. (See generally paragraphs **3.3.39–3.3.41** below.) Depending on the precise circumstances, including relevant values generally, that may be a result that is preferred (particularly with a surviving spouse claimant, so that spouse relief on the first death is attainable), or at least not inconvenient (especially in lower value cases). But if the new beneficiary is thought to have a relatively short life expectancy (which may be one reason a life interest is being considered anyway), and the value of the property concerned is such that a charge in two successive estates in comparatively quick succession might be at risk, it may be preferred to establish the life interest trust as a relevant property trust, of which no doubt the original beneficiary would be the settlor but perhaps with an argument that there is no gift or chargeable transfer on entry because the compromise has been hard fought and there is no gratuitous intent. The transaction may yet be framed as a deed of variation in order to avoid a chargeable disposal by the original beneficiary for CGT purposes; but omitting an IHT statement of intent would bring about a different IHT result from a Tomlin order. See generally paragraphs **3.3.47, 3.3.48** below.

CGT

3.1.161 There may be a slightly larger number of cases in which circumstances might make it advantageous to omit a CGT statement of intent. For the reasons explained in paragraphs **3.1.89–3.1.98** above, it will be advisable to include such a statement in all cases where the variation is taking place while the subject matter of the original disposition is still in the hands of the deceased's personal representatives at the date of the variation. (In such cases it will also be worth considering whether an assent before the variation, even if subject to a charge for outstanding administrative expenses under the AEA 1925 s 36(10), would improve matters by allowing the original beneficiary then to dispense with a CGT statement of intent if the circumstances were right.) Aside from that situation, the question will usually turn on the nature of the consequences of a CGT disposal of the property concerned by the original beneficiary. (Because the backdating effect for CGT is only limited, issues such as the identity of the settlor of any trust that results from the variation will, for practical purposes, be almost entirely unaffected by the presence or absence of a CGT statement of intent, even though the conclusion may follow by a different technical route depending on whether or not such a statement is included, see paragraph **3.1.109** above.)

3.1.162 Thus the following circumstances may indicate that, where the asset in question is already vested in the original beneficiary, a CGT statement of intent may be at best unnecessary, and at worst wasteful—

(a) variation relating to original beneficiary's principal private residence, standing at a gain over probate value; the new beneficiary will take with a higher base cost without a CGT statement of intent, while the original beneficiary's gain is exempt under TCGA 1992 s 223;

(b) variation in favour of a charity in circumstances where share aid relief can be obtained in consequence (see paragraphs **3.1.182**, **3.1.183** below); or

(c) variation relating to an asset standing at a gain which—

   (i) (with other anticipated gains during the remainder of the tax year) does not exceed the original beneficiary's annual CGT exemption; clearly this will be harder to judge early in the tax year; or

   (ii) can be offset by losses available to the original beneficiary and which he does not anticipate being able to utilise elsewhere; possibly more relevant to elderly original beneficiaries than younger ones, and not necessarily as strong a counter indicator to a CGT statement of intent as the other situations above since it will frequently be thought better to preserve losses for future use.

3.1.163 Although there are comparatively few cases these days where a UK-based family will see an offshore trust as more than an expensive and complicated luxury, there can still be occasions – particularly where family members are spread across the world – when basing a trust overseas has the capacity to achieve a better result than having UK resident trustees. The ideal, where that is a possibility, is obviously for a UK testator to think ahead and create a trust under his will of which he specifically appoints overseas trustees from the start; if this is brought about by means of a variation made by a UK-based original beneficiary, the latter will remain subject to CGT, by virtue of the offshore settlor charge in TCGA 1992 s 86, Sch 5, for so long as he is living and UK resident or ordinarily resident, if either he or any of the next two generations of his descendants, or any spouse or civil partner of any of these, is capable of benefiting under the trust. (For income tax his exposure arises only if he or his civil partner are capable of benefiting: see paragraphs **3.1.122**, **3.1.132** above.) But if the original beneficiary may not live for many years – or in occasional other situations – a variation that puts property in trust, with overseas trustees and incorporating a CGT statement of intent, may yet have a function in the longer term where early asset disposals are not in prospect.

Some particular examples

Passing value down a generation

By a grandparent

3.1.164

Example

Assume that Fred, a childless bachelor aged 69, died intestate, and that he was survived by his younger brother George, but by neither of their parents. George therefore inherits Fred's whole estate under the English intestacy laws (AEA 1925 s 46(1)(v)). George is not in particularly good health, but is well enough off in retirement, and both of George's two children Harry and Isobel are well set up in life, with school age families. In consultation with his children, therefore, George executes a deed of variation redirecting Fred's estate into trust for his (George's) grandchildren's benefit.

3.1.165 The consequences of George's variation include the following—

(a) The IHT charge on Fred's death is unaffected – the transfer of value was fully chargeable both before and after the variation.

(b) The IHT charge on George's estate in due course is unaffected, even if he dies quite soon after making the variation.

(c) The trust will be a relevant property trust, unless the variation confers IIPs on the grandchildren (which would be IPDIs) or the trust is a bare trust for them despite minority; and it is treated for IHT purposes as made by Fred. Distributions of capital within the remainder of the two year period since Fred's death will attract no further IHT charge by reason of IHTA 1984 s 144 (see paragraphs **3.2.2**, **3.2.3**, but also paragraph **3.2.37**); subject to that, the cumulative total used in calculating future periodic and exit charges in the trust will be Fred's total chargeable transfers in the seven years prior to his death.

(d) As a relevant property trust in any event, it matters not whether the trust lays down particular ages for vesting of capital in the grandchildren or is fully discretionary for their benefit; or even whether it restricts the class of eligible beneficiaries to the grandchildren or includes any other members of the family (or others) that George may wish to include.

(e) To the extent that income distributions are made from the trust for the benefit of George's grandchildren, their individual income tax personal allowances and lower tax bands will enable refunds to be claimed on their behalf against the tax pool that builds up as the trustees are liable for tax at the trust rate or (subject to non-repayment of the original dividend tax credit) at the dividend trust rate. This can be of obvious advantage in enabling distributions to be made (and in due course the related tax refunds to be claimed) to assist with school fees or other educational or maintenance requirements.

(f) Assuming that George had made no other settlements that are still current, the trustees of the trust will have a standard trust exemption for CGT purposes, of half that of an individual. The number of extant settlements made by Fred during his lifetime is irrelevant for this purpose, as he is not the settlor for CGT purposes: see paragraphs **3.1.104–3.1.106** above.

By a parent

3.1.166

Taking the same family as in the example in paragraph 3.1.164, let us assume instead that George predeceased his brother Fred. Thus Fred's estate passes equally to Harry and Isobel under English intestacy law. Harry decides to redirect his share to a trust for his own children, ensuring that Harry and any spouse or civil partner of his are excluded from benefit.

3.1.167 The consequences of Harry's variation include the following—

(a) As in the case of George's variation—

   (i) the IHT charge on Fred's death is unaffected – the transfer of value was fully chargeable both before and after the variation;

   (ii) the IHT charge on Harry's estate would be unaffected if he were to die within seven years after making the variation;

   (iii) the trust will be a relevant property trust, whatever its terms other than as conferring immediate IIPs or bare trusts; and it will be treated for IHT purposes as made by Fred, with implications as in points (c) and (d) of paragraph **3.1.165** above;

   (iv) as a relevant property trust in any event, it matters not whether the trust lays down particular ages for vesting of capital in the grandchildren or is fully discretionary for their benefit; or even whether it restricts the class of eligible beneficiaries to the grandchildren or includes any other members of the family (or others) that George may wish to include.

(b) The individual income tax personal allowances and lower tax bands of Harry's children will not be available against income distributions until after they have married, entered into civil partnership or attained their majority. Instead, under the settlor attribution rules noted in paragraph **3.1.122** above, point (b), Harry, as the settlor with minor children as beneficiaries, would be taxed on such distributions prior to that time; and similarly even if distributions were in capital form but could be matched against accumulated income within the trust.

(c) Correspondingly, as Harry's children are eligible to receive benefits while they are under age, chargeable gains realised by the trustees during that period will be assessable on Harry (who in turn will have a right of recovery against the trustees), under the CGT onshore (or offshore, as the case may be) settlor charge, see paragraph **3.1.103** above. Only after the last of the children has attained his majority (or married etc while still under age 18) will the trustees be subject to CGT in their own right and with a trust exemption.

3.1.168 Such a trust is therefore of less immediate benefit than where established by George as in the preceding example; but it may yet have income tax advantages when Harry's children are in higher education after age 18. The key immediate function of the variation is to ensure that the property has not entered Harry's estate for IHT purposes. Ironically, too, if Harry is not realising gains of his own during that period, the trust may pay *less* CGT in reimbursement of the settlor charge, while it lasts, than it will after that, because Harry's full individual annual allowance will be available against gains attributed to him. (Until the flat CGT rate of 18% announced in the Pre-Budget Report 2007, another reason might have been that, in some years at least, Harry's income may not necessarily fully exhaust his basic rate band.)

Increasing provision for the surviving spouse/civil partner

3.1.169 If the chargeable part of the estate exceeds the available NRB, so that there is a net IHT liability under the will or other dispositions taking effect on death, any variation or disclaimer which results in a reduction in that liability by an increase in spouse exemption is likely to give rise to enquiries from HMRC in line with IHTM35093 (and see paragraph **3.1.44** above). Such enquiries were even received in a case (in fact involving an appointment from a relevant property trust established by the will) in which the surviving spouse was at the time still pursuing a claim under the I(PFD)A 1975, even after the making of the appointment. Provided negative answers can truthfully be given to the questions foreshadowed, and the parties concerned retain full freedom of action in relation to the property or powers vested in them, that should not preclude the increased exemption. It remains to be seen how far this practice, of questioning the possible onward transfer of property varied or appointed in favour of an exempt beneficiary, continues after the introduction of the transferable NRB (see APPENDIX 7); it is thought that caution should still be exercised in this regard.

3.1.170 As discussed in paragraphs 2.2.22 ff, 2.3.10 ff, a common strategy in the case of a married testator who has children from an earlier relationship is for him to leave an IIP for the benefit of his spouse, with capital passing ultimately for the benefit of his own children, and often a power of appointment under which the trustees can override the IPDI of the surviving spouse (though the latter power, if not the fact of only income provision, may well prompt a well advised surviving spouse to initiate a claim under the I(PFD)A 1975). Even after the IHT changes in FA 2006 Sch 20, the exercise of such a power to pass funds on to other beneficiaries absolutely (including by way of bare trust) – or on BMT terms where capital will vest by age 18 – will divest funds from the surviving spouse's estate by way of PET, not chargeable transfer.

3.1.171 To the extent that the testator in that family situation has bypassed the surviving spouse altogether and left assets direct for the benefit of his children, to an extent which creates an IHT liability on the death, there may therefore be a temptation for the children to replicate that planning by way of a variation of the will, with the aim of, at worst, deferring any IHT liability until the death of the surviving spouse, and at best eliminating it if the IPDI is later overridden (or surrendered) at least seven years before the death of the surviving spouse. Such a case is obviously directly within the scope of the enquiries that may be expected from HMRC, and it may be preferable to ensure that an IIP under a variation of this sort will definitely last (if not overtaken by the death of the surviving spouse) for a minimum period of time, and that the income interest will genuinely yield more than a token amount of income for the benefit of the survivor – postponing the exercisability (not merely the exercise) of an overriding power of appointment for that period, or possibly building the time limit into the terms of the IIP itself. That period must in any event exceed two years from the testator's death, see paragraphs **3.1.43** ff above; it is recommended in addition that a year or more be allowed from the date of the variation (longer if the administration of the estate is expected to remain incomplete beyond that such that income distributions might not be made within that period). Even then, HMRC's interest is aroused by income interests that do not extend more than "slightly" beyond the two year period (see IHTM35095 and paragraph **3.1.44** above) – hence the recommendation that the interest conferred must be seen to have a guaranteed financial reality in practice.

3.1.172 Plainly, if the surviving spouse is claiming under the I(PFD)A 1975 that the provision made for her under the will is inadequate, rejection by her of such an arrangement in itself would be dangerous, though it would do little to dissuade her from continuing with such a claim. However, where she is not planning such a claim (but relationships are strained such that she may resent the possibility of her own NRB being hijacked at the expense of the intended beneficiaries of her own estate), the risk should be recognised that she could seek to defeat the expected IHT savings by simply disclaiming the income interest created by a variation on the above lines (or, for that matter, created for her by the will itself). As a technical matter, it would appear that – in contrast to the situation where the IIP in question had arisen under the will itself – the IHT effects of such a disclaimer, following a variation, may not be quite as clear as might be thought—

(a) If the IIP arose under the will, the disclaimer, to have IHT effect, would have to be made within two years after the testator's death (see paragraph **3.1.69** above), taking effect if at all under IHTA 1984 s 142, unless the conclusion in paragraphs **3.1.72–3.1.74** above is wrong (that IHTA 1984 s 93 is unavailable where IHTA 1984 s 142 is capable of applying). That much is uncontentious.

(b) Where however the IIP was created by a variation, the decision in *Russell and anor v IRC* [1988] STC 195, [1988] 2 All ER 405 (see paragraph **3.1.31** above) would preclude the use of IHTA 1984 s 142 to backdate the effect of a disclaimer, because it would relate to the same property as had already been the subject of statutory backdating under that section. Therefore reliance would need to be placed on IHTA 1984 s 93. As seen in paragraph **3.1.70** above, the condition that must be satisfied, if IHTA 1984 s 93 is to apply IHT as though the disclaiming beneficiary had not become entitled to the interest, is that "a person becomes entitled to an interest in settled property but disclaims the interest". It was suggested in paragraph **3.1.73** above that this should be read as requiring that the property in question was settled property immediately before the person became entitled to the interest; in the circumstances of a variation by the children who had been absolutely entitled under the will, that is not so as a matter of fact, though obviously the result of IHTA 1984 s 142 applying to the variation is that the property is treated as having become settled on the testator's death. But IHTA 1984 s 142 has the further result that the IIP created under the variation is also treated as having had effect since the death (so as to be an IPDI in the first place), and the property was not settled property immediately before that deemed acquisition of the IIP.

It is thought that a court would strain to avoid an interpretation that imposed a potential IHT disadvantage on the surviving spouse and her estate in the way described, by allowing her disclaimer to have backdated effect. However, if it is right that the property must have been settled property immediately before the beneficiary's entitlement, then backdating under IHTA 1984 s 93 could not apply in this scenario, either by reference to the factual position (the property was not settled immediately before the variation) or by reference to the position as backdated for all IHT purposes under IHTA 1984 s 142 (it was not settled immediately before the deceased's death). This may well be one of those anomalous situations where a reading of the provision that produces a coherent result generally has results that the court would rather avoid; if this were the context in which the interaction between IHTA 1984 s 93 and s 142 came to be litigated, it is just possible that – to prevent that result – IHTA 1984 s 93 would be held to be available even where the property was not settled immediately before the beneficiary became entitled to the interest disclaimed. If that were so, it would after all give rise to a potential overlap between the two sections where property was actually settled by the deceased's will, and would allow backdated effect for a disclaimer of an interest under that settlement even after the second anniversary of death provided no benefit had been received from the interest in question.

(c) As an interesting comparison, if the IIP had been appointed within two years after the death out of a relevant property trust established by the will – which would take effect as an IPDI by virtue of IHTA 1984 s 144, see paragraph 3.2.2 below – it is clear that IHTA 1984 s 142 would be capable of applying to a disclaimer of that IIP if made within the remainder of the two years after the death (see paragraphs 3.2.41 ff below). However, if the appointment was not made until immediately before the two year period expired, a disclaimer within s 142 would not be feasible, and the question would arise whether the interest appointed could be disclaimed instead under IHTA 1984 s 93, which contains no time limit as such (see point (a) in paragraph 3.1.71 above). Clearly the property in such a case *was* settled property immediately before the beneficiary became entitled to the IIP as a matter of fact; but not if that condition must be assessed by reference to the backdated status of the IIP by virtue of IHTA 1984 s 144.

Diverting value without affecting the IHT position on the death

Growth in value since the death

3.1.173

Example

Suppose that Paula died in May 2007 leaving an estate worth £1,000,000. Her will provided legacies of £100,000 each for her three adult children, and left the residue of her estate to her husband Quentin. The administration of Paula's estate is nearing an end. Since her death, planning permission has been granted – somewhat contrary to expectations at the time she died – for a housing development on an area of land behind her house; and it now appears that an area of her garden over which the developer had taken an option for access purposes – which was valued at her death at £200,000 subject to the option – is now likely to fetch £500,000 on exercise of the option. Quentin states that he will have no need for the additional £300,000 (before CGT) that would be generated on that sale, and would like to pass it on for the children's benefit.

3.1.174 Quentin and the children could enter into a deed of variation that provides for the estate to be distributed as if Paula had left Quentin a legacy of £700,000 and the residue to the children equally. The IHT position on Paula's death is unchanged by this; the £1,000,000 value on death is undisturbed, and the £700,000 substituted legacy attracts spouse exemption, leaving £300,000 of chargeable estate which is within the NRB. But there is a real difference in the devolution of the estate, because the growth in value since death passes with residue and thus to the children. (There is also a difference in entitlements to income or interest.) The value of what is distributed to the children (shortly before the option is expected to be exercised) is therefore £600,000, in place of the £300,000 they would have been entitled to between them under the will as it stood. Furthermore, when the option is then exercised, the sale will be made by the three of them, and therefore three separate annual CGT exemptions will be available.

3.1.175 The principle is the same where the chargeable part of the estate exceeds the NRB; the substitute legacy for the surviving spouse, to leave the IHT position unaffected in either direction, would still equate to the value of the estate for IHT after deducting the original legacies to the children and the IHT payable on them. The latter figure would of course be calculated on a grossed up basis where the legacies did not bear their own tax. Thus if in the above example the tax free legacies from Paula's estate to the children had totalled £400,000 instead of £300,000, with a NRB of £300,000, the IHT charge (in round pounds) would have been £66,667; the £100,000 excess of net legacies over the NRB would be charged at 40/(100–40), or $\frac{2}{3}$. Net residue for Quentin would then have been £533,333 (£1,000,000 – £400,000 – £66,667). If under a corresponding variation Quentin were given a legacy of £533,333 (exempt) with residue to the children, residue before tax for the IHT calculation would be £466,667, and tax on the £166,667 excess over the NRB at 40% would be £66,667.

Income within the two year period

3.1.176

Example

Suppose Brian died a few months ago leaving his residuary estate to his widow Caroline. Apart from his own house, which was of significant value, he owned 80% of the shares in Brian's Properties Limited, a property investment company that he had run successfully for many years and which had built up substantial undistributed reserves. Coincidentally Brian had negotiated a major sale not long before he died, and the company is cash rich. Caroline, who has recently had a poor medical diagnosis, is worried about IHT in the event of her own death; she seeks advice about what she can do to pass value on to their adult children. Brian's NRB for IHT had been fully exhausted by failed PETs, and Caroline is concerned that she too may not survive for seven years from any gifts she might make now.

3.1.177 Caroline is advised – with suitable risk warnings – to enter into a deed of variation under which Brian's shareholding in Brian's Properties Limited is to be held in trust to pay the income to the children equally for a period of 23 months from Brian's death, with the trust then terminating and Caroline (or her estate if she has died in the meantime) being absolutely entitled in remainder. This plan relies on the difficult rule in IHTA 1984 s 142(4), explored in paragraphs **3.1.43–3.1.50** above; although the variation is within the basic backdating provisions of IHTA 1984 s 142(1), treating the varied dispositions as made by Brian, the rule in IHTA 1984 s 142(4) is grafted on to that. The 23-month IIPs conferred on the children involve the shares being held in trust for the children for a period that ends less than two years from the death; in those circumstances, IHTA 1984 s 142(4) provides for the disposition which takes effect at the end of the 23 months (in favour of Caroline absolutely) to be treated as if it had had effect from the beginning of that period (the date of death, having regard to the basic backdating rule in IHTA 1984 s 142(1)). Thus, as confirmed in Example 2 set out in IHTM35133, HMRC regard the provision as requiring the short term interests of the children to be disregarded for IHT purposes: the Manual confirms that the estate remains wholly spouse-exempt.

3.1.178 So what, it may be asked, is achieved by this variation? The answer is apparent when the trustees exercise their control over the company, once the shares have been released from the administration by the personal representatives, to procure the declaration of a large dividend while the children's short term interests continue. The amount due to the trustees in respect of their 80% holding is in trust law terms income payable to the children as beneficiaries with IIPs, though it will be taxed in the hands of Caroline as settlor with a retained interest. (She in turn is in a position to reclaim that tax from the trustees, once she has paid it, under ITTOIA 2005 s 646; the trustees, aware of this, do not mandate the dividend to the children, and ensure that they retain enough to cover Caroline's demand in due course.) The amount of income tax involved will be no different if the children are themselves higher rate taxpayers; but the effect of the arrangement is that the net amount of the dividend after tax belongs to the children, without losing the existing IHT exemption on Brian's death, and without the variation constituting a transfer of value on Caroline's part since that is precluded by IHTA 1984 s 142(1)(a).

3.1.179   The main issue is concerned with whether there are any IHT consequences of the income distribution to the children. The position is sufficiently confusing to make risk warnings advisable, and there may be further questions not identified here—

(a)   As a result of the first half of IHTA 1984 s 142(4), for IHT purposes the shares are held for Caroline absolutely throughout. Can the exercise of control by the trustees [sc as bare trustees for Caroline] to procure a large dividend, so as to milk the company of its distributable reserves, amount to a transfer of value by Caroline – a disposition by her as a result of which the value of the shares is reduced? Seemingly not – that exercise did not involve a disposition by her at all as a matter of fact, and in the real world the trustees had every right to procure the payment of a dividend in whatever sum they thought fit. (The terms of the trust would need to be such that there was no question of Caroline as remainderman having an equitable claim against the trustees on account of the size of the dividend.) To attribute the action of the trustees to Caroline would be stretching the deeming effects of IHTA 1984 s 142 far further than the analysis in *Marshall v Kerr* [1995] 1 AC 148 would allow (admittedly for a different tax, though the principle is no different). As noted in paragraph **3.1.111** above, the House of Lords' approach was to see what has happened in the "real world", and then ask whether there is anything in the statutory fiction which *requires* one to assume a state of facts inconsistent with the real world analysis so identified.

(b)   The closing words of IHTA 1984 s 142(4), examined in paragraphs **3.1.46** ff above, preserve the application of IHTA 1984 (notwithstanding the basic rule ignoring the short term interests) "in relation to any distribution or application of property occurring before [Caroline's remainder interest] takes effect [in possession]". So what would be the IHT effect of what has taken place apart from the first half of that subsection? HMRC interpret this in IHTM35134 as referring to applications or distributions of trust capital (not income) – this must be correct – and as requiring the IHT treatment that would apply to "the trusts actually applying from the death" (which paragraph **3.1.46** above suggested should be taken as meaning, of necessity, "deemed to apply from the death under IHTA 1984 s 142(1)"). So even if capital had been distributed to the children, ostensibly there would have been no IHT consequence (IHTA 1984 s 53(2), (2A)), still less with just an income distribution which would have been ignored for IHT under IHTA 1984 s 65(5)(b) even if the trust had been in the relevant property regime.

Provision for charities

Gift aid

3.1.180   It was at one time suggested that obtaining the IHT charity exemption, through a variation by a non-exempt beneficiary creating a retrospective legacy in favour of a charity, could be combined with gift aid relief for income tax purposes. The theory was that, provided the legacy was redirected by the original beneficiary after distribution to him, in the "real world" which applies for income tax he was making a personal cash gift to the charity (see paragraphs **3.1.17, 3.1.117** above). Thus, for a £3,900 legacy provided for a charity out of the chargeable estate by means of a variation in those circumstances, tax savings totalling £3,560 would allegedly be generated—

(a) a saving of £1,560 (40%) would have been created in the estate's IHT bill; and

(b) in addition, the original beneficiary would provide the charity with a gift aid declaration, as a result of which the contention was that—

    (i) the charity could recover £1,100 from HMRC of income tax treated as deducted from the £3,900 "cash gift" (22/78 × £3,900, or 22% of the grossed-up gift of £5,000), and

    (ii) the beneficiary would claim a further £900 (18% of the grossed-up gift of £5,000) as a deduction against his income tax bill.

3.1.181 However, it was held by the Special Commissioner in *St Dunstan's v Major (Inspector of Taxes)* [1997] STC (SCD) 212 that if an IHT saving (in most cases at 40%) is generated which accrues to the benefit of the original beneficiary – or, for that matter, of any person connected with him – then that constitutes a "benefit associated with the gift" within what is now ITA 2007 s 417, at a level that exceeds the variable limit in ITA 2007 s 418(2) and thereby denies gift aid relief under ITA 2007 s 416(7). (Significant quantities of text appear to have been withheld under the FOIA 2000 from the published versions of IHTM35121 and IHTM35122, dealing with property redirected to a charity, and with gift aid relief, respectively.) Note that this decision would not preclude gift aid relief for a cash gift made by way of variation, where the IHT benefit of the variation accrues to someone not connected with the original beneficiary (eg where he was a pecuniary legatee, unrelated to the residuary beneficiary).

Share aid

3.1.182 Under ITA 2007 ss 431–446, income tax relief is given in connection with gifts (or other disposals other than by way of bargain made at arm's length) of the whole beneficial interest in a qualifying investment. (By virtue of ITA 2007 ss 432, 433, a qualifying investment can be quoted investments of various kinds or freehold or leasehold interests in land, though subject in the latter case to various conditions in ITA 2007 ss 441–444; the designation "share aid", convenient though it is, is perhaps misleadingly narrow.) The relief is similar to gift aid in that the transferor receives an income tax deduction. In a simple case, the amount of the deduction is the value of the net benefit received by the charity, plus the transferor's incidental costs of the disposal; where the transferor receives some consideration, the calculation is more complex taking account of that consideration and also of the deemed consideration on his transfer to the charity (a no gain, no loss transfer under TCGA 1992, s 257). Unlike gift aid, however, the transferor is not disqualified from relief if he (or a connected person) receives a benefit in consequence of making the disposal; instead the income tax deduction, calculated under the rules just mentioned, is reduced by the total value of that benefit. (See generally ITA 2007 s 434.)

3.1.183   It follows that there is scope for share aid relief to be combined with the IHT charity exemption by means of a variation. Assume that Ben has inherited his father's estate, and a portfolio of quoted investments has been distributed to him from the estate. Ben enters into a deed of variation before the second anniversary of death, under (the real world effect of) which he transfers shares from that portfolio worth £20,000 to his favoured charity, unconditionally. At his father's death the shares in question were worth £17,500. He pays his advisers £500 for preparing the deed. By including an IHT statement of intent in the deed, he secures a refund of £7,000 to the estate (and thus for his eventual credit, which in accordance with the St Dunstan's case is a benefit to him, see paragraph **3.1.181** above). Provided he does not retain any part of the holdings from which the transfer is made, Ben can claim share aid relief; on these figures, subject to the notes below, his relievable amount is calculated under ITA 2007 s 434(1) as £13,500 (£20,000 net value to the charity, plus £500 incidental costs of Ben's disposal, minus £7,000 benefit received by Ben). If Ben is a higher rate taxpayer, his income tax bill is reduced by £5,400 as a result, so the total tax benefits of the £20,000 gift amount to £12,400. Note however that—

(a) any interest on the IHT refund will probably have to be taken into account as a benefit to Ben as well;

(b) it may be necessary to exclude from the incidental costs of the disposal any element of the advisers' charge which properly relates to the advice given to Ben in relation to the contents of the deed, as distinct from simply preparing the deed and giving effect to it by transfer of the shares); and

(c) although the share aid provisions do not require that Ben's disposal of the whole of the beneficial interest in the qualifying investments in question must be a disposal for CGT purposes – this is an income tax relief and from the income tax point of view the deed of variation operates in the real world without reference to any statutory counterfactual treatment that applies for CGT or IHT purposes – it will be preferable *not* to include a CGT statement of intent in the deed (leading to the charity being treated as legatee of the shares for CGT purposes), so as to avoid any scope for debate on that issue. The deed will therefore bring about a CGT disposal of the shares, which is a gift as Ben does not obtain any consideration for it; he will still have no CGT liability in consequence, as his disposal will be on a no gain, no loss basis.

Business and agricultural property

Generally

3.1.184   A general principle of IHT planning in wills – which obviously must be tempered to the family circumstances and needs in individual cases, and in the process governed not least by the sufficiency of the estate generally – is to make maximum use of reliefs by leaving to chargeable beneficiaries property that attracts BPR or APR, and to make maximum use of exemptions by leaving non-relievable property to exempt benefici-aries. This will remain so even with the transferable NRB, at any rate to the extent that the combined estates of the two spouses or civil partners exceed twice the statutory NRB, or where property attracting BPR or APR on the first death is thought unlikely to do so by the time of the second death. (See generally CHAPTER 2.8). Chargeable beneficiaries of course include the trustees of a trust that does not confer an IPDI or DPI on an exempt beneficiary (typically the testator's surviving spouse or civil partner). Care is obviously needed where an asset is relievable at less than 100%, or where a relief extends to only part of the value of a particular asset (eg by virtue of the excepted assets rule for business property relief, in IHTA 1984 s 112, or because the value of agricultural property exceeds its agricultural value, cf IHTA 1984 s 116(1)).

3.1.185   Clearly it is not always possible to predict, at the time a will is prepared, the extent of the reliefs that will be accepted by HMRC after the testator's eventual death. Indeed, the definitive position may yet be far from clear as the end of the two year period allowed for variations approaches. Often a variation (or an appointment from a relevant property trust established by the will, see (CHAPTER 3.2) will need to be based on the advisers' best predictions of the eventual outcome of incomplete negotiations with HMRC on more than one front. No general advice can be given as to the basis for a variation in such cases, but the central question for the clients will be whether—

(a)   the objective should be to ensure (as can be done by skilled drafting, even if sometimes leaving an untidy asset ownership result) that as much underlying value as possible is worked through into "charge-able" hands without giving rise to any actual IHT liability on the death; or

(b)   an IHT liability on the death is still to be avoided, but on a more practical ownership basis; or

(c)   an allocation between chargeable and exempt beneficiaries should be planned which (unlike the above two options) does require the extent of the available reliefs to be fully worked out in negotiations with

HMRC, accepting that this will mean that some IHT may end up being payable. Frustration is often expressed that the estate planning of the surviving spouse or civil partner would be easier if it had been feasible to obtain agreement from HMRC that a particular asset or assets, passing to the survivor as part of residue, did or did not qualify for relief, at any rate by reference to the circumstances at the first death; but that, because the will and/or any variation had been planned with a specific view to ensuring that no actual IHT liability would remain on the first death, HMRC decided to close their file without completing negotiations on the issue since no tax liability depended on the outcome.

Planning for a double dip

3.1.186 One popular strategy where the deceased is survived by a spouse or civil partner, and there is relievable property which is likely to be retained (and to retain its relievable character) for the time being, is to set up a "double dip" of relief. On the first death the relievable property is left to chargeable beneficiaries in accordance with the principle in paragraph **3.1.184** above, and non-relievable property is left to the exempt survivor (or to trustees for the survivor on an IPDI basis). In due course, the survivor or the IPDI trustees look to improve the IHT profile of the survivor's estate on the survivor's eventual death, and might arrange to buy the relievable property from the beneficiaries to whom it was left on the first death. This may involve a charge to stamp duty (shares) or SDLT (land), and potentially a CGT charge in the hands of the original beneficiaries; so everything will have to be left to be looked at in the light of the circumstances at the time. If such a sale takes place, however, then subject to the usual minimum periods of ownership or occupation (IHTA 1984 s 106 for BPR, IHTA 1984 s 117 for APR) the survivor can hope to obtain relief for the same assets on his or her eventual death as well. If that is achieved, tax charges on the sale may seem a small price to pay in return for securing that the relievable property, and the open market price paid on its transfer, pass to the next generation for the minimum IHT cost. Placing relievable, and non-relievable, assets in suitable hands, preparatory to a sale of this sort, is really only an extension of the more general philosophy of maximising reliefs on the first death.

Avoiding loss of relief through the apportionment rules

3.1.187 If the value of the estate is reduced to any extent by APR or BPR, IHTA 1984 s 39A lays down rules as to how the reduced value is to be attributed between specific gifts and relievable gifts. It must be borne in mind that for this purpose a "specific gift" is "any gift [of property comprised in the deceased's estate for IHT purposes] other than a gift or residue or of a share of residue"; and "gift" means "the benefit of any disposition or rule of law by which, on the [death], any property becomes ... the property of any person or applicable for any purpose":

IHTA 1984 s 42(1). Thus a trust fund in which the deceased had an estate IIP, and which devolves in accordance with the terms of that trust, is just as much a specific gift for this purpose as a specific devise or a pecuniary legacy given by the deceased's will. (It is open to question how far property that is charged to IHT on the deceased's death through having fallen foul of the GROB rules is the subject of a "gift" at all within this definition, as it does not "become" the property of any person, or applicable for any purpose, on the making of the transfer of value on the deceased's death: its ownership and applicability is unchanged by the death.)

3.1.188 If no part of the estate is the subject of an exempt transfer (typically but not exclusively by virtue of the spouse or charity exemptions), IHTA 1984 s 39A will not make a difference to the total IHT liability of the estate, though the detail of its rules, combined with those in IHTA 1984 ss 38, 39, may affect the incidence of the total liability as between different funds if not all of them bear their own tax. But where part of the estate is exempt, IHTA 1984 s 39A can give rise to a wastage of APR or BPR through part of the relief being attributed to the exempt transfer. In other circumstances (not least, prior to the introduction of the transferable NRB, in the context of a "classic" will giving a NRB discretionary legacy and residue to the surviving spouse, depending on the precise drafting of the NRB legacy), it is capable of giving rise to unexpected results in the allocation of the estate between the legacy trustees and the spouse. The rule deals with the attribution of APR and BPR to specific gifts for the purpose of applying the rules in IHTA 1984 ss 38, 39 as to the calculation of IHT as a result; the basic operation of IHTA 1984 s 39A(2)–(4) is that—

(a) a specific gift of relievable property unsurprisingly attracts the full benefit of the relief it attracts; but

(b) if relievable property is not the subject of a specific gift, the relief on it is apportioned between all other specific gifts and residue.

3.1.189 To illustrate this, consider three examples, each of which assumes that Mike died leaving a free estate comprising £400,000 of fully relievable business property plus £600,000 of non-relievable property, and an unused NRB of £300,000. Mike's estate is to be shared between his widow Naomi and his son Oliver in the ways indicated in each example.

3.1.190

Example 1

Legacy to Naomi of £400,000 and residue to Oliver – the expectation being that the £400,000 legacy would be exempt and leave £600,000 of residue to attract BPR and (as to the excess) to be covered (with room to spare) by the available NRB. That is not the way IHTA 1984 s 39A operates. It requires that the value of the pecuniary legacy to Naomi be taken (for the purpose of IHTA

1984 ss 38, 39) as the appropriate fraction of itself. The appropriate fraction, in these circumstances, is 600,000/1,000,000, or 6/10: £600,000 being the value transferred on the death after taking account of BPR, and £1,000,000 being the "unreduced value transferred" ie the value of the estate for IHT before applying the relief. Thus the estate as a whole is taxed on the basis that the legacy to Naomi net of BPR is £240,000 and the residue passing to Oliver is worth £360,000 net of BPR: £60,000 of which would thus be subject to IHT at 40%.

3.1.191

Example 2

Legacy to Oliver of the maximum cash sum that Mike could leave him without giving rise to an actual IHT liability attributable to it, and residue to Naomi – the expectation here being that Oliver would receive £300,000 if (as was the case at the time the will was prepared) Mike had indeed made no chargeable transfers in the last seven years of his life, and so Naomi would receive £700,000. Again, IHTA 1984 s 39A does not work in accordance with that expectation. The appropriate fraction is still 6/10 as in Example 1; but, because the NRB legacy is expressed as the maximum amount that will avoid an actual IHT liability, the result will be an actual legacy of £500,000 to Oliver (reduced for IHT purposes by IHTA 1984 s 39A to a value net of relief of £300,000 covered by the NRB), and residue of only the remaining £500,000 to Naomi.

3.1.192

Example 3

In this example Mike's free estate is as above, but in addition he had an estate IIP under the will of his previous wife Lilian (Oliver's mother) in a fund worth £200,000 on Mike's death, which does not contain any relievable property and which passes to Oliver as remainderman under Lilian's will. Mike's will is as in Example 2, with a NRB legacy to Oliver and residue to Naomi. The IIP fund under Lilian's will itself comprises a specific gift within the meaning of IHTA 1984 s 42(1). Mike's total gross estate on death is now £1,200,000, and the total value transferred after BPR is £800,000, so the appropriate fraction used for apportioning the BPR is now 800,000/1,200,000 or 2/3. The IHT adjusted value of the IIP fund (gross £200,000) is thus £133,333, leaving relieved value of £166,667 available for the NRB legacy. That means the gross NRB legacy is £250,000, and residue is £750,000.

3.1.193   Any unacceptable consequences of the rules in IHTA 1984 s 39A can be resolved by means of a post-death variation (or, in cases where an NRB legacy is left on typical discretionary trusts, by an exercise of a power of appointment) within two years of death. The important thing is to understand how the rules work, in order to plan the optimum result in terms of family objectives and IHT objectives (which may of course not coincide).

Excluded property

Generally

3.1.194 A deceased who is not UK domiciled, though UK resident, may well die with a mix of excluded and non-excluded property in his estate. In the same way as with APR and BPR, the optimum result for IHT purposes is for any gifts to chargeable beneficiaries to take effect out of excluded property, and for non-excluded property to pass (with the possible exception of the available NRB) to the deceased's surviving spouse or civil partner with the benefit of that exemption. In relation to the devolution of the estate on the death itself, there may well be the added complication of foreign law succession requirements, and foreign tax systems, to take into account, which both often work rather differently from the English or UK systems; in particular, in many civil law countries, gifts to the testator's spouse (so far as not invalidated anyway by local forced heirship rules) may, in contrast to the UK system, attract a *heavier* tax charge in the succession than gifts to the testator's children. Additionally, with property in foreign jurisdictions and sometimes a number of countries' succession laws potentially relevant, complex questions of private international law will often arise as to which legal system should govern the devolution of which part of the overall worldwide estate.

3.1.195 In cases where the family are willing to work together, a variation can sometimes be worked out to improve the UK IHT results. (Foreign taxes on death will probably be unaffected since backdating effect under the provisions discussed in this chapter is of course a matter of UK tax law only.) As indicated in paragraph **3.1.18** above, point (a), beneficiaries entering into a variation must have capacity to do so under their own personal law; but this means capacity to enter into the underlying "real world" disposition; references to "rewriting the deceased's will" are particularly misleading in this context, and will only give rise to added confusion if used in communications with foreign lawyers involved. Additionally, if and so far as property affected by the variation is located outside the UK, it is necessary to check that the underlying disposition is not going to give rise to tax liabilities for either party in the jurisdiction of *situs*. Transfer duties and gift taxes are prime possibilities, though others such as capital gains taxation should also be checked.

3.1.196 There may be a temptation to propose a variation which leaves exempt and non-exempt beneficiaries with effectively the same entitlements in cash terms, but specified to be paid from UK assets in the case of the exempt beneficiary and overseas (excluded property) assets in the case of beneficiaries who do not qualify for UK IHT exemptions. Planning of that sort is the subject of an instruction in IHTM35094, which requires examiners to notify IHT Technical Group immediately of a variation which appears to have those characteristics, without preliminary enquiries. The allegation, no doubt, would be that if each party is entitled to cash both before and after the variation, of broadly unchanged amount, there is not in a true sense a variation of the dispositions taking effect on death, taken as a whole. But if the different parties take different assets (in kind) there seems no room for criticism on those lines, even if the values of the respective assets as at the deceased's death are broadly similar, since there is a real switch of entitlement, and potentially very different prospects for growth or income generation in the hands of each beneficiary affected.

Establishing an excluded property trust

3.1.197   A testator who is UK resident but not UK domiciled (and also not caught by the IHT deemed domicile rule in IHTA 1984 s 267) will generally be alert to the potential advantages of settling his estate, where possible, in a trust where the value can be broadly insulated from future IHT charges by being invested in a suitable manner. If that has not been done by his will, it is always open to the original beneficiary to bring it about by means of a variation, though where (as would usually be expected) the original beneficiary is to remain an important beneficiary of the trust, the income tax and CGT implications of the trust will be very different under a variation from what they would be if the deceased had established the trust direct under his will. A choice can be made in the process as to whether the trust should be established with UK or overseas trustees, as discussed in paragraph **3.1.163** above.

3.1.198   Establishing such a trust by deed of variation needs particular care where the original beneficiary is the deceased's surviving spouse. To the extent that the estate assets are UK-situated and worth more than the NRB, there will be a temptation to route those assets into an IPDI for the spouse, with a view to preserving the spouse exemption on the deceased's death. That course gives a hostage to fortune in relation to the domicile (and deemed domicile) status of the survivor at the time such IPDI comes (or is brought) to an end; by virtue of IHTA 1984 ss 80, 82, excluded property status for the trust in any form thereafter other than a DPI (most unlikely, not least since the beneficiary in question would have had to have disabled person status at the original testator's death, see IHTA 1984 s 89(4)–(6)) would be dependent not just on the domicile status of the original testator, but also of the spouse as IPDI beneficiary when the IPDI comes to an end. If, on the other hand, UK-situated property is redirected by the spouse into trust on a non-IPDI basis – effectively, as a relevant property trust and almost certainly fully discretionary – then the spouse exemption will be lost on the deceased's death, and some IHT may become payable as a result.

3.1.199   The foregoing comments relate to the situation with, typically, a UK resident but foreign domiciled testator. There are however plenty of occasions where a UK-based client inherits property from a relative with no current UK connection, and wishes to redirect his inheritance into a trust as a shelter against future IHT. Such planning is entirely valid; as explained in paragraph **3.1.18** above, point (a), so long as a transfer of assets into trust, by a UK (actual) settlor, will be valid in the country where the assets concerned are currently situated and will not incur unacceptable tax liabilities there, the deed by which the planning is implemented can take English form and be governed by English law, or for that matter by the law of the place where the intended trustees reside. Typically the original beneficiary or his immediate family will be beneficiaries of such a trust, and for this reason the original beneficiary as settlor will be vulnerable to income tax and CGT on trust income and gains whether or not they belong or are distributed to him (see paragraphs **3.1.103**, **3.1.129**, **3.1.132** above). But that is little different from the position were he to retain the inheritance personally, and the IHT shelter will often be an adequate justification for the expense.

Double estate variations

Reducing the estate of a beneficiary who has since died

3.1.200   It is not all that uncommon to find that a deceased person (let us call him Robert) had inherited something on the death of another person (Simon) not very long beforehand. Assume that Robert's estate passes to his brother Thomas. This could be IHT-inefficient in one of two ways—

(a)   If Robert and Simon were civil partners, Robert's inheritance from Simon will have been exempt on Simon's death, but will increase the amount that is taxable on Robert's death. Until the introduction of the transferable NRB, if Simon had not made full use of his available NRB (through other legacies or otherwise), IHT will be wasted – see Example 1 below.

(b)   If they were not civil partners but, say, brothers, effectively the same value will have been chargeable to IHT on both deaths. Quick succession relief under IHTA 1984 s 141 can provide some help in these circumstances, but it is not usually seen to be a full solution to the double taxation issue, see Example 2 below. (Its benefits are also spread between different taxable funds on the second death, for example if Robert was life tenant under a separate trust – part of the benefit of the relief would be taken in those circumstances by the beneficiaries of that trust, see IHTM22045.)

3.1.201

Example 1: Robert and Simon civil partners

Simon's estate was worth £450,000 when he died in January 2007, and he left one third of it to his sister Vanessa and two thirds to Robert. Simon had made no previous inroads into his NRB of £285,000, so no IHT was due on his estate: Vanessa's £150,000 was within the NRB, Robert's £300,000 was exempt.

Aside from his share of Simon's estate, which had not been paid over to him by the time of his death in June 2008, Robert's own estate was worth £362,000. So in all (ignoring intervening changes in value since Simon's death) Robert's taxable estate passing to Thomas was £662,000, against which his NRB of £312,000 was fully available. IHT at 40% on the excess of £350,000 is therefore £140,000.

Thomas realises that if Simon had left the two-thirds share of his estate on terms that £135,000 should pass direct to Thomas, and only the balance to Robert, the £135,000 would have been within Simon's NRB, of which only £150,000 had been used against Vanessa's share of the estate. Tax on Simon's estate would have remained at nil, but Robert's taxable estate would have been reduced by £135,000 accordingly, resulting in a saving of £54,000.

3.1.202

Example 2: Robert and Simon brothers

With the same values and dates of death as in Example 1, Simon's estate now attracts an IHT charge of £66,000 (40% of £165,000 excess over the £285,000 NRB). £22,000 of that is borne by Vanessa's £150,000 share of gross residue, and £44,000 by Robert's gross £300,000 – so the increase in Robert's estate was £256,000.

Robert's death estate in total is therefore £618,000 (his "separate" £362,000 plus £256,000). The excess over his NRB of £312,000 is £306,000; tax on this at 40%, before quick succession relief, is therefore £122,400.

The quick succession relief is worked out as 80% (on Robert's having survived Simon by between one and two years) of the tax on Simon's death that is attributable to the increase in Robert's estate as a result of his inheritance. There is, therefore, an immediate dilution of relief, in that part of the tax on Simon's death is attributable to the part of his estate that is paid away in tax. The tax attributable to the increase in Robert's estate is thus (in round pounds) £37,547 (calculated as 66,000/450,000 × 256,000); so 80% of that amount, or £30,038, falls to be deducted from the basic tax on Robert's death, leaving a net liability of £92,362. Thomas's inheritance is thus £525,638 (£618,000 –£92,362).

Thomas calculates what would have happened if Simon had left the two thirds share of his estate direct to Thomas. From Simon's estate Thomas would have received the £256,000, net of IHT, that was in fact payable to Robert. Robert's estate on death would have been limited to his "separate" £362,000, on which tax of just £20,000 would have been due (40% × (£362,000 −£312,000), leaving a net receipt for Thomas of £342,000. Thomas's combined inheritances from Simon and Robert would then have been £598,000 – a tax saving of £72,362.

3.1.203 In both cases a variation can be effected in relation to Simon's estate so far as it passed to Robert, so long as this is done within two years from Simon's death. In Example 1 (see paragraph **3.1.201** above), this strategy should now often be unnecessary where the second death occurred on or after 9 October 2007; in those circumstances, the unused proportion of Simon's NRB can be used to increase Robert's NRB at his death, and – with static values anyway – that may lead to a better end result. But if assets in Simon's estate have increased substantially in value since his death, it may yet be advisable to ensure that they are regarded as passing to chargeable, not exempt, beneficiaries on his death (see paragraphs **3.1.173–3.1.175** above).

3.1.204 Where such a variation is to be entered into, strictly speaking it is Robert's personal representatives – no doubt with Thomas' authority – who must enter into the variation, as "the persons who benefit under [Simon's] disposition" (cf IHTA 1984 s 142(1)). Certainly HMRC take the view that, where a deceased beneficiary's interest is to be disclaimed, both the personal representatives and the beneficiaries of Robert's estate are necessary parties (see IHTM35164, discussed in paragraph **3.1.9** above, where it was doubted that the beneficiaries are necessary parties as such on the basis that they could provide the necessary authority separately to the personal representatives). Of course, in a case where the two deaths are nearly two years apart, participation by the personal representatives could present problems in the absence of a grant in Robert's estate, particularly if he died intestate. It may be that this realisation explains the more relaxed view indicated in IHTM35042 – which may be no more than concessionary, and is certainly impossible to reconcile with IHTM35164 – that it is the beneficiaries of the second estate (Thomas in the present examples, without needing to involve Robert's personal representatives) who can make the variation in these circumstances. The example given in IHTM35042 is essentially on all fours with Example 1 in paragraph **3.1.201** above. HMRC go on in the same paragraph to resolve an issue to which some had thought they might object—

"In such cases, the redirection effected by the IoV made by [Robert's] beneficiaries may be to themselves directly or to others. We do not regard a redirection by [Robert's] beneficiaries to themselves directly as infringing the requirement to change the destination of the property. Though the final destination of the property in the hands of [Robert's] beneficiaries may not in fact be changed by the variation, the variation is still regarded as effecting a change in the disposition of the property in [Simon's] estate."

3.1.205 The August 2007 issue of HMRC's IHT and Trusts Newsletter (accessible at *www.hmrc.gov.uk/cto/newsletter-august07.htm*) draws attention to an issue that had obviously arisen in practice in the completion of form IHT200 in relation to the second estate where a variation of this kind has been made before probate to reduce the IHT value of the survivor's estate. They state—

"The hypothesis created by IHTA 1984 s 142 applies **only** for IHT (& CGT where those making the variation invoke TCGA 1992 s 62(6)) purposes – it does not and cannot alter the fact that at death, the estate of the survivor includes the assets inherited on the first death. The estate for which Probate/ Confirmation is required is the 'combined' estate and the assets from both estates must be taken into account to establish the gross value of the estate on the second death. Where this gross value exceeds the IHT nil-rate band the second death cannot qualify as an excepted estate. The correct process is to complete form IHT200 for the 'combined' estate, so the correct values are carried forward for Probate/Confirmation and then deduct the assets that are being redirected away from the second estate as a relief. This way, the correct position is reported for Probate/Confirmation and the impact of the IoV is correctly applied for tax purposes only."

Increasing the estate of a person who has since died

3.1.206 For similar reasons to those discussed in paragraphs **3.1.17**, **3.1.18** above, it might be argued that it is logically impossible for an original beneficiary to redirect property in favour of a person who has died by the time the variation is made. A gift in favour of someone who has already died – as opposed to a gift in favour of those who benefit from the deceased person's estate – has, it is submitted, no reality to it. However, HMRC do appear to accept that this type of variation is nevertheless possible for IHT purposes: they say in IHTM35110—

"Although in these circumstances the effect of the variation is (usually) to reduce the entitlement of the second spouse or civil partner, a variation may also be used to increase the entitlement of someone who has died after the person whose estate is being varied".

This approach can be seen to be justified if the effect "in the real world" is analysed as a gift to the (deceased) surviving spouse's personal representatives, to be held and administered as part of the estate, which is a perfectly valid concept, even though no layman would think of making a gift in that way apart from the tax reliefs to be gained from a variation.

3.1.207 That comment in IHTM35110 does not spell out, in terms, acceptance by HMRC that such a variation will secure spouse exemption on the first death that was not available under the will of the first spouse to die. However, it may be inferred that they do take this view; it is hard to see why a variation should be expressed in those terms at all (rather than in favour of the ultimate beneficiaries) for any other reason. Once the variation has been accepted as valid in principle under the analysis outlined above, the only rational way of then giving effect to the IHT backdating provided for by IHTA 1984 s 142(1) is to see it as a gift, as at the testator's death, to the surviving spouse herself, and therefore devolving under her will.

3.1.208   What should be avoided, however, is the temptation to control the devolution of the redirected property (if the surviving spouse's will is not in favour of the "correct" beneficiaries) by providing for the surviving spouse simply to be deemed to have taken a life interest, leaving the capital to devolve thereafter under the original provisions of the will or in some varied way. This would be open to more sustainable "real world" objections, and would in addition seem to fall foul of the rule for short term interests in IHTA 1984 s 142(4) (as to which see paragraphs **3.1.43** ff above).

Drafting approaches

3.1.209   No particular form is prescribed for a variation or disclaimer to attract the special tax treatment discussed in this chapter, beyond the requirement that (save in respect of IHTA 1984 s 93, see paragraph **3.1.71**, point (c)) it must be effected by an instrument in writing made by the specified parties and (for IHT and CGT) containing the necessary statement of intent. It is however as good as universal practice in England and Wales for the instrument to take the form of a deed, with a view to avoiding any suggestion of revocability unless otherwise expressly spelt out.

3.1.210   HMRC indicate in IHTM35025 that they regard the expression "any of the dispositions … are varied" in IHTA 1984 s 142(1) as connoting two requirements—

(a)   "that the document which constitutes the variation clearly identifies the original dispositions and so establishes the linkage between their dispositive effect and the redistribution now intended", and

(b)   "that the destination of the property subject to the specified dispositions be changed".

The second of those requirements does not go to the form of the document, and is touched on in different ways in paragraphs **3.1.33**, **3.1.34**, **3.1.36** ff above. On the first requirement, the HMRC guidance in IHTM35025 is considered realistic—

> "A document such as a deed of assignment/assignation which merely transfers property in fact received by A under the will of X to the donee B without mention of that will does not satisfy this requirement.
>
> However, the more usual deed of gift which recites the derivation of property under a will or intestacy or by survivorship in joint tenancy or under a

survivorship destination in Scotland and then in the operative part simply disposes of all or part of that property to its new beneficial destination will qualify both under this and the second requirement."

3.1.211 There is, therefore, no particular format which must be followed. Indeed this is spelt out even more specifically in IHTM35022, which reads—

"The only stipulation in IHTA 1984 s 142 about the form of an instrument is that it must be in writing. It does not have to be a formal deed or even writing that is signed as a deed. You can accept a letter or note from the beneficiary redirecting their inheritance as a valid variation so long as the document conforms to the guidelines and otherwise meets the conditions of IHTA 1984 s 142."

(The guidelines referred to were originally set out in a letter from the Inland Revenue to The Law Society dated 11 April 1985 and published in the Law Society Gazette on 22 May 1985; they are reproduced in IHTM35021, and expanded on in IHTM35022–IHTM35029.)

Make believe drafting – inserting or substituting clauses in the will

3.1.212 The author of the relevant section of the CGT Manual appears not to have registered this guidance (quite possibly because the CGT Manual predates this version of the IHT Manual); he describes a variation as follows in CG31600—

"A person who executes an instrument of variation in relation to a will or intestacy provisions gives up his or her right to receive assets or interests or a share of residue that he or she would otherwise have received. In addition the person gives directions as to how the assets etc involved shall devolve following the variation. If the estate is governed by a will the instrument does this by deeming certain clauses to have been removed from the will and certain other clauses to have been inserted in their place. For intestacies it does it by deeming assets to pass under a will having clauses containing the new conditions."

3.1.213 This description – deeming clauses to be omitted from and/or inserted into the deceased's will – certainly fits a large number of the deeds of variation that are seen in practice; perhaps even a large majority of them. But if it is meant as a definition of when a document will constitute a variation eligible for the special statutory treatment, it is unjustifiably restrictive. The more flexible approach of the author of the IHT Manual, quoted in paragraphs **3.1.210**, **3.1.211** above, is much more in accord with the requirements of the various statutory provisions discussed above, which in this respect are identical.

3.1.214 There seem to be many draftsmen who, in common perhaps with the author of the CGT Manual, adopt make believe drafting of this sort – "the Will shall be deemed to have effect with the substitution of clauses X and Y set out in the Schedule to this deed in place of clause X as contained in the Testator's Will as admitted to probate" – as the only possible format when preparing a deed of variation, however artificial the end result may look. There are indeed occasions when this approach may be tolerably convenient; but equally it can be taken to extremes, and in any event it does nothing to dispel common misunderstandings as to the true nature of what is taking place – see paragraph **3.1.18** above.

Real world drafting – making a gift or a bargain incorporating general words of variation

3.1.215   It will be apparent from the above comments that the present author prefers, where circumstances allow, to adopt a format which reflects much more closely the gift, or bargain, that the original beneficiary is making. Wording will clearly have to be included so as to demonstrate that this is indeed by way of variation of the (identified) original disposition; but there will be a good deal less room for misunderstanding, on the part of clients or others, if the drafting focuses on what is going on in the "real world" and less on the fictional world of the statutory results sought. Parliament has provided for the fictional effect where the real world transaction meets the required conditions, and there is usually no need to resort to make-believe drafting in the fullest sense described in CG31600.

A middle course

3.1.216   Sometimes a purely "real world" approach – even with the incorporation of a recital as to the background so as to explain what is being varied – may not prove the most practical format. This may apply particularly to the more complex variations. In such cases, a degree of fictional "as if" drafting, falling short of the purported deletion and insertion of clauses, is unexceptionable. In the case of some of the precedents in PART B2, it will be seen that alternative forms are offered, one as close as possible to the real world and the other treading this suggested middle course. Both are equally valid for the purpose of attracting the tax treatment provided for in IHTA 1984 s 142 and TCGA 1992 s 62(6).

Chapter 3.2

Conversion or distribution of relevant property trusts established by will

IHT treatment

Legislative background

3.2.1   At the same time as the old relief for deeds of family arrangement was clarified and extended in 1978 to cover variations and disclaimers (see paragraph **3.1.1** above), a provision was introduced to allow equivalent backdating treatment for capital transfer tax purposes – similar to that allowed for variations and disclaimers – where distributions or appointments are made from discretionary will trusts within the first two years after death. This was then modified in FA 1982 to fit with the revised regime for non-IIP settlements; and it is this rule which became the pre-2006 version of IHTA 1984 s 144. On to this were then grafted two additional provisions – both driving at the same result as the original provisions, but by a different route and in unnecessarily long-winded terms – as part of the government's scramble, during the passage of FA 2006, to rectify the most obvious unintended consequences of the major changes to the IHT settlements legislation contained in that Act. The terms in which the backdating takes effect, where the relevant conditions are satisfied, will be dealt with first, followed by a summary of the conditions that must be satisfied in order to attract this backdating treatment.

IHT effects where relevant conditions are met

3.2.2   If an event (referred to in this chapter as a "trigger event") occurs that is within one or other set of conditions below, then—

(a) for all IHT purposes the property affected is treated as though the deceased's will had provided that on his death the property should be held as it is held after the trigger event (IHTA 1984 s 144(2), (4)(a)), with equivalent effect to a variation as described in paragraph **3.1.41** above; and

(b) any tax charge otherwise arising on the trigger event under IHTA 1984 Pt 3 Ch 3 is abrogated (IHTA 1984 s 144(2), (4)(b)).

3.2.3 Note that this treatment is automatic if the conditions for a trigger event are met. It is not optional in the way that backdated IHT treatment for variations (though not disclaimers) is optional, depending as the latter does on the inclusion in the relevant instrument of an IHT statement of intent (see paragraphs **3.1.63** ff above).

The conditions to be satisfied for IHT backdating

Common conditions to the original and post-2006 provisions

3.2.4 There are three core requirements that apply in all cases—

(a) Property comprised in the deceased's estate immediately before his death is settled by his will (IHTA 1984 s 144(1), (3)(b), (5)(b)). Although ostensibly "estate" has the wide meaning given by IHTA 1984 s 5, the requirement that the property be settled by the will narrows the context significantly. Two points arise—

  (i) by analogy with the HMRC view expressed in IHTM35165 (quoted in paragraph **3.1.74** above), property that was settled property prior to the deceased's death, but over which the deceased had, and exercised by will, a general power of appointment, should be accepted as fulfilling the condition of being settled by his will if the terms on which it is to be held under that appointment are such that it remains settled property; this is also consistent with the HMRC affirmative reply to question 15 in the STEP/HMRC original IHT correspondence (APPENDIX 3) that an IIP appointed in these circumstances will be an IPDI; and

  (ii) property added by will to an existing settlement – whether a purely "pilot" settlement with token funds or a fully-funded and active trust – should be accepted as "settled by the will" for this purpose, by analogy with HMRC's reply to question 18 in the STEP/HMRC original IHT correspondence (APPENDIX 3).

(b) The trigger event occurs within two years after the deceased's death (IHTA 1984 s 144(1), (3)(c), (5)(c)(ii)).

(c) No estate IIP subsisted in the property concerned between the death and the trigger event (IHTA 1984 s 144(1), (1A), (3)(c), (5)(d), (e)). This is a highly condensed summary of the three separate provisions just mentioned, but is nevertheless accurate because—

  (i) for a death before 22 March 2006 any IIP, even in favour of a company, resulted in the settled property being comprised in the beneficiary's estate; and

  (ii) for a death on or after that date, although only two of the four possible types of IIP are referred to in those provisions, the other two types, a pre-Budget interest and a TSI, are logically impossible in respect of property which was settled by the will.

3.2.5 Where the core conditions are satisfied, IHTA 1984 s 144(1) provides that an event is a trigger event for backdating treatment if—

(a) it would occasion an IHT charge under any provision of IHTA 1984 Pt 3 Ch 3 other than IHTA 1984 s 64 (ten yearly charge) or IHTA 1984 s 79 (claw-back charges in respect of heritage property previously exempt from a ten-yearly charge); or

(b) it would have triggered such a charge but for exemption provided by IHTA 1984 s 75 or s 76, or Sch 4 para 16(1) (employee trusts, charities and heritage maintenance funds).

3.2.6 The most likely would-be IHT charge to be in point as a trigger event under this provision is the exit charge on property ceasing to be relevant property (or, though less likely, on a depreciatory transaction made by the trustees), under IHTA 1984 s 65(1). (For an unfortunate exception see paragraph **3.2.20** below.) Other charging provisions that could be relevant in theory – but for the most part only in theory unless the circumstances are most unusual, and as to (c) and (d) below see also paragraphs **3.2.14** ff below – would be the exit (or depreciatory transaction) charges under the regimes for—

(a) temporary charitable trusts, under IHTA 1984 s 70(3);

(b) A&M trusts, under IHTA 1984 s 71(3) – only now applicable to deaths before 22 March 2006, and therefore not capable of giving rise to a trigger event later than 21 March 2008;

(c) bereaved minor's trusts, under IHTA 1984 s 71B(1);

(d) age 18-to-25 trusts, under IHTA 1984 s 71E(1); or

(e) employee and newspaper trusts, under IHTA 1984 s 72(2).

3.2.7 The exception for ten-yearly charges, and claw-back charges after a ten-yearly charge, referred to in paragraph **3.2.5**, point (a), above, is at first sight puzzling: it may be wondered quite how property settled by the will could be subject to a ten-yearly charge – let alone a charge that presupposes a ten yearly charge in the past – in the first two years after the death on which it was settled. The probable explanation arises essentially from the possibility that the property was already settled property before the death and is resettled by will in exercise of a general power of appointment (see paragraph **3.2.4**, point (a)(i), above), read with IHTA 1984 s 81. The latter section treats property that has passed from one settlement to another as remaining in the same settlement, unless in the meantime a beneficiary has been absolutely entitled to it; so ten-yearly charges for the transferee settlement (in the present example, the settlement established by exercise of the general power of appointment) will arise by reference to the commencement date of the transferor settlement (the one under which the general power of appointment was conferred).

Alternative trigger event: the additional provisions post-FA 2006

3.2.8   Until the changes to the IHT regime for trusts in FA 2006, the conversion of a discretionary will trust to IIP or A&M form would operate as a trigger event under the primary conditions in IHTA 1984 s 144(1), because that conversion would result in the property in question leaving the relevant property regime. It rapidly became apparent that the conditions in IHTA 1984 s 144(1) could not give rise to a trigger event on an attempted conversion to IPDI format, because one requirement for this is that the beneficiary must have become beneficially entitled to the IIP on the testator's death (IHTA 1984 s 49A(3)). That could not be the case without the very backdating that was sought – an unbreakable circle of failure, under which the appointed IIP would remain within the relevant property regime and (if it was in favour of the testator's surviving spouse or civil partner) exemption under IHTA 1984 s 18 would remain unavailable. The government conceded that this was an unintended result, and by the time FA 2006 received Royal Assent IHTA 1984 s 144(3)–(6) had been added to cure this problem.

3.2.9   The added provisions – which, confusingly, appear separately for deaths before, and on or after, 22 March 2006, solely because the draftsman found drafting added provisions easier than drafting amendments to those already inserted, when the government was persuaded that its initial attempt to rectify the problem failed to deal properly with deaths before that date – lay down a cumbersome, but nevertheless effective, alternative trigger event for backdating the interests that apply after the event. (The backdating itself operates, in this case, under IHTA 1984 s 144(4), but the effect is identical to IHTA 1984 s 144(2), see paragraph **3.2.2** above.) Under these rules, an event will operate as a trigger event if it causes property to be held on trusts which would have been of one of the three types referred to in paragraph **3.2.10** below, on the assumptions—

(a)   that those trusts had in fact been established under the testator's will, and

(b)   (in cases where the testator in fact died before 22 March 2006) that the testator had instead died at the time of the event in question.

3.2.10   The types of trust which would have applied, on the assumptions in points (a) and where relevant (b) in paragraph **3.2.9** above, (and which will therefore secure this status on a backdated basis under this alternative trigger event, if appointed from a relevant property will trust within two years after the testator's death), are not limited to an IPDI. The legislation in fact specifies three types, namely—

(a)   an IPDI,

(b) a BMT , and

(c) an age 18-to-25 trust.

Why were BMTs and age 18-to-25 trusts included?

3.2.11 The inclusion of BMTs and age 18-to-25 trusts in this context may seem unnecessary; certainly, the drafting used to include them creates potential confusion, as explored in paragraphs **3.2.14** ff below. The relevant requirement for status as one or other of those types is simply that the trusts providing for the property to be held on the appropriate terms (for application of the BMT or age 18-to-25 trust regime as applicable) should have been "established under the will of a deceased parent" of the beneficiary in question (see IHTA 1984 ss 71A(2)(a), 71D(2)(a)). Unlike the IPDI requirement, that the beneficiary "became beneficially entitled to the interest in possession on the death", provisions that are appointed in exercise of a power of appointment conferred by the will can be argued to have been established "under" the will even, it is submitted, if the exercise (of a power in "the wider form" as discussed in *Bond v Pickford* [1983] STC 517) is such that the property passes out of the will trust into a separate settlement. Because property subject to a BMT or an age 18-to-25 trust is not relevant property (IHTA 1984 s 58(1)(b)), it follows that an appointment from a relevant property trust established by the beneficiary's parent's will, onto terms that satisfy IHTA 1984 s 71A or s 71D, will cause the property in question to cease to be relevant property, and will therefore in principle be capable of constituting a primary trigger event within IHTA 1984 s 144(1) (see paragraph **3.2.5** above).

3.2.12 This much is implicit in HMRC's confirmation, in their reply to question 19 in the STEP/HMRC original IHT correspondence (APPENDIX 3), that IHTA 1984 s 71A or s 71D would apply where trusts in appropriate terms are appointed under powers contained in the will – though they limited this confirmation to appointments in exercise of a special, as opposed to general, power of appointment. (A power of appointment in the "wider form" is, of course, still a special power and not a general power.) However, it is apparent from HMRC's subsequent response to Question 16 in the Law Society/HMRC IHT correspondence (APPENDIX 6) that, where the exercise (necessarily, of a "wider-form" power) results in property passing from one trust to another, they would see the resultant trusts as no longer being "established under" the will in question. (In fact their reply states that they consider the position is likely to be different [ie that the trusts at least might not be established under the testator's will] "if the trustees *have* wide powers, including the power to appoint property on new trusts" – emphasis added. That appears to be going far too far, and if the same view were to surface with reference to the PET example used in the HMRC reply to make that point then it should be strongly resisted. It is understood that this issue will be the subject of further correspondence with HMRC.)

3.2.13 If the basic proposition is accepted, however, there is at first sight at least some rationale for the express mention of IHTA 1984 ss 71A and 71D. However, remembering that property passing from one settlement to another is treated as remaining within the first settlement for all purposes of IHTA 1984 Pt 3, Ch 3 (see IHTA 1984 s 81), and that IHTA 1984 ss 71A and 71D are comprised within that Chapter, it is thought that a court would hold that trusts are "established under the will" for the purpose of those sections if IHTA 1984 s 81 treats the property as remaining within the settlement established by the will, even if as a matter of trust law (and for CGT purposes) it has passed into a separate settlement. At best, therefore, the express inclusion of IHTA 1984 ss 71A and 71D in the new IHTA 1984 s 144(3)–(6) is precautionary (albeit with one marginal benefit, see paragraph **3.2.23**, point (a), below); where the property remains in any case within the will trust, it results in an overlap between IHTA 1984 s 144(1)–(2) and s 144(3)–(6), and backdating will in virtually all cases be provided for by both IHTA 1984 s 144(2) and s 144(4).

Ambiguity arising from inclusion of BMTs and age 18-to-25 trusts

3.2.14 An overlap of that sort, albeit untidy conceptually, is of course not a serious problem. Less excusable is the ambiguity that arises from the particular drafting approach used to introduce it. It has been suggested that backdating treatment under IHTA 1984 s 144 could apply where the beneficiary of an age 18-to-25 trust established by his parent's will becomes entitled to an IIP within two years of the death – for example, where he was aged between 16 and 18 at the death and the Trustee Act 1925 s 31 results in the intermediate income becoming payable to him from age 18, even though capital is to vest at a later age up to 25. The somewhat peculiar result, if that were correct, would be that the beneficiary would, on survival to age 18, be treated for IHT purposes as though he had had an IPDI from the testator's death.

3.2.15 Certainly that reading of IHTA 1984 s 144(3), (5), (6) is not impossible semantically; but it is not the only possible interpretation, as it is equally realistic to read IHTA 1984 s 144(3)(i), (ii) (and the equivalent provisions for a pre-22 March 2006 death, in IHTA 1984 s 144(6)(a), (b)) as setting out a single group of results. On the latter reading, an event cannot "cause" property to be held on terms falling within that group if it was already held on terms that fell within that group from the death. On the other hand, the relevant core condition, summarised in paragraph **3.2.4**, point (c), above, is simply that no estate IIP has subsisted – no mention is made of a BMT or an age 18-to-25 trust as precluding an alternative trigger event.

3.2.16 The tax implications of the two competing interpretations differ significantly from each other, as shown in the following table—

	Backdating applies to create retrospective IPDI	*No backdating: trust remains an age 18-to-25 trust though now with IIP*
Beneficiary dies (over age 18, by definition) before becoming entitled to capital	• IHT charged under IHTA 1984 s 4 as part of his estate, maximum rate 40%	• IHT charged under IHTA 1984 s 71E, maximum rate 4·05% (in last 3 months before 25th birthday)
	• CGT base cost uplifted without chargeable gain	• no CGT uplift, but, if property vests absolutely in successor beneficiary, holdover relief under TCGA 1992 s 260 available subject to UK residence of successor beneficiary
Beneficiary survives to become entitled to capital by age 25	• No IHT charge: IHTA 1984 s 53(2); property comprised in his IHT estate both before and after absolute entitlement	• IHT charged under IHTA 1984 s 71E, maximum rate 4·2%
	• CGT charged on absolute entitlement – no holdover available unless property qualifies under TCGA 1992 s 165, Sch 7	• holdover relief available subject to beneficiary being UK resident

3.2.17   This issue was raised in Question 16 in the Law Society/HMRC IHT correspondence (**APPENDIX 6**), where it was pointed out that the "no backdating" interpretation seems more in keeping with the purpose of the amendments by which IHTA 1984 s 144(3), (4) were introduced, as set out in the Explanatory Notes issued with the amendments, which refer to appointments from discretionary trusts. Reference to that material is a legitimate aid to interpretation once an ambiguity has been established in the wording actually used. HMRC in their reply come down – like the authors but by different reasoning – in favour of the second interpretation described (paragraph **3.2.15** above, and the final column of the table in paragraph **3.2.16** above).

3.2.18   HMRC base this conclusion, somewhat shakily, on the proposition that "s 144 as a whole is predicated on the assumption that the property settled by a testator's will is relevant property – s 144(1)". That smacks of generalising from the majority situation to the extent of excluding the rarer possibilities; if it really were only relevant property that was in point, IHTA 1984 s 144(1)(a) could simply have referred to an event on which tax would have been chargeable under IHTA 1984 s 65. As it stands, however, s 144(1)(a) is wider in referring to "any provision ... of [IHTA 1984 Pt 3 Ch 3]" (see paragraph **3.2.5**, point (a), above), and there is no doubt in the authors' minds that occasions of charge under the various provisions listed in paragraph **3.2.6** above can in theory constitute trigger events within IHTA 1984 s 144(1). That is not inconsistent with the conclusion in paragraph **3.2.17** above, which is concerned with the "alternative" trigger event (see paragraphs **3.2.8** ff above); but (unlike the position of A&M trusts before FA 2006) it does leave a contrast with the consequences of an IIP arising within two years of death, where the trusts in the will are within IHTA 1984 s 71D. If capital is applied for the benefit of the beneficiary of the age 18-to-25 trust (or he becomes absolutely entitled to it) within two years after the testator's death, and the beneficiary is over age 18 at the time, this (apart from IHTA 1984 s 144) will be an occasion of charge under IHTA 1984 s 71E, as noted in paragraph **3.2.24** below, and will therefore constitute a "primary" trigger event (see paragraph **3.2.5** above). This therefore has the effect of backdating that absolute entitlement, for IHT purposes, to the testator's death under IHTA 1984 s 144(2), and in the process negating the s 71E charge on that application or entitlement; but from the CGT point of view, of course, that could in certain circumstances be a poisoned chalice, see paragraph **3.2.30**, point (a), below.

The Frankland case and later changes: When must trustees wait three months from death?

Position before 22 March 2006

3.2.19 If property leaves the relevant property regime within the first three months since the commencement of the settlement, the rate of IHT under the formula in IHTA 1984 s 68, if an exit charge were imposed under IHTA 1984 s 65, would be 0% in all cases, because no complete quarter years would have expired prior to the exit charge arising; whatever the effective rate calculated on the notional chargeable transfer detailed in IHTA 1984 s 68(4), the appropriate fraction of 0/40 would by definition always produce a nil-rate. Perhaps recognising this – but, as subsequent events showed, rather unhelpfully – the draftsman of FA 1982 provided, in what became on consolidation IHTA 1984 s 65(4), that the exit charge does not arise at all "if the event in question occurs in a quarter beginning with the day on which the settlement commenced or with a ten year anniversary".

3.2.20 This provision was recognised by some to set a serious trap for the trustees of a discretionary will wishing to appoint property in favour of the testator's surviving spouse, or in favour of a charity. The expectation in such a case would be to obtain the spouse exemption or charity exemption retrospectively to the death, in reliance on what became IHTA 1984 s 144. However, as was seen in paragraph **3.2.5** above, prior to the 2006 changes an event could only be a trigger event for backdating under IHTA 1984 s 144 if it would otherwise give rise to an IHT charge under a provision of IHTA 1984 Pt 3 Ch 3. Accordingly, IHTA 1984 s 65(4) meant that this condition could not be fulfilled if the settlement commenced on the testator's death and the appointment was made within the first three months after the death. This was confirmed by the Court of Appeal in *Frankland v IRC* [1997] STC 1450, where the trustees had not been warned of this trap before transferring the shares to an IIP trust for the deceased's widower. Noting that the amount of IHT at stake in that case was of the order of £2 million, Peter Gibson LJ remarked "It is not in dispute that if they had delayed that transfer for five days, that relief would have been available. *Hinc illae lacrimae*" [Hence these tears].

3.2.21   There is one, rare, situation in which under the pre-2006 law an appointment by trustees within three months after the death would not necessarily fall foul of this trap – or alternatively might fall foul of it, but at a different stage in the two year period from the deceased's death. This is the case envisaged in paragraph **3.2.7** above, where the property settled by the deceased on relevant property terms was in fact settled by the exercise by him, by will, of a general power of appointment conferred on him under a pre-existing settlement. Because of the operation of IHTA 1984 s 81, the ten year anniversary cycle in such a case is determined by the commencement date of the original settlement under which the general power of appointment subsisted. It is obviously possible that part or all of a three month period immediately after the commencement, or a ten year anniversary, of the original settlement could fall within the two year period from the deceased's death; an appointment within that three month period could not constitute a trigger event under IHTA 1984 s 144(1), whenever it fell in relation to the death itself.

How far did this change with the FA 2006 changes?

3.2.22   Because of the different working of the alternative trigger event in IHTA 1984 s 144(3)–(6), focusing purely on whether the new trusts would have qualified if actually contained in the will, and not on whether a tax charge would have arisen, an event can be a trigger event under this alternative at whatever time it occurs during the two years from the death.

3.2.23   Nevertheless, the *Frankland* trap still survives, despite attempts to persuade HMRC that it should be abolished in the process of amending IHTA 1984 s 144 during the passage of FA 2006 (which could have been done extremely easily, simply by adding a reference to IHTA 1984 s 65(4) to IHTA 1984 s 144(1)(b) (see paragraph **3.2.5** POINT (b) above). This is because there are certain types of restructuring of a relevant property will trust which still rely on the primary trigger event, rather than the alternative trigger event, for their backdating. Thus—

(a) conversion to the following can be made at any time, even within the first three months from death—

 (i) IPDI,
 (ii) BMT, or
 (iii) age 18-to-25 trust;

(b) conversion to the following remains subject to the *Frankland* trap and, if effected within the first three months (or as indicated in paragraph **3.2.13** above for the rare circumstances there described), will fail to achieve backdating—

 (i) absolute interest free of trust,
 (ii) charity, or
 (iii) DPI (which may look identical to an IPDI on paper – it will depend purely on whether the beneficiary is within the "disabled person" definition in IHTA 1984 s 89(4)–(6) at the date of the deceased's death – but may equally remain discretionary as to income, if distributions during the lifetime of the disabled person are restricted as mentioned in IHTA 1984 s 89(1)(b)).

3.2.24 For completeness, it can be noted that an absolute entitlement arising (over age 18) from an age 18-to-25 trust will technically secure backdating under IHTA 1984 s 144(2) even if it does occur within the 3-month window that, for relevant property, gives rise to the *Frankland* trap. There is no equivalent, within IHTA 1984 s 71E, of IHTA 1984 s 65(4) which creates the problem for relevant property trusts. However, this is essentially academic in the IHT context (contrast CGT, see paragraphs **3.2.18** above, **3.2.30** point (a) below), since there can by definition be no question of spouse or charity relief being at stake, and the rate of tax under IHTA 1984 s 71E will always be 0% within the first three months after the commencement of the settlement (ie with no complete quarters elapsed since then), whether it is s 71F or s 71G which applies to determine the rate of tax.

Pre-22 March 2006 deaths

Appointments onto IIP terms

3.2.25 Because the backdating effect under IHTA 1984 s 144 (in all its variants) is for the purposes of the IHTA 1984 as a whole, it follows that, if an IIP is appointed from the discretionary will of a testator who died before 22 March 2006, not only will it be an IPDI, but also the beneficiary will be treated as having become entitled to it before 22 March 2006. Therefore a subsequent switch to a different IIP (for the same or another beneficiary) would qualify as a TSI (with any transfer of value being a PET accordingly) provided the switch took place before 6 April 2008. This is of course the same result that would – as confirmed by HMRC in the STEP/HMRC original IHT correspondence (**APPENDIX** 3) – be available if an IIP were brought into effect by deed of variation under IHTA 1984 s 142 in respect of a death before 22 March 2006 (see paragraph **3.1.41**, point (c)(iv), above).

Appointments onto A&M terms

3.2.26   It will be noticed that – in contrast to what is possible using a variation under IHTA 1984 s 142 (see paragraph **3.1.41**, point (c)(v), above) – the conditions for backdating under s 144, in relation to a pre-22 March 2006 death, do not allow for the creation of a trust that would have met the pre-2006 conditions for an A&M trust. An appointment onto such terms (other than where in fact also satisfying the conditions for a BMT or an age 18-to-25 trust), even under the will of someone who died before 22 March 2006—

(a)   will not constitute an alternative trigger event, but

(b)   will also not constitute a primary trigger event, because (apart from IHTA 1984 s 144) it would not result in property leaving the relevant property regime. The result of IHTA 1984 s 71(1A) is that property cannot enter the A&M trust regime on or after 22 March 2006, and there is no exit charge for IHTA 1984 s 144(1)–(2) to disapply if the property remains relevant property.

3.2.27   If, despite that analysis, an appointment in such a case has in fact been made since 22 March 2006 on terms that would have constituted an A&M trust before that date, it does not follow that the appointment itself can be disregarded and a further attempt made to bring the trust within the backdating provisions. In terms of IHT law as such, that could certainly be done during the remainder of the two year period, since the property concerned remains relevant property. But the appointment will already have taken effect according to its terms, and may therefore have restricted or even removed altogether the trustees' freedom of action in respect of any further restructuring, unless and until set aside by the court pursuant to the Hastings-Bass line of cases (see Re Hastings-Bass (dec'd); Hastings and others v IRC [1974] STC 211 as reviewed most recently in Sieff v Fox [2005] EWHC 1312 (Ch), [2005] 3 All ER 693). There would now scarcely be time for that: by definition, for a pre-22 March 2006 death, the two year period allowed by IHTA 1984 s 144(5)(c)(ii) cannot last beyond 21 March 2008.

CGT treatment

3.2.28   There is no statutory provision in the CGT legislation which provides for backdating treatment of any sort in respect of appointments out of discretionary will trusts. Nevertheless, in certain circumstances, a degree of backdating treatment is given by HMRC published practice, see paragraphs **3.2.31**, **3.2.32** below.

Distribution of property already vested in trustees

3.2.29   If property has been vested in the trustees by the date of the appointment, it will carry the normal CGT consequences; no disposal if property remains within the same settlement, but a deemed disposal at market value, under TCGA 1992 s 71, if it results in a person (including the trustees of a separate settlement, even if composed of the same actual persons as the appointing trustees) becoming absolutely entitled as against the trustees.

3.2.30   The "normal CGT consequences" for an absolute entitlement under a discretionary trust (or certain other types of trust) of course generally include an entitlement to claim holdover relief under TCGA 1992 s 260 provided the beneficiary (or recipient trustees) is UK resident. However, relief under that section is unlikely to be available (though it may be under TCGA 1992 s 165, Sch 7, depending on the nature of the assets involved) in the case of an appointment, or other distribution, from a will trust within the two years following the testator's death. The reason is that holdover relief under TCGA 1992 s 260 depends on the absolute entitlement coinciding with an event that gives rise to a charge to IHT, or being excepted from such a charge by specified provisions relating to particular types of trust. However—

(a)   if backdated effect is given to the terms of the appointment for IHT purposes, by virtue of IHTA 1984 s 144, as described in the earlier part of this chapter, then for IHT purposes the resultant position is deemed to have applied since the death, and so there is no IHT event of the sort required to trigger the operation of TCGA 1992 s 260 (see paragraph **3.1.100**, point (a), above); this would apply as much to backdating from IHTA 1984 s 71D format to absolute entitlement as described in paragraphs **3.2.18**, **3.2.24** above as to an absolute entitlement arising from a fully discretionary will trust; and

(b)   even if backdated effect is not given, this would be either—

(i)   because the trust already conferred an IPDI or an IIP that is a DPI, and distributions from these sorts of trust do not carry an entitlement to claim holdover relief; or

(ii)   because the appointment or distribution was caught by the *Frankland* trap (see paragraphs **3.2.20**, **3.2.21** above), resulting from an IHT exit charge being expressly disapplied by IHTA 1984 s 65(4). As before, if there is no IHT exit charge, there can be no holdover under TCGA 1992 s 260.

Appointments where residuary estate not yet vested in trustees

3.2.31   HMRC have long since accepted that the trustees of a will can validly exercise a power of appointment over residue before property has been vested in them by the personal representatives – whether or not the same persons occupy both offices. There was at one time a concern that the trustees in those circumstances would be regarded as making an appointment in respect of the *chose in action* vested in them as being prospectively entitled to receive the residuary estate from the personal representatives (see paragraph **3.1.20** above) – which, in the case of an absolute appointment, would then make the appointee absolutely entitled to that *chose in action* as against the trustees and trigger a CGT charge, by reference to a potential nil base cost for the *chose in action* (see paragraph **3.1.91** above). Moreover, when the appointee came to receive a distribution from the personal representatives, that analysis would involve a chargeable disposal by the personal representatives of any assets distributed in kind, since the appointee would not take as legatee and therefore TCGA 1992 s 62(4) would be inapplicable.

3.2.32   However, it was seen in paragraph **3.1.100**, point (b), above that HMRC operate a slightly more favourable practice than might be thought in the case of a trust that is eliminated during the administration by means of a variation, as set out in CG32081–CG32100. Where a trust is eliminated during the administration by means of an exercise of a power of appointment, their published practice is more favourable still (and arguably not easy to reconcile logically with their approach to variations), amounting as noted in paragraph **3.2.28** above to a non-statutory backdating effect. The practice is stated in CG31432–CG31433 as follows (cross references omitted)—

> "Where the trustees exercise their powers of appointment before the assets have vested in them then the assets are still in the hands of the personal representatives at the time of exercise. Even though these may be the same individuals as the trustees they are different bodies of persons for CGT purposes. If, in these circumstances, the trustees make an appointment under the specific powers given to them in the will, then when the asset(s) vest they should be treated as passing direct to the appointee.
>
> The asset(s) appointed should be treated as never becoming subject to the trust. In effect, the appointment is read back into the will. It is treated as though the deceased had intended the assets concerned to pass directly to the legatee rather than into trust. The appointee then takes those asset(s) as legatee and therefore acquires the asset(s) at probate value by reason of TCGA 1992 s 62(4)."

Not just for discretionary wills

3.2.33   Where a testator contemplates that use might be made of the restructuring relief in IHTA 1984 s 144, the classic form of will he would be advised to use is a fully discretionary will (ie with a discretionary trust of income and provision for accumulation of income not distributed, as well as a wide power of appointment over capital). This would sometimes be drafted with a built-in two year time limit so that default interests vest automatically within that time to attract the relief if the trustees have not appointed otherwise, or sometimes on a discretionary basis for the full perpetuity period (see generally CHAPTER 2.5).

3.2.34 However, another type of will may well feature in this context over the years following the FA 2006 changes. If a will was drawn up before 22 March 2006 on a basis that was expected to qualify for A&M trust treatment, then on the testator's death on or after that date the trust in question will be in the relevant property regime, except to the extent that the beneficiary/ies—

(a) are children of the testator and are to take capital no later than age 25, with other terms of the trust sufficiently restrictive to satisfy the requirements for BMT or age 18-to-25 trust treatment, or

(b) have attained such an age by the testator's death that they take IIPs or absolute interests under the trusts of the will (read if necessary with the Trustee Act 1925 s 31).

3.2.35 Because the terms of a will trust of that description are now within the relevant property regime, it follows that a restructuring that is effected under any powers contained in the will, within two years after the testator's death, will qualify for backdating treatment under IHTA 1984 s 144 just as much as if the will had been drafted from the outset on a fully discretionary basis. What must be noted, of course, is that if the will was prepared with a view to attracting A&M trust status, the flexibility that it confers on the trustees is likely to be less than under a fully discretionary will; a similar point to the one made in a different context in paragraph **3.2.27** above. But so long as such a will does incorporate sufficient flexibility to allow a restructuring after the death onto terms that suit the testator's objectives, it is not necessarily vital for it to be revised by the testator prior to the time he would in any case need to revisit his testamentary planning. Restructuring under such a power is likely to be less costly, where minor or unborn potential beneficiaries are involved as there may often be in a would-be A&M trust, than having to resort to a deed of variation that would require the approval of the court on behalf of those beneficiaries.

Not just for written instruments

3.2.36 The discussion in this chapter has envisaged that any restructuring that takes advantage of backdating relief under IHTA 1984 s 144 is likely to involve the conscious exercise of a power arising under the will, in writing for evidential purposes and typically taking the form of a formal deed of appointment. However, a written instrument is not essential from the point of view of the application of backdating treatment. Although this may be seen as helpful in occasional cases, it can also operate as a trap, given that the backdating treatment is automatic, not optional, where the relevant circumstances are fulfilled (see paragraph **3.2.3** above). Consider the following possibilities—

3.2.37

Example 1

A discretionary will contains a power for the trustees to pay or apply capital to or for the benefit of members of the discretionary class, not merely a fully-fledged overriding power of appointment. Distributions, in cash or in kind, that are made under that power within the two year period will be given backdated effect under IHTA 1984 s 144, even if not decided on in writing, unless—

(a) they rank as distributions of income, which would not incur an exit charge under the IHT relevant property regime (IHTA 1984 s 65(5)(b)), or

(b) they are made within the first three months after the death and thus caught by the *Frankland* trap (see paragraph 3.2.20 above).

3.2.38 Whilst this may be thought helpful in saving the expense otherwise incurred in preparing a suitable deed of appointment, it does carry the danger that such a power might be used to make payments or other distributions to the testator's surviving spouse (especially of furniture, car and other personal possessions, if not left by a separate direct legacy of personal chattels) within the three months following death, as indeed happened in the *Frankland* case itself, and thus miss out on spouse exemption. It is thought that a will under which a deed of appointment is needed in order to make an effective distribution of capital is a safer drafting approach, to ensure that issues of that sort are considered in the process of preparing it. Where the surviving spouse requires an early release of financial or other resources, a loan from the executors will generally be preferable until after the three month period has expired. However, where a loan has been made with an eye to converting that to an outright entitlement by appointment in due course, it is advisable not to delay the appointment too long after any immediate tax reason for deferral has passed, because it would be too late if the borrower were to die before an appointment had been made: the loan would then fall to be repaid or returned by the borrower's estate. Just as with variations, before a question can arise as to the application of a statutory backdating provision to it, the validity of an appointment has to be assessed in the "real world" – in which a deceased person can no longer be a member of a class of eligible appointees.

3.2.39

Example 2

A NRB discretionary trust under a will contains a power to allow beneficiaries to occupy, or have the use of, property comprised in the trust fund. The matrimonial home had been owned by the testator alone, and the testator's surviving spouse remains in occupation after the death, without objection from the personal representatives or trustees. It has become clear that the net value of the estate is within the testator's available NRB, and there is sufficient liquidity to cover debts, administration expenses and any legacies.

3.2.40 Unless steps have been taken to establish some clear basis for the surviving spouse's continued occupation that negates this suggestion (such as implementation of a charge or debt scheme – see CHAPTER 2.7), there has to be some risk of an argument by HMRC – even now, despite Judge (PRs of Walden) v HMRC, [2005] STC (SCD) 863 – that the survivor occupies by virtue of an implicit exercise of the power to allow him or her to do so on a sufficiently permanent basis as to constitute a *de facto* revocable IIP. If that argument were to succeed then it would follow that an IIP arising in this way within two years after the death would be an IPDI – thereby negating to that extent the testator's careful NRB planning. Although there are some relatively helpful confirmations in this area by HMRC in reply to question 14 in the STEP/HMRC original IHT correspondence (APPENDIX 3), the final point under that question confirms that the circumstances that will or will not give rise to an IPDI in a property left on NRB discretionary trusts where the surviving spouse is already in occupation "will depend on the precise terms of the testator's will or any deed of appointment exercised [*sic*] by the trustees after the testator's death, and [HMRC] will continue to examine each case on its particular facts". In the authors' view, continued caution is needed on this front when dealing with an estate in that position.

Combination of appointment with variation or disclaimer

3.2.41 As was seen in paragraph **3.1.31** above, the decision in Russell and anor v IRC [1988] STC 195, [1988] 2 All ER 405 established that a second variation is incapable of attracting backdating treatment under IHTA 1984 s 142 if it relates to the same property as a variation already effected. However, even though it might be possible to construct arguments to the contrary on the basis of comments in that case and in *Marshall v Kerr* [1995] 1 AC 148, HMRC accept that backdating treatment under IHTA 1984 s 142 can be used, for the same property, in combination with that provided by IHTA 1984 s 144. IHTM35085 states—

"You may accept that—

— there can be a IHTA 1984 s 142(1) variation or disclaimer after a IHTA 1984 s 144 event, such as the exercise by trustees of powers of appointment and advancement, and

— a IHTA 1984 s 144 event after a IHTA 1984 s 142(1) variation has created a discretionary trust, or a disclaimer has caused property to be added to a discretionary trust set up under the will."

3.2.42 One particular situation in which this double backdating could prove helpful – so long as those concerned are satisfied that the trustees are not in the process exercising a fiduciary power for an improper purpose such as to render the exercise liable to attack by a disgruntled beneficiary – is to overcome unwanted, and perhaps unintended, restrictions on the scope of a trust established by the will, assuming that the trust does fall within the relevant property regime. Consider the following example—

3.2.43

Ken's will left his residuary estate on discretionary trusts for a class comprising his widow Jill and their issue. After Ken made this will, but some years before he died, he and Jill had taken in the two children of Ken's younger brother and sister-in-law Mike and Lorna, who had both just been killed in a road accident. Ken had been meaning to amend his will to add these extra beneficiaries, since he had been much better off than Mike, and Ken's own children were now getting well established themselves, but somehow he had never got round to doing this.

The trustees of Ken's will appoint the whole of his estate to Jill absolutely just as they, in their capacity as executors, are ready to apply for probate four months after Ken's death. This appointment attracts backdating under IHTA 1984 s 144(1)–(2). A little while later (long before the administration of the estate has been completed), Jill (an addition to making a similar settlement outside the variation rules) resettles £300,000 from Ken's estate on discretionary trusts for a class including Mike's children as well as her and Ken's issue. This resettlement is expressed to be by way of variation of Ken's will as affected by the appointment in Jill's favour, and attracts backdating to Ken's death under IHTA 1984 s 142(1).

Jill specifies in the resettlement that she, and any spouse or civil partner she might have at a later stage, are to be excluded from the class, so that the trust is not settlor-interested for income tax and CGT purposes. She considers that the balance of Ken's estate which she retains for herself is adequate for her own future requirements.

3.2.44 It should be noted that it is far from clear how HMRC would approach this sequence of events from the CGT point of view. It does not fit clearly within their practice as described in CG31432, CG31433 (see paragraph **3.2.32** above) or CG32000–CG32030 (see paragraphs **3.1.25**, point (e), and **3.1.97**, point (c), above). In terms of technical analysis there could be doubts about that practice in any event, see paragraphs **3.2.32**, **3.1.89** ff above. However, it is thought that HMRC would probably apply these two passages from the CGT Manual in combination, with the effect that—

(a) the appointment to Jill occasions no disposal for CGT but, in accordance with CG31433, Jill would be treated as the legatee;

(b) Jill's resettlement also occasions no disposal by her at that time, based on the HMRC analysis that it can operate as no more than an agreement, without consideration (and so apparently unenforceable), to assign the assets that vest from the estate (CG32001);

(c) when the executors release assets to the trustees of the resettlement, this is treated as vesting them in Jill as the legatee, so no chargeable gain accrues to the executors (CG32030); and

(d) to the extent that assets, not cash, are released to the trustees, Jill is treated as disposing of those assets to the trustees at that time (by virtue of the previously "ineffective" resettlement), for their market value at the time of vesting but with a base cost and acquisition date (as "legatee") inherited from the executors (CG32002) – so that the trustees' base cost and acquisition date is as at the date of vesting (CG32010).

3.2.45 The following scenario illustrates another possible use of the two sections together, this time in reverse order from the example just discussed.

> Anne's will left a discretionary trust of her NRB, with residue passing to her widower Bernard. A few months after her death, Bernard executed a deed of variation directing that Anne's minority shareholding in Services Limited, a sizeable unquoted trading company, should also pass into the discretionary trust, so as to take advantage of maximum BPR (paragraphs 3.1.184, 3.1.185 above).

> Towards the end of the two year period from Anne's death, Bernard dies unexpectedly, and the trustees agree with the family's view that there is no continued purpose for the discretionary trust. The question is whether to wind up the trust before or after the second anniversary of the death.

3.2.46 CGT considerations are not examined in detail in this example, but would also have to be considered carefully. The nature of Services Limited suggests that holdover relief under TCGA 1992 s 165 may be available even if there is no IHT event such as to attract similar relief under TCGA 1992 s 260; and to the extent that holdover relief does not apply, business taper relief may be available on those shares. (Much may depend on how soon it is likely that the recipients of the shares might look to dispose of them.) However, the IHT consequences of the two alternative courses are as follows—

(a) If distributions are left until after the second anniversary, the trustees will have completed two years of ownership (as a result of the backdating effect of Bernard's variation), so should qualify for 100% BPR on a distribution of the shares provided the company's business has not changed materially since Anne's death. However, this would leave a positive IHT charge on the original NRB fund itself, because the notional chargeable transfer used to work out the rate of tax for the IHT exit charge, under IHTA 1984 s 68(5), would be of an amount equal to the available NRB at Anne's death plus the *unrelieved* value, immediately after that death, of the Services Limited shares.

(b) By contrast, if the trust is brought to an end before the second anniversary of death – at least in relation to the assets other than the Services Limited shares, if CGT considerations suggest that it might be better to defer distribution of those shares until after the two year mark – the distribution would attract backdating to Anne's death by virtue of IHTA 1984 s 144(1)–(2), and the recipient beneficiaries would therefore be regarded for IHT purposes as having become absolutely entitled at that time. No additional IHT would be payable in respect of Anne's death estate.

Chapter 3.3

Other cases of special IHT treatment

3.3.1 In addition to the two sections discussed in CHAPTERS 3.1, 3.2, IHTA 1984 contains four further sections under the cross heading "changes in distribution of deceased's estate, etc" within IHTA 1984 Pt 5 Ch 5. One of these, IHTA 1984 s 147, relates to certain rights under Scots law and is outside the scope of this book; the other three are dealt with in this chapter (not in the order in which they appear in the Act), namely—

(a) IHTA 1984 s 146 relating to the I(PFD)A 1975 (see paragraphs **3.3.2** ff below);

(b) IHTA 1984 s 143 entitled "Compliance with testator's request" (see paragraphs **3.3.53** ff below); and

(c) IHTA 1984 s 145 dealing with the redemption of a life interest conferred by English intestacy law on a deceased's surviving spouse or civil partner (see paragraphs **3.3.61** ff below).

I(PFD)A 1975

The basics of the I(PFD)A 1975

What is the I(PFD)A 1975 about?

3.3.2 Unlike many legal systems, English succession law contains no fixed inheritance rights for any relative of a deceased person. To the extent that English law applies to the devolution of his estate – a sometimes complex subject outside the scope of this book – a testator has, nominally, complete freedom of testamentary disposition. However, if he fails to make reasonable provision for certain categories of person for whom the law considers that he ought to make such provision, the courts can intervene at the instance of a disappointed claimant and order reasonable provision to be made, in priority to the dispositions actually made by the will. Indeed, it is not just provision by the deceased's will which can be upset in this way; provision made by the law of intestacy can also be attacked as unreasonable in appropriate circumstances.

Who can claim and in what estates?

3.3.3 The first thing to be aware of is that a claim under the I(PFD)A 1975, is only possible if the deceased died domiciled in England and

Wales: I(PFD)A 1975 s 1(1). Unless the court allows a late claim, court proceedings must be commenced within six months after the first grant of probate or letters of administration in the deceased's estate – which could include a grant for a limited purpose such as *ad colligenda bona*. Those eligible to make such a claim can be summarised in outline as follows—

(a) a current or former spouse or civil partner of the deceased (but not one who has remarried or formed a subsequent civil partnership);

(b) a person who was living with the deceased, in the same household and as spouse or civil partner, for the whole of the last two years of the deceased's life;

(c) a child of the deceased;

(d) a person who was at any time in the deceased's lifetime treated as a child of the family in relation to any marriage or civil partnership to which the deceased was party;

(e) anyone who was being maintained wholly or partly by the deceased immediately before his death – meaning that the deceased, otherwise than for full valuable consideration, was making a substantial contribution in money or money's worth towards the reasonable needs of that person.

What orders can the court make?

3.3.4 A range of available financial orders which the court may make, if it finds that reasonable financial provision has not been made for the claimant, is set out in I(PFD)A 1975 s 2. These include—

(a) payment of a lump sum;

(b) transfer or settlement of property (including the acquisition of property for that purpose);

(c) periodical payments; or

(d) variation of certain descriptions of settlement made (by any person and whether in lifetime or by will) on the parties to any marriage or civil partnership to which the deceased was a party.

3.3.5 Reference should be made to books on the subject of the I(PFD)A 1975 for fuller details, and for the level of provision that the courts may judge to meet, or to fail to meet, the standard of reasonable provision, on the part of each category of claimant. Suffice it to say that for all categories other than the deceased's spouse or civil partner at the time of his death it is judged purely by what is reasonable for that person's maintenance in all the circumstances. For the spouse or civil partner, the test is wider and is what financial provision it would be reasonable for that person to receive, whether or not it is required for his or her maintenance.

Source of provision for those orders

3.3.6   The orders in categories (a) to (c) in paragraph **3.3.4** above can all be made in relation to the "net estate" of the deceased, as defined in I(PFD)A 1975 s 25(1). This is not confined to property passing under his will or intestacy (point (a) below); in particular, it extends to the following—

(a)   all property of which the deceased had power to dispose by will, other than in exercise of a special power of appointment (and so including property over which he had a testamentary general power of appointment, whether or not he exercised it), less

   (i)   his funeral, testamentary and administration expenses and
   (ii) his debts and liabilities including IHT payable out of his estate on his death;

(b)   any property over which he had a non-testamentary general power of appointment that was not exercised by him;

(c)   by virtue of I(PFD)A 1975 s 8, any property that was the subject of a nomination or a *donatio mortis causa* made by the deceased, less any IHT payable on that property as a result of the death and borne by the recipient;

(d)   if the court so orders under I(PFD)A 1975 s 9 (again on application made within the same six month time limit as applies for applications under I(PFD)A 1975 s 2, see paragraph **3.3.3** above), the deceased's severable share of any property of which he was a beneficial joint tenant immediately before his death, but only to the extent that the court thinks just in all the circumstances, taking into account *inter alia* any IHT payable in respect of that share;

(e)   any property which the court orders under I(PFD)A 1975 s 11 to be provided by a person who has already received it pursuant to a contract made by the deceased (otherwise than for full valuable consideration) and with the intention of defeating a possible application for financial provision under the I(PFD)A 1975 after his death (though in practice usually the personal representatives will not have made a distribution to such a person and any order under s 11 will simply direct them not to make such distribution, so that the property remains available within the core definition of net estate); and

(f)   any property which the court orders under I(PFD)A 1975 s 10 to be provided by a person ("the donee") to whom or for whose benefit the deceased made a disposition within six years before his death and with the intention of defeating a possible application for financial provision under the I(PFD)A 1975 after his death, unless that disposition was made for full valuable consideration. ("Disposition" for this purpose is widely defined in I(PFD)A 1975 s 10(7), and would inter alia include the exercise, otherwise than by will, of a general power of appointment (cf point (b) above); but it will not include the exercise of a special power of appointment, nor a nomination or donation *mortis causa*, nor any provision in a will.) Such an order under I(PFD)A 1975 s 10—

(i) is limited to the amount of the deceased's payment, or the value of the property disposed of by him, less in each case any IHT borne in respect of it by the donee; for this purpose the property is to be valued at the date of the deceased's death or, if earlier, the date on which it was disposed of by the donee; and

(ii) can be made not only at the instance of the person pursuing the underlying claim for financial provision, but also at the instance of the donee under a disposition attacked by that claimant under I(PFD)A 1975 s 10; the purpose of this, obviously, is to prevent the claimant targeting a particular lifetime disposition to the prejudice of that donee when there was another disposition in favour of a less "deserving" donee which could be more reasonably used as a source of funds for financial provision where the estate at death is insufficient on its own.

Universal backdating under the I(PFD)A 1975 itself

3.3.7 An order made under I(PFD)A 1975 s 2 has general backdated effect for all purposes – not merely those of tax – by virtue of I(PFD)A 1975 s 19(1), which provides as follows—

"Where an order is made under section 2 of this Act then for all purposes, including the purposes of the enactments relating to inheritance tax, the will or the law relating to intestacy, or both the will and the law relating to intestacy, as the case may be, shall have effect and be deemed to have had effect as from the deceased's death subject to the provisions of the order."

The scope of the general backdating effect

3.3.8 Where, and to the extent that, I(PFD)A 1975 s 19(1) applies, the backdated effect for tax purposes of an order under I(PFD)A 1975 s 2 is thus wider than in respect of deeds of variation and disclaimers, in that it extends not merely to IHT and the CGT death provisions (as to which, in the variation context, see paragraphs **3.1.41, 3.1.81** ff above; corresponding effects will apply here), but also for all other CGT purposes and for income tax purposes too; also, from the point of view of the claimant becoming treated as the legatee, for stamp duty and SDLT purposes. (So, for example, an order for transfer of a specific income-producing asset forming part of the estate will shift the income tax liability on the income generated from the original beneficiary to the successful claimant.) Furthermore, backdating in this context applies irrespective of how long has elapsed since the death when the order is made. However, the scope of I(PFD)A 1975 s 19(1) (see paragraph **3.3.7** above) is limited by its own wording in two ways—

(a) it is confined to orders made by the court under I(PFD)A 1975, s 2, and so will not extend to an out-of-court compromise: but see paragraphs **3.3.37** ff below; and

(b) it is confined to the altered effect of the will or the intestacy law, and so to property which did actually devolve under the will or intestacy, ie in the deceased's free estate: but see paragraphs **3.3.13** ff below. Accordingly it cannot of itself extend to—

  (i) property that is brought in to the deceased's "net estate" only as a result of I(PFD)A 1975 ss 8–11 (paragraph **3.3.6**, points (c) to (f), above): such property does not pass via the will or intestacy, whether before or after the order; or

  (ii) an order under I(PFD)A 1975 s 2(1)(f) or (g) varying a settlement (paragraph **3.3.4**, point (d), above).

3.3.9 The application of the statutory backdating under I(PFD)A 1975 s 19(1) is automatic – there is no need for any election or statement of intent, whether or not backdating increases the amount of IHT payable by the deceased's personal representatives. Given that they are necessary parties to the proceedings, they will certainly be aware of the risks in this connection, and will almost certainly have made no distributions once they were made aware of the claim; indeed, proper advice to the personal representatives in any estate where there might be any possibility of a claim under I(PFD)A 1975 will usually be to defer any distribution at all (at any rate, other than to the only potential claimant) until after the six month time limit for commencing proceedings (see paragraph **3.3.3** above).

The effect on requirements for status as an IPDI, BMT or age 18-to-25 trust

3.3.10 Because I(PFD)A 1975, s 19(1) deems the will or intestacy to have effect subject to the terms of the order, it follows that if such an order establishes a trust with an IIP in respect of property that passed under the will or intestacy, that IIP will be an IPDI: not only will the beneficiary be deemed to have been entitled to it from the deceased's death (condition 2 under IHTA 1984 s 49A(3)), but also the trust so established will be deemed to have been effected by the will or intestacy law – thus satisfying condition 1 under IHTA 1984 s 49A(2).

3.3.11 If an order under I(PFD)A 1975 s 2 establishes a trust for the benefit of someone to whom the deceased was a "parent" (within the extended meaning given to that word by IHTA 1984 s 71H), the terms of which meet the conditions for a BMT or an age 18-to-25 trust (not limited to providing for capital entitlement by age 18 or 25), then where it is the deceased's will that is being modified it will be clear, as a result of the backdating effect of I(PFD)A 1975 s 19(1), that that trust is to be treated as meeting the remaining condition for the status in question: namely that the trust should have been "established under the will" of the deceased parent as referred to in IHTA 1984 s 71A(2)(a) or s 71D(2)(a) as the case may be.

3.3.12 However, given the way that IHTA 1984 s 71A is drafted in relation to an intestacy – not looking at the terms of the trust and its origin, but requiring that the property "is held on statutory trusts for the benefit of [the] bereaved minor under [AEA 1925 ss 46, 47(1)]", it is less clear that backdating under I(PFD)A 1975 s 19(1) can bring about BMT status if it is purely the devolution of the estate on the deceased's intestacy that failed to make reasonable provision for the minor and is therefore affected by a financial provision order under I(PFD)A 1975 s 2. The circumstances where this might apply are likely to be rare, given that the children of the deceased take second place only to the surviving spouse or civil partner under the law of intestacy; but it is possible, at least in theory, to conceive of a case where a child (perhaps a disabled child) for whom the deceased had parental responsibility, and for whom the deceased had been providing financially in the years leading up to his death, might claim provision which overrides the statutory legacy, and/or the life interest in residue, given to the deceased's surviving spouse or civil partner by the intestacy law. If in such a case the court orders a trust for the minor on terms which, if in the deceased's will, would constitute a BMT – or for that matter an age 18-to-25 trust – there does seem to be technical scope for that trust to miss out on that status because the trust does not take effect under AEA 1925 ss 46, 47(1) as such, nor did the deceased leave a will under which (as modified by the order) it was established. Almost certainly this is not a point that HMRC would seek to take, as it would patently have no merit whatever in policy terms; but if the circumstances are likely to arise it would be prudent to seek specific confirmation in relation to the facts of the particular case, before the order is finalised.

Further limited backdating provisions for orders under I(PFD)A 1975

Orders under I(PFD)A 1975 s 2

IHT

3.3.13 The general backdating rule in I(PFD)A 1975 s 19(1) in relation to orders of the court under I(PFD)A 1975 s 2 is duplicated, and extended, for IHT purposes only by IHTA 1984 s 146(1), which provides as follows—

> "Where an order is made under [I(PFD)A 1975 s 2] in relation to any property forming part of the net estate of a deceased person, then, without prejudice to [I(PFD)A 1975 s 19(1)], the property shall for the purposes of this Act be treated as if it had on his death devolved subject to the provisions of the order".

3.3.14 This provision – which is again unlimited in terms of the period elapsed since the death – goes beyond the "will and intestacy" limitation of I(PFD)A 1975 s 19(1) (see paragraph **3.3.8**, point (b), above), in extending to an order made in respect of any of the deceased's "net estate". That expression is not defined for the purpose of IHTA 1984 s 146; but the context pins it squarely to the net estate in respect of which an order under I(PFD)A 1975 s 2 can be made, namely as defined in I(PFD)A 1975 s 25(1) – see paragraph **3.3.6** above. This includes, therefore, not only nominated property and joint property (I(PFD)A 1975 ss 8(1), 9, see paragraph **3.3.6**, points (c) and (d), above), which would be part of the deceased's death estate for IHT purposes in any case, but also—

(a) *donationes mortis causa* (I(PFD)A 1975 s 8(2), see paragraph **3.3.6**, point (c), above). IHTM14900 sees these as part of the death estate anyway, analysing them as held in trust for the transferor (confusingly printed as the transferee) until made absolute by the death; but that analysis entails the gift being in trust for persons in succession, and so a settlement (albeit a very short lived one), and clearly depends on the transferor's interest being an estate IIP. This would be the case if the transferor were a disabled person at the time; but otherwise, since FA 2006, the HMRC analysis would lead to the *donatio* taking effect as a gift to a relevant property trust and thus a chargeable lifetime transfer which is therefore not within the death estate. The latter conclusion – more common, obviously, than a DPI for the transferor – could lead to different consequences in relation to accountability for IHT; and

(b) property retrieved from a lifetime disposition for the purpose of a financial provision order, by means of an order under I(PFD)A 1975 s 10.

3.3.15 However, even though an order varying a settlement (paragraph **3.3.4**, point (d), above) is made under I(PFD)A 1975 s 2 (in particular, I(PFD)A 1975 s 2(1)(f) or (g)), IHTA 1984 s 146(1) clearly cannot provide backdated effect for such an order, since the settled property of such a settlement is not part of the deceased's "net estate" as defined (see paragraph **3.3.6** above).

3.3.16 In contrast to the terms in which I(PFD)A 1975 s 19(1) is couched – that the will or intestacy are deemed to have had effect as from the deceased's death subject to the provisions of the order – IHTA 1984 s 146 simply treats property as having devolved on the death subject to the provisions of the order. It does not treat it as though it had devolved under the will of the deceased. It would therefore appear that, insofar as an order under I(PFD)A 1975 s 2 affects property that is comprised in the net estate of the deceased that did not in fact devolve originally under his will or intestacy – so that backdating takes effect under IHTA 1984 s 146(1) and not under I(PFD)A 1975 s 19(1) – there is no obvious basis on which the backdating could extend so far as to confer IPDI or BMT or age 18-to-25 trust status on any resultant settlement, even if its terms otherwise fitted the mould for the relevant status (see paragraphs **3.3.10** ff above). This is effectively the same issue as was highlighted, for variations that relate to property not forming part of the deceased's free estate as such, in paragraph **3.1.42** above; and, in the same way as in that context, HMRC take the view that the conditions for that status are not met unless the property affected was in fact part of the deceased's free estate on death: see their response to Question 2 in the Law Society/HMRC IHT correspondence (**APPENDIX 6**).

CGT

3.3.17   Nominated property and the deceased's severable share of joint property are within the CGT concept of property of which the deceased was competent to dispose (TCGA 1992 s 62(1), see paragraphs **3.1.77**, **3.1.78** above). They therefore benefit from the tax-free uplift in base cost under TCGA 1992 s 62(1). Similarly, although a *donatio mortis causa* is not within that definition, a corresponding effect is achieved by TCGA 1992 s 62(5) which provides that "notwithstanding [TCGA 1992 s 17(1) – the market value rule] no chargeable gain shall accrue to any person on his making a disposal by way of *donatio mortis causa*". However, because I(PFD)A 1975 s 19(1) extends only to property dealt with by the will or the law of intestacy, it will not protect from the normal consequences of a CGT disposal – at market value – when property within one of those categories is transferred pursuant to an order of the court under I(PFD)A 1975 s 2. (The considerations are the same as on the transfer of an asset by the original donee ordered to provide that asset under I(PFD)A 1975 s 10, see paragraphs **3.3.21** ff below.)

Orders under I(PFD)A 1975 s 10

3.3.18   By definition any lifetime disposition which is the occasion for an order under I(PFD)A 1975 s 10 must have been made within six years before the death (see paragraph **3.3.6**, point (f), above); so, unless it was exempt in all circumstances (eg through the annual exemption or the normal income expenditure exemption in IHTA 1984 s 19 or s 22 respectively), it will have been a chargeable transfer for IHT purposes, either from the outset or as a result of the failure of a PET. It may also (depending on the property involved) have constituted a chargeable disposal for CGT purposes.

The original donee

IHT

3.3.19   Save perhaps in collusive circumstances, it stands to reason that a donee (or purchaser at an undervalue) who is ordered under I(PFD)A

1975 s 10 to provide property for the purpose of a financial provision order in favour of another claimant will do so against his will. Thus any disposition he makes in order to comply with the order is at arm's length and without gratuitous intent, so protected from IHT consequences by IHTA 1984 s 10. No additional provision in that regard is needed in the part of IHTA 1984 dealing with changes to the distribution of the deceased's estate.

3.3.20 If the transfer to the donee was a chargeable transfer and the donee has already borne IHT on it by the time the order under I(PFD)A 1975 s 10 is made, the amount so borne is excluded from the order (see paragraph **3.3.6**, point (f)(i), above), so he is not left out of pocket. There can nevertheless be complications if he paid the tax out of his own pocket and the application is for, essentially, the provision of a gifted asset *in specie*.

CGT

3.3.21 If the property to be provided by the donee is in cash form, no CGT consequence should ensue. If on the other hand it involves the transfer of an asset *in specie*, there is nothing to prevent that transfer from constituting a disposal by him for CGT purposes. In general the order will be for payment or transfer to the deceased's personal representatives, who (in their collective capacity as such, cf TCGA 1992 s 62(3)) cannot be connected persons with the donee providing the property: the connected persons definition in TCGA 1992 s 286 makes no mention of personal representatives, and they can only be connected with another person in connection with the control of a company under TCGA 1992 s 286(6), (7). Although the donee's disposal is thus unlikely to be to a connected person, and is made very much at arm's length (in the absence of collusion), it seems arguable nevertheless that it is not made by way of a "bargain" at arm's length – in which case it would take place at market value under TCGA 1992 s 17(1)(a), with the potential to give rise to a chargeable gain for the original donee. (At least, in the absence of connected persons implications, any loss computed on this disposal would not be blocked under TCGA 1992 s 18(3).) It is to be hoped that HMRC would not seek to place excessive weight on the "bargain" element of that phrase in the present context.

3.3.22 The position in this respect appears less than satisfactory (and see further paragraphs **3.3.26, 3.3.27** below), and it is vital that the court be apprised of the potential consequences on the donee's behalf before an order is made, so that those consequences can be taken into account as "other circumstances of the case" under I(PFD)A 1975 s 10(6) when the court is deciding what order to make. The seven short paragraphs in the CGT Manual relating to I(PFD)A 1975 deal only with the basic orders under I(PFD)A 1975 s 2 and with compromises by way of Tomlin order; they give no coverage to orders retrieving property from a lifetime disposition, nor (unsurprisingly) is this dealt with in the Help Sheet IR 282 ("Death, personal representatives and legatees") to the capital gains pages of the self-assessment tax return.

3.3.23 In this regard the Court of Appeal decision in *Dixit v Dixit* (1988, unreported; see Sidney Ross, *Inheritance Act Claims—Law and Practice*, A4–011, Sweet & Maxwell, December 2005) should be borne in mind. In slightly complex circumstances, the judge at first instance had made an order which in effect switched beneficial interests between two trusts, granting liberty to apply to any party who might be assessed to CGT arising out of the terms of his order. It emerged that the CGT effect of the order was to give rise to a chargeable gain on the part of the trustees of one of the trusts. The Court of Appeal decided that an order made without adverting to true tax implications cannot have been made in a proper exercise of the court's discretion; they were therefore able to make a substitute order without needing to determine whether the actual order made at first instance was within the jurisdiction given by I(PFD)A 1975.

The deceased and his estate

IHT

3.3.24 The remaining IHT consequences where a chargeable transfer is retrieved for the estate under I(PFD)A 1975 s 10 comprise the unscrambling of the chargeable transfer under IHTA 1984 s 146(2) (or its proportional unscrambling under IHTA 1984 s 146(3), if the donee is not ordered to provide the maximum amount authorised by I(PFD)A 1975 s 10), and the adding back to the deceased's death estate of the property provided by the donee—

(a) any tax payable on the lifetime chargeable transfer is discharged (and, if any has already been paid, it is refundable by HMRC to the deceased's personal representatives even if it was actually paid by someone else); tax so repaid is then included both in the deceased's death estate for IHT purposes and in the deceased's net estate for the purposes of the I(PFD)A 1975: IHTA 1984 s 146(5);

(b) the chargeable transfer is removed from the lifetime cumulation relevant to determine the rate of IHT payable on the chargeable transfer made on the deceased's death; and

(c) the money or property which the donee was required to provide is also included in the deceased's death estate for IHT purposes.

3.3.25 Both the property provided by the donee, and any IHT repayable by HMRC to the personal representatives, are thus part of the deceased's net estate out of which a financial provision order can be made under I(PFD)A 1975 s 2 (see I(PFD)A 1975 s 25(1) and paragraph **3.3.6**, point (f), above, and IHTA 1984 s 146(5) and paragraph **3.3.24**, point (a), above). As such, the order that is made under I(PFD)A 1975 s 2 carries backdated IHT consequences by virtue of IHTA 1984 s 146(1), which will lead to the reworking of exemptions in the estate according to the revised destination of the property. As noted at paragraph **3.3.16** above, IHTA 1984 s 146 appears not to extend to giving IPDI status to an IIP (under a trust established pursuant to such an order), such as to attract spouse relief in appropriate circumstances. It seems doubtful, too, whether I(PFD)A 1975 s 19(1) could achieve that result, either, since if it could operate on property that did not of itself pass under the will or intestacy (which obviously property brought in by the donee does not), IHTA 1984 s 146(1) would have been otiose.

CGT

3.3.26 The CGT implications of any disposal made by the deceased to the donee, on the lifetime transaction which is being unscrambled, are unaffected by the making of an order under I(PFD)A 1975 s 10. Insofar as the donee disposes of an asset to the deceased's personal representatives (see paragraph **3.3.21** above), the same considerations that create the potential for the donee to be faced with realising a chargeable gain on that disposal appear to leave the personal representatives with the prospect of a nil base cost for the asset in question, by reference to TCGA 1992 s 17(2)(b).

3.3.27 If the order made under I(PFD)A 1975 s 2 is for the personal representatives to transfer to the claimant (or to trustees for the claimant) the asset retrieved from the original donee, the other CGT question that arises is the status of that transfer when made. For the same reason as in paragraph **3.3.25** above – that the property provided by the original donee is not affected by the will or intestacy, merely by the orders under I(PFD)A 1975 ss 10, 2 – the general backdating effect of I(PFD)A 1975 s 19(1) does not seem to apply; so the claimant would not take as legatee, and the personal representatives would therefore realise a chargeable gain (seemingly from their nil base cost as in paragraph **3.3.26** above) when transferring the asset to the claimant pursuant to the order. Even if the successful claimant did take as legatee, the nil base cost would clearly be an issue for him too.

An inheritance tax illustration

3.3.28 An example may help illustrate the IHT effects described in paragraphs **3.3.19**, **3.3.20**, **3.3.24** above. CGT complications are not covered.

Example

Suppose that Ronnie was estranged from his wife Sarah, and in March 2004 secretly gave £505,000 to the trustees of a newly formed discretionary trust, intending to put those funds beyond Sarah's reach. Ronnie had made no previous chargeable transfers. The terms of his gift required that the trustees bear any IHT on the gift out of the fund settled; as this was a chargeable transfer, lifetime IHT of £50,000 was paid by the trustees (20% × (£505,000 −£255,000)).

Ronnie died in June 2006 leaving his estate worth £200,000, net of debts, to a recently acquired girlfriend Tamsin, who is a wealthy woman in her own right. Ronnie's executors obtained probate in February 2007, paying IHT of £80,000 (40% × £200,000, the NRB having been fully exhausted by the gift into trust), and soon afterwards Sarah issued proceedings claiming reasonable provision out of his estate under I(PFD)A 1975. On being provided by the executors with a copy of the IHT return submitted in respect of the estate, which discloses the March 2004 gift, she applied in May 2007 for an order under I(PFD)A 1975 s 10 to gain access to the trust fund in support of her primary claim.

Meanwhile, the additional IHT on the gift to the trustees, resulting from his death within seven years, had fallen due at the end of January 2007, and the trustees had paid the additional £38,000 accordingly (calculated as (40% × (£505,000 −£285,000)) −£50,000: note the impact of the higher NRB at the date of death, by virtue of IHTA 1984 Sch 2 para 2). The trustees had invested the net gift of £455,000 successfully, and the trust fund at Ronnie's death was worth £538,000, so after paying the additional IHT the remaining fund is £500,000.

3.3.29   The maximum order that can be made in the circumstances against the trustees under I(PFD)A 1975 s 10 is £412,000 (£500,000 originally settled in cash, less total IHT paid by the trustees of £88,000; unlike the position where the lifetime disposition was something other than a payment of money, the increase in value between the date of the gift and the date of death is irrelevant): see I(PFD)A 1975 s 10(3). The court decides that it is right to make the maximum order; and on considering all the circumstances orders that the whole of Ronnie's estate, including the money thus recovered from the trust fund, should be transferred to Sarah.

The net effect of these adjustments is as set out in the following table.

	Ronnie's Executors	Discretionary Trustees	HMRC
	£	£	£
At Ronnie's death	200,000	538,000	*50,000
Payment of IHT following death	−80,000	−38,000	118,000
	120,000	500,000	168,000

	Ronnie's Executors £	Discretionary Trustees £	HMRC £
Maximum order under I(PFD)A 1975 s 10	412,000	– 412,000	
Repayment of trustees' IHT to executors (IHTA 1984 s 146(2)(a)(i))	88,000	n/a	–88,000
	620,000	88,000	80,000
Repayment of executors' IHT: whole estate (£200,000 + £412,000 + £88,000) now spouse exempt: I(PFD)A 1975 s 19(1) and IHTA 1984 s 146(1)	80,000	n/a	–80,000
	700,000	88,000	0

* from 2004 IHT payment

Allowances for IHT in applying I(PFD)A 1975 s 8 or s 9

3.3.30   As was seen above (paragraph **3.3.6**, points (c) and (d), above)—

— nominated property and *donationes mortis causa* that come into the deceased's net estate for I(PFD)A 1975 purposes by virtue of I(PFD)A 1975 s 8 are brought in net of any IHT borne by the recipient; and

— correspondingly, though more flexibly because the circumstances could be more complex, if the deceased's severable share of joint property is ordered to be brought in under I(PFD)A 1975 s 9, the court in making that order is to have regard to any IHT payable in respect of that severable share.

It is provided by IHTA 1984 s 146(4) (to avoid circularity) that the backdating provided for by I(PFD)A 1975 s 19(1) and the other provisions of IHTA 1984 s 146 is not to affect the amount of the IHT deduction under I(PFD)A 1975 s 8 or the amount of the IHT to be taken into account under I(PFD)A 1975 s 9(2). Further – and in parallel with I(PFD)A 1975 s 10 as already examined (see paragraph **3.3.24**, point (a), above) – IHTA 1984 s 146(4) also provides that where a person is ordered to make a payment, or to transfer property, by reason of his holding property that comes into the net estate in one of these ways, any repayment of the tax for which allowance was made as above is to be made to the personal representatives and not to the person who paid or bore it.

Orders varying a settlement under I(PFD)A 1975 s 2(1)(f), (g)

3.3.31   It has already been seen (see paragraph 3.3.8, point (b)(ii) and paragraph 3.3.15 above) that an order varying a nuptial settlement (or the equivalent for civil partnership) does not affect the deceased's will or intestacy, or relate to his "net estate", and so is not covered by the backdating provisions of I(PFD)A 1975 s 19(1) or IHTA 1984 s 146(1), even though it is made under I(PFD)A 1975 s 2.

IHT

3.3.32   Relief from the IHT consequences that might otherwise flow from such an order is provided not by way of backdating its effects to the deceased's death; indeed, backdating as such would not always be a suitable relief given the variety of possible circumstances within such a settlement. Although it might be thought that this sometimes would be suitable in cases where the deceased had been the life tenant of the settlement, to provide a backdating relief as such in these circumstances would be inconsistent with the policy that excludes from the more general relief for variations settled property in which the deceased had an estate IIP at his death, see paragraph 3.1.30, point (c), above.

3.3.33   Instead, tax charges under the IHT settled property regime, to which the coming into force, or implementation, of the order might give rise, are cancelled by IHTA 1984 s 146(6). (This relief is significantly different from backdating – less favourable in some circumstances, more so in others – as it will not, for example, retrospectively secure (or lose) spouse exemption on the death if the deceased had an estate IIP, nor will it backdate the ownership of a successful claimant for the purpose of qualifying periods of ownership for APR or BPR.) Specifically, IHTA 1984 s 146(6) is in two parts—

(a) the first part deals with charges under the non-estate-IIP provisions in IHTA 1984 Pt 3 Ch 3 (other than IHTA 1984 s 79 relating to clawback charges where heritage exemption from a ten yearly charge has previously been claimed), preventing a charge on "anything which is done in compliance with an order under [I(PFD)A 1975] or occurs on the coming into force of such an order"; and

(b) the second part prevents a deemed transfer of value (on termination of an estate IIP) under IHTA 1984 s 52(1) on the coming into force of "an order under [I(PFD)A 1975] [which] provides for property to be settled or for the variation of a settlement".

3.3.34 The draftsman of IHTA 1984 s 146(6) clearly contemplated, in the second part of that provision, that where an order is made "for the settlement for the benefit of the applicant" of property comprised in the deceased's net estate, under I(PFD)A 1975 s 2(1)(d) (paragraph **3.3.4**, point (b), above), the settlement would take effect automatically on the coming into force of the order, without the need for any person to take further steps in compliance with the order; there is a clear contrast with the first part of the provision (paragraph **3.3.33**, point (a), above), which protects things done in compliance with an order as well as the coming into force of the order itself. On the other hand, since an order for settlement can only be made in respect of property comprised in the deceased's net estate, and which thus must have devolved on his death in some way (even if just as a result of being provided by the donee of a lifetime disposition under I(PFD)A 1975 s 10), its effect will be backdated by virtue of IHTA 1984 s 146(1) anyway, if not by I(PFD)A 1975 s 19(1), thus making it unnecessary to make further provision dealing with steps taken to comply with the order.

3.3.35 It should of course be appreciated that this relief in IHTA 1984 s 146(6) relates only to charges that would arise on the coming into force, or compliance with, the order. On any later changes of beneficial interest, or other events, within the settlement, or its termination, the usual IHT rules will apply at the time.

CGT

3.3.36 On an order for the variation of a settlement coming into force, there would ordinarily be no disposal for CGT purposes unless the result of the order was to make some person absolutely entitled as against the trustees (TCGA 1992 s 71). If this does occur, there is nothing to prevent the application of the usual CGT rules in relation to that absolute entitlement – be it on the part of an individual or of the trustees of a separate settlement.

Compromise of I(PFD)A 1975 claims

Tomlin orders

3.3.37 A common method of finalising a compromise of pending court proceedings is a "Tomlin order", whereby the terms of the compromise agreed between the parties are set out in a Schedule to an order of the court, the only operative part of the order being to stay or dismiss the proceedings. If the parties are all of full capacity, the court does not need to consider the adequacy of the terms of the compromise; to the extent that any party is not of full capacity, or is representing unborn persons, the court's approval of the terms is necessary.

3.3.38 Without special statutory treatment, a compromise reached by way of a Tomlin order would attract no different treatment from a compromise agreement reached out of court, or for that matter from a deed of variation not containing (or not eligible to contain) an IHT statement of intent as contemplated by IHTA 1984 s 142 (paragraphs **3.1.51**, point (d), and **3.1.63** ff above).

IHT

3.3.39 Backdated effect, for IHT purposes only, is given to a compromise reached by a Tomlin order by IHTA 1984 s 146(8), reproduced below, subject to an important limitation identified by the words italicised—

> "Where an order is made staying or dismissing proceedings under the [I(PFD)A 1975] on terms set out in or scheduled to the order, this section shall have effect as if any of those terms *which could have been included in an order under [I(PFD)A 1975 s 2 or s 10]* were provisions of such an order." [emphasis added]

3.3.40 With the exception of terms that go beyond that limitation, this therefore brings into play IHTA 1984 s 146(1) (see paragraphs **3.3.13** ff above) – again without limit as to the time elapsed since the death – and IHTA 1984 s 146(2), (3) (paragraphs **3.3.24**, **3.3.25** above);but only, of course, so far as those provisions extend in themselves, see paragraphs **3.3.15**, **3.3.16** above.

3.3.41 Insofar as any term of the compromise does provide for something that was not within the jurisdiction of the court to order under I(PFD)A 1975 s 2 or s 10, the question arises whether those terms can attract variation treatment under IHTA 1984 s 142 provided they include an IHT statement of intent and the Tomlin order is made within two years after the death. On the basis of the HMRC practice in connection with CGT (see paragraph **3.3.42** below), it would seem in principle that the terms scheduled to a Tomlin order will be accepted as an instrument in writing "made" by the parties, even though it would not generally be signed by them. The issue will essentially be whether anything contained in the terms will constitute extraneous consideration; it is thought that there is no reason why changes to the devolution of the estate that are already backdated under IHTA 1984 s 146(8) should then be seen as extraneous for this purpose. Care would however be needed over matters such as costs of the proceedings (see paragraph **3.1.58** above.)

CGT

3.3.42 No provision is made in the CGT legislation, let alone in the I(PFD)A 1975 itself, for backdating the effect of a compromise reached by way of a Tomlin order. However, HMRC accept in CG31821 that the terms scheduled to such an order, if made within two years after the death, are capable of attracting CGT treatment as a variation, provided the terms actually include a CGT statement of intent (as to which see paragraph **3.1.76**, point (a)(iv), above). (The version of this passage in the CGT Manual that was current at the time of writing had not been updated to reflect the change from election to statement of intent made by FA 2002 s 52, but the principle remains the same; however there is a considerable practical difference in the requirement that the statement of intent must be actually embodied in the instrument, which puts the onus on the litigators handling a compromise to get the wording of the Tomlin order right rather than relying on tax colleagues to deal with election and notification after the event.) As with any variation, if backdated treatment is required, care must be taken to avoid terms which could be taken as involving consideration that does not consist of the variation of some other disposition taking effect on the death. At least HMRC are willing to accept (in the IHT context, but the principle must be the same for the equivalent CGT provision) that giving up a claim under I(PFD)A 1975 is not "extraneous" consideration in this context (see IHTM35100, commented on in paragraphs **3.1.61**, **3.1.62** above).

3.3.43 Variation treatment as above is obviously not possible if the compromise is reached outside the two year period from death. In such a case – or if one of the other bars to CGT variation treatment (extraneous consideration or no statement of intent) exists – the compromise will be treated for CGT in the same way as a variation that fails to achieve backdating under TCGA 1992 s 62(6). As discussed in paragraphs **3.1.81–3.1.101** above, HMRC's practice seems to be a good deal less unfavourable than a technical analysis of the position would suggest; but even then it is not as helpful as backdating treatment.

Compromise by other means while proceedings are pending

3.3.44 If the absence of backdating treatment for the purpose of the CGT death provisions is going to be a problem – or, for that matter, in the SDLT context, where a property is being transferred that is subject to outstanding indebtedness – then the parties would do well (so long as the terms of the compromise are indeed within the court's jurisdiction) to seek to have the compromise given effect by means of an order made by the court itself under I(PFD)A 1975 s 2, rather than by means of a Tomlin order. At least where the order relates to the deceased's free estate passing under his will or intestacy, that will then trigger the general backdating effect of I(PFD)A 1975 s 19(1), which applies for CGT and SDLT as much as for other purposes, and which has no two year time limit from death (see paragraphs **3.3.7** ff above).

Consent order

3.3.45   Where that is required, the approach available generally would be to ask the court to make a consent order. This differs from a Tomlin order in that the judge will need to consider the terms of the compromise as such, decide that they represent reasonable provision for the claimant, and ensure that he has jurisdiction to make all the orders sought. Where the terms of compromise involve some specific tax planning feature, the judge will doubtless have in mind the observations of Morritt LJ in the Court of Appeal decision in *Goodchild v Goodchild* [1997] 1 WLR 1216 at 1231, with which both other judges concurred. The judge in that case at first instance had ordered provision for the claimant (where residue had passed to the surviving spouse) on a basis that the sum in question was to be regarded as held in trust to pay the income to the surviving spouse for life or until about two weeks after the date of the order, whichever was shorter, and then for the claimant; the order was made well after the two year period since the death. Morritt LJ said—

> "If the order made is properly within the jurisdiction of the court the fact that it was sought with the motive of seeking to achieve a better tax position is usually irrelevant: In re *Sainsbury's Settlement* (Practice Note) [1967] 1 WLR 476. But where the effect of the order is to confer a substantial advantage on the parties at the expense of the revenue it is in my view important that the court should be satisfied that the order is not only within its jurisdiction but also one which may properly be made.

> It formed no part of either the appeal or the cross appeal to challenge the manner in which the provision the judge thought was appropriate for the maintenance of Gary was made. Obviously it was in the interests of both parties that if the judge were to make any order it should be in this form. We have heard no argument on whether the order was or was not warranted by the terms of [I(PFD)A 1975 s 2(4) – consequential and supplemental provisions]; that would be a matter for the revenue. However, I think that it is important for the future that if an order such as this is to be made the grounds on which it is thought to be authorised by section 2(4) should be clearly demonstrated, for the consent and wishes of the parties is not enough."

Approved Tomlin order

3.3.46   In cases where the interests of one or more minors or unborn beneficiaries are at stake (on either side of the claim), compromise terms agreed between the adult parties and the minors' litigation friends cannot take effect by way of a Tomlin order unless approved by the court. Here again the judge must consider the suitability of the terms, to ensure that the interests of the minor or unborn beneficiaries are adequately pro-tected. If all the judge does is to approve the terms, and order a stay or dismissal of the proceedings on the approved terms, then the order is no different in its tax effects from a Tomlin order to which no court approval is required. If, on the other hand, the parties are looking to secure backdating treatment under I(PFD)A 1975 s 19(1), then the judge can be invited not merely to approve the compromise terms as such but also to order the personal representatives to carry them into effect. HMRC make clear in CG31813 that such an order will be accepted as being an order made under I(PFD)A 1975 s 2 (though in turn they would doubtless want to verify that jurisdiction existed under that section for the court to make orders to the effect indicated in the compromise terms).

Non-backdated variation

3.3.47 Just occasionally, backdating treatment for IHT purposes might lead to a *less* favourable result than without backdating; as where a non-exempt claimant is seeking provision at the expense of an exempt beneficiary such as the surviving spouse/civil partner or a charity. Another example might be where provision is agreed in the form of an IIP in settled property, and IPDI status for that IIP appears less favourable than relevant property status for the trust (typically where the fund is not especially large and the claimant's life expectancy is not enormous), see paragraph **3.1.160** above.

3.3.48 Where IHT backdating is to be avoided, and the court's approval to the compromise terms is not needed, a different procedure can be adopted. The agreed terms can be set out in a simple compromise agreement (or deed of variation), which specifically does not contain an IHT statement of intent. Completion of that deed can be linked, temporally (and no doubt as a condition of its being executed in escrow) to the discontinuance of the claimant's proceedings. This way both an order under I(PFD)A 1975 s 2 and a Tomlin order are avoided. If the compromise is reached within two years after the death and backdating treatment is required for CGT purposes, then a CGT statement of intent can be included – this decision is independent of the inclusion or non-inclusion of an IHT statement of intent (see paragraph **3.1.63** above); but in such a case care would, as always, have to be taken to avoid extraneous consideration.

Compromise before commencement of proceedings

3.3.49 Sometimes negotiations are commenced in relation to an obvious I(PFD)A 1975 claim before any proceedings are launched. If a compromise is reached without proceedings on foot, then a compromise agreement – typically drawn up as a deed of variation – is the natural vehicle for disposing of the claim. As in the case where proceedings have already been started, and provided all the usual conditions for a tax backdated variation are fulfilled (see paragraphs **3.1.51**, **3.1.76** above), the parties can determine whether or not to include statements of intent for IHT and/or CGT purposes.

3.3.50 It is sometimes suggested on behalf of charity beneficiaries under a will, where a financial provision claim is pursued by a non-exempt beneficiary, that it is highly desirable to secure a solution that does not

219

involve backdating for IHT purposes, and that the way to do this is by means of a deed of variation before commencement of proceedings, with no IHT statement of intent even if a CGT statement of intent is to be included. The charity may well in such a case seek to put pressure on the claimant to defer issuing proceedings while negotiations are taking place, even if this involves delaying beyond the normal six month time limit (see paragraph **3.3.3** above), through offers to consent to an extension of time by the court. Claimants may well feel some difficulty in acceding to this pressure, since an extension of time is a purely discretionary matter. As was seen in paragraph **3.3.48** above, the issue of proceedings does not preclude a non-backdated variation, and it is suggested that there is thus no reason to hold back from starting proceedings within the time limit, subject to usual costs constraints.

Will IHT exemption be preserved anyway in the absence of backdating?

3.3.51 If a surviving spouse (or civil partner) compromises a non-exempt beneficiary's claim by giving up part of the estate, without IHT backdating, then provided the negotiations are fully at arm's length and there is no element of gratuitous intent the surviving spouse will not make a transfer of value, independently of IHTA 1984 s 17: see IHTA 1984 s 10. In those circumstances exemption should be preserved. It will be different if the spouse seeks to buy off the claim using his or her own resources; in that case, IHTA 1984 s 29A will lead to a proportional loss of the spouse exemption.

3.3.52 The position where the exempt beneficiary defending the claim is a charity is slightly more complicated. IHTA 1984 s 29A will still be a factor if the charity's own resources are used – with a possible exception where the charity is constituted as a charitable trust rather than as a company or (in time to come) charitable incorporated organisation, since IHTA 1984 s 29A depends on a reduction in the estate of the exempt beneficiary, and a charitable trust (unlike a charity that is a corporate body in its own right) appears not to be capable of having an "estate" within IHTA 1984 s 5. However, apart from IHTA 1984 s 29A, there is a further issue that is not present in the case of an attempt to preserve spouse exemption. The charity exemption depends on the property in question not becoming applicable for purposes other than charitable purposes: IHTA 1984 s 23(5). There would seem to be a strong argument that a portion of the estate that is diverted to a non-charitable beneficiary, even as part of an arm's length bargain in the light of the prospective claim under I(PFD)A 1975, would lose charity exemption by this means in any case. Attempting to preserve it by means of a separate payment by the charity would then run into IHTA 1984 s 29A territory, subject to the point just made concerning the estate of a charity that happens to be constituted as a charitable trust.

Transfer of property by a legatee

The scope of the IHT backdating

3.3.53   Under the heading "compliance with testator's request", IHTA 1984 s 143 provides automatic backdating effect for IHT purposes where property bequeathed by the deceased's will is transferred by the legatee to other persons within two years after the death in accordance with a wish expressed by the testator to that effect. The IHTA 1984 is then to have effect as if the property in question had been bequeathed by the will to the transferee. Where that section applies, IHTA 1984 s 17(b) then provides in addition that the original legatee making the transfer does not thereby make a transfer of value.

3.3.54   It should be noted that IHTA 1984 s 143 has no application in the case of property passing to a person under the intestacy laws, even if the intestacy was conscious and deliberate on the part of the deceased: it refers only to a transfer of "property bequeathed by [the deceased's] will".

3.3.55   The context of IHTA 1984 s 143, speaking of a "transfer" by a "legatee" "to other persons", seems to confine its effect to outright transfers, and it may be questionable whether it is capable of applying to a transfer into settlement. On the other hand, although the provision is most commonly seen as applicable to the distribution of personal chattels, it is not confined to any particular kind of property (except possibly by implication through the word "bequeathed" which may, anyway in England and Wales, arguably exclude realty that is devised certainly that view appears to be implicit in the instruction in IHTM35173 that a case should be referred to IHT Technical Group if a claim is made that IHTA 1984 s 143 applies to a transfer of freehold land or an interest in it).

3.3.56   Nor, importantly, is the effect of IHTA 1984 s 143 confined to a wish that is expressed in the will, or even that was communicated in writing at all, though inevitably if there is no written evidence of the deceased's request then it may be less easy to deal with enquiries by HMRC as to the destination of property passed on by a legatee who then himself dies within seven years after that. IHTM35171 states—

> "The request need not be in writing, but it should have been made in terms sufficiently certain for a court to have given effect to it had it been binding. Cases in which a legatee has made a transfer allegedly in pursuance of a non-binding request, but the existence or effect of the wish appears to be uncertain, should be referred at an early stage to [IHT Technical Group]".

Potential problems for the personal representatives

3.3.57   As mentioned, the application of IHTA 1984 s 143 is automatic: no election, statement of intent or notification to HMRC is required.

(Equally it is not possible to opt out of its effect.) That is certainly convenient in the sense of posing minimal difficulties in the way of the original legatee seeking to avoid the making of a transfer of value. But the very same features make the section capable of causing trouble for personal representatives – at least in theory!

3.3.58

Example 1

If, in a case where the testator had utilised his entire NRB in his lifetime, the personal representatives have distributed the whole estate to the testator's surviving spouse or civil partner and wound up the estate, it is still possible for that person, within the remainder of the two year period from death, to pass items on to third parties. If that transfer was, as a pure matter of fact, made in accordance with a wish expressed by the testator, then IHTA 1984 s 143 will lead to the deceased being treated as having bequeathed those items direct to the third parties – with a consequent backdated IHT charge on the death estate, for which the personal representatives are the primary persons accountable. Even a statutory certificate of discharge under IHTA 1984 s 239(2) will not preclude HMRC from seeking payment of the tax (or additional tax) found to be payable as a result (see IHTA 1984 s 239(4)(a)), though it is possible that they may in practice be persuaded on a concessionary basis to seek payment in the first instance from the surviving spouse, as the person to whom residue had been distributed, rather than putting the personal representatives in the front line. (No indication of such willingness is however evident from the IHT Manual.)

3.3.59

Example 2

Suppose Anne died in May 2007, leaving her personal chattels and residue to her widower Ben absolutely, and a NRB legacy on discretionary trusts. The personal representatives wind up and distribute the estate in 15 months, having appropriated an investment fund worth £300,000 to the NRB legacy as Anne had no cumulative total. However, unbeknown to them, Ben had, quite soon after the death, handed over Anne's jewellery worth £20,000 to her daughters; furthermore, shortly before the second anniversary of death, he makes over to them the leasehold holiday flat that Anne had bought during her lifetime.

If in fact Anne had told Ben she would like him to pass on either or both of those items of property, then IHTA 1984 s 143 will treat the daughters as having inherited direct under the will – giving rise to additional chargeable transfers on the death. Whether the NRB trust will have been over-funded, or alternatively a debt be outstanding for IHT payable on the NRB legacy plus the two transfers under IHTA 1984 s 143, will depend on whether the NRB legacy is properly to be quantified (having regard to the precise drafting) without reference to events occurring after the death.

3.3.60   It follows that it would be prudent for personal representatives, before finalising distributions to the deceased's surviving spouse or civil partner, to seek assurances from him or her as to whether or not the deceased expressed any wish as to the onward transfer of any property bequeathed to him or her by the will, with details of any such wishes and of whether or not he or she has complied with them or intends to comply with them.

Redemption of life interest under intestacy rules

3.3.61   Under the intestacy law applicable in England and Wales, the surviving spouse or civil partner ("the survivor") of the deceased may in certain circumstances be given a life interest in a part of the estate. This applies where the deceased left children or remoter issue, as well as the survivor, and the net value of the estate at the end of the administration (less the personal chattels which pass to the survivor) exceeds the amount of the "fixed net sum" due to the survivor (presently, in these circumstances, £125,000 under the Family Provision (Intestate Succession) Order, SI 1993/2906 art 2). The residue in such a case, by virtue of paragraph (2) in the Table in AEA 1925 s 46(1)(i), is held—

(a)   as to one half on the statutory trusts for the deceased's issue (as amplified in AEA 1925 s 47), and

(b)   as to the other half in trust for the survivor for life, and subject to that on the statutory trusts for the deceased's issue.

3.3.62   The survivor is however given the right, by AEA 1925 s 47A, to elect for that life interest to be redeemed for a capital sum calculated in accordance with subordinate legislation (see the Intestate Succession (Interest and Capitalisation) Order, SI 1977/1491). That election must normally be made within 12 months after the issue of the first grant of probate or letters of administration in the estate, though the court does have jurisdiction to extend that time limit in certain circumstances under the proviso to AEA 1925 s 47A(5).

3.3.63   This facility to redeem the life interest is reflected in the IHT legislation by IHTA 1984 s 145, which provides straightforwardly that—

> "Where an election is made by a surviving spouse or civil partner under [AEA 1925 s 47A], this Act shall have effect as if the surviving spouse or civil partner, instead of being entitled to the life interest, had been entitled to a sum equal to the capital value mentioned in that section."

The making of the election does not constitute a transfer of value: IHTA 1984 s 17(c). The changed (lump sum) entitlement will be a specific gift for the purpose of IHTA 1984 ss 38–39A, in contrast to the life interest in residue which would have been an interest in residue; this could in certain circumstances have an impact on the incidence of BPR or APR (see paragraphs **3.1.187** ff).

3.3.64 This backdating is not time limited, except so far as that is implicit in the (extendable) time limit imposed under AEA 1925 (the purpose of which is obviously to enable the personal representatives to finalise the administration of the estate without undue delay). The effect of the section (except where the deceased was UK domiciled but the survivor was neither domiciled nor deemed domiciled within the UK, so that spouse exemption is restricted to £55,000) will obviously be to reduce the extent to which the estate is exempt from IHT on the death, and thereby (where the value of the estate and previous chargeable transfers is sufficient) to increase the amount of IHT chargeable on the death. As with the transfer of property in accordance with a wish expressed by the deceased, and for that matter variations, disclaimers and distributions from property settled by the will, a certificate of discharge will not preclude collection of any such increased IHT charge: IHTA 1984 s 239(4)(a). So personal representatives administering an intestate estate will generally wish to defer distributions to the deceased's issue until after the expiry of the time limit for such an election by the survivor.

Chapter 4.1

Trusts

Types of trust

4.1.1   There are various types of trust which can be created by a testator. These trusts are—

— fixed interest trusts;

— discretionary trusts;

— trusts for bereaved minors;

— trusts for disabled persons.

The creation and operation of all these trusts have IHT, CGT and income tax consequences. These consequences are considered in paragraphs **4.1.5–4.1.19.**

Precedent clauses for each of the above trusts, and for the other types of trusts mentioned in this book, as they can be incorporated into Wills or Deeds of Variation to Wills, are to be found as follows—

— Fixed interest trusts—PRECEDENTS 1, 6

— Discretionary trusts—PRECEDENTS 1, 6

— Trusts for bereaved minors—PRECEDENT 5

— 18–25 trusts—PRECEDENT 25

— Trusts for disabled persons—PRECEDENT 4

— Protective trusts—PRECEDENT 3

Fixed interest trusts or life interest trusts are frequently created by testators who have children from previous relationships. It is of course necessary for them to provide for a surviving spouse, civil partner or cohabitee, but ultimately they may want the bulk of their assets to go to children of their previous relationships. In these circumstances, it is very common for testators to give the surviving spouse, civil partner or cohabitee a life interest possibly in the whole of their estate, but if the estate mainly consists of the matrimonial or family home, only a life interest in the house.

A discretionary trust is one where there is a class of beneficiaries, and the trustees have a discretion as to which beneficiary they benefit. The nil-rate band (NRB) discretionary trust coupled with the power to accept an IOU, or to impose a charge for the NRB is very common in wills these days; these are discussed in more detail in CHAPTER 2.7.

Trusts for bereaved minors must be created by parents on their own children, and the trust must be in a will. These trusts receive special treatment as far as IHT is concerned, and to a certain extent as far as CGT is concerned. They are discussed in more detail in paragraphs **4.1.9**, **4.1.14**.

Trusts for disabled persons receive special treatment as far as IHT is concerned. They are discussed in more detail in paragraphs **4.1.10, 4.1.15**.

Trusts for vulnerable persons receive special treatment as far as income tax and CGT is concerned, and trusts for bereaved minors and trusts for disabled persons may qualify as trusts for vulnerable persons. The income tax and CGT treatment is described in paragraph **4.1.19**.

The distinction between fixed trusts and discretionary trusts

4.1.2   The distinction between fixed trusts and discretionary trusts was very important as far as IHT is concerned, but its importance is much diminished by the changes to the IHT treatment of trusts in FA 2006. However, the distinction is still important as far as income tax is concerned.

As far as IHT is concerned, there is now a very restricted definition of what is meant by a fixed interest trust or an interest in possession trust. The interest in possession trust must either be an immediate post death interest or a trust for a disabled person. Such a trust is treated as far as IHT is concerned as if the beneficiary who is entitled to the immediate post death interest or the disabled person owns the underlying trust assets.

As far as income tax is concerned, if there is a beneficiary entitled to the income, the trustees pay basic rate income tax, even though they may be in receipt of an income of several million pounds. If there is no beneficiary entitled to the income, then the trustees must pay the special rate applicable to trusts; the current rate for income apart from a dividend income is 40%, for dividend income 32·5%.

The essential elements of a trust

4.1.3   The essential elements of a trust are—

— certainty of intention;

— certainty of subject matter;

— certainty of objects;

— certainty of beneficial interest if it is a fixed interest trust.

With regard to certainty of intention, the test is whether the testator intended to create a trust. It is immaterial whether or not the word "trust" has been used; if the testator intended to create a trust, even though that word has not been used, then a trust will be created.

With regard to the certainty of subject matter, it is necessary to specify the property which is the subject of the trust with a reasonable degree of certainty so that it can be identified. In most wills, this will frequently not be a problem. The trust may be of the residuary estate, or a legacy may be given to the trustees. Alternatively, it may be that a spouse, civil partner or cohabitee is given a life interest in whatever property the testator is living in at the date of death or if the testator is a tenant in common, a life interest in the testator's interest in the property.

The test for certainty of objects depends on whether it is a fixed interest trust or a discretionary trust. If it is a fixed interest trust, then it must be possible to make a list of all possible beneficiaries. If that is not the case, then the trust will be void.

If it is a discretionary trust, then it is necessary to have a class of beneficiaries, and the definition of the class of beneficiaries must be linguistically certain. This means that if someone alleges that he is within the class of beneficiaries, it must be possible to say whether or not that person is within the class of beneficiaries. It is immaterial that there may be evidential problems as to whether or not a person comes within the class of beneficiaries. However, if the class of beneficiaries is too widely drawn, then it may be void as being administratively unworkable.

With the great majority of discretionary trusts in wills, there will be no problem over certainty of objects. Frequently, the class of beneficiaries includes the spouse, children and grandchildren of the testator. Such wording is clearly linguistically certain. There could be doubts as to whether a person is actually the child or grandchild of the testator, but this can be resolved by evidence in the form of DNA tests if necessary. It is also clear that the class is administratively workable.

However, a discretionary trust for "all my friends" will probably be void for linguistic uncertainty. It is possible to avoid this problem by giving the trustees or some third party the power to determine if someone was a friend of the testator and therefore within the class of beneficiaries under the discretionary trust.

A discretionary trust for "everyone in the world who does not own a car" would be administratively unworkable as millions of people would qualify.

If it is a fixed interest trust, then it is necessary to define the beneficial interest given to the beneficiaries. Again, frequently there will be no problem with this in wills as a spouse may be given a life interest in a house or the residuary estate. However, a trust providing that the trustees should pay the life tenant a reasonable income, or whatever minimum is required to maintain their standard of living may very well be void on the grounds of uncertainty.

Typical issues

4.1.4   The main issue with trusts in wills is the taxation treatment of the different kinds of trust. However, other problems can arise with regard to the powers of the trustees, and the rights of beneficiaries. Frequently, it is members of the family who are the trustees of these trusts, and in the great majority of trusts, there is no problem. However, unfortunately some families do fall out, and then litigation may result.

Tax implications of trusts

4.1.5

Inheritance tax

All trusts are now subject to "the relevant property regime" with three exceptions – IPDI, BMTs and trusts for disabled persons.

The relevant property regime means that IHT may be payable on the creation of a trust depending on the size of the estate of the deceased and lifetime gifts within seven years of death. If the trust is created during the lifetime of a settlor, IHT will be payable at one half of the death rate, currently 20%, in so far as the reduction in value of the settlor's estate is in excess of the NRB, or is in excess of what is left of the NRB having deducted the amounts transferred to other settlements subject to the relevant property regime the seven years prior to the date of creation.

In addition, there will be ten yearly or principal charges to IHT, and also exit or proportionate charges to IHT whenever the trustees distribute any of the capital in the trust, or a beneficiary becomes entitled under the terms of the trust. The rate of these charges is very low – IHTA 1984 states that the rate of ten yearly or principal charge is 30% of the lifetime rate. As the lifetime rate is 20% once the NRB has been exhausted, it follows that the ten yearly charge is a maximum of 6%. Exit or proportionate charges cannot be more than 6%, and will often be considerably less than this because of the way they are calculated.

If the deceased creates an immediate post death interest (these are discussed in more detail at paragraph **4.1.8**), then the beneficiary entitled to the interest in possession is deemed to own the underlying trust assets as far as IHT is concerned. This means that all the assets in the trust will be aggregated with the remainder of the beneficiary's estate, and if the combined total is in excess of the NRB, or what is left of the NRB, IHT will be payable.

Inheritance tax on the creation of a settlement on death

4.1.6   Any part of the estate of the deceased person over the NRB, which is currently £300,000, for 2007–08, is subject to IHT at 40%. In addition, if the deceased has made lifetime gifts in the seven years before the date of death which are not covered by some lifetime exemption from IHT, then those must be cumulated or added together in order to determine the rate of tax which applies to the death estate. At the moment there are only two rates of tax, 0% or 40%, then the previous gifts must be added together to see if there is anything left of the NRB.

Thus, if the deceased had merely made use of the lifetime exemptions from IHT by making use of the annual exemption of £3,000, or gifts on the occasion of the marriage of a child, such gifts will not reduce the NRB. However, if the deceased has made a gift of £500,000, that would clearly absorb the whole of a £300,000 rate band, and will mean that the whole of the deceased's estate will be subject to IHT at 40%. If the gift was of £200,000, and the deceased had also made gifts of £3,000 in the previous tax year and the tax year of the gift so that there is no annual exemption available to offset against the £200,000, then the £200,000 will reduce the NRB which is available to offset against the death estate to £100,000 assuming that the NRB is £300,000.

It may be that various exemptions and reliefs will reduce the amount of IHT payable on the estate of the deceased person. The most common reliefs applying to the estate of a deceased person are—

— spouse or civil partner exemption;

— agricultural property relief;

— business property relief;

— charities.

The Government is proposing that if a spouse dies, and has not used up the whole of his or her nil-rate band, then this can be claimed by the surviving spouse. The nil-rate band is increased by the percentage of the nil-rate band left unclaimed on the death of the first spouse.

Example

Assume that NRB is £300,000 on death of S1. S1 uses up £100,000 of the NRB—

— S2 dies when NRB is £360,000.

— S2'S NRB will be increased by: 200,000/300,000 = ⅔.

— Increase will be ⅔ x £360,000 = £240,000

If the surviving spouse remarries, and the next spouse dies, then the unused percentage of the nil-rate band can be used on the death of the surviving spouse, with a limit of double the nil-rate band which is available on the death of that spouse.

If the testator creates an IPDI in favour of a spouse or civil partner who is domiciled in the UK, then no IHT will be payable on the assets subject to the immediate post death interest. However, at the moment, if the testator creates an IPDI in favour of a cohabitee, there is no exemption from IHT.

Agricultural property relief and business property relief (see CHAPTER 2.8) are very valuable reliefs as far as farmers and businessmen are concerned. These reliefs operate by reducing the value transferred by 50% or 100%. If it is business assets which qualify for 100% relief, then it is a complete exemption from IHT. If it is agricultural property which qualifies for 100% relief, the relief is only on the agricultural value of the land, which means that it will not be a complete exemption. The agricultural value of the land is defined as the value of land subject to a covenant that it can only be used in perpetuity for agricultural purposes.

If the testator creates a trust for a disabled person, then the disabled person is deemed to have an interest in possession in all the assets which are the subject of the trust. This means that if the disabled person is a spouse or civil partner of the testator, and is domiciled in the UK, then spouse or civil partner exemption will operate on the death of the testator.

There have been problems in recent years as to the calculation of IHT on mixed gifts of the residuary estate to non-exempt beneficiaries, for example children, and exempt beneficiaries, the spouse of the testator or charities. It is not permissible to pay the IHT from the share going to the exempt beneficiary, and such gifts can be construed either as a gift of residue to be divided between the non-exempt beneficiary and the exempt beneficiary, with the non-exempt beneficiary paying the IHT due on that share from it so that the non-exempt beneficiary receives less than the exempt beneficiary, or if equality is required, then the following formula can be used—

— r = tax rate (currently 40%) and $r = R/100$

— n = nil-rate amount

— V = amount left in estate

— U = amount to be received by party which is not taxed

— T = amount to be received by party subject to IHT

— f = fraction to non-taxpayer

Assuming $V(1-f) > n$ (if $V(1-f) <= n$ then non-taxpayer receives Vf and taxpayer receives $V(1-f)$) then—

— $U = (Vf(1-r) + nrf) / (1-rf)$

— $T = (V(1-f)-nrf) / (1-rf)$

eg V= £700,000 left, nil-rate amount n = £300,000, fraction to non-taxpayer f = ⅓ then—

— U = £207,692

— T = £492,308 (after tax = £415,385)

The author is indebted to his daughter, Fiona Kolbert, for this formula.

There is a slightly more complicated variation on this theme, showing the effect of reliefs for business or agricultural property, see paragraph **2.8.53**.

If there is a mixed gift of this nature, the will should make it clear how the IHT is to be calculated.

The relevant property regime

4.1.7 This regime now applies to all trusts in a will apart from immediate post death interests, trusts for bereaved minors, and trusts for disabled persons.

The relevant property regime means that there will be a ten yearly or principal charge to IHT, and also an exit or proportionate charge to IHT whenever the trustees distribute any of the capital, or a beneficiary becomes absolutely entitled to any part of the capital under the terms of the trust, or if the trustees take any action which reduces the value of the trust assets. However, the rate of IHT is very low – it cannot be more than 6% for the current tax year, and with exit or proportionate charges the rate will frequently be considerably less than that because of the way it is calculated.

If a trust is created in a will, and it is not an immediate post death interest, a trust for a bereaved minor or a trust for a disabled person, then it will be subject to the relevant property regime, and on the 10th anniversary of the death of the deceased and every subsequent 10th anniversary there will be a ten yearly or principal charge to IHT. How is the charge calculated?

IHTA 1984 s 64 provides that where all or any part of the property comprised in the settlement is relevant property, tax is to be charged at the rate applicable under IHTA 1984 ss 66, 67 on the value of the property.

Section 66 provides that in order to determine the rate of tax which applies on a ten year anniversary it is necessary to aggregate—

— the value of the assets in the trust on the 10th anniversary;

— the value immediately after it became comprised in the settlement of any property which was not then relevant property and has not subsequently become relevant property while remaining comprised in the settlement;

— the value immediately after a related settlement commenced of the property being comprised in it;

— the values transferred by any chargeable transfers made by the settlor in the period of seven years ending with the day on which the settlement commenced, disregarding transfers made on that day or before 27 March 1974;

231

and the amounts on which any charges to tax were imposed under IHTA 1984 s 65 in respect of the settlement in the ten years before the anniversary concerned.

"Relevant property" is defined by IHTA 1984 s 58(1) as settled property in which no qualifying interest in possession subsists, subject to various exceptions. IHTA 1984 s 59(1) provides that a qualifying interest in possession means an interest in possession—

(i) to which an individual is beneficially entitled; and

(ii) which, if the individual became beneficially entitled to the interest in possession on or after 2 March 2006, is an IPDI, a disabled person's trust or a transitional serial interest.

IHTA 1984 s 62(1) provides that two settlements are related if and only if the settlor is the same in each case, and they commenced on the same day.

This means that on the 10th anniversary of the death of any testator who has created any trust apart from an immediate post death interest, a trust for a bereaved minor and the trust for a disabled person, it will be necessary to value all the assets in the trust. In many trusts, all the assets in the settlement will be relevant property, and the deceased will not have created any other settlement by will, or created any lifetime settlements. If that is the case, then in order to determine the tax rate, or that anything is left of the NRB, it will only be necessary to aggregate the values subject to an exit or proportionate charge in the ten years leading up to the anniversary charge.

Example

T creates a discretionary trust in his will. The trustees vest assets worth £100,000 in a beneficiary six years after the death of the testator. On the 10th anniversary the assets in the trust are valued at £700,000. The NRB for the tax year when the 10th anniversary falls is £400,000. The NRB is reduced to £300,000 because of the distribution of £100,000. As the assets in the trust on the 10th anniversary are worth £700,000, this means that IHT at 6% is payable on £400,000 = £24,000.

If the testator has created other settlements in his lifetime, it will be necessary to aggregate the values transferred by any chargeable transfers by the deceased in the seven years prior to the date death. Chargeable transfers include failed PETS, and since 22 March 2006, all trusts created by the deceased during his lifetime which are not trusts for disabled persons. For trusts prior to 22 March 2006, it will be necessary to aggregate those where there is no beneficiary with an interest in possession, and any failed PETs. In addition, it will also be necessary to aggregate the value on which any exit or proportionate charge has been paid in the ten years leading up to the anniversary.

Example

T creates a discretionary trust five years before death and transfers £200,000 to the trustees. He also creates a discretionary trust in his will. The trustees of the will discretionary trust vest assets worth £100,000 in a beneficiary six years after the death of the testator. On the 10th anniversary the assets in the trust are valued at £700,000. The NRB for the tax year when the 10th anniversary falls is £400,000. The NRB is reduced to £100,000 because of the distribution of £100,000 and the lifetime settlement. As the assets in the trust on the 10th anniversary are worth £700,000, this means that IHT at 6% is payable on £600,000 = £36,000.

With regard to exit or proportionate charges, IHTA 1984 s 65(1) provides that there shall be a charge to tax under this section—

(a) where the property comprised in a settlement or any part of that property ceases to be relevant property (whether because it ceases to be comprised in the settlement or otherwise); and

(b) in a case in which paragraph (a) above does not apply, where the trustees of the settlement make a disposition as a result of which the value of relevant property comprised in the settlement is less than it would be but for the disposition.

This means that IHT may be payable if the trustees decide to distribute any of the capital in the trust, or a beneficiary becomes absolutely entitled to it under the terms of the trust. In addition, if the trustees take any action which reduces the value of the trust assets, that could also give rise to an exit or proportionate charge. One situation where the trustees may reduce the value of the assets in the trust is if they are holding a house as part of the assets in the trust. There is no one living in the house, so the trustees could sell it and obtain full vacant possession value. However if they agree that a member of the class of beneficiaries under the trust can live in the house rent-free for the rest of that beneficiary's life, there will be a reduction in the value of the assets in the trust as they cannot now sell it with full vacant possession, and they have encumbered the property by agreeing that the beneficiary can live in the house rent-free.

How are these exit or proportionate charges calculated?

The first stage is to calculate the reduction in value of the assets in the trust. Frequently the reduction in value will be the same as the value of the assets the trustees are distributing. If the trustees are distributing cash or quoted shares, then the reduction in value of the assets in the trust will be the same as the cash or the value of the quoted shares. However, there are exceptional circumstances, the reduction in value of the assets in the trust will be more than the value of the assets being distributed.

The next stage is to determine the rate of tax. As far as exit charges after a ten year anniversary are concerned, IHTA 1984 s 69(1) provides that the rate is the appropriate fraction of the rate which was charged on the last ten year anniversary. IHTA 1984 s 69(4) provides that for the purposes of s 69 the appropriate fraction is so many fortieths as are complete successive quarters in the period beginning with the most recent ten year anniversary and ending with the day before the occasion of the charge.

Thus if the trustees distribute the assets in the trust five years after the last ten year anniversary, or a beneficiary becomes absolutely entitled to any part of the trust assets five years after the last ten year anniversary, the IHT rate would be $20/40$ths or one half of the rate paid on the last ten year anniversary.

Example

T creates a discretionary trust in his will. The trustees vest assets worth £100,000 in a beneficiary six years after the death of the testator. On the 10th anniversary the assets in the trust are valued at £700,000. The NRB for the tax year when the 10th anniversary falls is £400,000. The NRB is reduced to £300,000 because of the distribution of £100,000. As the assets in the trust on the 10th anniversary are worth £700,000, this means that IHT at 6% is payable on £400,000 = £24,000. The average rate is £24,000/£700,000 = 3·42%.

Six years after the ten year anniversary, the trustees vest quoted shares worth £100,000 in a beneficiary. The reduction in value of the trust assets is £100,000. The number of quarters which has elapsed since the last ten year anniversary is 24. The exit charge is £100,000 x 3·42% x $24/40$ = £2,052.

If there is a distribution within the first ten years of the creation of the settlement, then as there has been no ten year charge, it is necessary to do a special calculation in order to determine the average rate. IHTA 1984 s 68(4), (5) provides that it is necessary to calculate the IHT which would be payable on the following chargeable transfer—

— the value, immediately after the settlement commenced, of the property comprised in it;

— the value, immediately after a related settlement commenced, of the property comprised in it; and

— the value, immediately after it became comprised in the settlement, of any property which became so comprised after the settlement commenced before the commencement of the charge under IHTA 1984 s 65 (whether or not it has remained so comprised); and

— the chargeable transfers made by the settlor in the period of seven years ending with the day on which the settlement commenced disregarding transfers made on the day or before 27 March 1974.

The rate is $3/10$ of the rate produced by this calculation. It is then necessary to multiply that by as many fortieths as there are complete successive quarters in the period beginning with the day on which the settlement commenced and ending with the day before the occasion of the charge.

This means that if there is a distribution within the first ten years of the commencement of the settlement, or the trustees reduce the value of the trust assets, it will be necessary to work out the reduction in value of the assets. Frequently the reduction in value will be the same as the value of the assets handed out.

In order to determine the rate of tax, whether there is anything left of the NRB, provided that there is no other settlement in the will, and the testator has not created any settlements in the seven years before death, it will be necessary to add the value of the assets in the trust as at the date of death to the chargeable transfers made by the settlor in the seven years prior to the date of death. It will then be necessary to work out $3/10$ths of this rate, and then to multiply that by the number of complete quarters that have elapsed since the commencement of the settlement divided by 40.

Example

T creates a discretionary trust in his will; the assets subject to the trust are worth £700,000 at the date of death. The trustees vest assets worth £100,000 in a beneficiary six years after the death of the testator. NRB is £400,000. IHT at 20% on £700,000–£400,000 = £60,000.

— £60,000/£700,000 = 8·57%

— 8·57% x $3/10$ = 2·57%

— Exit charge is £100,000 x 2·57% x $36/40$ = £2,313

Inheritance tax treatment of IPDIs

4.1.8   A beneficiary entitled to an interest in possession under an immediate post death interest is deemed to own the underlying assets as far as IHT is concerned. This means that when the beneficiary dies, the assets in the trust will be aggregated with the assets owned by the beneficiary in his personal capacity, and if the combined total exceeds the NRB, or the NRB has been exhausted by lifetime gifts in the seven years up to the date of death, then IHT will be payable. In addition, if the life tenant decides to surrender any part of the life interest, the life tenant will be deemed to have made a PET of whatever proportion of the trust assets are surrendered. So if the trust assets comprise cash or investments to the value of £900,000, and the beneficiary gives up one half of the interest in possession under an immediate post death interest, the beneficiary will be deemed to have made a PET of one half of the underlying trust assets.

IHTA 1984 s 49A provides that an interest is an immediate post death interest if the following for conditions are satisfied—

1   The settlement must be affected by will or under the law relating to intestacy.

2   The beneficiary must have become beneficially entitled to the interest in possession on the death of the testator or intestate.

3   IHTA 1984 s 71A does not apply to the property in which the interest subsists, and the interest is not a disabled person's interest.

4   Condition 3 must have been satisfied at all times since the beneficiary becoming beneficially entitled to the interest in possession.

The first condition requires that the interest must arise under a will or the law relating to intestacy. If someone dies intestate or partially intestate, and leaves a spouse or civil partner and children, and his estate is large enough, then the surviving spouse or civil partner will be entitled to a life interest in one half of the residuary estate. That life interest is an immediate post death interest.

The second condition requires that the beneficiary must become beneficially entitled to the interest in possession on the death of the testator or intestate. This condition is not infringed if the beneficiary has to satisfy a survivorship condition of not more than six months, and indeed a surviving spouse or civil partner entitled under the intestacy rules must survive for 28 days after the death of the other spouse or civil partner before they can take under the intestacy of that spouse or civil partner.

However, if the testator creates successive life interests, then the first life interest can be an immediate post death interest, but not the life interests after the first unless a transitional serial interest comes into existence. (It is beyond the scope of this book to discuss transitional serial interests as these only arise if the trust was created before 22 March 2006.) So if a testator creates a life interest trust in favour of a spouse, with a subsequent life interest trust for a child, then the life interest trust in favour of the spouse will be an immediate post death interest, and the spouse will be deemed to own all the underlying trust assets, but the subsequent life interest trust will not be an immediate post death interest, and will be subject to the relevant property regime. This means that where the spouse dies, the assets in the trust will be aggregated with the assets owned by the spouse, and IHT will be payable if the combined total is in excess of the NRB, or the spouse's NRB has been exhausted by lifetime gifts in the seven years prior to the date of death of the spouse. However, the subsequent interest in possession trust will be subject to the relevant property regime, which means that there will be ten yearly or proportionate charges to IHT, and in addition exit or proportionate charges whenever the trustees distribute any of the capital either exercising a power of advancement or because a beneficiary has become absolutely entitled to the assets of the trust under the terms of the trust. However, the assets in the trust will not be aggregated with the remainder of the estate of subsequent life tenants. So when any life tenant after the first dies, then on the death of the subsequent life tenant, the assets in the trust will not be aggregated with the personal assets of the life tenant. Instead, there will be an exit or proportionate charge.

The third and fourth conditions require that the settlement must never have been a trust for a bereaved minor or a trust for a disabled person.

Inheritance tax treatment of BMTs

4.1.9   BMTs replaced accumulation and maintenance settlements. Whereas anyone could create an accumulation and maintenance settlement either *inter vivos* or by will, BMTs can only be created by parents, and must be in the will of the parents on their own children. Alternatively, these trusts can arise under the intestacy rules.

BMTs receive special treatment as far as IHT is concerned. The special treatment is that whilst IHT may be payable on the estate of the parents, there are no ten yearly or principal charges or exit or proportionate charges.

IHTA 1984 s 71(A) provides that a BMT is one where settled property—

— is held on statutory trusts for the benefit of a bereaved minor under AEA 1925 ss 46, 47(1); or

— is established under the will of the deceased parent of the bereaved minor; and

— the bereaved minor, if he has not done so before attaining the age of 18, will on attaining that age become absolutely entitled to the settled property, any income arising from it and any income that has arisen from the property held in the trust for his benefit and being accumulated before that time;

— that for so long as the bereaved minor is living and under the age of 18, if any of the settled property is applied for the benefit of a beneficiary, it is applied to the benefit of the bereaved minor; and

— that, for so long as a bereaved minor is living and under the age of 18, either the bereaved minor is entitled to all of the income (if there is any) arising from any of the settled property, or no such income may be applied for the benefit of any other person.

"Parent" includes stepparent and someone with parental responsibility for a child under the law of England and Wales.

"A bereaved minor" is defined as a person who has not yet attained the age of 18 and at least one of whose parents has died.

As the statutory trusts which arise under the intestacy rules qualify as a trust for a bereaved minor, it seems that if grandparents die intestate, and grandchildren are entitled under the intestacy rules because a parent is dead, then that would qualify as a BMT. However, if grandparents create a trust in their wills for grandchildren, then such trust will not qualify as trusts for a bereaved minor, and will be subject to the relevant property regime.

If a BMT is created, IHT may be payable on the death of a parent or possibly grandparent. However, usually there will be no further charge to IHT, so there will be no ten yearly or principal charge to IHT and no exit or proportionate charge when a child satisfies the contingency and becomes absolutely entitled.

It is also possible to have 18-to-25 trusts. IHTA 1984 s 71D provides that an 18-to-25 trust is one where—

— the property is held on trusts for the benefit of a person who has not yet attained the age of 25;

— at least one of the person's parents has died;

— the trust is established under the will of the parent of the child.

Whilst there is no ten yearly or principal charge to IHT on an 18-to-25 trust, there will be a charge when the beneficiary satisfies the contingency and becomes absolutely entitled.

In order to calculate this charge, it is necessary to determine the chargeable amount. This is defined by IHTA 1984 s 71F(4) as the amount by which the value of the property which is comprised in the settlement is less immediately after the event giving rise to the charge than it would be but for the event. Normally the reduction in value when a child satisfies the contingency will be the same as the value of the assets or cash handed to the child.

In order to determine the rate of tax, it is necessary to calculate a settlement rate, and also a relevant fraction. The settlement rate is determined by aggregating—

— the value, immediately after the settlement commenced, of the property being comprised in it;

— the value immediately after a related settlement commenced, of the property being comprised in it; and

— the value immediately after it became comprised in the settlement of any property which became so comprised after the settlement commenced and before the occasion of the charge under IHTA 1984 s 71E (whether or not it has remained so comprised); and

— the chargeable transfers made by the deceased in the period of seven years ending with the date on which the settlement commenced, disregarding transfers made on that day.

Having calculated the IHT using the lifetime rate, 20%, and worked out the average rate applying, it is unnecessary to multiply that by 3/10ths.

It is then necessary to multiply that by so many fortieths as there are complete successive quarters in a period beginning with the day on which the child attains the age of 18, or if later, the day on which the property became subject to s 71D.

Assuming that the NRB has been exhausted, the average rate will therefore be 6% ($^3/_{10}$ths of 20%). If a child is entitled on attaining the age of 25, then the rate of the exit or proportionate charge will be 6% multiplied by $^{28}/_{40}$ as there are 28 quarters in seven years. This means that the maximum IHT payable on these 18-to-25 trusts is 4·2%.

Example

Assume the NRB is always £300,000. T creates a BMT for his three children and gives the trustees quoted shares to the value of £900,000 contingent on them attaining 21. Assume the shares do not drop or increase in value. T has not created any lifetime settlements. IHT will be payable on his death. When each child attains 21, the rate of IHT payable will be—

£900,000 – NRB £300,000	= £600,000
IHT at 20% on £600,000	= £120,000
Average rate is £120,000/£900,000	= 13·33%
30% of 13·33%	= 3·99%
Number of quarters which have elapsed since 18	= 12
IHT payable when a child attains 21 is therefore £300,000 x 3·99% x 12/40	= £3,591

Inheritance tax treatment of trusts for disabled persons

4.1.10 Trusts for disabled persons received a special treatment as far as IHT is concerned. The disabled person is deemed to have an interest in possession in the assets subject of the trust, and accordingly there are no ten yearly or principal charges to IHT and no exit or proportionate charges. However, when the disabled person dies, the assets in the trust will be deemed to be part of the estate for IHT purposes, and so IHT will be payable on both the personal assets of the disabled person and the assets in the trust if the combined estate is large enough, or the NRB has been absorbed by lifetime gifts in the seven years prior to the date of death. In addition, the lifetime creation of such a trust is not a chargeable disposal for IHT purposes, but instead is a PET.

In order for a trust to qualify as a trust for a disabled person, various conditions have to be satisfied.

IHTA 1984 s 89(1) provides that a trust for a disabled person is one where settled property has been transferred into a settlement after 9 March 1981 and held on trusts—

(a) under which, during the life of a disabled person, no interest in possession in the set tled property subsists; and

(b) which secure that not less than half of the settled property which is applied during his life is applied for his benefit.

It does not matter that the trustees have the power of advancement conferred on them by TA 1925 s 32 (IHTA 1984 s 89(3)).

IHTA 1984 s 89(4) provides that a disabled person is, in relation to any settled property, a reference to a person who, when the property was transferred into settlement, was—

(a) incapable, by reason of mental disorder within the meaning of MHA 1983 of administering his property or managing his affairs; or

(b) in receipt of an attendance allowance under the SSCBA 1992 s 64; or

(c) in receipt of disability living allowance under the SSCBA 1992 s 71 by virtue of entitlement to the care component at the highest or middle rate.

IHTA 1984 s 89(5), (6) further extend the definition of what is meant by a disabled person.

IHTA 1984 s 49 provides that where a person becomes beneficially entitled to an interest in possession in settled property on or after 22 March 2006 that person is to be treated as beneficially entitled to the property in which the interest subsists provided it is *inter alia* a disabled person's interest. IHTA 1984 s 89B provides that an interest in possession in settled property to which a disabled person became beneficially entitled on or after 22 March 2006 is a disabled person's interest. The effect of these sections is that it is possible to establish a lifetime settlement creating a life interest trust for a disabled person which will not be subject to the relevant property regime. This means that if a settlor creates a lifetime settlement, and gives a disabled person a life interest, the initial creation will be a PET, and there will not be any ten yearly or principal charges to IHT, or exit or proportionate charges. Instead, when the disabled person dies, all the assets in the trust will be aggregated with the personal estate of the disabled person.

Protective trusts

4.1.11 Protective trusts are sometimes established where a beneficiary is or may be in financial difficulty. Model protective trusts are set out in the Trustee Act 1925 s 33. In general terms, the principal beneficiary has a life interest, but if he becomes bankrupt etc, then his life interest terminates, and it becomes a discretionary trust for the beneficiary and members of his family.

Protective trusts receive special treatment as far as IHT is concerned if they are created in a will, but they do not receive special treatment for income tax and CGT. IHTA 1984 s 88 provides that if the protective trusts is created by will, and the principal beneficiary has an immediate post death interest, or a disabled person's interest, then if the principal beneficiary's interest terminates, it is still treated as if the principal beneficiary had an immediate post death interest. This means that there are no ten yearly or principal charges or exit or proportionate charges, but when the principal beneficiary dies, whatever is in the trust will be part of the principal beneficiary's estate.

A protective trust created during the lifetime of a settlor does not receive any special treatment, and accordingly it will be subject to the relevant property regime. This means that the creation will be a chargeable disposal, and in addition there will be ten yearly or principal charges, and also exit or proportionate charges.

CGT

4.1.12

Death

When a person dies, there is no liability to CGT. Instead, there is a deemed disposal at market value of all the assets owned by the deceased, but no chargeable gain accrues to the personal representatives. Accordingly, CGT is not an issue on death.

CGT implications of IPDI

4.1.13 As an immediate post death interest must be created by will, or arise under intestacy rules, the CGT implications of creation are as outlined in the preceding paragraph.

The trustees will be deemed to acquire the assets subject of the trust at market value at the date of death of the deceased. If they sell those assets for more than the market value at the date of death, there is a potential liability for CGT after allowing for any exemptions and reliefs. It may also be that they will acquire assets during the currency of the trust, and if they sell those assets for more than the purchase price or the value at which they were acquired, again there will be a potential liability for CGT.

When the life tenant dies, there will be a deemed disposal at market value, but no chargeable gain will accrue to the trustees. Whoever is entitled to the reversion will then acquire the assets at market value as at the date of death of the life tenant.

CGT implications of BMTs

4.1.14 Again, as with the immediate post death interests, these must be created either in a will, or they can also arise under the intestacy rules. As outlined in the previous paragraph, the trustees will be deemed to acquire the assets subject to the trust at market value as at the date of death of the deceased.

Whenever a child satisfies the contingency, provided the assets in the trust can be divided easily between the beneficiaries, the trustees will be deemed to dispose of the assets the child is entitled to at market value on the date when the child satisfies the contingency. Accordingly, if the assets have increased in value, there is a potential liability for CGT on the trustees. However, holdover relief will be available whatever the nature of the assets provided the trustees and the child agree that the gain should be held over.

If the assets in the trust cannot be divided between the children easily, an example is a house, then there will not be deemed disposal when the older children satisfied the contingency. Instead, the deemed disposal will not take place until the youngest child satisfies the contingency, and in that situation holdover relief will be limited to business assets as far as the older children are concerned. Unrestricted holdover relief should be available as far as a youngest child's interest is concerned however.

CGT implications of trust for disabled persons

4.1.15   A trust for a disabled person can be created by a settlor either *inter vivos* or by will. If it is created by will, the consequences are as outlined in paragraph **4.1.10**.

As far as IHT is concerned, a trust for a disabled person can take the form of a discretionary trust or a life interest trust.

If the trust for the disabled person takes the form of a life interest trust, when the disabled person dies, there will be a free uplift to market value for CGT purposes of all the assets in the trust. Accordingly, the trustees will not incur any CGT liability, and the remainderman will be deemed to acquire the assets in the trust at market value at the date of death of the life tenant. If the trust takes the form of a discretionary trust, when the disabled person dies, there will not be any CGT consequences, and no free uplift to market value for the assets in the trust. Instead, when the trustees vest any of the assets in the trust in a beneficiary, that will be a deemed disposal at market value for CGT purposes of those assets.

Income tax

4.1.16

The liability of the personal representatives

The personal representatives only pay basic rate income tax, even though the income of the personal representatives may be in the millions. However, the personal representatives cannot claim any personal allowances. This means that trustees must pay income tax at 10% on all dividend income received, 20% on savings income and 22% on or other income, for example rental income on a buy to let property owned by the deceased.

Once the personal representatives have completed the administration of the estate, they may become trustees, and then the rules described in paragraphs **4.1.18–4.1.19** will apply.

The entitlement of beneficiaries or trustees to income during the administration period

4.1.17   It goes without saying that the personal representatives have to account to the beneficiaries for the income received during the administration period. The income tax treatment depends on the type of the gift.

Specific gifts

The beneficiary of a specific gift, for example, quoted shares, is entitled to all the dividends accruing from the date of death.

General legacies

Beneficiaries entitled to general legacies are not usually entitled to any interest as long as the general legacy is paid within 12 months of death. If it is paid more than 12 months after death, then the beneficiary is entitled to interest. There are also some circumstances when interest will be payable from the moment of death; this is discussed in more detail in paragraph **4.1.39**.

The rate of interest is the basic rate payable on funds in court, and if the interest is paid, then it should be paid gross without deduction of tax. The beneficiary must include the income in his or her tax return for the year when the interest is paid.

The personal representatives cannot deduct the gross interest when calculating their income tax liability.

Residuary beneficiaries with a limited interest

The income tax liability of a residuary beneficiary depends on whether any income has been paid to him or her. If any income has been paid to the residuary beneficiary, the personal representatives will have paid basic rate tax on that income, and the beneficiary will get a credit for that basic rate tax. Accordingly if the beneficiary is still a basic rate taxpayer even after the income from the estate is added to the beneficiaries own income, there will be no further income tax liability. On the other hand, if the beneficiary is already a higher rate taxpayer, or the income from the estate means that the beneficiaries total gross income is above the upper limit for basic rate tax, then the beneficiary will have to pay extra tax to HMRC.

Discretionary interest in residue

I(TTOI)A 2005 s 655(1) provides that income is treated as arising in the tax year from a person's discretionary interest in the whole or part of the residue of an estate if a payment is made in the tax year in exercise of the discretion in that persons favour.

The liability of the trustees and beneficiaries once the administration period has terminated

4.1.18   FA 2006 did not change the rules with regard to the taxation of the income of trusts. It is therefore necessary to distinguish between trusts where there is a beneficiary entitled to the income and those where there is no beneficiary entitled to the income, however those trusts may be treated for IHT purposes.

Income tax implications of trusts where a beneficiary is entitled to the income

If there is a beneficiary entitled to the income, then the trustees are liable for basic rate income tax on all the income they receive. Trustees are not entitled to any personal allowance, but they do not pay higher rate tax, however large the income of the trust is.

The trustees are of course under a duty to pay the income to the beneficiary who is entitled to it. The beneficiary must then include that income grossed up at basic rate in his or her income tax return. Thus if the beneficiary is already a higher rate taxpayer, the beneficiary will have to pay extra income tax on the income received. If the beneficiary does not have any income, then they may be entitled to a refund of the income tax paid by the trustees.

Income tax applications of trusts where no beneficiary is entitled to the income

If there is no beneficiary entitled to the income, then the trustees must pay the special rate applicable to trusts, which, in 2007–08, is 32·5% on the dividends and 40% for other income.

ITA 2007 s 479, which imposes this special rate to tax, provides that it applies to accumulated or discretionary income arising to the trustees of a settlement, where the income does not arise under a trust established for charitable purposes only.

ITA 2007 s 480(1) provides that income is accumulated or discretionary income so far as—

(a)   it must be accumulated; or

(b)   it is payable at the discretion of the trustees or any other person,

and it is not excluded by s 480(3).

ITA 2007 s 480(2) provides that the cases covered by s 480(1)(b) include cases where the trustees have, or any other person has, any discretion over one or more of the following matters—

(a)   whether, or the extent to which, the income is to be accumulated;

(b)   the persons to whom the income is to be paid; and

(c)   how much of the income is to be paid to any person.

ITA 2007 s 480(3) provides that income is excluded for the purposes of s 480(1) so far as *inter alia* before being distributed, it is the income of any person other than the trustees.

ITA 2007 s 491 provides that so much of the special trust tax rate income as does not exceed £1,000 is not chargeable to income tax at the dividend trust rate or the rate applicable to trusts (but is instead chargeable to income tax at the basic rate, the lower rate or the dividend ordinary rate, depending on the nature of the income). This means that the first £1,000 of all income that the trustees of a trust receive where there is no beneficiary entitled to the income receive will be taxed at basic rate, the lower rate of a dividend ordinary rate, depending on the nature of the income. However, the income above £1,000 will be subject to the special trust tax rate.

Tax pools and distributions to beneficiaries

ITA 2007 s 497 provides for "tax pools". The trustees of a discretionary trust have to pay income tax on any untaxed income they receive, and this becomes part of the tax pool. In addition, the income tax deducted at source by a payer also forms part of the tax pool.

If the trustees decide to distribute any income, then it must be grossed up at 40%, and the trustees must account to HMRC for the 40% income tax. However, if there is any tax left in the tax pool, then the trustees can offset any further income tax act which is due against the tax in the tax pool. If there is no tax left in the pool, then any further tax will have to be paid from capital or income.

If the trustees decide to distribute any of the income to members of the class of beneficiaries under the trust, then the beneficiary will receive a credit for the tax paid by the trustees. This means that if the beneficiary is a higher rate taxpayer, there will be nothing further to pay. However, if the beneficiary is a basic rate taxpayer, or does not pay income tax, then the beneficiary will be able to obtain a refund of tax.

Expenses

The trustees' expenses relating to income are not deductible in calculating the basic rate liability of trustees, but they are deductible when calculating the special rate applicable to trusts.

Example

Trustees of discretionary trust have the following income—

—   Dividends: £2,000

—   Savings income: £1,000

—   Rental income: £10,000

— The expenses amount to £3,000

Calculate the amount of expenses grossed up at the dividend ordinary rate is equal to £2,000 = £1,800. The grossed up amount is set against the dividend income and so there is no further tax liability on that income.

Calculate the amount of expenses grossed up at the savings rate is equal to £1,000 = £800. The grossed up amount is set against the savings income and so there is no further tax liability on that income.

Calculate the amount of expenses left = £400. This should be grossed up at the basic rate = £512·85. The grossed up amount is set against the rental income.

Trusts for vulnerable persons

4.1.19 FA 2005 introduced trusts with vulnerable beneficiaries, which receive special treatment for income tax and CGT. The effect of these provisions is that it is assumed that any income or capital gains accruing to the trustees of a trust for a vulnerable beneficiary has been paid over to the vulnerable beneficiary, even though the trustees may still be retaining the income or the capital gain. This means that if the vulnerable person is a higher rate taxpayer, the trustees will still be liable for higher rate tax. If the beneficiary is a basic rate taxpayer, then that is what trustees will pay.

In order for these provisions to apply, FA 2005 s 24 provides that a claim to special tax treatment for a tax year may be made by the trustees of a settlement and the vulnerable person or someone acting on behalf of the vulnerable person, for example the parent or guardian of an infant, if in any tax year they hold property on qualifying trusts for the benefit of a vulnerable person. If that is the case, a vulnerable person election has effect for all or part of the tax year in relation to those trusts and that person.

A "vulnerable person" is defined as a "disabled person" or a "relevant minor". A "disabled person" is defined in FA 2005 s 38(1) as—

(a) a person who by reason of mental disorder within the meaning of the Mental Health Act 1983 is incapable of administering his property or managing his affairs; or

(b) a person in receipt of attendance allowance or of a disability living allowance by virtue of entitlement to the care component at the highest or middle rate. FA 2005 s 38(2) provides that a person is to be treated as a disabled person under s 38(1)(b) if he satisfies the Inland HMRC:

   (i) that if he were to meet the prescribed conditions as to residence under SSCBA 1992 s 64(1) he would be entitled to receive attendance allowance; or

   (ii) that if he were to meet the prescribed conditions as to residence under the SSCBA 1992 s 71(6) he would be entitled to receive a disability living allowance by virtue of entitlement to the care component at the highest or middle rate.

FA 2005 s 39 provides that a relevant minor is a person who has not yet attained the age of 18; in addition at least one of the person's parents must have died.

FA 2005 s 34(1) provides that a disabled person's trust is one where property is held on trusts for the benefit of a disabled person which secure that the conditions specified in s 34(2) are met during the lifetime of the disabled person, or until the termination of the trusts (if that occurs before his death). Section 34(2) provides that those conditions are—

(a)   that if any of the property is applied for the benefit of a beneficiary, it is applied for the benefit of the disabled person; and

(b)   either that the disabled person is entitled to all the income (if there is any) arising from any of the property or that no such income may be applied for the benefit of any other person.

FA 2005 s 34(3) provides that the trust on which property is held is not to be treated as failing to secure that the conditions in s 34(2) are met by reason only of *inter alia* a power conferred on the trustees by TA 1925 s 32.

FA 2005 s 35(1) provides that where property is held on trusts for the benefit of a relevant minor those trusts are qualifying trusts if they are—

(a)   statutory trusts for the relevant minor under the AEA 1925 ss 46, 47(1) (succession on intestacy and statutory trusts in favour of relatives of the intestate); or

(b)   trusts to which FA 2005 s 35(2) applies.

Section 35(2) provides that the subsection applies to trusts established under the will of a deceased parent of the relevant minor, or established under the Criminal Injuries Compensation Scheme which secure that the conditions in s 35(3) are met.

Section 35(3) provides that those conditions are—

(a)   that the relevant minor will, on attaining the age of 18, become absolutely entitled to the property, any income arising from it and any income that has arisen from property held on trust for his benefit and being accumulated before that time;

(b)   that, until that time, as long as the relevant minor is living, if any of the property is applied for the benefit of a beneficiary, it is applied for the benefit of the relevant minor; and

(c)   that, until that time, for so long as the relevant minor is living, either—

(i) the relevant minor is entitled to all the income (if there is any) arising from any of the property; or

(ii) no such income may be applied for the benefit of any other person.

FA 2005 s 35(4) provides that trusts to which s 35(2) applies are not to be treated as failing to secure that the conditions in s 35(3) are met by reason only of a power conferred on the trustees by the Trustee Act 1925 s 32.

FA 2005 s 26 provides that the trustees liability to income tax for the tax year is to be reduced by an amount equal to: TQT1 – VQT1

— TQT1 is defined as an amount determined in accordance with FA 2005 s 27 (income tax liability of trustees in respect of qualifying trust's income).

— VQT1 is defined as an amount determined in accordance with FA 2005 s 28 (extra tax to which a vulnerable person would be liable if qualifying trust income were income of his).

Section 27 defines TQT1 as the amount of income tax to which the trustees would be liable for the tax year in respect of the qualifying trust income arising or treated as arising to them in that year.

Section 28 defines VQT1 as an amount equal to: TLV1 – TLV2

TLV2 is defined as the total amount of income tax and CGT to which the vulnerable person would be liable for the tax year if his income tax liability were computed in accordance with ss 28(5), 28 (6).

Section 28(5) provides that in a case where income has arisen to the trustees (whenever it arose) is distributed to the vulnerable person in the tax year, that income is to be disregarded in computing income tax to which he would be liable for the tax year for the purposes of determining TLV1 and TLV2.

Section 28(6) provides that in computing income tax to which the vulnerable person would be liable for the tax year for the purposes of determining TLV1 and TLV2, there is to be disregarded any relief which is given by way of reduction in the amount of income tax to which the vulnerable person would be liable apart from that relief.

TLV1 is defined as what TLV2 would be if the qualifying trust income arising (or treated as arising) to the trustees in the tax year in respect of which the trustees are liable to income tax were income of the vulnerable person for the tax year.

FA 2005 s 30 deals with CGT, and provides that it applies if—

(a) in the tax year chargeable gains accrue to the trustees of a settlement from the disposal of settled property which is held on qualifying trusts for the benefit of a vulnerable person ("the qualifying trusts gains");

(b) the trustees would be chargeable to CGT in respect of those gains;

(c) the trustees are either resident in the UK during any part of the tax year, or ordinarily resident in the UK during the tax year; and

(d) a claim for special tax treatment under this chapter for the tax year is made by the trustees.

If the section applies, the effect is that any gains made by the trustees are treated as the top slice of the income of the vulnerable person. Accordingly, if the vulnerable person is a higher rate taxpayer, then the trustees will pay higher rate CGT.

The perils of flexibility

4.1.20 The disadvantages of discretionary trusts or a fixed interest trust where the trustees have power to advance capital is that the settlor or testator loses control over the ultimate destination of the assets in the trust. It is common with discretionary trusts in wills for testators either to express a wish in the will as to how they would like the trustees to exercise their discretion, or alternatively to have a separate letter of wishes. The problem with expression of wishes is that they do not bind the trustees, although most trustees will feel a considerable moral obligation to give effect to the wishes of the testator.

It may be that letters of wishes could be dangerous. It is possible that a letter which is couched in demanding terms could constitute a secret trust. For example, if there was a discretionary trust, and the surviving spouse was a member of the class of beneficiaries, and the testator in his letter of wishes insists that the trustees must give priority to looking after the surviving spouse, it may be that HMRC could argue that this was a secret trust, and that an immediate post death interest in favour of the surviving spouse has been created. However, as long as the letter of wishes makes it plain that the testator is not seeking to bind the trustees in the exercise of their discretion in any manner, then it is difficult to see how HMRC could argue that there was a secret trust.

What rights do beneficiaries have?

4.1.21 It is clear that if the trustees have not complied with the terms of the trust, or have broken some duty imposed on them by law, then the beneficiaries will have a remedy against the trustees.

What duties are imposed on trustees?

4.1.22

Core duties

In *Armitage v Nurse and others* [1997] EWCA Civ 1279 Millett LJ made it clear that trustees owe an irreducible core of obligations to beneficiaries, to perform the trusts honestly and in good faith, but he did not accept that these obligations included the duties of skill and care, prudence and diligence.

In *Bartlett v Barclays Trust Co (No 1)* [1980] Ch 515 Brightman J considered the duties of a bank trustee. He said at page 532: "The bank, as trustee, was bound to act in relation to the shares and to the controlling position which they conferred, in the same manner as a prudent man of business. The prudent man of business will act in such manner as is necessary to safeguard his investment."

Later the learned judge made it clear that a professional trustee owes a higher duty of care to the beneficiaries than lay trustees. He said that "a professional person possessed of a particular skill is liable for breach of contract if he neglects to use the skill and experience which he professes."

In *West v Lazard 1993* JLR the court had to consider exemption clauses in a trust document, and made it clear that for an exemption clause to be effective, it must be drawn to the attention of the settlor. The court also made it clear that an exemption clause which purported to relieve trustees from all liablilty would not be effective as there would be no trust – the trustee could apply the trust assets as he liked.

Duty to comply with the terms of the trust

4.1.23   It almost goes without saying that the trustees must comply with the terms of the trust, and if they fail to do so, will be liable to compensate any beneficiary who suffers loss as a result. This duty to comply with the terms of the trust is a very onerous duty as it is no defence to the trustees to prove that they were mistaken as to the interpretation of the will. In addition, it is no defence to the trustees to prove that they paid out to the wrong beneficiary relying on a forged document.

Duty of reasonable care

4.1.24   The Trustees Act 2000 s 1 provides that whenever the duty under this subsection applies to a trustee, he must exercise such care and skill as is reasonable in the circumstances, having regard in particular—

(a) to any special knowledge or experience that he has or holds itself out as having; and

(b) if he acts as trustee in the course of a business or profession, to any special knowledge or experience that it is reasonable to expect of a person acting in the course of that kind of business or profession.

TA 2000 Sch 1 then lists the situations to which the duty of care applies: investment, acquisition of land, entering into arrangements with agents, nominees and custodians, compounding liabilities, insurance.

Schedule 1 para 7 provides that the duty of care does not apply if or in so far as it appears from the trust instrument that the duty is not meant to apply.

Duty to keep accounts

4.1.25 There is a duty on trustees to keep accurate accounts and investment records. In addition, there is also a duty on trustees to record the decisions made at meetings of trustees.

Duties with regard to investment

4.1.26 TA 2000 s 4 prescribes standard investment criteria. These apply whether or not the trustees are exercising an express power of investment, or the general power of investment under the TA 2000 s 3 (for more details of the power of investment, see paragraph **4.1.37**). Section 4(1) provides that in exercising any power of investment whether express or implied a trustee must have regard to the standard investment criteria. Section 4(3) provides that the standard investment criteria, in relation to a trust are—

(a) the suitability to the trust of investments of the same kind as any particular investment proposed to be made or retained and of that particular investment as an investment of that kind; and

(b) the need for diversification of investments of the trust, in so far as is appropriate to the circumstances of the trust.

This means that trustees have various decisions to make about investment. The first decision is whether they want to keep the trust assets as cash, or whether they wish to invest on the Stock Exchange, or whether they would prefer indirect investment on the Stock Exchange. Having decided that they require investment on the Stock Exchange, they must then decide whether they wish to invest, for example in the retail food sector. Having decided they wish to invest in the retail food sector, the next question is in what company they wish to invest.

Section 4(2) provides that a trustee must from time to time review the investments of the trust and consider whether having regard to the standard investment criteria they should be varied.

TA 2000 s 5(1) provides that before exercising any power of investment, a trustee must obtain and consider proper advice about the way in which, having regard to the standard investment criteria, the power should be exercised. Section 5(2) provides that when reviewing the investments of the trust, trustees must obtain and consider proper advice about whether, having regard to the standard investment criteria, the investment should be varied. Under s 5(3) this does not have to be done if the trustees reasonably conclude that in all the circumstances it is unnecessary or inappropriate to do so. "Proper advice" is defined as the advice of a person who is reasonably believed by the trustees to be qualified to give it by his ability in and practical experience of financial and other matters relating to the proposed investment.

The effect of these provisions is that the trustees will have to take advice from someone who is authorised to advise about investments under FSMA 2000. In addition, they must believe that the person is qualified by his ability in and practical experience of financial other matters relating to the proposed investment to give the advice. Such person giving advice must have regard to the standard investment criteria.

Duties when exercising discretions

4.1.27 Trustees of a discretionary trust have a special power of appointment over the assets in the trust. The trustees must not commit a fraud on the power when exercising it. This means that the trustees must not benefit a member of the class beneficiaries under the trust indirectly as a result of the exercise of the power. In *Netherton v Netherton* [2000] WTLR 1171 H was ordered to transfer some property to his ex-wife. He was also the beneficiary under a settlement, and the trustees proposed to transfer a percentage of the trust assets to him. It was held that it would not be a fraud on the power to do so as it was for the benefit of H, and not the former wife.

In *Wong v Burt* [2005] WTLR 291, a decision of the Court of Appeal of New Zealand, H died leaving a will giving his residuary estate to trustees to pay the income to his wife, W, for life, and then to such of his daughters as were then living. On the death of the surviving daughter the residuary estate passed to the children of one of his daughters, Phillipa. The trustees also had a power of advancement. Phillipa died aged 43, and W became concerned about Phillipa's two teenage children. The trustees purported to exercise the power of advancement, and handed NZ$250,000 of the capital to W, who then lent it to a trust for the benefit of Phillipa's children.

It was held—

1   The distribution was a fraud on the power, and the trustees were personally liable to repay the amount with interest. "The central principle is that if the power is exercised with the intention of benefiting some non-object of the discretionary power, whether that person is the person exercising it, or anybody else for that matter, the exercise is void. If, on the other hand, there is no such improper intention, even although the exercise does in fact benefit a non-object, it is valid."

2   The court could relieve the trustees from liability under the Trustee Act 1956 s 73 if the trustees had acted honestly and reasonably and ought fairly to be excused. However, the trustees had behaved in a foolish manner, and would not be relieved from liability by the court.

3   Clause 13 of the will provided that no trustee was to be liable for any loss not attributable to their own dishonesty or to the wilful commission by them of an act known to be a breach of trust. This did not protect the trustees as they had not acted as an honest person would.

The judge at first instance had held that a distribution made before a company was liquidated was income, but if made after liquidation was capital. The Court of Appeal refused to review this order.

The trustees may also seek directions as to how a discretion should be exercised. In *The Public Trustee v Paul Cooper* [2001] WTLR 901 some trusts were established holding shares in the Mansfield Brewery Company. An offer was received for the shares, and the trustees of one of the trusts sought directions as to whether the offer should be accepted. The trustees made it clear that they did not intend to surrender any of their discretionary powers.

It was held that the court could rule on a course of action proposed to be taken by trustees in four situations—

1   Whether a proposed course of action was within the powers of the trustees.

2   Whether the proposed course of action was a proper exercise of the powers of the trustees.

3   Where the trustees were surrendering their powers. The court would only exercise its powers in this situation if there were good reasons for the trustees surrendering their powers, for example the trustees were deadlocked, or there was conflict of interest.

4   Where the trustees had actually taken action, but it was being challenged.

However, trustees cannot surrender all decisions to the court.

What is the position if the trustees of a discretionary trust cannot agree on how the assets should be distributed, probably because they are also within the class of beneficiaries under the trust? It is to be hoped that the trustees would come to their senses, and ultimately would agree as to how the asset should be divided. If that is not the case, presumably one or all of the beneficiaries could apply to the court. If all the members of the class of beneficiaries are of age and full capacity, and there is no possibility of under age beneficiaries, then it may be that a judge would adjourn the proceedings to see if some compromise could be reached. If that was not the case, the judge could exercise his discretion, but the judge might also remove the existing trustees and appoint new trustees in their place.

Duty to hold the balance fairly between the beneficiaries

4.1.28   It is a general principle that the trustees must hold the balance fairly between the beneficiaries. This duty becomes particularly important if the trust is a life interest trust as the life tenant is of course entitled to the income, whereas the remainderman is interested in capital appreciation. It is the duty of the trustees to hold the balance fairly between the life tenant and the remainderman, to strike a balance between income and capital appreciation.

Equity developed some rules to ensure that trustees held the balance fairly between the life tenant and the remainder men. These rules are the rule in *Howe v Dartmouth* (1802) 7 Ves Jr 137, the rule in *Re Earl of Chesterfield's Trusts* (1883) 24 Ch D 643 and the rule in *Allhusen v Whittell* (1867) LR 4EQ 295.

Howe v Dartmouth provides that if there is a residuary gift of personalty for persons in succession, the trustees are under a duty to sell any trust assets which are wasting, hazardous or unauthorised, and any reversionary interests. The trustees must then invest the proceeds of sale in more suitable investments. This rule is of very limited application as it only applies to gifts in wills, and to gifts of personalty. It does not apply to lifetime settlements, or gifts of realty.

Whether or not there is a duty to convert under *Howe v Dartmouth*, if there is a duty to convert, then the life tenant is entitled to income at 4% calculated on the value of the assets in the trust as at the date of death if there is an immediate duty to convert. If there is a power to postpone the sale, then the 4% is calculated on the value one year after death

The rule in *Re Earl of Chesterfield's Trust* provides that if trustees hold reversionary interest, they do not yield any income, and accordingly when the reversionary interest is sold, it must be assumed that the life tenant is entitled to income at 4% from the testator's death and accumulating at compound interest calculated at that rate with yearly rests and deduction of income tax.

The rule in *Allhusen v Whittell* deals with liability for debts. It would be very unfair to a life tenant if the debts were paid out of the income of the estate of the deceased person, and the rule requires that they should be apportioned between the income and the capital.

The Apportionment Act 1870 requires that "all rents, annuities, dividends and other periodical payments in the nature of income …shall …be considered as accruing from day to day and shall be apportionable in respect of time accordingly".

Thus if rent is paid on a yearly basis in arrear, and the person entitled to it dies, it has to be apportioned between the period up to the date of death, and the period after the date of death. If it is a life tenant who dies, the life tenant's estate would be entitled to the rental income up to the date of death, but thereafter the remainderman would be entitled. If the rental income was paid in advance, then no apportionment is required.

The equitable rules of apportionment are frequently excluded by settlements and wills as they are difficult to operate. However, the duty to hold the balance fairly between beneficiaries can still cause difficulties for trustees in connection with bonus shares, scrip dividends, and mergers or demutualisation by building societies and insurance companies.

With regard to bonus shares, it was held in *Bouch v Sproule* (1887) 12 App Cas 385 that they were capital. Scrip dividends are also usually treated as capital. As far as mergers and demutualisation is concerned, in *Re Lee (deceased)* [1993] 3WLR 498 the shareholders of ICI were given shares in Zeneca in satisfaction of the dividend to be declared by ICI. It was held that the shares were capital.

Sir Donald Nicholls VC said at page 510—

> "Having regard to these considerations, in my view to regard the ICI trans-action as a distribution of profits, akin to payment of dividend in specie and hence income, would be to exalt company form over commercial substance to an unacceptable extent. In the last analysis, the rationale underlying the general principles enunciated in *Hills* case (1930) AC 70 CH is an endeavour by the law to give effect to the check instrument intention of the testator or settlor in respect of a particular distribution to shareholders. When the inflexible application of these principles would produce a result manifestly inconsistent with the presumed intention of the testator or settlor, the court should not be required to apply them slavishly. In origin they were guidelines. They should not be applied in circumstances, or in a manner, which would defeat the very purpose they are designed to achieve. Unless constrained by binding authority to the contrary, I consider the ICI transaction is to be characterised as a company reconstruction, with two capital assets (shares in ICI and; Zeneca group in the trustees hands replacing one capital asset (shares in ICI)."

Duty to ensure that the assets are distributed to the correct beneficiaries

4.1.29 The trustees are under a duty to ensure that the assets are distributed to the correct beneficiaries. If it is the children of the settlor who are entitled to the assets, then the trustees must ensure that they distribute the assets to the settlor's children. As this is quite an onerous duty, the trustees could mitigate the severity of it by making use of the following provisions—

Advertisements under TA 1925 s 27

TA 1925 s 27 provides that trustees may give notice by advertisement in the *Gazette*, and in a newspaper circulating in the district in which any land forming part of the estate of a deceased person or part of the trust assets is situated and such other like notices, including notices elsewhere than in England and Wales, as would in any special case, have been directed by a court of competent jurisdiction in an action for administra-tion, of the intention to make a conveyance or distribution to beneficiar-ies. The advertisement must require any person interested to send to the trustees within the time, not being less than two months, fixed in the notice, or where more than one notice is given in the last of the notices, particulars of his claim in respect of the property or any part to which the notice relates. In addition the trustees are under an obligation to make the searches and to obtain official certificates of search similar to those which an intending purchaser would be advised to make or obtain.

Section 27(2) provides that at the expiration of the time fixed by the notice the trustees may distribute the property or any part thereof to which the notice relates, to or among the persons entitled thereto, having regard only to the claims, whether formal or not, of which the trustees or personal representatives then had notice and shall not, as respects the property so conveyed or distributed, be liable to any person of whose claim the trustees or personal representatives have not had notice at the time of conveyance or distribution. However, nothing in the section is to prejudice the right of any person to follow the property, or any property representing the same, into the hands of any person, other than a purchaser, who may have received it.

Section 27 advertisements clearly protect trustees from claims of which they have no knowledge. If they have knowledge of claims, but those claims are not being pursued, then s 27 advertisements will not protect them. There is a grey area where trustees may think that there is a claim in the offing, but do not definitely know about it. In such circumstances, it is best to assume that s 27 advertisements will not protect the trustees.

Children

If the trust benefits children, it is clear that legitimate, legitimated, illegitimate and adopted children are all included, subject to any contrary intention. How are trustees to be satisfied that they have identified all the children of a settlor or testator? Frequently this will not be an issue, but there is some protection for trustees as far as adopted children are concerned. The Adoption Act 1976 s 45 provides—

(i) a trustee or personal representative is not under a duty, by virtue of the law relating to trusts or the administration of estates, to enquire before conveying or distributing any property, whether any adoption has been effected or revoked if that fact would affect entitlement to the property;

(ii) a trustee or personal representative shall not be liable to any person by reason of a conveyance or distribution of the property made without regard to any such fact if he has not received notice of the fact before the conveyance or distribution;

(iii) this section does not prejudice the right of a person to follow the property, or any property representing it, into the hands of another person other than a purchaser, who has received it.

With regard to illegitimate children there is no such protection. Trustees must then relying upon s 27 advertisements to protect them from claims from children of which they are not aware.

The Administration of Justice Act 1985 s 48(1)

This subsection provides that where—

(i) any question of construction has arisen out of the terms of a will or a trust, and

(ii) an opinion in writing given by a person who has a ten year High Court qualification within the meaning of the Courts and Legal Services Act 1990 s 71, has been obtained on that question by the personal representatives or trustees under the will or trust, the High Court may, on the application of the personal representatives or trustees and without hearing argument, make an order authorising those persons to take such steps in reliance on the said opinion as are specified in the order.

Section 48(2) provides that the High Court shall not make an order if it appears that a dispute exists which would make it inappropriate for the court to make the order without hearing argument.

TA 1925 s 61

This section enables a court to relieve a trustee from liability for breach of trust if the trustee has acted honestly and reasonably and ought fairly to be excused.

The court

If all else fails, money can be lodged in court, or there can be an application to the court for directions as to how the asset should be distributed.

Rights of beneficiaries to inspect the documents relating to the trust

4.1.30   There have been several cases in recent years over the rights of beneficiaries to inspect the trust documents, and whether there is a difference between trusts where the beneficiaries have fixed interest and discretionary trusts where there is a class of beneficiaries. It is clear from these cases that there is no difference between the rights of beneficiaries under a fixed trust and the members of a class of beneficiaries under a discretionary trust. However, the beneficiaries do not have an absolute right to see all the documents relating to the trust in the possession of the trustees. It is clear that the trustees would be justified in withholding some trust documents.

In *Rouse v IOOF Australia Trustees Limited* 2000 WTLR 111 it was stated that beneficiaries have a right to inspect trust documents, but that this was not an unqualified right. Trustees could refuse to disclose documents on the ground of confidentiality, and on the ground that it would not be in the best interests of all the beneficiaries.

In the matter of the *Rabaiotti Settlement and other settlements* [2000] WTLR 953, a decision of the Jersey Royal Court, there were four discretionary trusts. One of the persons within the class of beneficiaries was involved in divorce proceedings, and was ordered to disclose various documents relating to the trusts. It was held that a beneficiary was entitled to inspect the documents relating to the trust and that there was no good ground for refusing disclosure. However, the right of a beneficiary to see trust documents was not absolute, and the court could refuse disclosure in an appropriate case. A beneficiary was not normally entitled to see a letter of wishes, but in this case, it would be disclosed.

Schmidt v Rosewood Trust Ltd [2003] WTLR 565 is a decision of the Privy Council on appeal from the Isle of Man. It is concerned with disclosure of trust documents to beneficiaries. The Privy Council stated that no beneficiary had a right to disclosure of trust documents, but the court could order disclosure in appropriate circumstances.

In *Foreman v Kingstone* [2005] WTLR 823, a decision of the High Court of New Zealand, the plaintiffs were members of the class of beneficiaries under several family trusts. They sought disclosure of various documents concerning the trust. It was held that the beneficiaries were entitled to receive information which would enable them to ensure accountability in terms of the trust deed, but they were not entitled to be given the reasons for the decisions of the trustees.

It was directed that the trustees should disclose the following—

(a) financial statements;

(b) accounts and details of beneficiaries to whom assets had been provided;

(c) copies of all deeds appointing trustees;

(d) details of all distributions of income and capital;

(e) information as to the amount and state of the property in trust funds;

(f) information about the management of trust property;

(g) details of changes in the structure of the trusts;

(h) memoranda of wishes or like communications from the settlor.

The following did not have to be disclosed—

(i) information as to their change of policy with regard to the application of provisions in the trust document regarding distributions made to one beneficiary;

(ii) legal opinions obtained by the trustees, but not necessarily all communications between the trustees and their legal advisers;

(iii) information as to the basis on which they had made their decision.

In *Broere v Mourant* [2004] WTLR 1417, a decision of the Jersey Court of Appeal, J and C were beneficiaries under a trust. J alleged that he had been unfairly treated by the trustees, who had shown favouritism to C. J issued a summons requiring C to disclose certain documents. C alleged that these documents had come into his possession in capacities other than as a beneficiary, and that therefore they did not need to be disclosed. It was held that if the documents were relevant, they should be disclosed. It was immaterial in what capacity they were held.

Can trustees be forced to disclose the terms of the trust in proceedings to which they were not parties, for example divorce proceedings between a beneficiary and his or her spouse?

In *Charman v Charman* [2006] WTLR 1, H was very wealthy. He separated from his wife, and moved to Bermuda. In divorce proceedings, the wife applied to the court for an order for the issue of a letter to the Bermudian court to cause H's Bermudian solicitor to produce documents to the court. H argued that this was a "fishing expedition", and should not be allowed. The application was granted.

Wilson LJ quoted with approval the statement of the law by Kerr LJ in In *Re State of Norway's Application* [1987] 1 QB 433. In that case Kerr LJ said—

> "... although fishing has become a term of art for the purposes of many of our procedural rules dealing with applications for particulars of pleadings, interrogatories and discovery, illustrations of the concept are more easily recognised than defined. It arises in cases where what is sought is not evidence as such, but information which may lead to a line of enquiry which would disclose evidence. It is the search for material in the hope of being able to raise allegations of fact, as opposed to the elicitation of evidence to support allegations of fact, which have been raised *bona fide* with adequate particularisation ... It is perhaps best described as a roving enquiry, by means of the examination and cross-examination of witnesses, which is not designed to establish by means of their evidence allegations of fact which have been raised *bona fide* with adequate particulars, but to obtain information which may lead to obtaining evidence in general support of a party's case."

Powers of trustees

4.1.31 Trustees have various powers conferred on them by TA 1925, the Trusts of Land and Appointment of Trustees Act 1996, the Trustee Delegation Act 1999 and the Trustee Act 2000. The powers implied by law, and common alterations to those powers are considered in this section.

Advancement

4.1.32 TA 1925 s 32 enables trustees to advance one half of the capital to which that beneficiary will ultimately be entitled to that beneficiary.

When the beneficiary becomes absolutely entitled, then the advance must be brought into account in the final distribution. If there is a beneficiary with a prior interest, then no advance can be made to subsequent beneficiaries without the consent of the beneficiary entitled to a prior interest.

The application of the capital must be for the advancement or benefit of the beneficiary. This has been given a wide meaning, and may permit the resettlement of capital the subject of the trust. In *Pilkington v Inland Revenue Commissioners* [1964] AC 612 Viscount Radcliffe said—

> "I have not been able to find in the words of section 32, to which I have now referred, anything which in terms where or by implication restricts the width of the manner or purpose of advancement. It is true that, if the settlement is made, Penelope's children, who are not objects of the power, are given a possible interest in the event of her dying under 30 leaving surviving issue. But if the disposition itself, by which I mean the whole provision made, is for her benefit, it is no objection to the exercise of the power that other persons benefit incidentally as a result of the exercise."

If the trustees advance money for a particular purpose, it is not necessary for them to ensure that the money is applied for that particular purpose, for example the payment of school fees. However, if in the past they have advanced money for a particular purpose, and it has been misapplied then they must ensure that any future advance is applied for that particular purpose.

Note that there is no implied power to advance capital to the life tenant under a life interest trust.

Common alterations

(1) To permit the trustees to advance the whole of the capital. See PRECEDENT 9 for a further extension to the power to advance.

(2) Dispense with the requirement that the advance should be brought into account, or give the trustees a discretion as to whether it should be brought into account.

(3) If there are successive interests, to dispense with the requirement to obtain the consent of any beneficiary with a prior interest.

(4) If it is a life interest trust, to advance capital to the life tenant.

Charging clauses

4.1.33 It has for a long time been a rule of equity that trustees are not entitled to be remunerated for the work that they do; they are only entitled to be reimbursed for the expenses. This rule had become inappropriate for modern day circumstances as trusts need trustees who are professionally qualified, and such trustees will have to be paid.

TA 2000 s 29 does authorise a trustee or executor who is a trust corporation, or acts in a professional capacity to be remunerated. However, it is not an absolute entitlement to remuneration, as the consent of the other trustees must be obtained. In view of this, it is common for wills appointing professional persons as executors and trustees to include the usual charging clause; see PRECEDENT 1 CLAUSE 15.

Professional trustees should take heed of the salutary judicial comments about the extent to which they must retain a balance between clauses which exonerate trustees from liability for negligence and/or misfeasance, their level of fees, and the expectation that trustees will perform their fiduciary duties competently: *West v Lazard Brothers & Co Jersey Limited* [1993] JLR 165.

The power to delegate

4.1.34 TA 1925 contained provisions authorising trustees to delegate their powers, but these powers needed updating. The Trustee Act 2000 repealed the provisions in TA 1925 authorising trustees to delegate their powers.

The intention behind TA 2000 was that trustees should be able to delegate all their powers apart from those powers which deal with the distribution of the assets in the trust. Section 11(1) provides that trustees may authorise any person to exercise any or all of their delegable functions as their agent. Section 11(2) defines the trustees delegable functions. These are any function other than—

(a) any function relating to whether or in what way any assets of the trust should be distributed;

(b) any power to decide whether any fees or other payments due to be made out of the trust funds should be made out of income or capital;

(c) any power to appoint a person to be a trustee of the trust; or

(d) any power conferred by any other enactment or the trust instrument which permits the trustees to delegate any of their functions or to appoint a person to act as nominee or custodian.

Section 11(2) does not apply to charitable trustees. Instead s 11(3) sets out the functions that the trustees of a charity can delegate.

There is no objection to the trustees appointing one of their number as their agent, but trustees are not allowed to appoint one of the beneficiaries under the trust as their agent, even if that beneficiary is a trustee as well

An agent appointed by the trustees to exercise a specific function is subject to the same duties that the trustees owe to the beneficiaries if the trustees were carrying out that function themselves. So if trustees delegate investment decisions to an agent, the agent will be under the same duties as the trustees with regard to the standard investment criteria and taking advice about investments; the powers and duties of trustees with regard to investment are discussed in more detail in paragraph **4.1.26**. If the person to whom the trustees delegate investment decisions is qualified to advise about them, then they need not consult anyone else (Trustee Act 2000 s 13)

The Trusts of Land and Appointment of Trustees Act 1996 s 11(1) requires trustees to consult the beneficiaries of a trust of land and to give effect to the wishes of the beneficiaries so far as possible. TA 2000 s 13 makes it clear that trustees cannot delegate this duty to consult. This may be of little practical importance as frequently the duty to consult is expressly excluded by the terms of the will.

TA 2000 s 14 prescribes the terms on which trustees can employ agents. Section 14(1) provides that trustees may authorise a person to exercise trustee functions as their agent on such terms as to remuneration and other matters as they may determine. This wide discretion is then restricted by ss 14(2), (3). Section 14(2) provides that the trustees may not authorise a person to exercise functions as their agent on any of the terms mentioned in s 14(3) unless it is reasonably necessary for them to do so. Section 14(3) lists these semi-forbidding terms; they are—

(a) a term permitting the agent to appoint a substitute;

(b) a term restricting the liability of the agent or his substitute to the trustees or any beneficiary;

(c) a term permitting the agent to act in circumstances capable of giving rise to a conflict of interest.

Trustees seeking to appoint agents should be wary of standard conditions of contract as they may contain the semi-forbidding terms. See the Precedents section of this work for an example of how these practically necessary powers of delegation can be more specifically given to trustees in the body of any trust instrument.

Asset management functions

TA 2000 s 15 authorises trustees to delegate their asset management functions to an agent. There must be an agreement which is either in writing or evidenced in writing. Section 15(2) provides that the trustees may not authorise a person to exercise any of their asset management functions as their agent unless—

(a) they have prepared a statement (known as a policy statement) that gives guidance as to how the functions should be exercised; and

(b) the agreement under which the agent is to act includes a term to the effect that he will secure compliance with—

(i) the policy statement; or
(ii) if the policy statement is revised or replaced under s 22, the revised or replacement policy statement.

Section 15(3) provides that the trustees must formulate any guidance given in the policy statement with a view to ensuring that the functions will be exercised in the best interests of the trust. Section 15(4) provides that the policy statement must be in, or evidenced in, writing. Under s 22 trustees must review the performance of the agent, and if they have delegated asset management functions, then they have the following duties—

(a) a duty to consider whether there is any need to revise or replace a policy statement made for the purposes of s 15;

(b) if they consider that there is a need to revise or replace a policy statement, a duty to do so; and

(c) a duty to assess whether the terms of the policy statement are being complied with.

When reviewing the policy statement, the trustees must comply with ss 15(3), (4); any guidance given in the policy statement must be with a view to ensuring that the functions will be exercised in the best interests of the trust, and the policy statement must be in, or evidenced in, writing.

Section 15 (5) defines asset management functions of the trustees widely. They are—

(a) the investment of assets subject to the trust;

(b) the acquisition of property which is to be subject to the trust; and

(c) managing property which is subject to the trust and disposing of, or creating or disposing of an interest in, such property.

Appointment of nominees and custodians

The Trustees Act 2000 empowers trustees to appoint nominees and custodians. Section 16(1) provides that the trustees of a trust may—

(a) appoint a person to act as their nominee in relation to such of the assets of the trust as they determine; and

(b) take such steps as are necessary to secure that those assets are vested in the person so appointed.

Any appointment under this section must be in, or evidenced in, writing.

Section 17(1) provides that the trustees of the trust may appoint a person to act as custodian in relation to such assets of the trust as they have determined. Section 17(2) provides that a person is the custodian in relation to assets if he undertakes safe custody of the assets or of any documents or records concerning the assets. Section 17(3) provides that an appointment under the section must be in, or evidenced in, writing. If the trustees hold bearer securities, then under s 18 the trustees must appoint a person to act as a custodian of the securities, unless the trust instrument contains a provision which permits the trustees to retain or invest in securities payable to the bearer without appointing a person to act as a custodian. Section 18(3) provides that an appointment under the section must be in, or evidenced in, writing.

Section 19(1) provides that a person may not be appointed under ss 16, 17 or 18 as a nominee or custodian unless one of the relevant conditions is satisfied. Section 19(2) provides that the relevant conditions are that—

(a) the person carries on business which consists of or includes acting as a nominee or custodian; or

(b) the person is a body corporate which is controlled by the trustees; or

(c) the person is a body corporate recognised under the Administration of Justice Act 1985 s 9 (this is concerned with the incorporation of solicitors practices).

Section 19(3) provides that the question of whether a body corporate is controlled by trustees is to be determined in accordance with TA 1988 s 840.

Section 19(5) provides that subject to subsections (1), (4), the persons whom the trustees may appoint as a nominee or custodian under ss 16, 17 or 18 include—

(a) one of their number, if that one is a trust corporation; or

(b) two (or more) of their number, if they are to act as joint nominees or joint custodians.

Section 19(6) provides that the trustees may under s 16 appoint a person to act as their nominee even though he is also—

(a) appointed as their custodian (under ss 17 or 18 or any other powers); or

(b) authorised to exercise functions as their agent under s 11 or any other power.

Section 19(7) provides that the trustees may under those sections appoint a person to act as their custodian even though he is also—

(a) appointed to act as their nominee (under s 16 or any other power); or

(b) authorised to exercise functions as their agent (under s 11 or any other power).

Section 20(1) provides that the trustees may appoint a person to act as nominee or custodian on such terms as to remuneration and other matters as they may determine. However, s 20(2) provides that the trustees may not appoint a person to act as a nominee or custodian on any of the terms mentioned in subsection (3) unless it is reasonably necessary for them to do so. Section 20(3) contains the semi-forbidden terms; they are—

(a) a term permitting the nominee or custodian to appoint a substitute;

(b) a term restricting the liability of the nominee or custodian or his substitute to the trustees or to any beneficiary;

(c) a term permitting the nominee or custodian to act in circumstances capable of giving rise to a conflict of interest.

Remuneration of agent, nominee or custodian

If a trustee is appointed, his or her right to remuneration is governed by s 29; see above.

Section 32(1) applies if a person other than a trustee has been—

(a) authorised to exercise functions as an agent of the trustee; or

(b) appointed to act as a nominee or custodian.

Section 32(2) provides that the trustees may remunerate the agent, nominee or custodian out of the trust fund for services if—

(a) he is engaged on terms entitling him to be remunerated for those services; and

(b) the amount does not exceed such remuneration as is reasonable in the circumstances for the provision of the services by him on a half of that trust.

Section 32(3) provides that the trustees may reimburse the agent, nominee or custodian out of the trust funds for any expenses properly incurred by him in exercising functions as an agent, nominee or custodian.

Review of and liability for agents, nominees and custodians

TA 2000 ss 22 or 23 imposes a duty on trustees to review the arrangements under which the agent, nominee or custodian acts and how those arrangements are being put into effect. The trustees must intervene if they consider that it is necessary to do so. Section 23 provides that a trustee is not liable for the default of an agent, nominee or custodian provided they have complied with the duty of care when selecting the agent, nominee or custodian and when supervising the agent, nominee or custodian.

Delegation by individual trustees

4.1.35 TA 1925 s 25 as amended by the Trustee Delegation Act 1999 enables individual trustees to delegate the execution or exercise of all any of the trust, powers and discretions vested in him as trustee either alone or jointly with any other person. The delegation can only be for a maximum of 12 months after the commencement of the power. Section 25(4) provides that before or within seven days after giving a power of attorney the donor must give written notice of it (specifying the date on which the power comes into operation and its duration; the donee of the power; the reason why the power is given and where some only are delegated, the trust, powers and discretions delegated) to—

(a) each person (other than himself), if any, who under any instrument creating the trust has power (whether alone or jointly) to appoint a new trustee; and

(b) each of the other trustees, if any.

However, failure to comply with this subsection does not, in favour of the person dealing with the donee of the power, invalidate any act done or instrument executed by the donee.

Section 25(6) has a form of power of attorney, and if the form is used, or a form to the like effect but expressed to be made under s 25(5), it will operate to delegate to the person identified in the form as the single donee of the power the execution and exercise of all trusts, powers and discretions vested in the donor as trustee (either alone or jointly with any other person or persons).

Delegation to beneficiary with an interest in possession

The Trusts of Land and Appointment of Trustee Act 1996 s 9 authorises trustees to delegate any their functions by power of attorney to a beneficiary of full age and entitled to an interest in possession in land subject to the trust. It is believed that little use is made of this provision.

Delegation by a trustee who is also beneficially interested

The Trustee Delegation Act 1999 s 1(1)as amended provides that the donee of an ordinary or an enduring power of attorney or lasting power of attorney can exercise the trustee functions of the donor in relation to land, the capital proceeds of a conveyance of land or income from land. This section enables spouses, civil partners or cohabitees who are joint owners of a house to delegate trustee powers by means of an enduring power of attorney or a lasting power of attorney. However, it is still necessary for two persons to sign any transfer or conveyance.

Insurance

4.1.36 TA 1925 s 19 as amended by the TA 2000 provides that a trustee may insure any property which is subject to the trust against risk of loss or damage due to any event, and pay the premiums out of the trust funds. Note that s 19 does not impose any duty on trustees to insure the trust property, but if they fail to do so, and could have obtained insurance, and the property is destroyed, almost certainly the trustees would be liable for breach of the duty of care owed to the beneficiaries. If the trustees have tried to obtain insurance, but have not been able to do so, then of course there would be no breach of the duty of care owed to beneficiaries. Section 20 contains provisions dealing with the application of insurance money.

Investment

4.1.37   Frequently, wills will contain an express power of investment. If there is no such power, then TA 2000 s 3 provides that a trustee may make any kind of investment that he could make if he were absolutely entitled to the assets of the trust. This is known as the ' the general power of investment '. Note that the general power of investment does not permit a trustee to make investments in land other than loans secured on land; there is a separate provision authorising trustees to invest in land, which is considered below. Section 3(4) provides that a person invest in a loan secured on land if he has rights under any contract under which—

(a)   one person provides another with credit; and

(b)   the obligation of the borrower to repay is secured on land. "Credit" is defined as including any cash loan or other financial accommodation, and "cash" includes money in any form.

The trustees when exercising any power of investment whether it is an express power or the power implied by TA 2000 must have regard to the standard investment criteria, and to the requirement to obtain advice; these are considered in paragraph **4.1.26** above.

Acquisition of land

4.1.38   TA s 8(1) provides that a trustee may acquire freehold or leasehold land in the UK—

(a)   as an investment; or

(b)   for occupation by a beneficiary; or

(c)   for any other reason.

"Freehold or leasehold land" means in relation to England and Wales a legal estate in land.

Section 8(3) provides that for the purposes of exercising his functions as a trustee, a trustee who acquires land under this section has the powers of an absolute owner in relation to the land.

Maintenance

4.1.39   TA 1925 s 31 authorises trustees holding any property in trust for any person for any interest whether vested or contingent, then, subject to any prior interest or charge as affecting that property, during infancy of such person, the trustees may, at their sole discretion, pay to his parent or guardian, if any, or otherwise apply for or towards his maintenance educational benefit the whole or such part, if any, of that income of that property as may in all the circumstances be reasonable, whether or not there is—

(a) any other fund applicable to the same purpose; or

(b) any person bound by law to provide for his maintenance or education.

If the infant is entitled to a vested interest at an age greater than 18, then if s 31 applies, the infant is entitled to the income from the age of 18. Section 31 does not give the trustees a complete discretion as to whether the income is applied for the maintenance, education or benefit of the beneficiary. The trustees are directed to have regard to the age of the infant and his requirements and generally to the circumstances of the case, and in particular to what other income, if any, is applicable for the same purposes. Where the trustees have notice that the income of more than one fund is applicable for those purposes, then, so far as practicable, unless the entire income of the funds is paid or applied or the court otherwise directs, a proportionate part only of the income of each fund is to be paid or applied.

If the trustees do not apply the income for the maintenance, education or benefit of the beneficiary, then it must be accumulated. The accumulations must be held if any such person—

(a) attains the age of 18 years, or marries under that age, or forms a civil partnership under that age and his interest in such income during his infancy or until his marriage or his formation of a civil partnership is a vested interest; or

(b) on attaining the age of 18 years or on marriage or formation of a civil partnership under that age becomes entitled to the property from which such income arose in fee simple, absolute or determinable, or absolutely, or for an entailed interest.

In these circumstances, the trustees must hold the accumulations in trust for such person absolutely, but without prejudice to any provision with respect to thereto contained in any settlement by him made under any statutory powers during his infancy. The receipt of such person after marriage or formation of a civil partnership, and though still an infant, is a good discharge.

In any other case the trustees must hold the accumulations as an accretion to the capital of the property from which such accumulations arose, and as one fund with such capital for purposes, and so that, if such property is settled land, such accumulation shall be held upon the same trusts as if the same were capital money arising therefrom. However, the trustees may at any time during infancy or such person if his interest so long continues, apply as accumulations or any part thereof as if they were income arising in the then current year.

Section 31(3) provides that the section applies in the case of a contingent interest only if the limitation or trust carries the intermediate income of the property. The section also applies to a future or contingent legacy by the parent of, or a person standing in loco parentis to, the legatee, if and for such period as, under the general law, the legacy carries interest to the maintenance of the legatee.

Which contingent interests carried the intermediate income? The Law of Property Act 1925 s 175 provides that a contingent or future specific devise or bequest of property, whether real or personal, and a contingent residuary devise of freehold land, and a specific or residuary devise of freehold land to trustees upon trust for persons whose interests are contingent or executory shall, subject to the statutory provisions relating to accumulations, carry the intermediate income of that property from the death of the testator, except so far as such income, or any part may be otherwise expressly disposed of. A contingent bequest of residuary personalty will also carry the intermediate income (*Re Adams* 1893 1 Ch 329).

A contingent pecuniary legacy does not normally carry interest until the time when it is payable, and so is outside s 31. However, interest will be payable on such a legacy, and it will therefore carry the intermediate income—

(i) if the donor has shown an intention that the income should be applied for the maintenance of the beneficiary;

(ii) if the testator is the parent of the beneficiary, or stands in *loco parentis* to the beneficiary, the testator has not made any other provision for the beneficiary, the gift is directly to the beneficiary, and the condition to be satisfied is attaining an age no greater than 18;

(iii) if the testator has directed that the legacy should be set aside for the benefit of a beneficiary.

Common variations

(1) The trustees have an absolute discretion as to whether or not the income should be applied for the benefit of a beneficiary.

(2) The entitlement to income may be postponed until a greater age.

Sale

4.1.40   The Trusts of Land and Appointment of Trustees Act 1996 s 6(1) authorises trustees to sell any land subject to the trust. Section 8(2) provides that if the disposition creating such a trust makes provision requiring any consent to be obtained to the exercise of any power conferred by s 6 or s 7, the power may not be exercised without that consent. Section 10(1) provides that if the disposition creating a trust of land requires consent of more than two persons to the exercise by the trustees of any function relating to the land the consent of any two of them to the exercise of the function is sufficient in favour of a purchaser. This does not apply to the exercise of a function by trustees of land held on charitable, ecclesiastical or public trusts (section 10(2)).

The 1996 Act also imposed a duty on trustees to consult the beneficiaries of full age and absolutely entitled of a trust of land as to what should happen with the land. This duty is frequently excluded by wills.

Mode of sale

TA 1925 s 12 gives trustees a wide discretion as to how they sell the assets which are the subject of the trust. However, s 6(9) provides that the duty of care under the TA 2000 s 1 applies to trustees of land when exercising the power of sale conferred by that section. This of course means that trustees must obtain the best possible price, and that means selecting the method of sale which is going to yield the best possible price.

Power to convey the land to beneficiaries

4.1.41   The Trusts of Land and Appointment of Trustees Act 1996 s 6(2) provides that where in the case of any land subject to a trust of land each of the beneficiaries interested in the land is a person of full age and capacity who is absolutely entitled to the land, the trustees may convey the land to the beneficiaries even though they have not required the trustees to do so. Where land is conveyed by virtue of this subsection, the beneficiaries must do whatever is necessary to secure that the land is vested in them, and if they fail to do so the court may make an order requiring them to do so.

This provision may be useful to trustees holding land on trust for beneficiaries who are of full age and capacity, and cannot agree as to what should happen to the land. The trustees could transfer the land to those beneficiaries.

Part B1

Precedents: Wills and Will Clauses

Precedent 1

Model will

THIS IS THE LAST WILL and TESTAMENT of [ME]

1   I HEREBY REVOKE all previous wills and testamentary dispositions made by me and DECLARE that this Will deals with all my property real and personal [*except my real estate situate in France/Spain/Portugal*][1]

2   I APPOINT my wife[2] [*Winifrid*] ("*Winifrid*") and [*A N Other*] of [*address*] to be the Executors of this my Will (hereinafter called "my Executors" which expression shall include any executor or executors for the time being hereof)

3   I APPOINT [*Winifrid and T2 and T3/Offshore Trustee Company Ltd whose registered office is at ...*] or the successor company to that company to be the Trustees of the trusts established by this my Will and any Codicil to it AND I DECLARE that the expression "my Trustees" means the trustees hereof for the time being

4   I GIVE the following pecuniary legacies

4.1   to my godson Frederick the sum of £5,000 (five thousand pounds)

4.2   etc etc

5   I GIVE the following

5.1   my diamond solitaire engagement ring to my daughter Eloise

5.2   my largest diamond tiara to my god-daughter Princess Zoe

5.3   etc etc (not that the testator in this model is a cross-dresser)

6   IN this my Will and in the Schedule hereto "Fund" means such sum as is equal to the amount which is the upper limit at the date of my death of the first nil-rate portion of value referred to in Section 7(3) of the Inheritance Tax Act 1984 in accordance with Section 8 of that Act but reduced by the aggregate of the values transferred by previous chargeable transfers made by me in the period of seven years ending with the date of my death and the value of any legacies in this Will or any Codicil hereto to the extent that they are not exempt from inheritance tax and the terms "values transferred" and "chargeable transfers" have the same meanings as in the Inheritance Tax Act 1984 and references to any statute shall mean such statute modified or re-enacted from time to time and words and phrases defined in the Schedule hereto shall have the same meaning as in this my Will

7   IF my wife [*Winifrid*] shall survive me by thirty days at least[3] then I GIVE the Fund free of inheritance tax and all other duties payable on or in

respect of my death to my Trustees to hold upon trust with and subject to the powers and provisions set out in the Schedule which forms part of this my Will and my Executors may require my Trustees to accept in satisfaction of all or part of the Fund a binding promise of payment whether secured or unsecured made personally by my wife [*Winifrid*] or by my Executors which debt shall be payable on demand and my Trustees shall accept such as the whole or as part (as the case may be) of the Fund

8   I BEQUEATH AND DEVISE all the residue of my real and personal property wheresoever and whatsoever to which this Will applies ("my Residuary Estate") to my Executors to hold UPON TRUST to sell call in and convert the same into money (with power to postpone such sale calling in and conversion for so long as my Executors think fit without being responsible for any consequent loss and with power to distribute assets in specie) and to hold the same together with any ready money belonging to me at the date of my death to pay thereout my just debts and my funeral and testamentary expenses and any inheritance tax or other taxes arising on or by reason of my death and to pay or transfer the balance of my Residuary Estate to my Trustees TO HOLD upon trust for my wife [*Winifrid*] for life if she shall have survived me by thirty days at least (except that such conditional survivorship shall not apply where our deaths are simultaneous or our deaths occur in circumstances rendering it uncertain which one of us survived the other) and subject thereto and if she shall not so survive me (or otherwise as aforesaid and in any event after her death) UPON THE TRUSTS specified in the Schedule hereto which forms part of this my Will

9   MY TRUSTEES may in their discretion from time to time pay to [*Winifrid*] free of the trusts hereof the whole or any part or parts of the capital of my Residuary Estate

10   THE POWER of appointing and removing Trustees in respect of the trust of my Residuary Estate shall be vested in the person or persons for the time being who may be the Appointor in accordance with the Schedule to this my Will

11   SUBJECT always to the life interest of my wife [*Winifrid*] given by clause 6 above in dealing with my Residuary Estate my Trustees shall in addition have all the powers and discretions set out in the Schedule to this my Will (including without limitation and without the need to obtain the consent of any person[4] the power of appointment given to them by paragraph 5 of that Schedule)

12   I DECLARE that the receipt of the parent or guardian of any infant beneficiary hereunder and the receipt of the secretary or other proper officer of any charity or other organisation taking benefit hereunder shall be a full discharge to my Executors and Trustees in respect of the same

13   I DECLARE that all income of my estate shall be treated as arising at the time of its receipt by my Executors and shall not be apportioned to any other time or period under the Apportionment Acts 1834 and 1870

and I hereby exclude for the purposes of this my Will the rules of equitable apportionment and any other technical rules of administration[5]

14 MY EXECUTORS and MY TRUSTEES shall have power at any time to exercise the power of appropriation conferred upon personal representatives by Section 41 of the Administration of Estates Act 1925 and to exercise such power without the consent of any person whose consent could or might but for this present provision be or have been made requisite[6]

15 Any of my Executors and any of my Trustees who is engaged in any profession or business shall be entitled to charge and be paid all usual reasonable professional and other charges for work or business done or transacted by him or his firm in connection with acting as an Executor hereof including acts which Executors or Trustees not being engaged in any profession or business could do personally[5]

16 SUBJECT TO paragraph 15 of the Schedule hereto this Will shall be construed in accordance with the laws of England

Schedule

1 Name

This Trust shall be known as **The #### Will Trust** or by such other name as the Trustees shall from time to time determine.

2 Definitions

In this Trust where the context admits—

2.1 The following expressions mean and include the following—

Expression	Meaning
"Appointor"	Winifrid during her lifetime unless and until and for such period as she is incapable of managing her own affairs by reason of mental or physical incapacity (such mental incapacity to be certified to the Trustees by a medical practitioner of at least 5 years standing and so certified at intervals of not longer than 12 months during such period of incapacity and such physical incapacity to be evidenced conclusively by Winifrid in the opinion of my Trustees being unable to sign a document or to give an oral or demonstrative instruction to another person to sign a document on her behalf) and during such period of Winifrid's incapacity and in any event after her death my Trustees.

"Beneficiaries"	The persons specified in the Appendix hereto (and "Beneficiary" shall include any one or more of the Beneficiaries).
"Trustees"	The Trustees for the time being of this Trust (and "Trustee" shall include any one or more of the Trustees).
"Trust Fund"	(1) For the purposes of Clause 6 of the Will, the Fund, and the purposes of Clause 8 of the Will, my Residuary Estate; and in either case; (2) all other (if any) money investments and other property which may in future be paid or transferred to or under the control of the Trustees by any person to be held on these trusts and which shall be accepted by the Trustees as an addition to the Trust Fund; (3) all other accretions to the Trust Fund by way of accumulation of income or otherwise; and (4) all money investments or other property for the time being representing all or any part of the above.
"Trust Period"	The period ending eighty years after the date of my death or such shorter period as the Trustees shall in their absolute discretion in writing decide and that period shall be the perpetuity period applicable hereto.
"Will"	The Will of [ME] to which this is the Schedule.

2.2 References to the singular shall include the plural and vice versa.

2.3 References to any gender shall include the other genders.

2.4 References to statutory provisions shall include statutory modifications and re-enactments of such provisions.

2.5 References to a particular power or discretion vested in the Trustees shall be construed without prejudice to the generality of any other powers or discretions.

2.6 Clause descriptions are included for reference only and shall not affect the interpretation of this Trust.

2.7 Words and phrases defined in the Will shall have the same meaning in this Schedule.

3 Trust for sale

The Trustees shall hold the Trust Fund upon trust in their absolute discretion either to retain the Trust Fund in its existing state or to sell call in or convert into money the whole or any part or parts of the Trust Fund (but with power to postpone such sale calling in and conversion) and in their absolute discretion to invest or apply the net proceeds of such sale calling in or conversion in any manner authorised by this Trust or by law with power at any time or times to vary or transpose any such investments or applications for others so authorised.

4 Trusts of added property

The Trustees may at any time or times during the Trust Period accept such additional property of whatever kind (including property of an onerous kind the acceptance of which the Trustees consider to be beneficial) as may be paid or transferred to them upon these trusts by any person in whatever manner.

5 Power of appointment over capital and income

5.1 The Trustees shall hold the capital and income of the Trust Fund upon trust for all or such one or more of the Beneficiaries at such ages or times in such shares and upon such trusts (whether created by the Trustees or not) for the benefit of all or any one or more of the Beneficiaries as the Trustees may in their absolute discretion decide at any time or times during the Trust Period to appoint and in making any such appointment the Trustees shall have powers as full as those which they could possess if they were the absolute beneficial owners of the Trust Fund including the power (in their absolute discretion subject to paragraph 8 hereof) to extend restrict amend vary or release all or any of the powers of administration or investment hereunder or (with the written consent of the Appointor) at any time(s) to add to the class of Beneficiaries hereunder and provided always that if the terms of any revocable appointment have not been revoked before the end of the Trust Period such appointment shall at that time become irrevocable.

5.2 In addition the Trustees may from time to time pay or transfer the whole or any part or parts of the capital or income of the Trust Fund to the Trustees for the time being of any other trust wheresoever established or existing and whether governed by the same proper law as this Trust or by the law of any other state or territory under which any one or more of the Beneficiaries is or are interested notwithstanding that such other trust may also contain trusts powers and provisions (discretionary or otherwise) in favour of some other person or persons or objects if the Trustees shall in their absolute discretion consider such payment to be for the benefit of such one or more of the Beneficiaries.

5.3 The receipt of the parent or guardian of any infant to whom assets may be appointed and the receipt of the secretary or other property officer of any charitable or other organisation to which assets may be appointed will be a conclusive and complete discharge to the Trustees.

6 Power to accumulate income

In default of and subject to any appointment made under the provisions of the preceding paragraph 5 during the Trust Period the Trustees shall pay or apply the income of the Trust Fund to or for the maintenance and support or otherwise for the benefit of all or any one or more of the Beneficiaries as the Trustees may in their absolute discretion think fit but during the period of twenty-one (21) years from the date of my death the Trustees may if they in their absolute discretion think fit accumulate such income or any part of it by way of compound interest by investing the same and its resulting income in any way hereby authorised and if they do so they shall hold such accumulations as part of the capital of the Trust Fund but may nonetheless in any future year during the Trust Period apply them or any part of them as if they were income arising in that year.

7   Ultimate default trusts

Subject as above the Trustees shall hold the Trust Fund and its income for the Beneficiaries described in paragraph 3 of the Appendix hereto living at the end of the Trust Period if more than one in equal shares absolutely.

8   Power to vary

The power to extend restrict amend vary or release any powers of administration or investment hereof or to add to or restrict in any way the class of Beneficiaries hereunder may be validly exercised by the Trustees only if prior to implementing any such act the Trustees shall have been advised in writing by a lawyer qualified for at least ten years in the jurisdiction to which the Trust Fund is then subject that it would be expedient for the purposes of the management and administration of the Trust Fund to act in the manner specified in such written advice and provided that acting in such manner will not be in breach of any relevant law against perpetuities. [*For an example of wider and more detailed Trustee powers see* APPENDIX 5 PRECEDENT 7]

9   Power to invest

The Trustees in their absolute discretion may retain any investments in which the Trust Fund is invested from time to time and may invest monies as if without restriction they were the absolute beneficial owners thereof and in particular they may purchase or lend at interest upon the security of any property real or personal of whatever nature and wheresoever situate in such manner as the Trustees think fit whether or not producing income or involving liabilities or not including in particular (but without prejudice to the generality of the foregoing) insurance policies on the life of any Beneficiary or other person shares stocks and land including any house or flat and its contents as a residence for any Beneficiary on whatever terms the Trustees in their discretion think appropriate and may vary or switch any such investment in all cases without being liable for loss and in all respects as if they were absolutely beneficially entitled and not subject to any restriction as to taking advice or otherwise in relation to investment.

10   Power to borrow and insure

In addition to their statutory powers the Trustees shall have the following powers—

10.1 to borrow money with or without giving security and on such terms as they think fit for any purpose (including investment);

10.2 to insure as they think fit any property which may form part of the Trust Fund, the cost of such insurance to be paid out of the income or capital of the Trust Fund as the Trustees shall think fit.

11   Liability for loss

In the professed execution of the trusts and powers hereof no trustee being an individual shall be liable for any loss to the trust fund or for breach of trust arising by reason of any improper investments made in good faith or for the negligence or fraud of any agent employed by him or by any other trustee hereof although the employment of such agent was not strictly necessary or expedient or by reason of any mistake or omission or commission made or suffered to be made in good faith by any trustee hereof or by reason of any other matter or thing except wilful and individual fraud of which he was personally conscious on the part of the trustee sought to be made so liable or gross negligence and no trustee shall be bound to take proceedings against a co-trustee or past trustee or his personal representatives for any breach or alleged breach of trust committed or suffered by such co-trustee or past trustee.

12   Appointment and removal of trustees

12.1   The power of appointing new and additional Trustees hereof shall be vested in the Appointor for the time being hereof and subject thereto in the Trustees for the time being.

12.2   The Appointor shall be entitled to remove Trustees (provided at all times that there remains a minimum of one Trustee acting) upon giving not less than 21 days written notice to the Trustees and by executing a Deed removing the Trustee. Any such removed Trustee shall do all that is necessary to effect the transfer of the Trust Fund to the remaining or newly appointed Trustee(s) and if such actions have not been completed within 30 days of the date of the Deed removing any Trustee from office the then Trustees for the time being hereof are hereby empowered in the name of the removed Trustee to do all acts and things necessary to effect the transfer of the Trust Fund into the name of the Trustees.

13   Indemnity to retiring trustees

13.1   Subject to paragraph 13.2 below any person ceasing to be a trustee of this Trust shall be entitled to an indemnity from the Trustees to the extent permitted by law from and against all and any actions proceedings or defaults accounts costs claims and demands including without prejudice to the generality of the foregoing any liability incurred or which may have been incurred whether of a fiscal nature or not and whether enforceable or not and arising in any part of the world.

13.2   No indemnity given pursuant to paragraph 13.1 above shall extend to provide indemnity to any person who has acted at any time as a Trustee of this Trust in respect of any act or omission of fraud or willful or gross negligence by such person.

14   Trustee charges

Any Trustee for the time being of this Trust being engaged in any profession or business shall be entitled to charge and be paid all usual reasonable professional and other charges for work or business done or transacted by him or his firm in connection with the trusts hereof including acts which a Trustee not being engaged in any profession or business could do personally and any corporate trustee hereof for the time being shall be entitled to charge in accordance with its published scale of fees for the time being in force PROVIDED THAT during the lifetime or the Appointor no fees shall be paid to any Trustee unless the amount of such fees are approved in writing by the Appointor.

15 Proper law

This Trust is subject to the law of England and Wales but the Trustees may in their discretion from time to time by Deed declare that this Trust shall thenceforth be subject to the laws of any other jurisdiction.

Appendix

The Beneficiaries

1   My wife Winifrid.

2   My children A (born on ###)[6] B (born on ###) and C (born on ###)

3   The issue of the Beneficiaries names or described in paragraph 2 above born before the end of the Trust Period

4   Any person added to the class of Beneficiaries by exercise of the power conferred by paragraph 5.1 of this Trust

IN WITNESS whereof I have signed my name this day of Two thousand and [###]

SIGNED by the above-named)

[testator])

and for his last Will in the presence of)

us both being present at the)

same time who at his request)

and in his presence and in the)

presence of each other have)

hereunto subscribed our names as)

witnesses:)

Witness Signature ....

Full Name ....

Address ....

....

Occupation ....

Witness Signature ....

Full Name ....

Address ....

....

Occupation ....

[1] As noted in paragraph **2.1.18** prudent advice is that real estate owned outside the UK should be subject to a separate will made in the jurisdiction where the property is situated.

[2] This model is drafted for a testator. Where a testatrix uses this model, appropriate changes will need to be made.

[3] A conditional survivorship clause is advisable, in order to keep average rates of IHT as low as possible between partners. Without the conditional survivorship clause, it if the wife were to die immediately after husband, the advantage of owning assets between them in approximately equal shares will be lost, so that distributions from will trusts will attract higher rates of IHT. See paragraphs **2.1.14–2.1.17**.

[4] Avoiding the need to obtain the consent of the surviving partner before making a capital advance within Trustee Act 1925 s 32(1), and avoiding the 50% advancement restriction in that section.

[5] The all-important clause to any professional will draftsman. Absent this clause no executor can charge fees for acting. *Re Barber* (1886) 34 Ch D 77; *Dale v IRC* [1954] AC 11,27.

[6] Appropriate only if children are infants when the Will is signed.

[7] There need to be a minimum of three trustees including A for this clause to operate effectively.

[8] Wording in square brackets appropriate where Appointor is also a trustee.

Precedent 2

Clause to ensure that agricultural property relief/business property relief property can form part of the NRB Trust

I DECLARE that my Executors may appropriate in or towards satisfaction of the Fund any relevant business property or agricultural property (as respectively defined by section 39(A)(7) of the Inheritance Tax Act 1984) which I own at my death reduced in accordance with section 104 or section 116 of that Act (as the case may be) or any statutory modification or re-enactment of them.

Precedent 3

Protective trust clauses for inclusion in a will

I BEQUEATH AND DEVISE all the residue of my real and personal property wheresoever and whatsoever to which this Will applies ('my Residuary Estate') to my Executors to hold UPON TRUST to sell call in and convert the same into money (with power to postpone such sale calling in and conversion for so long as my Executors think fit without being responsible for any consequent loss and with power to distribute assets in specie) and to hold the same together with any ready money belonging to me at the date of my death to pay thereout my just debts and my funeral and testamentary expenses and any inheritance tax or other taxes arising on or by reason of my death and to pay or transfer the balance of my Residuary Estate to my Trustees

1.1   TO HOLD (subject to clause #.2 below) upon protective trusts in accordance with Section 33 Trustee Act 1925 for my wife *Winifrid* for life if she shall have survived me by thirty days at least (except that such conditional survivorship shall not apply where our deaths are simultaneous or our deaths occur in circumstances rendering it uncertain which one of us survived the other) and subject thereto and if she shall not so survive me (or otherwise as aforesaid and in any event after her death) UPON THE TRUSTS specified in [...]

1.2   The provisions of this clause shall apply notwithstanding the provisions of clause 1.1

1.2.1—My Trustees may at any time while *Winifrid* is living by deed revocable during the Trust Period (as defined in clause ### hereof) or irrevocable declare that the income of my Residuary Estate or any part of it shall be paid to *Winifrid* during her lifetime freed from the protective trusts

1.2.2—Until my Trustees have notice of any act or event causing *Winifrid* to be deprived of the right to the income of the whole or any part of my Residuary Estate my Trustees shall not be liable if they continue to pay or apply such income to or for her benefit

1.2.3—MY TRUSTEES may in their discretion from time to time pay to *Winifrid* free of the trusts hereof the whole or any part or parts of the capital of my Residuary Estate and in exercising their discretion so to do my Trustees shall be entitled to have regard solely to

Winifrid's interests and to disregard all other interests or potential interests in the Trust Fund. The provisions of this clause shall apply notwithstanding the provisions of clause #.1

Alternative clause 1.1 to allow for determination of fixed interest in the event of remarriage or new civil partnership by surviving spouse

1.1 TO HOLD (subject to clause 1.2 below) upon protective trusts in accordance with Section 33 Trustee Act 1925 but as if the words "or if she shall re-marry or enter into a civil partnership with any person" were inserted in sub-section (1) thereof after the words "he would be deprived of the right to receive the same or any part thereof" for my wife Winifrid for life if she shall have survived me by thirty days at least (except that such conditional survivorship shall not apply where our deaths are simultaneous or our deaths occur in circumstances rendering it uncertain which one of us survived the other) and subject thereto and if she shall not so survive me (or otherwise as aforesaid and in any event after her death) UPON THE TRUSTS specified in […].

Precedent 4

Disabled person's trust

Definitions

"Principal Beneficiary"	AB [being a disabled person within IHTA 1984 s 89 – ie a person entitled to be in receipt of attendance allowance within the Social Security Contributions and Benefits Act 1992 s 64 or the Social Security (Northern Ireland) Contributions and Benefits Act 1992 – see IHTA 1984 s 89(4)–(7)
"Qualifying Settlement"	any settlement or trust, wherever and whenever established, which shall be for the benefit of all or any one or more of the Beneficiaries notwithstanding that other persons (other than Excluded Persons) may also benefit thereunder

1 Power of appointment over capital and income

1.1 The Trustees shall hold the Trust Fund and its income upon trust for all or any to the exclusion of the other or others of the Beneficiaries at such age or time and if more than one at such respective ages or times in such shares and with such trusts including protective trusts for their respective benefit and such provisions for their respective advancement maintenance education and benefit or for forfeiture in any event or to the trustees of any Qualifying Settlement and otherwise at the discretion of any person or persons and with such discretionary and administrative trusts and powers and generally in such manner in all respects as the Trustees may in their absolute and uncontrolled discretion at any time or times or from time to time during the Trust Period by any deed or deeds revocable before the end of the Trust Period or irrevocable appoint **PROVIDED ALWAYS that not less than one half of any distribution payments or benefits applied by the Trustees during the lifetime of the Principal Beneficiary shall be applied for the benefit of the Principal Beneficiary.**

1.2 No exercise of the power or powers conferred by this clause shall invalidate any previous payment or application of all or any part or parts of the Trust Fund or its income made under any other power conferred by this Trust or by law.

1.3 In any appointment under the above power the Trustees may delegate to any person or persons all or any of the powers and discretions vested in them by this Trust or by law.

2 Trusts in default of appointment

Until and subject to and in default of any exercise of the power or powers contained in Clause #, and provided always that during the lifetime of the Principal Beneficiary not less than one half of all distributions and applications of Trust monies and benefits shall be applied for the benefit of the Principal Beneficiary:

2.1 during the Trust Period the Trustees shall pay or apply the income of the Trust Fund to or for the benefit of all or such one or more to the exclusion of the other or others of the Beneficiaries for the time being in existence in such manner and if more than one in such shares as the Trustees in their absolute discretion from time to time think fit;

2.2 notwithstanding sub-clause 2.1—

2.2.1—the Trustees may at any time or times during the Accumulation Period in their absolute discretion accumulate any income of the Trust Fund by investing or applying that income and its resulting income in any manner authorised by this Trust or by law and subject to sub-clause 2.2.2 shall hold those accumulations as an accretion to the capital of the Trust Fund and as one fund with it for all purposes; and

2.2.2—the Trustees may at any time or times during the Accumulation Period apply the whole or any part or parts of the income accumulated under sub-clause 2.2.1 as if it were income arising in the then current year;

2.3 notwithstanding sub-clause 2.1 and 2.2 the Trustees may at any time or times during the Trust Period—

2.3.1—pay apply or transfer all or any part of the Trust Fund to or for the benefit of all or such one or more of the Beneficiaries exclusive of the others or other of them in such shares if more than one and in such manner generally as the Trustees shall in their absolute discretion think fit;

2.3.2—pay or transfer all or any part of the Trust Fund or its income to the trustees of any other trust wherever established or existing under which any one or more or all of the Beneficiaries is or are interested (whether or not such one or more or all of the Beneficiaries is or are the only persons interested in or capable of benefiting under such other trust but not so that any of the Excluded Persons shall be capable of benefiting under such trust) if the Trustees shall in their absolute discretion consider such payment or transfer to be for the benefit of such one or more or all of the Beneficiaries; and

2.3.3—lend all or any part of the Trust Fund upon such terms as to repayment and as to interest and with or without security and generally as they in their absolute discretion think fit to the trustees of any such trust as is described in sub–clause 2.3.2.

Precedent 5

Trust for bereaved minors—clauses for inclusion in a will

I BEQUEATH AND DEVISE all the residue of my real and personal property wheresoever and whatsoever to which this Will applies ('my Residuary Estate') to my Executors to hold UPON TRUST to sell call in and convert the same into money (with power to postpone such sale calling in and conversion for so long as my Executors think fit without being responsible for any consequent loss and with power to distribute assets in specie) and to hold the same together with any ready money belonging to me at the date of my death to pay thereout my just debts and my funeral and testamentary expenses and any inheritance tax or other taxes arising on or by reason of my death and to pay or transfer the balance of my Residuary Estate to my Trustees

1.1   TO HOLD (subject to clause #.2 below) upon trusts in accordance with Section 71A Inheritance Tax Act 1984 for my children A and B until they attain the age of 18 years when they shall become absolutely entitled in equal shares to my Residuary Estate

1.2   The administrative powers given to my Trustees by the Schedule to this my Will shall apply insofar as they do not conflict with the terms of the said Section 71A.

Precedent 6

Flexible will—two-year discretionary trust

1 I BEQUEATH AND DEVISE all the residue of my real and personal property wheresoever and whatsoever to which this Will applies ('my Residuary Estate') to my Executors to hold UPON TRUST to sell call in and convert the same into money (with power to postpone such sale calling in and conversion for so long as my Executors think fit without being responsible for any consequent loss and with power to distribute assets in specie) and to hold the same together with any ready money belonging to me at the date of my death to pay thereout my just debts and my funeral and testamentary expenses and any inheritance tax or other taxes arising on or by reason of my death and to pay or transfer the balance of my Residuary Estate to my Trustees TO HOLD UPON THE TRUSTS specified in the next following provisions of this my Will.

2 In the trusts applicable to this my Will the following expressions shall bear the following meanings—

2.1 'the Perpetuity Day' shall mean the day which is 80 years after the date of my death and no other day shall be the Perpetuity Day in relation to the trusts hereof;

2.2 'the Accumulation Day' shall mean the day which is 21 years after the date of my death;

2.3 'the Beneficiaries' shall mean the following persons for the living of my death or born thereafter but before the Perpetuity Day—

2.3.1—my wife Winifrid

2.3.2—my children and remoter issue

2.3.3—the spouses civil partners widows and widowers and surviving civil partners of such children and remoter issue

2.3.4—[others];

2.4 my Trustees shall stand possessed of my Residuary Estate and the income thereof upon such trusts for the benefit of the Beneficiaries or any one or more of them exclusive of the other or others in such shares and proportions and subject to such terms and limitations and with and subject to such provisions for maintenance education or advancement or for accumulation of income or for forfeiture in the event of bankruptcy or otherwise and with such discretionary trusts and powers exercisable by such persons as my Trustees shall at any time or times by deed or deeds revocable before the Perpetuity Day or irrevocable and executed before the Perpetuity Day in their absolute discretion appoint;

2.5   in default of and subject to any such appointment my Trustees shall until the Perpetuity Day pay apply or appropriate to the whole of the income of my Residuary Estate to or for the benefit of all or such one or more exclusive of the others or other of the Beneficiaries in such proportions and manner as my Trustees shall in their absolute discretion think fit provided always that until the Accumulation Day the Trustees shall have power instead to accumulate all or any of such income by capitalising it as an accretion to any part of my Residuary Estate;

2.6   in default of and subject to any such appointment on the date two years after the date of my death the Trustees shall stand possessed of my Residuary Estate UPON TRUST for my wife [*Winifrid*] for life if she shall have survived me by thirty days at least (except that such conditional survivorship shall not apply where our deaths are simultaneous or our deaths occur in circumstances rendering it uncertain which one of us survived the other) and subject thereto and if she shall not so survive me (or otherwise as aforesaid and in any event after her death) UPON THE TRUSTS specified in the previous paragraphs of this clause;

2.7   in default of and subject to any such appointment and the provisions of sub-clause 2.6 above the Trustees shall stand possessed of my Residuary Estate on the Perpetuity Day upon trust as to income and capital for all or such one or more of the Beneficiaries as shall then be living in such shares as my Trustees shall prior to on the Perpetuity Day determine and in the absence of such determination if more than one in equal shares absolutely.

Precedent 7

Powers of Trustees

1 Investment

1.1 The Trustees may to invest or apply any money subject to these trusts in any investments of whatever nature and wherever situate and whether producing income or not as the Trustees shall in their absolute discretion think fit so that the Trustees shall have the same full and unrestricted powers of making and changing investments as if they were absolute beneficial owners of such money or other property.

1.2 The acquisition of any reversionary interest or any life endowment sinking fund or other policy or any annuity or securities or other investments not producing income or of a wasting nature or for any other reason not within the meaning of the word 'Investment' strictly construed shall be an authorised investment of trust money if the Trustees shall consider such acquisition to be for the benefit of any one or more of the Beneficiaries.

1.3 The Trustees may exchange property for other property of a similar or different nature and for such consideration and on such conditions as they in their absolute discretion think fit.

1.4 The Trustees may retain any property in the form in which it is received by them without being responsible for any loss occasioned by such retention.

1.5 The Trustees shall have express power at their absolute discretion to invest or keep invested the whole of the Trust Fund in the securities of any one company unit trust investment trust or other fund and shall not be liable or accountable in any manner for any loss caused by failure to diversify or consider diversification of investments and shall not be bound to maintain a balance between capital and income.

2 Real property

Where the Trust Fund for the time being includes any real property or any interest in it ('the land')—

2.1 the Trustees shall in relation to the land have all the powers of granting entering into and accepting leases tenancies mortgages charges easements restrictive covenants options licences surrenders of leases and other rights of any nature for any purpose and whether involving waste or not and for any term and subject to any conditions and whether with or without consideration as the Trustees in their absolute discretion think fit and the Trustees shall have generally all the powers of disposition and management of a sole absolute beneficial owner of land;

2.2   the Trustees may from time to time expend any part of the Trust Fund or its income in improving developing erecting enlarging demolishing repairing rebuilding altering decorating and furnishing the land or any buildings or other structures on all or any part of the land to such extent and in such manner as they shall in their absolute discretion think fit;

2.3   the Trustees may pay from the Trust Fund or its income the costs of and incidental to obtaining permission for any development of the land or of any buildings or other structures on the land;

2.4   the Trustees shall not be bound to see nor be liable or accountable for omitting or neglecting to see to the repair or insurance of any buildings or other structures on the land or to the payment of any outgoings in respect of them or otherwise as to the maintenance of the land but may repair and insure any such buildings or other structures in such manner and to such extent as they shall in their absolute discretion think fit;

2.5   the Trustees may in relation to the land use any part of the Trust Fund or its income to stock equip and manage any commercial woodlands or any farm or other buildings and may engage in forestry and carry on any farming or other business whatever in any part of the world;

2.6   the Trustees may in executing any trust or power sell all or any part of the land either wholly or partly in consideration of any sum reserved or secured in such manner as the Trustees shall in their absolute discretion think fit;

2.7   the Trustees may in executing any trust or power of sale or leasing—

2.7.1—sell or lease all or any part of the land (however any division of the land may be made);

2.7.2—sell or lease or reserve any easement or right or privilege over all or any part of the land;

2.7.3—sell or lease or except or reserve any timber or mines or minerals on or in or under all or any part of the land together with any easements rights or privileges of cutting or working and carrying away the same or otherwise incidental to or connected with forestry or mining or other purposes;

2.7.4—impose and make binding for the benefit of all or any part of the land sold or leased any restrictions or stipulations as to user or otherwise affecting any part of the land retained;

2.7.5—accept in exchange for the land or any part of it to be sold or leased (either with or without any money paid or received for equality of exchange) any other real property or any lease of property; and

2.7.6—enter into any contract or grant any option for the sale or leasing of all or any part of the land or otherwise for the exercise by the Trustees of any of the above powers.

3 Personal property

Where the Trust Fund includes any personal property—

3.1 the Trustees may sell lease hire deposit store or otherwise deal with such property upon such terms as they shall in their absolute discretion think fit; and

3.2 the Trustees shall not be bound to see nor be liable or accountable for omitting or neglecting to see to the repair or insurance of such property but may repair and insure it in such manner and to such extent as they shall in their absolute discretion think fit.

4 Appropriation

4.1 The Trustees may at any time or times appropriate any part of the Trust Fund in its then actual state of investment or condition in or towards satisfaction of the whole or any part of any share or interest in the Trust Fund or its income as may in all the circumstances appear to them to be just and reasonable and so that any appropriation so made shall be final and binding on all persons who are or may be interested under these trusts.

4.2 In making any distribution or appropriation of any part of the Trust Fund the Trustees may at their absolute and uncontrolled discretion place such value on the Trust Fund or any part of it as to them shall seem fit.

5 Lending etc

5.1 The Trustees may lend let or hire any property real or personal for the time being forming part of the Trust Fund to any Beneficiary either gratuitously or for such consideration and with or without security and upon such terms and for such periods as the Trustees may in their absolute discretion think fit.

5.2 The Trustees may permit any Beneficiary to occupy or reside in or upon any real property or to have the enjoyment and use of personal property for the time being held upon these trusts upon such conditions (if any) as to payment of rent rates taxes and other expenses and outgoings and as to insurance and repair and decoration and for such period and generally upon such terms as the Trustees shall in their absolute discretion think fit and where any such property is lent let or hired to any Beneficiary or any Beneficiary is permitted to use and enjoy the same in kind the Trustees shall not be responsible for any loss incurred through any damage to the same caused by or through any sale or conversion of such property made by such person or otherwise incurred through any act or neglect or default of such person.

5.3   The Trustees may forgive or release in whole or in part any debt owing to them by any Beneficiary or by any trust under which any Beneficiary is interested whether during the life of such Beneficiary or after his death.

6   Borrowing

The Trustees may borrow and raise money on the security of the Trust Fund for any purpose for which they can apply the capital of the Trust Fund (including the investment of the money so raised as part of the Trust Fund and the payment of any fiscal or other liabilities) and may mortgage charge or pledge all or any part of the Trust Fund as security for any money so raised.

7   Guarantees and indemnities

7.1   The Trustees may guarantee the payment of money and the performance of obligations in respect of any existing or future borrowings or any other commitments of like nature given to third parties by any Beneficiary.

7.2   The Trustees may guarantee the payment of money and the performance of obligations in respect of borrowings by any company wholly or partly owned by the Trustees and in connection with such guarantees may enter into such indemnities as the Trustees shall in their absolute discretion think fit.

7.3   The Trustees may enter into any indemnity in favour of any former Trustee or any other person in respect of any fiscal imposition or other liability of any nature prospectively payable in connection with this Trust.

7.4   The Trustees may give or enter into any indemnity warranty guarantee undertaking or covenant or enter into any type of agreement that they shall in their absolute discretion think fit relating to the transfer or sale of a business or holding of securities forming part of the Trust Fund whether relating to the business or company itself its assets liabilities shares or employees or any other aspect of the business or company in favour of any transferee purchaser or other relevant party.

7.5   For any of the above purposes the Trustees may charge or deposit the whole or any part of the Trust Fund and may enter into such indemnities in connection with any such guarantee as they shall in their absolute discretion think fit.

8   Undertakings

The Trustees may give all such undertakings and enter into such contracts and incur all such obligations relating to the whole or any part or parts of the Trust Fund as the Trustees in their absolute discretion think fit.

9 Payment of taxes etc

If any probate succession estate or other duties or fees or any tax upon capital income or wealth or any other tax of whatever nature and wherever arising ('the tax') becomes payable in any part of the world in respect of any property transferred by or to or under the control of the Trustees or any Beneficiary the Trustees may pay all or any part of the tax out of the Trust Fund and shall have absolute discretion as to the time and manner in which the tax shall be paid (whether or not any such payment shall be capable of being enforced by law) and no person interested under this Trust shall be entitled to make any claim against the Trustees in respect of the Trustees making such payment.

10 Insurance policies

In relation to any insurance policy comprised in the Trust Fund ('the policy') the Trustees shall have power (notwithstanding that the sum assured under the policy may thereby be reduced)—

10.1 to pay from the Trust Fund or its income any premium whether single or periodic for effecting maintaining or restoring the policy (but without being obliged to maintain the policy);

10.2 to borrow on the security of the policy for any purpose;

10.3 to convert the policy into a fully paid-up policy for a reduced sum assured free from payment of future premiums;

10.4 to surrender wholly or in part the policy or any bonus attaching to the policy for its cash surrender value;

10.5 to sell the policy or any substituted policy on such terms as the Trustees shall in their absolute discretion think fit;

10.6 to agree to any variation in the terms of the policy; and

10.7 to exercise any of the powers conferred by the policy or to alter the amount or occasion of the payment of the sum assured or to increase or decrease the amount of any periodic premiums payable under the policy or to alter the period during which the premiums are payable.

11 Trading

11.1 The Trustees may engage in any business trade or enterprise whether solely or jointly with any other person and whether or not by way of partnership (limited or general) and for those purposes may make such arrangements as they shall in their absolute discretion think fit and may delegate any exercise of this power to any one or more of their number or to a company or partnership formed for this purpose.

11.2 The persons carrying on any such business trade or enterprise shall have power to determine what are its distributable profits.

11.3 Any power vested in the Trustees by this Trust shall (where applicable) extend to any arrangements in connection with any such business trade or enterprise and the Trustees' powers of borrowing and charging shall extend to any borrowing arrangements made in connection with such business trade or enterprise and whether or not made severally or jointly with others or with unequal liability.

11.4 The Trustees shall be entitled to be fully indemnified out of the Trust Fund against all personal liability to which they may become in any manner subject in connection with any such business trade or enterprise.

12 Promotion of companies

The Trustees may promote incorporate or establish any company in any part of the world or subscribe for or acquire any of the securities of any company in any part of the world for any purposes which may (but without limitation) include—

12.1 the establishment and carrying on by such company of a business trade or enterprise of any kind which the Trustees are for the time being authorised to carry on themselves and the acquisition of any of the assets comprised in the Trust Fund which may be required for the purposes of such business trade or enterprise;

12.2 the acquisition of the assets and undertaking of any business trade or enterprise being carried on by the Trustees under the above power; and

12.3 the acquisition of all or any of the property comprised in the Trust Fund to be held as investments of the company acquiring the same.

13 Corporate reorganisation

13.1 The Trustees may enter into any compromise or arrangement concerning all or any of their rights as holders of any securities (whether in connection with a scheme of reconstruction or amalgamation or otherwise) and accept in or towards satisfaction of all or any of such rights such consideration as they shall in their absolute discretion think fit whether in the form of cash or options debentures debenture stock stock shares obligations or securities of the same or of any other company or companies or in any other form whatever.

13.2 The Trustees may consent to and vote in favour of any resolution for the conversion of any company of which securities are comprised in the Trust Fund into an unlimited company notwithstanding that the Trustees may by so doing assume responsibility for the debts and liabilities of such company if in their absolute discretion they think fit to do so.

13.3 The Trustees may at any time or times obtain or join in obtaining from any Stock Exchange a quotation for or permission to deal in any securities which or some of which are comprised in the Trust Fund and to sell or join with any other person or persons in selling or disposing of any securities with a view to creating a market in such securities whether or not a sale or disposition would on any other ground be desirable or expedient.

13.4 The Trustees may concur in the winding up dissolution or liquidation of any company in which they are interested as holders of securities and may accept in satisfaction of all or any of their rights in such company a distribution in kind of the assets of any such company and may thereafter hold and carry on business with such assets either alone or in conjunction with any other person.

14 Voting and nominee powers

In respect of any property comprised in the Trust Fund the Trustees shall have power—

14.1 to vote upon or in respect of any securities in any company or the purchase or sale or lease of the assets of any company;

14.2 to deposit any securities in any voting trust or with any depository designated under such a voting trust;

14.3 to give proxies or powers of attorney with or without power of substitution for voting or acting on behalf of the Trustees as the owners of any such property; and

14.4 to hold any such property in bearer form or in the names of the Trustees or any one or more of them or in the name of some other person or partnership or in the name of nominees (whether or not resident in the United Kingdom) without disclosing the fiduciary relationship created by this Trust and to deposit the said securities and any documents belonging or relating to the Trust Fund in any part of the world with any bank firm trust company or other company that undertakes the safe custody of securities as part of its business without being responsible for the neglect or default of such organisation or for any consequent loss.

15 Overseeing management

15.1 The Trustees shall not be required to become directors or officers of nor to interfere in the management or conduct of the business of any company in which or in any subsidiary of which this Trust shall be interested notwithstanding that the Trustees have (whether directly or indirectly) a substantial holding in or control of any such company nor shall the Trustees be under any obligation to seek information about the affairs of any such company other than that normally available to or supplied to the holders of the relevant proportion of the securities of such company but the Trustees may leave the conduct of the affairs of any such company to its directors or other persons managing the company and so long as the Trustees shall have no actual notice of any act of dishonesty or misappropriation of monies on the part of the persons having the management of such company the Trustees may leave the conduct of its business (including the payment or non-payment of dividends) wholly to its directors.

15.2   No Beneficiary shall be entitled to require the distribution of any dividend by any company in which this Trust may be interested or to require the Trustees to exercise any powers they may have of compelling such distribution.

15.3   The Trustees may leave the entire management of any business trade or enterprise an interest in which forms part of the Trust Fund to the other partner or partners manager or other persons engaged in it so that the Trustees shall be under no obligation to attend personally to any such business trade or enterprise or be in any way responsible for any loss which may result from their omission to attend personally to any such business trade or enterprise or to interfere in it.

16   Acting as company officer or employee

Any of the Trustees may act as director or other officer or employee of any company in which any part of the Trust Fund may be invested in any part of the world or which is in any way connected with the Trust Fund and (unless he is one of the Excluded Persons) may retain for his own use any fees or other remuneration or benefits received in respect of any such directorship office or employment notwithstanding that it is held by virtue of voting rights attaching to securities comprised in the Trust Fund.

17   Agents and delegation

17.1   The Trustees instead of acting personally may employ and pay at the expense of the Trust Fund or its income any agent (other than any of the Excluded Persons) whether a lawyer banker accountant broker trust company valuer surveyor or land or other agent in any part of the world to transact any business or act as nominee or do any other act in connection with these trusts and the Trustees shall not be responsible for the neglect or default of any such agent if employed in good faith.

17.2   Any of the Trustees may delegate to any person (including to the other or any other or others of the Trustees) and on any terms (including except in the case of the Excluded Persons provision for reasonable remuneration) the exercise of all or any powers and discretions conferred on such Trustee notwithstanding the fiduciary nature of such power or powers without being liable for the acts or defaults of such person.

17.3   In particular (but without limitation of the above) the Trustees may employ any firm or company to provide professional administrative or other services to the Trustees in connection with the execution administration and management of this Trust (including any acts or matters which could be performed by the Trustees personally) upon such terms as to remuneration and otherwise as the Trustees may in their absolute discretion think fit notwithstanding that one or more of the Trustees or any officer or employee of a Trustee which is a company is a partner officer member or employee of the said firm or company and notwithstanding that (in the case of a Trustee which is a company) the issued share capital of such Trustee is wholly or partially owned by or held in trust for such firm or company.

17.4   Without limitation of the above the Trustees may delegate to any person (including any one or more of their number) the operation of any bank account in their names.

18   Investment advisers

18.1   The Trustees may engage the services of such investment adviser or advisers as the Trustees may from time to time think fit ('the investment adviser") to advise the Trustees in respect of the investment and reinvestment of the Trust Fund with power for the Trustees without being liable for any consequent loss to delegate to the investment adviser discretion to manage all or any part of the Trust Fund within the limits and for the period stipulated by the Trustees and to vest all or any of the Trust Fund in the name of the investment adviser as nominee for the Trustees.

18.2   The Trustees shall settle the terms and conditions for the remuneration of the investment adviser and the reimbursement of the investment adviser's expenses as the Trustees shall in their absolute discretion think fit and such remuneration and expenses shall be paid by the Trustees from the Trust Fund.

18.3   The Trustees shall not be bound to enquire into nor be in any manner responsible for any changes in the legal status of the investment adviser.

18.4   The Trustees shall incur no liability for any action taken pursuant to or for otherwise following the advice of the investment adviser however communicated.

19   Transactions in which Trustees have an interest

19.1   Subject to sub-clause 19.2 the Trustees shall have power to enter into any transaction concerning the Trust Fund without any such transaction being voidable notwithstanding that one or more of the Trustees may be interested in the transaction other than as one of the Trustees.

19.2   Sub-clause 19.1 shall not apply unless the transaction is—

19.2.1—in the case of a purchase or sale of securities listed on any stock exchange at the middle market price on the day on which such securities are purchased or sold;

19.2.2—in the case of a purchase or sale of securities not listed on any stock exchange at a price certified by the auditors of the company or if there are no auditors by a suitably qualified valuer to be their open market price; and

19.2.3—in the case of any other transaction at a price and on terms certified by a suitably qualified valuer to be such as would apply to such a transaction effected on fully commercial terms between unconnected persons.

19.3 The Trustees in their absolute discretion shall exercise all voting and other rights attached to or for the time being exercisable in respect of any securities held by the Trustees in that capacity in such manner as they may consider to be for the benefit of the Beneficiaries or any of them and notwithstanding that the Trustees or any of them may hold other securities in the same or any parent or subsidiary or allied company either beneficially or in some other fiduciary capacity.

20 Indemnity

20.1 In the professed execution of the trusts and powers of this Trust no Trustee shall be liable for any loss to the Trust Fund arising by reason of any improper investment made or retained in good faith or for the negligence or fraud of any agent employed by him or by any other Trustee although the employment of such agent was not strictly necessary or expedient or by reason of any mistake or omission made in good faith by any Trustee or by reason of any other matter or thing except wilful fraud or dishonesty on the part of the Trustee who is sought to be made liable.

20.2 A former Trustee (including the estate of a deceased Trustee) shall be entitled to be indemnified out of the Trust Fund for all (if any) obligations or liabilities which such former Trustee may have incurred as a Trustee or for which he may be liable as a former Trustee and for which he would have been entitled to an indemnity out of the Trust Fund had he still been a Trustee.

20.3 The Trustees shall not be obliged to ascertain before distributing amongst the Beneficiaries all or any part of the Trust Fund whether any person whose parents are not married to each other at the time of birth of such person or who claim through such a person is or may be entitled to an interest in the Trust Fund nor shall the Trustees be liable to any such person of whose existence the Trustees have no notice or who claims through such a person.

21 Transfer to non-UK Trustees

The Trustees may transfer all or any part of the Trust Fund to trustees who are not resident or ordinarily resident in the United Kingdom to the intent that thereafter the general administration of this Trust shall be ordinarily carried on (or continue to be so) outside the United Kingdom.

22 Transfer to trust under another jurisdiction

The Trustees may transfer all or any part of the Trust Fund to trustees of a new trust or Trust constituted under the law of a jurisdiction other than England and Wales to be held freed and discharged from the trusts of this Trust on the trusts of such new trust or Trust having the same effect under such law as near as may be as the trusts declared in this Trust being new trusts under which the only beneficiaries are some or all of the Beneficiaries and so that any deed executed by the Trustees declaring that the trusts of such new trust or Trust correspond as nearly as may be to the trusts powers and provisions which under the law of England and Wales are applicable to this Trust shall as against and between all persons who may be interested under this Trust be treated as conclusive evidence of that fact and shall be binding on them for all purposes and so that a declaration made by deed by the Trustees that they hold all or any part of the Trust Fund as trustees of such new trust or Trust shall for the purposes of this Clause be deemed to be a transfer to them as trustees on such new trusts and shall take effect accordingly.

23 Legal advice and proceedings

23.1   The Trustees may take legal advice in any part of the world concerning any matter relating to this Trust.

23.2   The Trustees may institute and defend legal proceedings and proceed to their final determination or compromise them as the Trustees shall consider advisable.

23.3   The Trustees may pay the costs of such advice and proceedings out of the Trust Fund or its income.

24 Insurance

24.1   The Trustees may insure against any loss or damage from any peril any property for the time being forming part of the Trust Fund for any amount and may pay the premiums for such insurance out of the Trust Fund or its income.

24.2   Money received by the Trustees in respect of any such insurance may be used at the discretion of the Trustees either towards making good the loss or damage in respect of which it was received or as if it were proceeds of sale of the insured property.

25 Capital and income

25.1   The Trustees may determine as they shall consider just and the Proper Law may permit whether any money should be considered as capital or income of the Trust Fund and whether any taxes expenses outgoings or losses should be paid or borne out of capital or out of income.

25.2 The statutory and equitable rules of apportionment shall not apply to this Trust and (unless the Trustees in their absolute discretion shall otherwise determine) the Trustees may treat all dividends and other payments in the nature of income received by them as income at the date of receipt irrespective of the period for which the dividend or other income is payable.

25.3 If and so long as any business trade or enterprise or any interest in any of them ('the business') forms part of the Trust Fund the net profits arising from the business shall be applied as if they were income arising from investments representing the proceeds of sale of the business.

26 Accounts and audit

The Trustees shall keep accurate accounts of the Trust Fund and may have them audited by suitably qualified accountants at whatever intervals the Trustees think fit.

27 Non-disclosure

27.1 The Trustees shall not be obliged to have any contact with any Beneficiary nor to make known to any Beneficiary the existence of this Trust nor any matter relating to it before such Beneficiary becomes absolutely and indefeasibly entitled to any part of the Trust Fund or its income.

27.2 The Trustees shall not be obliged to disclose to any person any documents or other matter relating to this Trust.

28 Variation of administrative provisions

28.1 Subject to sub-clause 28.2 the Trustees may at any time or times during the Trust Period by deed revoke or vary any of the administrative provisions of this Trust or add any further administrative provisions in such manner in all respects as the Trustees may consider expedient for the purposes of this Trust and in particular (but without limitation) for ensuring that at all times there shall be Trustees or a Trustee and that the Trust Fund shall be fully and effectively vested in or under the control of such Trustees or Trustee.

28.2 The power contained in sub-clause 28.1 shall only be exercisable—

28.2.1—if the Trustees shall have been advised in writing by a lawyer qualified for at least ten years in the Proper Law that it would be expedient for the purposes of this Trust to revoke vary or add to the administrative provisions of this Trust in the manner specified in such written advice; and

28.2.2—by the Trustees causing to be prepared and executed an instrument in writing in a form appropriate to implement such advice

29 Restriction

No power or discretion vested in the Trustees shall be capable of being exercised in such a way so as to infringe any rule against perpetuities or accumulations applicable to this Trust or so as to conflict with the beneficial provisions of this Trust.

30 Release of powers

The Trustees may (subject to any relevant consents specifically referred to elsewhere in this Deed) at any time or times before the expiration of the Trust Period by deed or deeds revocable during the Trust Period or irrevocable and so as to bind their successors as Trustees release or restrict the future exercise of all or any of the powers rights or discretions by this Trust or by law conferred on them (notwithstanding any fiduciary nature) either wholly or to the extent specified in any such deed or deeds.

Precedent 8

Trustee powers

(a) Appointment of and legacy to guardians

1   IF my wife Winifrid shall survive me by thirty days at least then I GIVE the Fund free of inheritance tax and all other duties payable on or in respect of my death to my Executors to hold upon trust with and subject to the powers and provisions set out in the Schedule which forms part of this my Will.

2   If Winifrid shall not survive me as specified in clause # above I APPOINT A and B of [*insert address*] as the joint guardians of my infant children and if they accept such appointment I GIVE to them for their own use the sum of £###.

(b) Trustee investment powers

1 Power of investment

1.1   The Trustees may apply any money to be invested in the purchase or acquisition (either alone or jointly with other persons) of such property, of whatever nature and wherever situate and whether of a wasting nature, involving liabilities or producing income or not, or in making such loans with or without security, as they think fit, so that they shall have the same powers to apply money to be invested as if they were an absolute beneficial owner.

1.2   The Trustees may exchange property for other property on such terms as they think fit.

1.3   The Trustees shall not be required to diversify the investment of the Trust Fund.

Alternative clause

2 Power of investment

2.1   The Trustees may invest or apply any money subject to these trusts in any investments of whatever nature and wherever situate and whether producing income or not as the Trustees shall in their absolute discretion think fit so that the Trustees shall have the same full and unrestricted powers of making and changing investments as if they were absolute beneficial owners of such money or other property.

2.2   The acquisition of any reversionary interest or any life endowment sinking fund or other policy or any annuity or securities or other investments not producing income or of a wasting nature or for any other reason not within the meaning of the word 'Investment' strictly construed shall be an authorised investment of trust money if the Trustees shall consider such acquisition to be for the benefit of any one or more of the Beneficiaries.

2.3   The Trustees may exchange property for other property of a similar or different nature and for such consideration and on such conditions as they in their absolute discretion think fit.

2.4   The Trustees may retain any property in the form in which it is received by them without being responsible for any loss occasioned by such retention.

2.5   The Trustees shall have express power at their absolute discretion to invest or keep invested the whole of the Trust Fund in the securities of any one company unit trust investment trust or other fund and shall not be liable or accountable in any manner for any loss caused by failure to diversify or consider diversification of investments and shall not be bound to maintain a balance between capital and income.

Precedent 9

Dispensing with beneficiary consent for capital advancement

Amendments to Trustee Act 1925 s 32

Section 32 of the Trustee Act 1925 shall be deemed to have effect in relation to a Beneficiary as if—

1.1   the words 'advancement maintenance education or benefit' were substituted for the words 'advancement or benefit' wherever those words occur in the said section; and

1.2   as if the words 'one-half of' were omitted from proviso (a) to sub-section (1) of the said section; and

1.3   as if paragraph (c) of sub-section (1) thereof were omitted in its entirety so that the Trustees may make capital appointments and advancements without obtaining the consent of any person.

Precedent 10

Dispensing with beneficiary consent for sale of a property

Consents

1 The Trustees shall not be obliged to consult with any Beneficiary for the purposes of section 11 of the Trusts of Land and Appointment of Trustees Act 1996.

Precedent 11

Share sale restriction

The Trustees may not, except with the written consent of the [*Appointor/ /Protector*][1], sell, distribute or transfer (other than as security or guarantee for any borrowing) nor cause to be sold, distributed or transferred (except as security for any guarantee or borrowing) [*any /more than 10%*] of any direct or indirect holding by the Trustees of [*shares in ABC Limited/PLC/ the Specified Shares*].

Note

An alternate drafting approach, subject to the requirements and wishes of the testator, would be to draft the Will Trust as being subject to the governing law of a jurisdiction which allows for purpose trusts, so that the purpose of the Will Trust would be "to retain my shareholding in ABC Limited and to ensure that that company continues to trade [*indefinitely/ for a period of not less than 50 years*]".

Since *Marlborough (Duke) v A-G* [1945] 1 All E R 165 academic opinion inclines to the principle that settlors have complete freedom of choice to select any governing trust law which they wish, if that is their clear intention demonstrated in the original instrument creating the trust – even if the testator/settlor does not have any personal connection with the selected jurisdiction.

Limitations imposed by perpetuity periods do not generally apply to purpose trusts in the majority of jurisdictions where they are permitted.

[1] The Will Trust must be drafted to in clued the nomination of an Appointor or Protector with certain specified powers, including the power to give consent to the sale of Specified Shares.

Precedent 12

Trustees' powers of delegation

1 Agents and delegation

1.1 The Trustees instead of acting personally may employ and pay at the expense of the Trust Fund or its income any agent (other than any of the Excluded Persons) whether a lawyer banker accountant broker trust company valuer surveyor or land or other agent in any part of the world to transact any business or act as nominee or do any other act in connection with these trusts and the Trustees shall not be responsible for the neglect or default of any such agent if employed in good faith.

1.2 Any of the Trustees may delegate to any person (including to the other or any other or others of the Trustees) and on any terms (including except in the case of the Excluded Persons provision for reasonable remuneration) the exercise of all or any powers and discretions conferred on such Trustee notwithstanding the fiduciary nature of such power or powers without being liable for the acts or defaults of such person.

1.3 In particular (but without limitation of the above) the Trustees may employ any firm or company to provide professional administrative or other services to the Trustees in connection with the execution administration and management of this Trust (including any acts or matters which could be performed by the Trustees personally) upon such terms as to remuneration and otherwise as the Trustees may in their absolute discretion think fit notwithstanding that one or more of the Trustees or any officer or employee of a Trustee which is a company is a partner officer member or employee of the said firm or company and notwithstanding that (in the case of a Trustee which is a company) the issued share capital of such Trustee is wholly or partially owned by or held in trust for such firm or company.

1.4 Without limitation of the above the Trustees may delegate to any person (including any one or more of their number) the operation of any bank account in their names.

2 Investment advisers

2.1 The Trustees may engage the services of such investment adviser or advisers as the Trustees may from time to time think fit ('the investment adviser") to advise the Trustees in respect of the investment and reinvestment of the Trust Fund with power for the Trustees without being liable for any consequent loss and to delegate to the investment adviser discretion to manage all or any part of the Trust Fund within the limits and for the period stipulated by the Trustees and to vest all or any of the Trust Fund in the name of the investment adviser or his nominee as nominee for the Trustees.

2.2   The Trustees shall settle the terms and conditions for the remuneration of the investment adviser and the reimbursement of the investment adviser's expenses as the Trustees shall in their absolute discretion think fit and such remuneration and expenses shall be paid by the Trustees from the Trust Fund.

2.3   The Trustees shall not be bound to enquire into nor be in any manner responsible for any changes in the legal status of the investment adviser.

2.4   The Trustees shall incur no liability for any action taken pursuant to or for otherwise following the advice of the investment adviser however communicated.

Precedent 13

Trustee powers to guarantee beneficiary obligations

1 Guarantees and indemnities

1.1   The Trustees may guarantee the payment of money and the performance of obligations in respect of any existing or future borrowings or any other commitments of like nature given to third parties by any Beneficiary.

1.2   The Trustees may guarantee the payment of money and the performance of obligations in respect of borrowings by any company wholly or partly owned by the Trustees and in connection with such guarantees may enter into such indemnities as the Trustees shall in their absolute discretion think fit.

1.3   The Trustees may enter into any indemnity in favour of any former Trustee or any other person in respect of any fiscal imposition or other liability of any nature prospectively payable in connection with this Trust.

1.4   The Trustees may give or enter into any indemnity warranty guarantee undertaking or covenant or enter into any type of agreement that they shall in their absolute discretion think fit relating to the transfer or sale of a business or holding of securities forming part of the Trust Fund whether relating to the business or company itself its assets liabilities shares or employees or any other aspect of the business or company in favour of any transferee purchaser or other relevant party.

1.5   For any of the above purposes the Trustees may charge or deposit the whole or any part of the Trust Fund and may enter into such indemnities in connection with any such guarantee as they shall in their absolute discretion think fit.

Precedent 14

Powers to lend to beneficiaries and to allow property occupation

1 Lending etc

1.1   The Trustees may lend let or hire any property real or personal for the time being forming part of the Trust Fund to any Beneficiary either gratuitously or for such consideration and with or without security and upon such terms and for such periods as the Trustees may in their absolute discretion think fit.

1.2   The Trustees may permit any Beneficiary to occupy or reside in or upon any real property or to have the enjoyment and use of personal property for the time being held upon these trusts upon such conditions (if any) as to payment of rent rates taxes and other expenses and outgoings and as to insurance and repair and decoration and for such period and generally upon such terms as the Trustees shall in their absolute discretion think fit and where any such property is lent let or hired to any Beneficiary or any Beneficiary is permitted to use and enjoy the same in kind the Trustees shall not be responsible for any loss incurred through any damage to the same caused by or through any sale or conversion of such property made by such person or otherwise incurred through any act or neglect or default of such person.

1.3   The Trustees may forgive or release in whole or in part any debt owing to them by any Beneficiary or by any trust under which any Beneficiary is interested whether during the life of such Beneficiary or after his death.

Precedent 15

Incapacity of trustee

If and for so long as at any time—

1.1 the [*the First Named Trustee/ABC*] (for the purposes of this clause 'A') is, in the unanimous opinion of the Trustees other than A[9], incapable of conducting his own affairs by reason of any mental or physical incapacity (such mental or physical incapacity to be certified to the Trustees, at the expense of the Trust Fund, by a medical practitioner of not less then 10 years' standing, and so certified at intervals not longer than [6/12] months); or

1.2 A is declared by a Court of competent jurisdiction to be no longer capable of managing his own affairs such that a guardian, trustee, protector or committee or any similar person or body is appointed to administer his personal estate, then until such time as the A is again able properly to conduct his own affairs the Trustees shall conduct the affairs of this Trust as if A were not a Trustee hereof—

Incapacity of appointor having power to remove and appoint trustees

"Appointor"

[*Surviving Partner*] during her lifetime unless and until and for such period as she is incapable of managing her own affairs by reason of mental or physical incapacity (such mental incapacity to be certified to the Trustees by a medical practitioner of at least 5 years standing and so certified at intervals of not longer than 12 months during such period of incapacity and such physical incapacity to be evidenced conclusively by [*Surviving Partner*] in the opinion of my Trustees [*other than Surviving Partner*][10] being unable to sign a document or to give an oral or demonstrative instruction to another person to sign a document on her behalf) and during such period of [*Surviving Partner's*] incapacity and in any event after her death my Trustees.

Precedent 16

Trustee self-dealing

1 Transactions in which Trustees have an interest

1.1 Subject to sub-clause 1.2 the Trustees shall have power to enter into any transaction concerning the Trust Fund without any such transaction being voidable notwithstanding that one or more of the Trustees may be interested in the transaction other than as one of the Trustees.

1.2 Sub-clause 1.1 shall not apply unless the transaction is—

1.2.1—in the case of a purchase or sale of securities listed on any stock exchange at the middle market price on the day on which such securities are purchased or sold;

1.2.2—in the case of a purchase or sale of securities not listed on any stock exchange at a price certified by the auditors of the company or if there are no auditors by a suitably qualified valuer to be their open market price; and

1.2.3—in the case of any other transaction at a price and on terms certified by a suitably qualified valuer to be such as would apply to such a transaction effected on fully commercial terms between unconnected persons.

1.3 The Trustees in their absolute discretion shall exercise all voting and other rights attached to or for the time being exercisable in respect of any securities held by the Trustees in that capacity in such manner as they may consider to be for the benefit of the Beneficiaries or any of them and notwithstanding that the Trustees or any of them may hold other securities in the same or any parent or subsidiary or allied company either beneficially or in some other fiduciary capacity.

Precedent 17

Trustee also beneficiary

No Trustee hereof shall by reason of the fact that he is also a Beneficiary or the object or one of the objects of any discretionary trust or power for the time being vested in exercisable by the Trustees be in any way debarred or precluded from exercising such discretionary trust or power and every discretionary trust power for the time being vested in or exercisable by the Trustees may be exercised in favour of themselves or himself, and in favour of any child or remoter issue of any such Trustee PROVIDED ALWAYS AND IT IS HEREBY AGREED that if a Beneficiary or Beneficiaries hereunder is or areTrustees the trusts and powers in this Trust contained or referred to (except the power to appoint new or additional Trustees) shall only be exercisable when the Trustees are not less than two in number and include at least one Trustee who is not a Beneficiary.

Precedent 18

Instructions for valid signing of wills and codicils

1   Read the Will or Codicil[1] through carefully to make sure it is in accordance with your wishes. If it is not correct, please do not attempt to alter it, but return it with your comments.

2   If there is any minor alteration required (such as a correction in the spelling of a name), make the alteration clearly in ink <u>before</u> the Will is signed, as no alterations can be made after signature.

3   DO NOT CLIP OR PIN ANYTHING TO THE WILL OR CODICIL AT ANY TIME (this means no paperclips or staples or anything else which might mark the Will paper).

4   If there is any alteration made, it must be initialled by you and both witnesses, in the margin opposite the alteration, at the time of signing.

5   In order for the Will to be valid, you must sign it in the presence of two witnesses. Apart from following these instructions, the witnesses to your signature must not be named in the Will[2], nor may they be the spouse of any person named in the document. The witnesses do not need to read your Will – all they are doing is watching you put your signature on the document.

6   The date of signing should be inserted by you, in words where indicated, immediately before you sign.

7   YOU AND BOTH WITNESSES MUST ALL SIGN IN ONE ANOTHER'S PRESENCE, AND EACH MUST WATCH EACH OTHER SIGN. <u>IT IS ESSENTIAL THAT NONE OF YOU LEAVES THE ROOM UNTIL ALL THREE OF YOU HAVE FINISHED SIGNING.</u>

8   Both witnesses must add their names, addresses and occupation. The reason for this is so that they can be contacted or traced at a later date if there is any dispute about the valid signing of the Will.

[1] These instructions refer equally to Wills and Codicils, but to make reading these instructions easier, they refer only to Wills from this point on.

[2] In the case of a Codicil, the witnesses must not be named in either the Will or any Codicil.

Part B2

Post death reallocation of property devolving on death

Precedent 19

Deed of Variation by legatee redirecting whole legacy to third party

Specific legacy

Precedent 19(a)—Drafting approach in the real world

[*Letterhead or address of original beneficiary*]

To [*full names of substitute beneficiary*] of [   ]

[*Date*]

Dear [   ]

[Your grandfather] [*full names of testator*], who died on [*date of death*][1], has left to me in his will [a canteen of fiddle pattern silver cutlery]. [It has been distributed to me and is currently in my possession.][2] <u>OR</u> [I understand his executors have no need of it for administration purposes.][3]

This [cutlery] is surplus to my requirements, and I would like you to have it.

By way of variation of that gift in his will, therefore, I now give you that [canteen and all its contents], [which I will deliver to you shortly accordingly][4] <u>OR</u> [and all my rights in respect of them; sight of this letter will serve as my authority to the executors to release them to you][5].

I intend section 142(1) of the Inheritance Tax Act 1984 [and section 62(6) of the Taxation of Chargeable Gains Act 1992][6] to apply to the variation effected by this letter, which I have executed as a deed[7,8,9].

Signed by [*full names of original beneficiary*][10]:[*original beneficiary's signature*]

Signed as witness in the presence
of the above signatory:[*witness's signature*]

Full names and address of witness:[   ]

Notes

[1] Although the drafting approach is as informal as possible, the date of death should be referred to in order to demonstrate that the variation is being effected within the two year period.

2 Care should be taken that any deed of variation is made before the articles in question are delivered to the substitute beneficiary; otherwise, unless a very clear intent can be demonstrated that he should not become the owner at that stage, such delivery is likely to be seen as a completed gift by delivery. The subsequent purported deed of variation would then be ineffective for IHT and CGT purposes; it could not operate "in the real world" because the original beneficiary no longer has any rights in respect of the articles which he can pass on by deed. The actual passing on of the articles, by delivery, would not attract backdated treatment for IHT or CGT purposes because it was not carried out by an instrument in writing. For this reason, if the articles are not still under the control of the executors for administration purposes, it is wise to include in the deed a record that the articles are at the time still in the original beneficiary's possession.

3 Include these words if the articles in question have not yet been distributed/released by the executors.

4 See note 2 above.

5 Include these words if the articles are still under the executors' control, or if there is any doubt as to whether the executors have released them from their right to resort to these articles for administration purposes even though they are in the original beneficiary's possession.

6 Unless the articles have lost value since the death, a CGT statement of intent may be better omitted – giving the substitute beneficiary a higher base cost than if it is included – if each article or set dealt with by the deed is within the £6,000 chattel exemption (TCGA 1992 s 262), or if the chargeable gains accruing as a result of the gift (taking account of the chattel exemption where relevant) will be covered by the original beneficiary's annual exemption and/or allowable losses.

7 Although the requirement for IHT and CGT purposes is merely an instrument in writing, if a gift of a chattel is to pass title by means of a document that document must be a deed. This is also seen as precluding revocation.

8 To take effect as a deed, the document must make it clear on its face that it is intended to be a deed, as well as being in fact executed as a deed (ie signed, witnessed and delivered): see the Law of Property (Miscellaneous Provisions) Act 1989 s 1(2), (3). For an example of the importance of this, see *HSBC Trust Company (UK) Limited v Quinn* [2007] All ER (D) 125 (Jul). The word "executed" is deliberately used in the text to mirror the statutory expression which includes delivery in addition to signature in the presence of the witness.

9 This form assumes that the original beneficiary is *not* the surviving spouse or civil partner of the deceased, otherwise the personal representatives would need to be signatories as well in relation to the IHT statement

of intent because of an increase in the IHT liability of the estate (see paragraph **3.1.65** above), unless the chargeable estate remains within the available NRB after the variation.

[10] When using a less formal approach in the form of a letter as here, do not forget to identify the original beneficiary who is making the variation.

Precedent 19(b)—Drafting approach in the misleading fictitious world

THIS DEED OF VARIATION which is made on [*date*] BETWEEN me [*full names of original beneficiary*] of [   ] and [*full names of substitute beneficiary*] of [   ] ("the Donee")[1,2]

WITNESSES as follows—

1   This deed is supplemental to the Will dated [   ] ("the Will") of the late [*full names of testator*] who died on [   ] ("the Testator") [, probate of which was granted on [   ] to [full *names of proving executors*] out of the [   ] Probate Registry][3]

2   I IRREVOCABLY DECLARE AND DIRECT that the Will shall take effect and the estate of the Testator shall be administered as though in place of my name in clause [   ] of it (bequest of [a canteen of fiddle pattern silver cutlery]) the Testator had specified the name of the Donee

3   I MAKE any assignment necessary to ensure the immediate vesting in the Donee of the subject matter of that bequest, and I UNDERTAKE with the Donee to deliver it or procure it to be delivered to him as soon as practicable accordingly[4]

4   I intend section 142(1) of the Inheritance Tax Act 1984 [and section 62(6) of the Taxation of Chargeable Gains Act 1992][5] to apply to the variation of the Will which is effected by this deed

IN WITNESS of which I have duly executed this deed which is delivered on the date first above written

[SIGNED as a deed, etc]

Notes

[1] The Donee is made a party to the deed so that he can if necessary enforce it directly. He does not need to execute it.

[2] See note 9 to PRECEDENT 19(A) above.

[3] It is customary to record the grant of probate where it has been granted, though not strictly necessary. If omitted, the address of the Testator ought to be included for better identification.

[4] See note 2 to PRECEDENT 19(A).

[5] See note 6 to PRECEDENT 19(A).

Pecuniary legacy

Precedent 19(c)—Drafting approach in the real world

[*Letterhead or address of original beneficiary*]

To [*full names of executors*] as executors[1] of the late [*full names of testator*] who died on [*date of death*][2] ("the Testator")

[*Date*]

Dear [   ]

I refer to the legacy of £10,000 given to me by clause [   ] of the Testator's will dated [   ].

Please accept this letter, which I have executed as a deed[3] by way of variation of the Testator's will, as my irrevocable instruction to pay £5,000 that legacy to [*full names of substitute beneficiary 1*] of [   ], and the remaining £5,000 of it to [*full names of substitute beneficiary 2*] of [   ], instead of paying any of it to me.

I intend section 142(1) of the Inheritance Tax Act 1984 and section 62(6) of the Taxation of Chargeable Gains Act 1992[4] to apply to the variation effected by this letter.

Signed by [*full names of original beneficiary*][5]:[*original beneficiary's signature*]

Signed as witness in the presence
of the above signatory:[*witness's signature*]

Full names and address of witness:[   ]

Notes

[1] No alternative is given for a legacy that has been already paid. Unless great care has been taken to keep the legacy payment separate from the original beneficiary's other funds, it will be difficult to demonstrate that it really is the original legacy that is being varied.

[2] See note 1 to PRECEDENT 19(A) above.

[3] See note 8 to PRECEDENT 19(A) above.

[4] A CGT statement of intent may be superfluous, but is included to forestall any suggestion by HMRC that an unpaid legatee's rights are (like those of a residuary beneficiary) a separate asset and not cash – involving a disposal of that asset with the risk of a nil base cost.

[5] See note 10 to PRECEDENT 1(A) above.

Precedent 19(d)—Drafting approach in the misleading fictitious world

THIS DEED OF VARIATION which is made on [*date*] BETWEEN—

(1)   me [full names of original beneficiary]¹ of [   ] and

(2)   [full names of substitute beneficiary 1] of [   ] and [full names of substitute beneficiary 2] of [   ] ("the Donees")²

WITNESSES as follows—

1   This deed is supplemental to the Will dated [   ] ("the Will") of the late [*full names of testator*] who died on [   ] ("the Testator") [, probate of which was granted on [   ] to [*full names of proving executors*] out of the [   ] Probate Registry]³

2   I IRREVOCABLY DECLARE AND DIRECT that the Will shall take effect and the estate of the Testator shall be administered as though the following clause were substituted in place of clause [   ] of it (legacy to me of £10,000) namely: "to [*full names of substitute beneficiary 1*] of [   ] and [*full names of substitute beneficiary 2*] of [   ] the respective sums of £5,000 each"

3   I MAKE any assignment necessary to ensure the immediate vesting in the Donees in equal shares of my rights in respect of the legacy originally bequeathed by clause [   ] of the Will

4   I intend section 142(1) of the Inheritance Tax Act 1984 and section 62(6) of the Taxation of Chargeable Gains Act 1992⁴ to apply to the variation of the Will which is effected by this deed

IN WITNESS of which I have duly executed this deed which is delivered on the date first above written

[SIGNED as a deed, etc]

Notes

¹ See note 9 to PRECEDENT 19(A) above.

² See note 1 to PRECEDENT 19(B) above.

³ See note 3 to PRECEDENT 19(B) above.

⁴ See note 4 to PRECEDENT 19(C) above.

Precedent 19(e)—Deed of Variation by residuary beneficiary/administrator under intestacy redirecting a cash sum, and holdings of shares and loan stock in a private company, to third party

THIS DEED OF VARIATION is made on [*date*] BETWEEN—

(1) [*full names of original beneficiary*] of [   ] ("the Original Beneficiary") and

(2) [*full names of substitute beneficiary*] of [   ] ("the New Beneficiary")[1]

WHEREAS—

A   The Original Beneficiary's uncle [*full names of deceased*] of [   ] ("the Deceased") died on [   ] intestate and domiciled in England and Wales[2]

B   In the events which happened the Original Beneficiary is the only person entitled to succeed to the Deceased's estate under the Administration of Estates Act 1925 and Letters of Administration in respect of the Deceased's estate were granted to the Original Beneficiary out of the [   ] Probate Registry on [   ]

C   Among the assets comprised in the Deceased's estate at his death were the shares and securities listed in the Schedule below ("the Scheduled Assets") which are now vested in the Original Beneficiary personally free from his rights in his capacity as Administrator of the Deceased's estate

D   Additionally the Original Beneficiary in his capacity as Administrator of the Deceased's estate still holds a sum of cash in excess of £10,000 which he has not transferred into his personal account

E   The Original Beneficiary wishes to vary in favour of the New Beneficiary in the manner appearing below the dispositions of the Deceased's estate that took effect under the law relating to intestacy

NOW THIS DEED WITNESSES as follows—

1   The Original Beneficiary IRREVOCABLY DECLARES AND DIRECTS that subject to clause 2 below the Deceased's estate shall be administered (and the Scheduled Assets already released from it shall be dealt with) as though the Deceased had left a Will bequeathing to the New Beneficiary free of inheritance tax—

1.1   the Scheduled Assets and

1.2   a cash legacy of £10,000 ("the deemed legacy")

[2   Notwithstanding clause 1 above the New Beneficiary shall have no entitlement to interest in respect of the deemed legacy in respect of any period before the date of this deed nor to any income paid or payable in respect of the Scheduled Assets before the date of this deed to the Original Beneficiary whether as Administrator or personally][3]

OR

[2   The New Beneficiary—

2.1   shall have no entitlement notwithstanding clause 1 above to interest in respect of the deemed legacy in respect of any period before the date of this deed but

2.2 shall be entitled by virtue of the variation effected by clause 1 above to receive payment of [all amounts (after deduction of tax at source where applicable) received or receivable by the Original Beneficiary (whether personally or as Administrator of the Deceased's estate) in respect of income of the Scheduled Assets payable before the date of this deed, to the intent that if and so far as the Original Beneficiary has paid or is liable for income tax in relation to such amounts he shall bear that tax out of his separate resources] OR [such a sum as equates to the net amount received or receivable by the Original Beneficiary (whether personally or as Administrator of the Deceased's estate) in respect of income of the Scheduled Assets payable before the date of this deed after deducting all income tax for which the Original Beneficiary is liable (or which he has already paid or borne by deduction) in respect of such income]][4]

3 The Original Beneficiary (in his personal capacity and so far as necessary in his capacity as Administrator of the Deceased's estate) accordingly UNDERTAKES with the New Beneficiary that he will as soon as practicable—

3.1 do all in his power to ensure that the Scheduled Assets are vested in the name of to the New Beneficiary and

3.2 pay the Deemed Legacy to the New Beneficiary from the estate of the Deceased [and

3.3 pay such amount to the New Beneficiary as is appropriate to give effect to the provisions of clause 2 above]

4 The Original Beneficiary intends section 142(1) of the Inheritance Tax Act 1984 [and section 62(6) of the Taxation of Chargeable Gains Act 1992][5] to apply to the variation of the dispositions of the Deceased's estate under the law relating to intestacy which is effected by this deed

5 It is hereby certified that this deed falls within category L in the Schedule to the Stamp Duty (Exempt Instruments) Regulations 1987[6]

IN WITNESS of which the Original Beneficiary has duly executed this deed which is delivered on the date first above written

The Schedule

(the Scheduled Assets)

45,650 ordinary shares of 10p each in Hermann's Widgets Limited

£200,000 5·5% Unsecured Loan Stock 2012 in Hermann's Widgets Limited

[SIGNED as a deed, etc]

Notes

[1] See note 1 to PRECEDENT **19**(B) above.

[2] To demonstrate that it is English/Welsh intestacy law that is relevant.

[3] See paragraph **3.1.119** above

[4] See paragraphs **3.1.120, 3.1.121** above

[5] The CGT statement of intent can be omitted if any gain on the shares (and loan stock, if not a qualifying corporate bond) is expected to remain within the Original Beneficiary's annual CGT exemption, or if he prefers to pay such CGT as may be due in order to give the New Beneficiary a higher base cost for the future. See generally paragraphs **3.1.161, 3.1.162** above.

[6] The stamp duty exemption certificate is necessary because the shares and loan stock have been distributed to the Original Beneficiary personally, so that the deed operates as a voluntary disposition of those assets. See generally paragraphs **3.1.137, 3.1.141** above.

Precedent 20

Deed of Variation by residuary beneficiaries absolutely entitled, establishing a life interest trust in respect of a dwelling-house

Precedent 20(a)—Drafting approach in the real world

THIS DEED OF VARIATION AND SETTLEMENT is made and delivered on [*date*]

BETWEEN—

(1) [full names and addresses of original beneficiaries] ("the Original Beneficiaries") and

(2) [ ] of [ ] and [ ] of [ ] ("the Original Trustees") and

(3) [full names and addresses of executors] ("the Executors")[1,2]

WHEREAS—

A This deed is supplemental to the Will dated [ ] of the late [*full names of testator*] ("the Testator") who died on [ ] and probate of whose said Will ("the Will") was granted out of the [ ] Probate Registry to the Executors on [ ]

B By the Will the Testator gave certain specific and pecuniary legacies and subject to that gave all the remainder of his real and personal estate to the Executors on trust for sale and conversion such that after payment of the Testator's debts and funeral and testamentary expenses the residue of the monies arising from such sale and conversion should be held upon trust for the Original Beneficiaries in equal shares absolutely

C The Testator's estate at his death included the Property as defined below which remains vested in the Executors and which the Original Beneficiaries anticipate the Executors will not require for administration purposes

D The Original Beneficiaries wish to vary the Will in the way set out below as respects the Property for the benefit of the Principal Beneficiary as defined below

NOW THIS DEED WITNESSES as follows—

1 Interpretation

1.1 The Settlement created by this deed shall unless and until the Trustees otherwise determine be known as "the [ ] Trust"

1.2 In this deed where the context admits—

1.2.1—"the Trustees" means the Original Trustees or other the trustee or trustees for the time being of this deed

1.2.2—"the Property" means the freehold dwelling-house known as [ ] (registered at HM Land Registry under title number [ ])

1.2.3—"the Trust Fund" means all rights of the Original Beneficiaries in respect of any assets receivable by the Trustees other than in respect of income[3] pursuant to the variation of the Will contained in clause 2 below all property at any time added to the foregoing by way of accumulation of income capital accretion or otherwise and all property from time to time representing the foregoing respectively

1.2.4—"the Principal Beneficiary" means the Testator's widow [*full names*]

1.2.5—"the Beneficiaries" means the following—

— the Principal Beneficiary
— the Original Beneficiaries and any spouse widow or widower of any of the Original Beneficiaries
— all children and remoter issue of the Original Beneficiaries (whenever born)
— [*insert any others required*]
— all trusts and bodies (corporate or unincorporate) established (whether before or after the date of this deed) exclusively for purposes which are charitable under the law of England and Wales and subject for the time being to the jurisdiction of the courts of any part of the United Kingdom

and "Beneficiary" has a corresponding meaning

1.2.6—"the Perpetuity Date" means the date of expiration of 80 years from and including the date of [this deed] [the Testator's death][4]

1.2.7—"the Trust Period" means the period commencing at the date of this deed and ending on the earlier (in relation to any given part of the Trust Fund) of—

— the Perpetuity Date and

— such date (if any) as the Trustees may in their absolute discretion by irrevocable deed or deeds specify for this purpose in relation to the whole or such part or parts of the Trust Fund as may be specified in such deed (not being in any case a date earlier than the date of execution of such deed)

1.2.8—"spouse" does not include former spouse or widow or widower

1.2.9—expressions importing a status by reference to marriage at any time include a corresponding status by reference to civil partnership within the meaning of the Civil Partnership Act 2004

1.2.10—expressions descriptive of relationship shall be construed in accordance with the general law in force at the date of this deed

1.3 In this deed references to the income of the Trust Fund shall include the net rents and profits pending sale of any land held on trust for sale such that the future proceeds of sale are for the time being comprised in the Trust Fund [and shall also include without apportionment any cash or other assets receivable by the Trustees in respect of income pursuant to the variation of the Will contained in clause 2 below][5]

1.4 The clause headings in this deed are for reference purposes only and shall not affect the construction or effect of any provision of this deed

2 Variation of the Will

2.1 The Will shall be varied and shall have effect and the Deceased's estate shall be administered and distributed as though the Property had been given to the Trustees to be held by them [free of tax] OR [subject to payment out of it of any inheritance tax properly falling to be borne by it in the circumstances][6] upon the trusts and with and subject to the powers and provisions declared and contained in the following clauses of this deed

2.2 The parties to this deed HEREBY DECLARE that they intend Section 142(1) of the Inheritance Tax Act 1984 and Section 62(6) of the Taxation of Chargeable Gains Act 1992[7] to apply to the variation effected by this deed of the dispositions of the property comprised in the Testator's estate that were effected by the Will as made by the Testator

2.3 The Original Beneficiaries make all such assignments as are requisite to give effect to the terms of this clause 2

2.4 The Executors—

2.4.1—acknowledge notice of the variation effected by this deed

2.4.2—confirm that they do not require the Property for administration purposes[8] and

2.4.3—accordingly agree to vest the Property in the Original Trustees as soon as practicable

3 Primary beneficial trusts and powers

3.1   The Trustees shall hold the Trust Fund and the income arising from it UPON TRUST as follows—

3.1.1—to permit the Principal Beneficiary to reside during her lifetime in the Property and in any dwelling-house which the Trustees may from time to time acquire as a residence for the Principal Beneficiary in succession to the Property[9]

3.1.2—to pay to the Principal Beneficiary any income of the Trust Fund during her life

3.1.3—subject to that for the Original Beneficiaries and their respective estates in equal shares absolutely

4 Overriding power of appointment

4.1   The following provisions of this clause 4 apply notwithstanding and in derogation of the trusts powers and provisions of clause 3 above

4.2   Subject to clause 7 below the Trustees (being if individuals not less than two in number) shall have power at any time or times during the Trust Period by any deed or deeds revocable or irrevocable in their absolute discretion to appoint that the whole or any part or parts of the Trust Fund and of the income arising from it shall be held upon such trusts and with and subject to such charges powers and provisions whatever in favour or for the benefit of all or any one or more exclusive of the others or other of the Beneficiaries as the Trustees shall think fit (due regard being had nevertheless to the law relating to remoteness and excessive accumulations)

4.3   In any such deed the Trustees may—

4.3.1—create protective or discretionary trusts or powers operative or exercisable over capital or income or both at the discretion of the Trustees or any other person or persons (and whether or not subject to any requirement for the consent of any other person or persons) wherever any of such persons may be resident domiciled or incorporated

4.3.2—delegate in any manner and to any extent to any person or persons wherever resident domiciled or incorporated the exercise at any time or times during the Trust Period of this power of appointment

4.3.3—direct or authorise the accumulation of income during any period or periods for the time being permitted by law

4.3.4—generally make or confer in favour of or for the benefit of all or any one or more of the Beneficiaries all such dispositions charges or powers of or in relation to any capital or income of the Trust Fund as an absolute owner could make or confer of or in relation to any property belonging to him beneficially (regard nonetheless being had to the law relating to remoteness)

4.4   No appointment in exercise of the foregoing power shall be made (and no such appointment previously made shall be revoked) so as to affect any income of the Trust Fund already received or then presently receivable by the Trustees (other than income lawfully accumulated prior to such appointment or revocation) or any capital of the Trust Fund previously paid transferred or applied to or for the benefit of any beneficiary by virtue of any other power conferred by or under this deed or by law

5   Non-apportionment of income

5.1   Unless the Trustees in any case see special reason to the contrary and subject to any appointment or appointments under any relevant power conferred by or under this deed all income of the Trust Fund shall be treated as arising at the time when it is receivable (and all outgoings chargeable to income of the Trust Fund shall be treated as incurred at the time they fall to be discharged) and no such income or outgoings shall be related or apportioned to any other time or period under the Apportionment Acts of 1834 or 1870 or under any other rule of general law

6   Administrative powers

6.1   The administrative and other powers and provisions set out in the Schedule below shall have effect in relation to the Trust Fund and the income arising from it as part of this deed

6.2   The Trustees shall have power at any time or times during the Trust Period by deed or deeds to add to vary or extend the particular administrative powers and provisions set out in the Schedule if in their absolute discretion they shall consider any such addition variation or extension to be for the benefit of all or any one or more of the persons (born or unborn and ascertained or unascertained) from time to time entitled or capable of becoming entitled under this deed

6.3   The power conferred by clause 6.2 above shall be exercisable whether or not any appointment is then made or contemplated in respect of the beneficial interests under this deed

6.4   Section 1 of the Trustee Delegation Act 1999 shall not apply in relation to land in which a trustee has a beneficial interest under this deed

7   Overriding restrictions on powers

7.1   The provisions of this clause 7 shall have effect notwithstanding anything expressed or implied in this deed

7.2   No exercise of the overriding power of appointment in clause 4 above shall be made to the prejudice of the interests of the Principal Beneficiary[10] without the prior written consent of the Principal Beneficiary

7.3   No power or discretion which is subject to the rule against perpetuities and is by or under this deed conferred on or reserved to the Trustees or any other person shall be exercisable in any circumstances after the Perpetuity Date

8   Release and restriction of powers

8.1   The Trustees (being if individuals not less than two in number) shall have power from time to time and at any time during the Trust Period by any deed or deeds revocable or irrevocable wholly or partially to release or restrict from the date of such deed or deeds onwards the exercise of all or any of the powers or discretions conferred upon them by or under this deed or by law whether of a dispositive or an administrative nature (including this present power, and notwithstanding that such power or discretion is vested in them in a fiduciary capacity)

9   Change of Trustees

9.1   The statutory powers of appointing new or additional trustees shall apply to this deed subject to the following provisions of this clause and shall be exercisable by such of the Original Beneficiaries as are for the time being living (jointly if more than one)

9.2   The statutory power of appointing additional trustees shall authorise the appointment of the person exercising the same (whether or not with any other person or persons)

9.3   Section 19 of the Trusts of Land and Appointment of Trustees Act 1996 (appointment and retirement of trustees at the instance of beneficiaries) shall not apply in relation to the trusts of this Settlement

10   Remuneration of Trustees

10.1   The Trustees shall have power to employ any of their number who may be engaged in any profession or business either alone or in partnership and any of the Trustees (other than any of the Original Beneficiaries or any spouse of any of the Original Beneficiaries) who is an individual so engaged may charge and be paid and may retain all professional or other proper charges for any business done or time spent or services rendered by him or his firm (and all usual commissions deriving in any way from the Trust Fund or any dealings with it) in connection with any of the trusts powers and provisions of this deed or of any assurance of land or buildings upon trust for sale such that the net proceeds of sale are held upon any of the trusts of this deed whether or not within the usual scope of his profession or business and although not of a nature requiring the employment of a professional or business person

11   Protection of Trustees

11.1   In the professed execution and exercise of the trusts powers and discretions of this deed and of any instrument executed pursuant to it no individual who is a trustee shall be liable for any loss arising by reason of any improper investment made in good faith or the retention of any improper investment or any failure to see to the insurance or preservation of any chattels or the making or revising of any inventory of them or for the negligence or fraud of any agent employed by him or it or by any other trustee of this deed (although the employment of such agent was not strictly necessary or expedient) or by reason of any other matter or thing whatsoever except wilful and individual fraud or wilful wrongdoing on the part of the trustee whom it is sought to make liable

IN WITNESS of which the parties have duly executed this deed which is delivered on the day and year first before written

The Schedule

Administrative Powers of the Trustees

[*insert the draftsman's preferred schedule of administrative powers*]

[SIGNED as a deed etc]

Notes

[1] On the basis that the trust is for the testator's widow, IHT will be reduced (or at any rate, if the widow is not UK domiciled at least for IHT purposes, not increased). The executors are joined only for the purpose apparent from clause 2.4, rather than because they are essential parties to the IHT statement of intent.

[2] This type of situation – a trust of a residence being formed for the testator's widow, by other residuary beneficiaries (probably children of a first marriage) – may well result from negotiations relating to a claim or potential claim under the I(PFD)A 1975. In that event the widow may also need to be a party to confirm acceptance of this provision in satisfaction of any claim she may have. Alternatively, if she had already commenced proceedings, completion of the deed could instead simply be made conditional on the filing of a notice of discontinuance in the proceedings (cf paragraph **3.3.48** above, though in the present situation the securing of spouse exemption will generally mean that an IHT statement of intent is unlikely to be omitted unless the estate as a whole is within the available NRB, even if relevant property status would otherwise be preferred over an IPDI).

[3] The definition of the Trust Fund cannot refer simply to the Property at this stage, as it has not yet been vested in the Original Beneficiaries or the Trustees (though it soon will be, see clause 2.4.3). The Original Beneficiaries have at this stage no more than the residuary beneficiary's *chose in*

action (see paragraph **3.1.20** above). Receipts in respect of income should anyway be excluded from the Trust Fund definition since the latter defines capital of the Trust Fund.

[4] There is no need to start the perpetuity period from the testator's death where the Original Beneficiaries are absolutely entitled under the Will, though some may prefer to do so: see paragraph **3.1.18**, point (b), above.

[5] Unless the Property has been let, which is improbable in the circumstances, it is unlikely that any income will be due to the Trustees from the executors. In circumstances where the executors are willing to release the Property immediately (see clause 2.4), and it has not generated income since the death, these words can be omitted.

[6] These words are likely to be superfluous if the surviving spouse is UK domiciled (or deemed domiciled) and the variation is effective to secure backdated spouse exemption. If tax may be payable, it is more likely that the "free of tax" alternative would be desired in practice in any case. If the "subject to tax" option is chosen in the first instance, thought must be given to the funding of that tax before the variation is finalised.

[7] On the footing that the widow was not given an interest in the property by the will, the executors will not be entitled to CGT main residence relief under TCGA 1992 s 225A as matters stand, so a CGT statement of intent will be necessary to avoid a chargeable disposal by them on vesting the property in the new beneficiary (the trustees). The Original Beneficiaries will in any case want to include a CGT statement of intent, because at the time of the variation they have merely the residuary beneficiary's chose in action: see paragraph **3.1.161** above.

[8] As a precaution in case it were alleged that this confirmation records a decision already reached (so that the deed operates to create a beneficial interest in the Property as such) it would be wise for form SDLT60 to be completed at the same time as the variation, relying on the exemption from SDLT in FA 2003 Sch 3 para 4; see paragraphs **3.1.152**, **3.1.156** above. If any indebtedness is secured on the Property, note also paragraph **3.1.155** above.

[9] This formulation will ensure that the Trustees are entitled to CGT main residence relief in respect of the property for periods during which the Property is the widow's only or main residence (taking account of any election that may be relevant), assuming (as in this precedent) that the Trustees own a 100% interest in the Property. For possible difficulties in relation to that relief where the deceased's estate, and so the Trust Fund, included only a part-interest in the Property, see "Trustees with a part interest in land: the impact of the Trusts of Land and Appointment of Trustees Act 1996", published in Private Client Business [2007] 4 PCB 263, Sweet & Maxwell 2007.

[10] This formulation allows the Trustees to make appointments without the widow's consent (or even knowledge) where the only effect of the appointment is in relation to what happens after the termination of the widow's life interest.

Precedent 20(b)—Drafting approach in the misleading fictitious world

THIS DEED OF VARIATION is made and delivered on [*date*]

BETWEEN—

(1)   [full names and addresses of original beneficiaries] ("the Original Beneficiaries") and

(2)   [   ] of [   ] and [   ] of [   ] ("the Property Trustees") and

(3)   [full names and addresses of executors] ("the Executors")[1]

WHEREAS—

A   This deed is supplemental to the Will dated [   ] of the late [*full names of testator*] ("the Testator") who died on [   ] and probate of whose said Will ("the Will") was granted out of the [   ] Probate Registry to the Executors on [   ]

B   By the Will the Testator gave certain specific and pecuniary legacies and subject to that gave all the remainder of his real and personal estate to the Executors on trust for sale and conversion such that after payment of the Testator's debts and funeral and testamentary expenses the residue of the monies arising from such sale and conversion should be held upon trust for the Original Beneficiaries in equal shares absolutely

C   The Testator's estate at his death included the freehold dwelling-house known as [   ] (registered at HM Land Registry under title number [   ]) ("the Property") which remains vested in the Executors and which the Original Beneficiaries anticipate the Executors will not require for administration purposes

D   The Original Beneficiaries wish to vary the Will in the way set out below as respects the Property for the benefit of the Testator's widow [*full names*]

NOW THIS DEED WITNESSES as follows—

1   Variation of the Will

1.1   The Will shall be varied and shall have effect and the Deceased's estate shall be administered and distributed as though the following clause [4A] had been included in the Will immediately before clause [5] as admitted to probate—

"[4A](1) I GIVE my dwelling-house known as [   ] ("the Property") [free of tax] <u>OR</u> [subject to payment out of it of any inheritance tax properly falling to be borne by it in the circumstances][2] to [   ] of [   ] and [   ] of [   ] ("the Property Trustees" which shall include the trustees or trustee for the time being of the trust established by this clause [4A]) to be held by them upon the trusts and with and subject to the powers and provisions declared and contained in the following sub-clauses of this clause [4A]

(2) In this clause [4A] where the context admits—

(a) "the Beneficiaries" means the following—

   (i) my wife [*full names*]
   (ii) my children [   ] [   ] and [   ][3]
   (iii) any spouse widow or widower of any of my said children
   (iv) all children and remoter issue (whenever born) of my said children
   (v) [insert any others required]
   (vi) all trusts and bodies (corporate or unincorporate) established (whether before or after my death) exclusively for purposes which are charitable under the law of England and Wales and subject for the time being to the jurisdiction of the courts of any part of the United Kingdom

and "Beneficiary" has a corresponding meaning

(b) "the Property Fund" means the Property and all property of any kind from time to time representing it

(c) "the Perpetuity Date" means the date of expiration of 80 years from and including the date of my death[4]

(d) "the Trust Period" means the period commencing at the date of my death and ending on the earlier (in relation to any given part of the Property Fund) of—

   (i) the Perpetuity Date and
   (ii) such date (if any) as the Property Trustees may in their absolute discretion by irrevocable deed or deeds specify for this purpose in relation to the whole or such part or parts of the Property Fund as may be specified in such deed (not being in any case a date earlier than the date of execution of such deed)

(e) "spouse" does not include former spouse or widow or widower

(f) expressions importing a status by reference to marriage at any time include a corresponding status by reference to civil partnership within the meaning of the Civil Partnership Act 2004

(g) expressions descriptive of relationship shall be construed in accordance with the general law in force at the date of this will

(3)   The Property Trustees shall hold the Property Fund and the income arising from it UPON TRUST as follows—

(a)   to permit my said wife to reside during her lifetime in the Property and in any dwelling-house which the Property Trustees may from time to time acquire as a residence for her in succession to the Property[5]

(b)   to pay to my said wife any income of the Property Fund during her life

(c)   subject to that for my said children and their respective estates in equal shares absolutely

(4)   Notwithstanding and in derogation of the trusts powers and provisions of sub-clause (3) above the Property Trustees (being if individuals not less than two in number) shall have power at any time or times during the Trust Period by any deed or deeds revocable or irrevocable in their absolute discretion to appoint that the whole or any part or parts of the Property Fund and of the income arising from it shall be held upon such trusts and with and subject to such charges powers and provisions whatever in favour or for the benefit of all or any one or more exclusive of the others or other of the Beneficiaries as the Property Trustees shall think fit (due regard being had nevertheless to the law relating to remoteness and excessive accumulations); and so that in any such deed the Property Trustees may—

(a)   create protective or discretionary trusts or powers operative or exercisable over capital or income or both at the discretion of the Property Trustees or any other person or persons (and whether or not subject to any requirement for the consent of any other person or persons) wherever any of such persons may be resident domiciled or incorporated

(b)   delegate in any manner and to any extent to any person or persons wherever resident domiciled or incorporated the exercise at any time or times during the Trust Period of this power of appointment

(c)   direct or authorise the accumulation of income during any period or periods for the time being permitted by law

(d)   generally make or confer in favour of or for the benefit of all or any one or more of the Beneficiaries all such dispositions charges or powers of or in relation to any capital or income of the Property Fund as an absolute owner could make or confer of or in relation to any property belonging to him beneficially (regard nonetheless being had to the law relating to remoteness)

PROVIDED that no appointment in exercise of the foregoing power shall be made—

(i)   to the prejudice of the interests of my said wife[6] without her prior written consent

(ii) (and no such appointment previously made shall be revoked) so as to affect any income of the Trust Fund already received or then presently receivable by the Property Trustees (other than income lawfully accumulated prior to such appointment or revocation) or any capital of the Property Fund previously paid transferred or applied to or for the benefit of any beneficiary by virtue of any other power conferred by or under this deed or by law

(5)   The Property Trustees (being if individuals not less than two in number) shall have power from time to time and at any time during the Trust Period by any deed or deeds revocable or irrevocable wholly or partially to release or restrict from the date of such deed or deeds onwards the exercise of all or any of the powers or discretions conferred upon them by or under this will or by law whether of a dispositive or an administrative nature (including this present power and notwithstanding that such power or discretion is vested in them in a fiduciary capacity)

(6)   Notwithstanding anything expressed or implied in this will no power or discretion which is subject to the rule against perpetuities and is by or under this will conferred on the Property Trustees or any other person shall be exercisable in any circumstances after the Perpetuity Date

(7)   Section 1 of the Trustee Delegation Act 1999 shall not apply in relation to land in which a trustee has a beneficial interest under this deed

(8)   The statutory powers of appointing new or additional trustees shall apply to the trusts of the Property Fund subject to the following provisions of this sub-clause and shall be exercisable by such of my said children as are for the time being living (jointly if more than one) PROVIDED that—

(a)   the statutory power of appointing additional trustees shall authorise the appointment of the person exercising the same (whether or not with any other person or persons)

(b)   section 19 of the Trusts of Land and Appointment of Trustees Act 1996 (appointment and retirement of trustees at the instance of beneficiaries) shall not apply in relation to the Property Fund

(9)   Clauses [   ] of this Will[7] shall apply to the Property Fund and the Property Trustees as they do to my Residuary Estate and my Trustees"

1.2   The Original Beneficiaries make all such assignments as are requisite to give effect to the terms of this clause 1

2   Tax treatment

The parties to this deed HEREBY DECLARE that that they intend Section 142(1) of the Inheritance Tax Act 1984 and Section 62(6) of the Taxation of Chargeable Gains Act 1992[8] to apply to the variation effected by this deed of the dispositions of the property comprised in the Testator's estate that were effected by the Will as made by the Testator

3 Acceptance by the Executors

The Executors—

3.1 acknowledge notice of the variation effected by this deed

3.2 confirm that they do not require the Property for administration purposes[9] and

3.3 accordingly agree to vest the Property in the Original Trustees as soon as practicable

IN WITNESS of which the parties have duly executed this deed which is delivered on the day and year first before written

[SIGNED as a deed etc]

Notes

[1] See notes 1 and 2 to PRECEDENT 21(A) above.

[2] See note 6 to PRECEDENT 21(A) above.

[3] Or as appropriate. These are of course the Original Beneficiaries, but the make believe style of drafting means that definitions used for the deed itself cannot be adopted in the clauses inserted into the will.

[4] With this drafting style, fixing the perpetuity period by reference to the date of the deed is not a practical option; cf note 4 to PRECEDENT 21(A) above.

[5] See note 9 to PRECEDENT 21(A) above.

[6] See note 10 to PRECEDENT 21(A) above.

[7] These clauses would include primarily—

— administrative powers;

— trustee remuneration;

— trustee protection or indemnity; and

— non-apportionment of income.

[8] See note 7 to PRECEDENT 21(A) above.

[9] See note 8 to PRECEDENT 21(A) above.

Precedent 21

Deed of Variation by surviving spouse and adult children of intestate, dividing the spouse's life interest fund between them[1]

THIS DEED OF VARIATION is made and delivered on [*date*]

BETWEEN—

(1)   [   ] of [   ] ("the Widower") and

(2)   [   ] of [   ] and [   ] of [   ] ("the Children") and

(3)   [   ] of [   ] and [   ] of [   ] ("the Administrators")[2]

WHEREAS—

A   [*full names of deceased*] of [   ] ("the Deceased"), who was the wife of the Widower and the mother of the Children, died on [   ] intestate and domiciled in England and Wales[3]

B   Letters of Administration in respect of the Deceased's estate were granted to the Administrators out of the [   ] Probate Registry on [   ]

C   Subject to providing for the fixed net sum payable to the Widower, one half of the Deceased's net estate ("the Settled Share") is under the Administration of Estates Act 1925 to be held in trust for the Widower for life and subject to that for the Children absolutely

D   The Widower and the Children have determined to divide the Settled Share between them in the manner appearing below

NOW THIS DEED WITNESSES as follows—

1   The parties HEREBY AGREE AND DECLARE

1.1 by way of variation of the devolution of the Deceased's estate under the law relating to intestacy that the Settled Share shall be distributed (as soon as may be in due course of administration) as to [%] to the Widower absolutely and as to [%] to the Children in equal shares absolutely and

1.2 that that they intend [Section 142(1) of the Inheritance Tax Act 1984][4] and Section 62(6) of the Taxation of Chargeable Gains Act 1992 to apply to the variation effected by this deed of the dispositions of the property comprised in the Testator's estate that were effected by the Will as made by the Testator

[2 It is hereby certified that this deed falls within category M in the Schedule to the Stamp Duty (Exempt Instruments) Regulations 1987][5]

IN WITNESS of which the parties have duly executed this deed which is delivered on the day and year first before written

[SIGNED as a deed etc]

Notes

[1] Where the parties are on reasonably good terms, this may be a more flexible approach than a capitalisation of the life interest under AEA 1925 s 47A (see paragraphs **3.3.61** ff above) – especially if backdated IHT effect is not desired (see note 4 below). However, if there was delay in extracting the grant, and backdated IHT effect *is* wanted, the time limit for a capitalisation may be later than the fixed two years allowed for a variation.

[2] The Administrators (who in the circumstances may well just be the Widower, or him and one of the Children) are joined primarily by way of notice. But if the estate is of sufficient size and an IHT statement of intent is included (see note 2) this deed will increase the IHT payable out of the estate, in which case they are necessary parties to the IHT statement of intent: see paragraph **3.1.65** above.

[3] See note 2 to PRECEDENT 20 above.

[4] Depending on how far the available NRB had already been absorbed in lifetime or by the half share of the estate (after the fixed net sum) that devolves in any event to the Children, and on the perceived chance of the Widower surviving seven years from the date of the deed, it may be thought preferable to preserve IHT exemption for the whole of the Settled Share (thus avoiding early payment of IHT) by omitting an IHT statement of intent, and allow the deed to operate as a PET in respect of the proportion being partitioned to the Children. (This may have added attractions in the light of the introduction of the transferable NRB by the Pre-Budget Report 2007 (see APPENDIX 7), since preserving the NRB on the first death will gain the benefit, proportionally, of any increase in the statutory NRB between the two deaths.) Another factor will be whether there is thought to be any possibility that the Widower may in future come to benefit from the Children's share in any case – which in the absence of an IHT statement of intent would risk potential GROB implications.

[5] A stamp duty exemption certificate is only needed if the deed may operate as a conveyance or transfer in relation to stock or marketable securities: see paragraph **3.1.138** above. This may depend *inter alia* on how far the administration of the estate has progressed.

Precedent 22

Deed of Variation by surviving joint owner absolutely entitled, creating a nil-rate band discretionary trust with ancillary powers

THIS DEED OF VARIATION is made and delivered on [*date*]

BETWEEN—

(**1**) [   ] of [   ] ("the Original Beneficiary")

(**2**) [   ] of [   ] and [   ] of [   ] ("the Original Trustees")[1] and

(**3**) [   ] of [   ] and [   ] of [   ] ("the Executors")

WHEREAS—

A   This deed is supplemental to the Will dated [   ] of the late [*full names of testator*] ("the Testator") who died on [   ] and probate of whose said Will ("the Will") was granted out of the [   ] Probate Registry to the Executors on [   ]

B   By the Will the Testator gave certain specific and pecuniary legacies and subject to that gave all the remainder of his real and personal estate to the Executors on trust for sale and conversion such that after payment of the Testator's debts and funeral and testamentary expenses the residue of the monies arising from such sale and conversion should be held upon trust for the Original Beneficiary absolutely

C   The Original Beneficiary wishes to vary the above mentioned disposition in the Will by providing for a sum to be set aside out of it and settled for the benefit of herself and her family in the way appearing below

NOW THIS DEED WITNESSES as follows—

1   Interpretation

1.1   The Settlement created by this deed shall unless and until the Legacy Trustees otherwise determine be known as "the [   ] Trust"

1.2   In this deed where the context admits—

1.2.1—"the Legacy Trustees" means the Original Trustees or other the trustee or trustees for the time being of this deed

1.2.2—"the Trust Legacy" means the legacy treated as given on the trusts of this deed (out of the property otherwise passing to the Original Beneficiary as the Testator's residuary estate) by virtue of clause 2.1 below

1.2.3—"the Nil-Tax Sum" means the maximum sum which in the light of the circumstances existing at [the Testator's death] OR [the date of this deed][2] could have been bequeathed by him as a pecuniary legacy by way of chargeable transfer without giving rise to any actual liability to inheritance tax attributable to such assumed legacy (and so that in ascertaining that sum [no account shall be taken of the statutory attribution of any exemption or relief from inheritance tax as between the Trust Legacy and any other property] [due account shall be taken of the statutory attribution (disregarding events occurring after [the Testator's death] OR [the date of this deed][3]) of any exemption or relief from inheritance tax as between the Trust Legacy and the dispositions or devolution (actual or deemed) of any other property comprised in the Testator's estate or treated for inheritance tax purposes as part of his estate at his death][4])

1.2.4—"the Beneficiaries" means the following—

—   the Original Beneficiary
—   all children and remoter issue of the Testator and/or of the Original Beneficiary[5] whenever born
—   the respective spouses widows and widowers (whether or not remarried) of all such children and remoter issue
—   [insert any others required]

and "Beneficiary" has a corresponding meaning

1.2.5—"Charity" means any trust foundation institution or other body corporate or unincorporate (whether existing at or established after the date of this deed) subject for the time being to the jurisdiction of the courts of any part of the United Kingdom and established exclusively for any objects or purposes recognised as charitable by the laws of England and Wales and "Charities" has a corresponding meaning

1.2.6—"the Discretionary Class" means the Beneficiaries and all Charities[6]

1.2.7—"the Trust Period" means the period of 80 years commencing on the date of [this deed] OR [the Testator's death][7] which shall be the perpetuity period applicable to the trusts of this deed

1.2.8—"the Accumulation Period" means the period of 21 years commencing on the same date as the Trust Period[8]

1.2.9—"the Legacy Fund" means the Trust Legacy all rights in respect of it pending its full payment or satisfaction and all investments and property for the time being derived from or representing it

1.2.10—"spouse" does not include former spouse or widow or widower

1.2.11—expressions importing a status by reference to marriage at any time include a corresponding status by reference to civil partnership within the meaning of the Civil Partnership Act 2004

1.2.12—expressions descriptive of relationship shall be construed in accordance with the general law in force at the date of this deed

1.3 The clause headings in this deed are for reference purposes only and shall not affect the construction or effect of any provision of this deed

2 Variation of the Will

2.1 The Will shall be varied and shall have effect and the Deceased's estate shall be administered and distributed as though the Will had included—

2.1.1—a legacy of the Nil-Tax Sum to the Legacy Trustees to be held by them in trust on the terms set out in this deed, and

2.1.2—the provisions relating to the fulfilment of the Trust Legacy set out in the First Schedule below

2.2 The Original Beneficiary makes all such assignments as are requisite to give effect to the terms of clause 2.1 above

2.3 The Executors acknowledge notice of the above variation and agree to give effect to it subject to due administration of the Testator's estate and to all rights of theirs in that connection

2.4 The parties to this deed HEREBY DECLARE that that they intend Section 142(1) of the Inheritance Tax Act 1984 and Section 62(6) of the Taxation of Chargeable Gains Act 1992 to apply to the variation effected by this deed of the dispositions of the property comprised in the Testator's estate that were effected by the Will as made by the Testator

3 Overriding power of appointment

3.1 The Legacy Trustees shall have power at any time or times during the Trust Period by any deed or deeds revocable or irrevocable in their absolute discretion to appoint that the whole or any part or parts of the Legacy Fund and of the income arising from it shall be held upon such trusts and with and subject to such charges powers and provisions whatever in favour or for the benefit of all or any one or more exclusive of the others or other of the Discretionary Class as the Legacy Trustees shall think fit (due regard being had nevertheless to the law relating to remoteness and excessive accumulations)

3.2　In any such deed the Legacy Trustees may—

3.2.1—create protective or discretionary trusts or powers operative or exercisable over capital or income or both at the discretion of the Legacy Trustees or any other person or persons (and whether or not subject to any requirements of consent of any other person or persons) wherever any of such persons may be resident domiciled or incorporated

3.2.2—delegate in any manner and to any extent to any person or persons wherever resident domiciled or incorporated the exercise at any time or times during the Trust Period of this power of appointment

3.2.3—direct or authorise the accumulation of income during any period or periods for the time being permitted by law

3.2.4—generally make or confer in favour of or for the benefit of all or any one or more of the Discretionary Class all such dispositions charges or powers of or in relation to any capital or income of the Legacy Fund as an absolute owner could make or confer of or in relation to any property belonging to him beneficially (regard nonetheless being had to the law relating to remoteness)

3.3　No appointment in exercise of the foregoing power—

3.3.1—shall be made (and no such appointment previously made shall be revoked) so as to affect any income of the Legacy Fund already received or then presently receivable by the Legacy Trustees (other than income lawfully accumulated prior to such appointment or revocation) or any capital of the Legacy Fund previously paid transferred or applied to or for the benefit of any beneficiary by virtue of any other power conferred by or under this deed[9] or by law; or

3.3.2—shall be revocable or revoked after the end of the Trust Period

4　Provisions in default of appointment

4.1　The following provisions of this clause 4 apply in default of and subject to any or every exercise of the power of appointment conferred on the Legacy Trustees by clause 3 above

4.2　The Legacy Trustees shall accumulate the income of the Legacy Fund arising during the Accumulation Period by investing such income and the resulting income arising from it in any investments authorised by this deed or by law (other than the purchase of land only) and adding the accumulations to the capital of the Legacy Fund BUT so that—

4.2.1—the Legacy Trustees shall during the Trust Period have power instead of accumulating such income as described above to deal with the whole or any part or parts of it under clause 4.3 below as if it arose after the expiration of the Accumulation Period; and

4.2.2—the whole or any part or parts of such accumulations may at any time or times during the Accumulation Period be dealt with under clause 4.2.1 above as if it were income of the then current year

4.3   The Legacy Trustees shall hold the income of the Legacy Fund arising during such part of the Trust Period as falls after the expiration of the Accumulation Period UPON TRUST from time to time to pay appropriate or apply the same to or for the maintenance or education or otherwise for the benefit of all or such one or more exclusive of the other or others of the Beneficiaries10 for the time being in existence in such shares and proportions if more than one and generally in such manner as the Legacy Trustees in their absolute discretion think fit and so that the Legacy Trustees may pay any such income to any persons or person to be applied for any purpose authorised by this deed without themselves being bound to see to its actual application PROVIDED ALWAYS that the Legacy Trustees shall during the Trust Period have power to pay or apply the whole or any part or parts of such income to such Charity or Charities or for such exclusively charitable objects or purposes in any part of the world as the Legacy Trustees may from time to time in their absolute discretion think fit

4.4   Subject as provided above the Trust Fund shall be held as to both capital and income UPON TRUST absolutely for such of the children and remoter issue of the Testator and/or of the Original Beneficiary[11] as are living at the date of expiration of the Trust Period and if more than one in equal shares *per stirpes* (so that no issue more remote than a child shall take in competition with a living ancestor)

4.5   Subject to all the trusts powers and provisions of this Deed and if and so far as (for any reason whatever) not wholly disposed of by or under those trusts powers and provisions the Legacy Fund shall be held as to both capital and income UPON TRUST for the children now living of the Testator's marriage to the Original Beneficiary[12] and their respective executors administrators and assigns absolutely

5   *Non-apportionment of income*

5.1   Unless the Legacy Trustees in any case see special reason to the contrary and subject to any appointment or appointments under any relevant power conferred by or under this deed all income of the Legacy Fund shall be treated as arising at the time when it is receivable (and all outgoings chargeable to income of the Legacy Fund shall be treated as incurred at the time they fall to be discharged) and no such income or outgoings shall be related or apportioned to any other time or period under the Apportionment Acts of 1834 or 1870 or under any other rule of general law

6 Administrative powers

6.1   The administrative and other powers and provisions set out in the Second Schedule below shall have effect in relation to the Legacy Fund and the income arising from it as part of this deed

6.2   The Legacy Trustees shall have power at any time or times during the Trust Period by deed or deeds to add to vary or extend the particular administrative powers and provisions set out in the Second Schedule if in their absolute discretion they shall consider any such addition variation or extension to be for the benefit of all or any one or more of the persons (born or unborn and ascertained or unascertained) from time to time entitled or capable of becoming entitled under this deed

6.3   The power conferred by clause 6.2 above shall be exercisable whether or not any appointment is then made or contemplated in respect of the beneficial interests under this deed

7 Release and restriction of powers

7.1   The Legacy Trustees (being if individuals not less than two in number) shall have power from time to time and at any time during the Trust Period by any deed or deeds revocable or irrevocable wholly or partially to release or restrict from the date of such deed or deeds onwards the exercise of all or any of the powers or discretions conferred upon them by or under this deed or by law whether of a dispositive or an administrative nature (including this present power and notwithstanding that such power or discretion is vested in them in a fiduciary capacity)

8 Change of Trustees

8.1   The statutory powers of appointing new or additional trustees shall apply to this deed subject to the following provisions of this clause and shall be exercisable by the Original Beneficiary

8.2   The statutory power of appointing additional trustees shall authorise the appointment of the person exercising the same (whether or not with any other person or persons)

8.3   The Original Beneficiary shall not be the sole trustee of this deed and shall be obliged to exercise without delay the power to appoint at least one new trustee if circumstances occur in which she is the sole trustee surviving or capable of acting[13]

9 Remuneration of Trustees

9.1   The Legacy Trustees shall have power to employ any of their number who may be engaged in any profession or business either alone or in partnership and any of the Legacy Trustees (other than the Original Beneficiary or any spouse of any of the Original Beneficiary) who is an individual so engaged may charge and be paid and may retain all professional or other proper charges for any business done or time spent or services rendered by him or his firm (and all usual commissions deriving in any way from the Legacy Fund or any dealings with it) in connection with any of the trusts powers and provisions of this deed or of any assurance of land or buildings upon trust for sale such that the net proceeds of sale are held upon any of the trusts of this deed whether or not within the usual scope of his profession or business and although not of a nature requiring the employment of a professional or business person

10   Protection of Trustees

10.1   In the professed execution and exercise of the trusts powers and discretions of this deed and of any instrument executed pursuant to it no individual who is a trustee shall be liable for any loss arising by reason of any improper investment made in good faith or the retention of any improper investment or any failure to see to the insurance or preservation of any chattels or the making or revising of any inventory of them or for the negligence or fraud of any agent employed by him or it or by any other trustee of this deed (although the employment of such agent was not strictly necessary or expedient) or by reason of any other matter or thing whatsoever except wilful and individual fraud or wilful wrongdoing on the part of the trustee whom it is sought to make liable

IN WITNESS of which the parties have duly executed this deed which is delivered on the day and year first before written

The First Schedule

Provisions relating to the fulfilment of the Trust Legacy

1   Powers for the Executors instead of satisfying the Trust Legacy wholly by the payment of cash (or by the appropriation of real or personal property) to the Legacy Trustees—

1.1   to require the Legacy Trustees to accept in place of all or any part of Trust Legacy a binding promise of payment on demand made by the person entitled (whether beneficially or as trustees) to the residue of the Testator's estate (a "Legacy Promise"), and (instead or in combination)

1.2   to charge all or any part of the Trust Legacy on any property forming (or which would but for the provision of the Trust Legacy form) part of the residue of the Testator's estate (a "Legacy Charge"); and to do so, if they think fit, on terms that no one in whom the charged property is from time to time vested shall be or become personally liable for the sum secured

2   A provision exonerating the Executors—

2.1   from any further responsibility to see that the Legacy Trustees receive the sum promised by any Legacy Promise, and

2.2 from any further responsibility (to the extent of the value at the Testator's death of the property charged) to see that the Legacy Trustees receive the sum secured by any Legacy Charge

3 A power for the Executors to give an assent of any property subject to a Legacy Charge in favour of the person who would be entitled to it (free of the Legacy Charge) if the Trust Legacy did not have to be provided for

4 Rights for the Legacy Trustees—

4.1 to require security to be given for the debt created by any Legacy Promise

4.2 to require or impose in relation to any such security, or in relation to a Legacy Charge, such terms if any (subject to the foregoing provisions) as they think fit including terms as to interest and the personal liability of the borrower and terms linking the debt to a published index or otherwise providing for its amount to vary with the passage of time according to a formula and

4.3 in relation to any debt created by a Legacy Promise and any amount payable under a Legacy Charge—

4.3.1 to leave it outstanding for as long as they think fit
4.3.2 to refrain from exercising their rights in relation to it
4.3.3 to waive the payment of all or any part of it or of any interest or indexation element due in respect of it

5 A provision exonerating the Legacy Trustees—

5.1 from any liability for loss to the Legacy Fund if—

5.1.1 the person making a Legacy Promise is or becomes unable to pay the debt created by it, or
5.1.2 a Legacy Charge or any security given for a Legacy Promise is or becomes inadequate; and

5.2 from any liability for any other loss which may occur through their exercising or choosing not to exercise any power treated as given to them by this clause 2.1.2

6 A provision confirming that—

6.1 the foregoing powers and exonerations—

6.1.1 are without prejudice to any other powers or exonerations given by the Testator's will or by the general law and
6.1.2 are exercisable even though the Executors and the Legacy Trustees may be or include the same persons and the Original Beneficiary may be among them (but without prejudice to clause 8.3 above they are not exercisable while the Original Beneficiary is the sole Legacy Trustee); and

6.2 any of the Legacy Trustees may exercise or concur in exercising all powers and discretions given to him or her by this clause or by law notwithstanding that he or she has a direct or other personal interest in the mode or result of any such exercise

The Second Schedule

Administrative Powers of the Legacy Trustees

[*insert the draftsman's preferred schedule of administrative powers*]

[SIGNED as a deed etc]

Notes

[1] The Original Beneficiary (usually the surviving spouse or civil partner) must not be the only trustee of the NRB discretionary trust. There are some who, fearing that HMRC will fail to appreciate the difference between the survivor's personal capacity and a separate fiduciary capacity as trustee, advocate that he/she should not even be *one* of the trustees (cf paragraph **2.6.18** above), especially where FA 1986, s 103 may be in point as it was in *Phizackerley v HMRC* (2007) SpC 591.

[2] It is important that the amount of an NRB legacy contained in the will itself should be capable of determination without reference to events occurring later than the death (eg deeds of variation, especially by other beneficiaries, or the passing on of legacies using IHTA 1984 s 143); otherwise the personal representatives will be unable to complete the administration of the estate until after the two year period during which retrospective adjustments to the IHT position are possible (cf paragraph **3.3.59** above). If as a result of post-death events it transpires that the NRB legacy as ascertained under the will is now excessive (because more chargeable gifts have been created on a backdated basis for IHT, and the total chargeable gifts therefore in fact exceed the available NRB), a distribution from the NRB discretionary trust can be made within two years from the death with backdated effect under IHTA 1984 s 144, thus rectifying the position. However, where an NRB legacy is itself being created by means of a variation, there is no objection to taking account of events occurring up to the date of the variation.

[3] The same option should be selected here as in relation to note 2 above. Again the aim is to fix the amount of the Nil-Tax Sum without reference to any changes in the IHT position of the estate resulting from events after the date specified.

[4] Where assets in the estate attract BPR or APR, and are not themselves the subject of a specific gift, IHTA 1984, s 39A will result in part of the relief being attributed to the NRB legacy, itself a specific gift. (Bear in mind that the amount of the NRB legacy may be being fixed by reference to the circumstances existing at the date of death, see note 2 above, so some other variation to create a specific gift of the BPR or APR property will not be taken into account.) That will often mean that the NRB legacy ends up at a figure greater than the available NRB itself: see paragraphs

3.1.188–3.1.193 above. Alternative formulations are given here to fix the amount of the nil-tax sum taking IHTA 1984 s 39A into account, or disregarding that section and taking solely the amount of the available NRB itself without relief (which would mean that, after applying IHTA 1984 s 39A, not all of the NRB was in fact utilised).

[5] There will be cases where the children of the family are children of one but not both of the couple. It is assumed that the surviving spouse in such a case will wish to ensure that children of his/her own are objects of the trust he/she is creating, while also including children of the deceased partner.

[6] In contrast to PRECEDENT 21 above (both versions), where the Beneficiaries feature only in an overriding power of appointment, a distinction is drawn here between the Beneficiaries and the Discretionary Class (the latter including Charities). This relates to the trust in clause 4.3 for distribution of income among the Beneficiaries; although that is supplemented by a power to distribute to Charities instead of to the Beneficiaries, making this distinction places a clear focus on the (family) Beneficiaries as primary objects. The distinction is not, however, necessary for the validity of the trust (or "trust power") in clause 4.3: *McPhail v Doulton* [1971] AC 424, and those unconcerned with nuances of this sort can, if they prefer, make do with a single class as in PRECEDENT 21 above, even in the present context. The overriding power of appointment in clause 3 is in favour of the Discretionary Class, thus allowing appointments which include charities.

[7] See note 4 to PRECEDENT 21(A) above. This choice of dates is technically independent of the linked choices to which notes 2 and 3 above relate.

[8] This is an unusual, though entirely valid, formulation, designed simply to avoid having to repeat the choice between the date of the deed or of the Testator's death, with the consequent risk of a mismatch.

[9] The powers are in truth conferred by this deed, whatever the formulation as to how the Legacy Fund becomes settled: see paragraph **3.1.17** above. The drafting of this precedent takes the middle course described in paragraph **3.1.216** above, albeit a course that is much closer to the "real world" drafting style referred to in paragraph **3.1.215** above than to the "make believe" style described in paragraphs **3.1.212–3.1.214** above.

[10] See note 6 above.

[11] See note 5 above.

[12] This ultimate default trust is consciously more restricted (in cases where the children do not all have the same two parents) than the references in clauses 1.2.4.2 and 4.4(see notes 5 and 11 above). In cases where the only children are those of both parties to the marriage, the simpler alternative "the Testator's children now living" may be preferable.

[13] See note 1 above.

Precedent 24

Deed of Variation by surviving spouse as joint holder of bank account creating additional "legacies"[1]

THIS DEED OF VARIATION AND DECLARATION OF TRUST is made and delivered on [*date*]

BY [*full names of original beneficiary*] of [   ] ("the Original Beneficiary")

WHEREAS—

A Expressions defined in the body of this deed are intended to have the same meanings in these recitals

B On the Deceased's death on [*date*] the Joint Accounts accrued wholly to the Original Beneficiary as surviving joint holder of those accounts

C Since the death of the Deceased—

(a) interest has been credited (net of income tax at source) to each of the Joint Accounts, but

(b) the Original Beneficiary has made no withdrawals or other additions from or to any of the Joint Accounts[2]

NOW THIS DEED WITNESSES as follows—

1 In this deed where the context so admits—

1.1 "the Deceased" means the Original Beneficiary's late husband [*full names*]

1.2 "the Joint Accounts" means the bank and building society accounts listed in the First Schedule which stood in the joint names of the Deceased and the Original Beneficiary immediately before the death of the Deceased, the balances on which at the date of the Deceased's death were as shown in the third column of the First Schedule[3]

1.3 "the Deceased's Interest" in relation to each of the Joint Accounts means the one-half share of the balance on each such account that would have belonged beneficially to the Deceased if he and the

Original Beneficiary had been entitled to the Joint Accounts as beneficial tenants in common in equal shares immediately before his death (as shown for convenience in the fourth column of the First Schedule)

2   By way of variation of the devolution of the Joint Accounts on the death of the Deceased (so far as provision is hereby made for interests on the part of others than the Original Beneficiary), the Original Beneficiary HEREBY DIRECTS AND DECLARES that each of the Joint Accounts shall be treated for all purposes as though:

2.1   the joint beneficial interest in it had been severed immediately before the death of the Deceased, and

2.2   the severed beneficial interest of the Deceased as tenant in common had devolved at the Deceased's death on the Original Beneficiary as trustee (but subject to clause 4 below) to be held by her as specified in the following provisions of this clause 2.2 (and so that she is to be treated accordingly subject to clause 4 below as having held each of the Joint Accounts following the death of the Deceased as to one half in trust for herself absolutely and as to the other one half, being the Deceased's Interest, in the amounts and for the beneficiaries shown in the Second Schedule)

3   For the purpose of giving effect to the provisions of clause 2 above in the events which have happened the Original Beneficiary HEREBY ACKNOWLEDGES her obligation as trustee to pay from the Joint Accounts as soon as practicable after the execution of this deed (as a first charge on such respective accounts) to the beneficiaries other than herself who are entitled in respect of the Deceased's Interest the respective sums due to them having regard to the terms of clause 2 above[4]

4   No provision of this deed shall confer on any person other than the Original Beneficiary any right to income or interest in respect of the Deceased's Share in any of the Joint Accounts in respect of any period before the date of this deed, nor shall it give rise to any liability on the part of the Original Beneficiary for not having paid before now the amounts due to beneficiaries other than herself in respect of the Deceased's Interest in the Joint Accounts

5   The Original Beneficiary HEREBY DECLARES that that she intends Section 142(1) of the Inheritance Tax Act 1984[5] [and Section 62(6) of the Taxation of Chargeable Gains Act 1992][5] to apply to the variation effected by clauses 2 to 4 above of the devolution of the Deceased's Interest in the Joint Accounts that took effect by law on the Deceased's death as a result of the beneficial joint tenancy in the Joint Accounts not in fact having been severed before then

IN WITNESS of which the Original Beneficiary has duly executed this deed which is delivered on the date first before written

The First Schedule

The Joint Accounts

Bank/Building Society	Account Number or other identification	Balance at the Deceased's death	Deceased's severable share at death

The Second Schedule

Varied devolution of the Deceased's Interest in the Joint Accounts as at the Deceased's death

["Balance" refers to the balance of the Deceased's Interest in each case]

[bank and account no]

[amount of "legacy"]	[full names of "legatee"]	[address of "legatee"]
etc		
Balance	the Original Beneficiary	

[SIGNED as a deed, etc]

Notes

[1] An exercise of this sort may now in fact be of mainly historic interest under the new regime for transferable NRBs (**APPENDIX 7**).

[2] This precedent is a simplified version of a deed used where the Original Beneficiary had in fact consolidated some of the Joint Accounts, and indeed added and withdrawn other sums. A complex tracing statement was drawn up to demonstrate that – even on the least favourable assumptions – the existing accounts contained enough money that was clearly traceable from the Deceased's Interest to cover the intended "legacies". See generally paragraphs **3.1.36** ff, **3.1.83** ff above.

[3] These balances should be the actual balances at death – ie without the accrued interest to death that will also feature in the IHT return.

[4] The terms of the accounts as to notice of withdrawal should be checked, also the mechanism of withdrawal – some accounts allow only withdrawals in favour of the holder of the account, others can issue bank or building society cheques in favour of the "legatees" direct.

[5] This precedent assumes that the "legacies" provided will remain within the unused NRB. Any payments above that limit can be dealt with separately by way of PET. If the variation results in the NRB being exceeded, the personal representatives will be necessary parties to the deed (even though they had nothing to do with the devolution or administration of the Joint Accounts), because they must join in the IHT statement of intent where the amount of IHT payable on the death is increased: see paragraphs **3.1.65**, **3.1.66** above.

[6] A CGT statement of intent is needed only where one or more of the Joint Accounts is designated in a non-sterling currency (and then only where any gain is likely to exceed the Original Beneficiary's available annual CGT exemption and the money in the account was not acquired merely for personal expenditure outside the UK, including the provision or maintenance of a residence outside the UK): see TCGA 1992 s 252. No gain will be realised on a sterling bank account debt, even if TCGA 1992 s 251 does not, in strictness, protect the survivor of joint holders of a debt represented by a bank balance from realising a chargeable gain (he acquires the deceased's severable share of the debt on death under TCGA 1992 s 62(1), (10), so is seemingly not the original creditor to that extent; certainly does not hold the debt as personal representative; and is arguably not a 'legatee', cf the inclusive definition in TCGA 1992 s 64(2)–(3)).

Precedent 24

Deed of Variation by personal representatives of deceased's widow, herself since deceased within two years[1]

THIS DEED OF VARIATION is made and delivered on [*date*]

BETWEEN—

(1) [   ] of [   ] and [   ] of [   ] ("the Second Executors") and

(2) [   ] of [   ] and [   ] of [   ] ("the Beneficiaries") and

(3) [   ] of [   ] and [   ] of [   ] ("the First Executors")

SUPPLEMENTAL to the will dated [   ] of the late [   ] ("the Testator") who died on [   ], and probate of which was granted to the First Executors out of the [   ] Probate Registry on [   ]

WHEREAS—

A By his said will after bequeathing charitable legacies totalling £4,000 and non-charitable legacies totalling £25,000 the Testator left his residuary estate in the events which happened to his widow [   ] ("the Widow") absolutely

B The Widow died on [   ] having by her will dated [   ]—

(a) appointed the Second Executors to be the executors and trustees of her said will and

(b) bequeathed her residuary estate to the Beneficiaries in equal shares absolutely

C The Second Executors intend to apply for probate of the Widow's said will as soon as practicable after the execution of this deed and are not aware of any reason why it should not be admitted to probate[2]

D The Second Executors wish to vary the devolution of the Testator's estate in the manner appearing below

NOW THIS DEED WITNESSES as follows—

1   The Second Executors (with the authority of the Beneficiaries as attested by their execution of this deed) and so far as necessary the Beneficiaries[3] HEREBY AGREE AND DECLARE, by way of variation of the disposition of the Testator's residuary estate made by his said will, that his estate shall be administered and distributed as though a legacy[4] of [£200,000][5] had been bequeathed by his said will to the Beneficiaries absolutely in equal shares free of tax

2   The First Executors acknowledge notice of the foregoing variation and agree to give effect to it subject to due administration of the Testator's estate and to all rights of theirs in that connection

3   The parties HEREBY DECLARE that that they intend Section 142(1) of the Inheritance Tax Act 1984 and Section 62(6) of the Taxation of Chargeable Gains Act 1992 to apply to the foregoing variation

IN WITNESS of which the parties have duly executed this deed which is delivered on the day and year first before written

[SIGNED as a deed etc]

Notes

[1] As with PRECEDENT 24 above, a double estate variation to reduce the estate of the first to die of a married couple or civil partners will generally not now be needed to provide for cash "legacies", having regard to the new transferable NRB (APPENDIX 7); but it may yet have relevance where assets can be identified which have increased substantially in value between the two deaths (or which qualified for BPR or APR on the first death but not on the second, eg where the first to die was in professional practice (whether as a sole practitioner or a partner) and his interest in the business (if not already distributed anyway) was therefore not relevant business property in the hands of the survivor (cf *Beckman v IRC* (2000) SpC 226); see paragraph **3.1.203** above.

[2] Effecting the variation before probate of the Widow's will should allow the benefit of the overall IHT reduction to be gained in relation to the IHT payable on application for the grant in her estate. (A variation to reduce the Widow's estate – as opposed to a variation of the Widow's will – is generally only of benefit for IHT where her estate, inclusive of what was derived, or is due, from the Testator's estate, exceeds her available NRB.) Additionally, effecting the variation before probate may be important with a view to ensuring that the two year limit is complied with, where the Widow died relatively close to the end of the two year period from the Testator's death.

[3] See paragraph **3.1.204** above as to the roles of the Beneficiaries and the Second Executors. Where there could be a dispute over the Widow's will, or where she died intestate, it appears from IHTM35042 that HMRC would accept a variation made solely by the Beneficiaries, but that is inconsistent with IHTM35164 relating to disclaimers, which insists that both the Second Executors and the Beneficiaries must make the variation.

The authors take the view that the Second Executors are the correct parties in principle, but that they will plainly need the authority of the Beneficiaries; and where time allows it is best for both to join in as a practical matter.

[4] As it is provided out of the residuary estate as ascertained in the light of the will itself, it is not a true legacy: if some late emerging liability were to reduce the net residue beneath the amount specified, the legacies left by the will itself will not abate, merely the one provided by the variation out of residue: see paragraph **3.1.22** above.

[5] Subject to note 1 above, unless IHT rates have *increased* between the two deaths, the amount of the deemed legacy (or the value at death, net of any APR or BPR, of any asset redirected in kind)—

— should not exceed the Testator's available NRB (taking account of lifetime dispositions and existing non-exempt gifts under his will, as well as estate IIP funds and GROB property); and subject to that

— need not exceed the amount by which the Widow's estate exceeds her available NRB.

If at the time the deed is prepared there is uncertainty as to the amount of the Testator's available NRB, it may be better to use an NRB formula (see PRECEDENTS **1** and **23** above), instead of a fixed sum.

Precedent 25

Deed of Appointment under fully discretionary will, creating immediate post-death interest for surviving spouse and subject to that age 18-to-25 trust for testator's children

THIS DEED OF APPOINTMENT is made and delivered on [*date*][1]

BY [   ] of [   ] and [   ] of [   ] ("the Appointors")

SUPPLEMENTAL to the Will ("the Will") dated [   ] of the late [   ] ("the Testator") who died on [   ]

WHEREAS—

A   Probate of the Will with one codicil was granted on [   ] out of the [   ] Probate Registry to the Appointors ([*name of executor who has died, whether before or since the Testator*] having died on [   ])

B   The Appointors having proved the Will as aforesaid have accepted office as both executors and trustees of it

C   By clause [   ] of the Will a special power of appointment ("the Overriding Power") is conferred on the persons referred to in the Will as "my Trustees"

D   It is expressly provided by clause [   ] of the Will that the Overriding Power (among other powers) should be exercisable by the executors and trustees for the time being of the Will notwithstanding (inter alia) that the Testator's estate may still be partly or wholly unadministered[2]

E   The Appointors have determined to make the appointment contained in this deed

NOW THIS DEED WITNESSES and IT IS HEREBY DECLARED as follows—

1 In this deed except where the context otherwise requires—

1.1 "the Appointed Fund" means a 75% share of the Testator's Residuary Estate (as defined in the Will)

1.2 "the Will Trustees" means the Appointors or other the trustees or trustee from time to time of the Will

1.3 "the Life Tenant" means the Testator's widow [*full names*]

1.4 "the Children" means the Testator's children [*full names of each*]

2 In exercise of the Overriding Power and of all (if any) other relevant powers the Appointors in their capacities as executors and as trustees (or either) of the Will and of the Testator's estate HEREBY APPOINT AND DECLARE that from and after the date of this deed the Will Trustees shall stand possessed of the Appointed Fund and the future income arising from it upon and with and subject to the trusts charges powers and provisions declared and contained in this deed TO THE INTENT that the rights interests and property of all kinds affected by it shall be held from the date of this deed and administered and applied and (where appropriate) distributed (subject only to all liens and rights from time to time of the Appointors or other the personal representatives of the Testator for the time being) in accordance with the following provisions of this deed and free from any beneficial interests of any person not consistent with those provisions

3 The income of the Appointed Fund shall be paid to the Life Tenant during her lifetime

4 Subject to that the Appointed Fund shall be held in trust for such of the Children as attain the age of 25 PROVIDED that if any of the Children dies under that age leaving a child or children then living who attain the age of 25 years[3] such child or children shall take (equally between them if more than one) the share of the Appointed Fund which his her or their parent would have taken if he or she had survived

5 The statutory provisions as to maintenance and accumulation and the statutory power of advancement shall apply to the foregoing trusts subject to the following modifications namely—

5.1 the power of maintenance shall be exercisable free from any obligation to apply a proportionate part only of income where other income is applicable for maintenance purposes and shall be exercisable generally in any amount or amounts the Will Trustees may think fit

5.[2 the provisions as to maintenance and accumulation shall apply as if the age of majority were not 18 years but 25 years or such lesser age (in years and days) as the beneficiary in question will have attained (if he or she so long lives) on the 21st anniversary of the Testator's death[4] BUT where the beneficiary in question has attained the age of

18 years references in those provisions to payment to the beneficiary's parent or guardian shall be read as references to payment to the beneficiary[5]

5.]3 the power of advancement shall authorise the application of the whole or any part (instead of being limited to one half) of the presumptive or vested share or interest of the person for whose benefit the same is exercised [and shall be exercisable by the Will Trustees without the consent of the Life Tenant if still living][6]

[6 All receipts in the nature of income shall for the purposes of the foregoing trusts be treated as income accruing at the date the same become receivable whatever the period in respect of which the same actually accrue or have accrued]

IN WITNESS of which the Appointors have duly executed this deed which is delivered on the date first before written

[Signed as a deed, etc]

Notes

[1] For the appointment of an IPDI, this appointment could be made within the first three months after the Testator's death if desired: see paragraph **3.2.22** above. But note carefully that if the Life Tenant was a disabled person at the Testator's death, within the definition in IHTA 1984 s 89(4)–(6), the life interest will be a DPI, not an IPDI (see IHTA 1984 s 49A(4)(b)). In that case, the appointment must be deferred until after the end of the first three months, because backdating under IHTA 1984 s 144 will then depend on a primary trigger event (see paragraph **3.2.5** above), not the alternative trigger event introduced by FA 2006 (see paragraphs **3.2.8–3.2.10** above), and therefore remains subject to the *Frankland* trap as noted in paragraph **3.2.23** above, point (b)(iii).

[2] This should be reviewed against the drafting of the particular Will under which the appointment is made.

[3] Assuming the Will set a perpetuity period of 80 years, as is typical where a discretionary trust is set out, no provision need be included here to ensure vesting under the age of 25 on perpetuity grounds, since the Testator's children were by definition living at his death (or at least born posthumously within about nine months afterwards), and children of those who die before age 25 must themselves reach age 25 within at most 50–51 years of the Testator's death. However if a fixed perpetuity period of adequate length was not prescribed by the Will, it will generally be necessary to add words on the lines "or are living and under that age at the end of [the Perpetuity Period as defined in the Will] [the perpetuity period applicable to the Overriding Power]". The admittedly vague formulation of the second option could be made more helpful to later readers if the basis for measuring the perpetuity period can be established with confidence at the time the deed of appointment is prepared, and reflected in a "Perpetuity Period" definition in the deed; however, if there

is any doubt over the matter, this wording will at least allow the appointment to be made without taking time to consider that issue, which may in any case never arise in practice assuming all the Children attain vested interests.

[4] Pending eventual enactment of the Law Commission's recommendation that accumulation of income should be permitted throughout the perpetuity period (LC251), it remains necessary to restrict accumulation to 21 years from the Testator's death or, if longer, the minority of the beneficiary from whose share it arises. This formulation defers the vesting of an income entitlement for the maximum period allowed – if a beneficiary whose interest in capital has not yet vested by the 21st anniversary of the Testator's death has reached age 18 by then (or on that anniversary), he will become entitled to the future income from his share with effect from that anniversary. Unless otherwise provided, an apportionment will be necessary of income accruing at that date.

[5] This clause is included on the assumption that trustees will often consider it more prudent to defer an income entitlement beyond age 18 in general terms – leaving open the option, of course, of accelerating it under the statutory power of advancement if they consider this right at the time. It is no longer the case (as it was with accumulation and maintenance trusts, see TCGA 1992 s 260(2)(d)) that CGT considerations also make it important to delay the vesting of an income interest for as long as possible. If the beneficiary takes under a BMT or an age 18-to-25 trust (basically confined to those to whom the deceased was a "parent" within the extended meaning in IHTA 1984 s 71H), holdover relief will be available, subject to the beneficiary being UK resident, under TCGA 1992 s 260(2)(da) or s 260(2)(db). If on the other hand the property concerned was relevant property immediately before the absolute entitlement – which no longer excludes the subsistence of an IIP – holdover relief is available (again subject to residence) under TCGA 1992 s 260(2)(a), subject to two exceptions (see paragraph **3.2.30** above): where the entitlement arises—

— within two years after the death on which the property was settled and no IPDI or DPI has subsisted before then (not relevant to the present appointment); or

— within three months after the commencement of the settlement or of a ten year anniversary.

[6] Retaining the ability for the Will Trustees to make advancements without the consent of the Life Tenant may be thought helpful in certain cases, or threatening to the Life Tenant in others. It will not however avoid potential GROB implications, as a result of FA 1986 s 102ZA. Bear in mind that a power of revocation, or an overriding power of appointment, exercisable over the interests appointed to the Children once the IPDI has ceased, will preclude age 18-to-25 trust status, as it will be inconsistent with the conditions in IHTA 1984 s 71D(6); but it would be possible, with care and if so desired, to include such a power so long as—

— its exercise was confined to the time while the Life Tenant's IPDI continues in force, or

— (in the light of the rather relaxed HMRC view confirmed in the STEP/HMRC children's trusts guidance, APPENDIX 5) its function after the termination of the Life Tenant's IPDI is purely as a method of varying the shares of Children who are still living and under age 25. At least the class of Children, in this precedent, is closed, as is necessary for the Children's interests to qualify as age 18-to-25 trusts after the IPDI has ceased; the substitutional proviso in clause 4 does not prejudice that status except to the extent that it actually takes effect on the death of one of the Children under age 25 (see paragraph 1.5 of the guidance).

Precedent 26

Deed of Disclaimer of legacy

[*Letterhead or address of original beneficiary*]

TO WHOM IT MAY CONCERN

[*Date*]

I hereby irrevocably renounce and disclaim[1] the legacy bequeathed to me by clause [ ] of the will of the late [*full names of testator*], who died on [*date of death*] [2].

Executed as a deed[3] by [*full names of original beneficiary*][4]:[*original beneficiary's signature*]

Signed as witness in the presence
of the above signatory:[*witness's signature*]

Full names and address of witness:[   ]

Note

[1] No statement of intent is needed for either IHT or CGT: see paragraphs **3.1.51** point (d), **3.1.63**, **3.1.67**, and **3.1.76** point (a)(iv), above.

[2] See note 1 to **PRECEDENT 19**(A) above.

[3] See note 8 to **PRECEDENT 19**(A) above, and paragraph **3.1.7** above.

[4] See note 10 to **PRECEDENT 19**(A) above.

Part C

Appendices

Appendix 1

Standard provisions of the Society of Trust and Estate Practitioners

1 Introductory

1(1) These Provisions may be called the standard provisions of the Society of Trust and Estate Practitioners (1st Edition).

1(2) These Provisions may be incorporated in a document by the words—

> "The standard provisions of the Society of Trust and Estate Practitioners (1st Edition) shall apply"

or in any manner indicating an intention to incorporate them.

2 Interpretation

2(1) In these Provisions, unless the context otherwise requires—

(a) **Income Beneficiary,** in relation to Trust Property, means a Person to whom income of the Trust Property is payable (as of right or at the discretion of the Trustees).

(b) **Person** includes a person anywhere in the world and includes a Trustee.

(c) **The Principal Document** means the document in which these Provisions are incorporated.

(d) **The Settlement** means any settlement created by the Principal Document and an estate of a deceased Person to which the Principal Document relates.

(e) **The Trustees** means the personal representatives or trustees of the Settlement for the time being.

(f) **The Trust Fund** means the property comprised in the Settlement for the time being.

(g) **Trust Property** means any property comprised in the Trust Fund.

(h) **A Professional Trustee** means a Trustee who is or has been carrying on a business which consists of or includes the management of trusts or the administration of estates.

2(2) These Provisions have effect subject to the provisions of the Principal Document.

3 Administrative powers

The Trustees shall have the following powers—

Investment

3(1)—

(a) The Trustees may invest Trust Property in any manner as if they were beneficial owners. In particular the Trustees may invest in unsecured loans.

(b) The Trustees may decide not to diversify the Trust Fund.

Management

3(2) The Trustees may effect any transaction relating to the management administration or disposition of Trust Property as if they were beneficial owners. In particular—

(a) The Trustees may repair and maintain Trust Property.

(b) The Trustees may develop or improve Trust Property.

Joint property

3(3) The Trustees may acquire property jointly with any Person.

Income and capital

3(4) The Trustees may decide not to hold a balance between conflicting interests of Persons interested in Trust Property. In particular—

(a) The Trustees may acquire

    (i) wasting assets and
    (ii) assets which yield little or no income

    for investment or any other purpose.

(b) The Trustees may decide not to procure distributions from a company in which they are interested.

(c) The Trustees may pay taxes and other expenses out of income although they would otherwise be paid out of capital.

Accumulated income

3(5)   The Trustees may apply accumulated income as if it were income arising in the current year.

Use of trust property

3(6)   The Trustees may permit an Income Beneficiary to occupy or enjoy the use of Trust Property on such terms as they think fit. The Trustees may acquire any property for this purpose.

Application of trust capital

3(7)   The Trustees may—

(a)   lend money which is Trust Property to an Income Beneficiary without security, on such terms as they think fit,

(b)   charge Trust Property as security for debts or obligations of an Income Beneficiary, or

(c)   pay money which is Trust Property to an Income Beneficiary as his income, for the purpose of augmenting his income

Provided that—

(i)   the Trustees have power to transfer such Property to that Beneficiary absolutely; or

(ii)   the Trustees have power to do so with the consent of another Person and the Trustees act with the written consent of that Person.

Trade

3(8)   The Trustees may carry on a trade, in any part of the world, alone or in partnership.

Borrowing

3(9)   The Trustees may borrow money for investment or any other purpose. Money borrowed shall be treated as Trust Property.

Insurance

3(10)   The Trustees may insure Trust Property for any amount against any risk.

Delegation

3(11)   A Trustee may delegate in writing any of his functions to any Person. A Trustee shall not be responsible for the default of that Person (even if the delegation was not strictly necessary or expedient) provided that he took reasonable care in his selection and supervision.

Deposit of documents

3(12)   The Trustees may deposit documents relating to the Settlement (including bearer securities) with any Person.

Nominees

3(13)   The Trustees may vest Trust Property in any Person as nominee, and may place Trust Property in the possession or control of any Person.

Offshore administration

3(14)   The Trustees may carry on the administration of the trusts of the Settlement outside the United Kingdom.

Payment of tax

3(15)   The Trustees may pay tax liabilities of the Settlement (and interest on such tax) even though such liabilities are not enforceable against the Trustees.

Indemnities

3(16)   The Trustees may indemnify any Person for any liability properly chargeable against Trust Property.

Security

3(17)   The Trustees may charge Trust Property as security for any liability properly incurred by them as Trustees.

Supervision of company

3(18)   The Trustees are under no duty to enquire into the conduct of a company in which they are interested, unless they have knowledge of circumstances which call for enquiry.

Appropriation

3(19)   The Trustees may appropriate Trust Property to any Person or class of Persons in or towards the satisfaction of their interest in the Trust Fund.

Receipt by charities

3(20)   Where Trust Property is to be paid or transferred to a charity, the receipt of the treasurer or appropriate officer of the charity shall be a complete discharge to the Trustees.

Release of powers

3(21)   The Trustees may by deed release any of their powers wholly or in part so as to bind future trustees.

Ancillary powers

3(22)   The Trustees may do anything which is incidental or conducive to the exercise of their functions.

4   Powers of maintenance and advancement

Sections 31 and 32 Trustee Act 1925 shall apply with the following modifications—

(a)   The Proviso to section 31(1) shall be deleted.

(b)   The words one-half of in section 32(1)(a) shall be deleted.

5   Trust for sale

The Trustees shall hold land in England and Wales on trust for sale.

6   Minors

6(1)   Where the Trustees may apply income for the benefit of a minor, they may do so by paying the income to the minor's parent or guardian on behalf of the minor, or to the minor if he has attained the age of 16. The Trustees are under no duty to enquire into the use of the income unless they have knowledge of circumstances which call for enquiry.

6(2)   Where the Trustees may apply income for the benefit of a minor, they may do so by resolving that they hold that income on trust for the minor absolutely and—

(a)   The Trustees may apply that income for the benefit of the minor during his minority.

(b)   The Trustees shall transfer the residue of that income to the minor on attaining the age of 18.

(c)   For investment and other administrative purposes that income shall be treated as Trust Property.

7 Disclaimer

A Person may disclaim his interest under the Settlement wholly or in part.

8 Apportionment

Income and expenditure shall be treated as arising when payable, and not from day to day, so that no apportionment shall take place.

9 Conflicts of interest

9(1)   In this paragraph—

(a) **A Fiduciary** means a Person subject to fiduciary duties under the Settlement.

(b) **An Independent Trustee**, in relation to a Person, means a Trustee who is not:

(i) a brother, sister, ancestor, descendant or dependent of the Person;
(ii) a spouse of the Person or of (i) above; or
(iii) a company controlled by one or more of any of the above.

9(2)   A Fiduciary may—

(a) enter into a transaction with the Trustees, or

(b) be interested in an arrangement in which the Trustees are or might have been interested, or

(c) act (or not act) in any other circumstances

even though his fiduciary duty under the Settlement conflicts with other duties or with his personal interest;

Provided that—

(i) The Fiduciary first discloses to the Trustees the nature and extent of any material interest conflicting with his fiduciary duties, and

(ii) there is an Independent Trustee in respect of whom there is no conflict of interest, and he considers that the transaction arrangement or action is not contrary to the general interest of the Settlement.

9(3)   The powers of the Trustees may be used to benefit a Trustee (to the same extent as if he were not a Trustee) provided that there is an Independent Trustee in respect of whom there is no conflict of interest.

10 Powers of trustees

The powers of the Trustees may be exercised—

(a) at their absolute discretion; and

(b) from time to time as occasion requires.

11 Trustee remuneration

11(1) A Trustee who is a solicitor or an accountant or who is engaged in a business may charge for work done by him or his firm in connection with the Settlement, including work not requiring professional assistance. This has priority to any disposition made in the Principal Document.

11(2) The Trustees may make arrangements to remunerate themselves for work done for a company connected with the Trust Fund.

12 Liability of Trustees

12(1) A Trustee (other than a Professional Trustee) shall not be liable for a loss to the Trust Fund unless that loss was caused by his own fraud or negligence.

12(2) A Trustee shall not be liable for acting in accordance with the advice of Counsel of at least five years standing, with respect to the Settlement, unless, when he does so—

(a) he knows or has reasonable cause to suspect that the advice was given in ignorance of material facts; or

(b) proceedings are pending to obtain the decision of the court on the matter.

13 Appointment and retirement of Trustees

13(1) A Person may be appointed trustee of the Settlement even though he has no connection with the United Kingdom.

13(2) A Professional Trustee who is an individual who has reached the age of 65 shall retire if—

(a) he is requested to do so by his co-trustees, or by a Person interested in Trust Property; and

(b) he is effectually indemnified against liabilities properly incurred as Trustee.

On that retirement a new Trustee shall be appointed if necessary to ensure that there will be two individuals or a Trust Corporation to act as Trustee.

In this sub-paragraph Trust Corporation has the same meaning as in the Trustee Act 1925.

This sub-paragraph does not apply to a Professional Trustee who is—

(a) a personal representative

(b) the settlor of the Settlement or

(c) a spouse or former spouse of the settlor or testator.

14   Protection for interest in possession and accumulation and maintenance settlements

These Provisions shall not have effect—

(a) so as to prevent a Person from being entitled to an interest in possession in Trust Property (within the meaning of the Inheritance Tax Act 1984);

(b) so as to cause the Settlement to be an accumulation or discretionary settlement (within the meaning of section 5 Taxation of Chargeable Gains Act 1992);

(c) so as to prevent the conditions of section 71(1) Inheritance Tax Act 1984 from applying to Trust Property.

Appendix 2

Inland Revenue statements

HMRC comments on protective trusts

Extract from HMRC letter published in the Law Society Gazette on 3 March 1976

In our view trusts 'to the like effect' as those set out in this 33(1) of the Trustee Act are trusts which are not materially different in their tax consequences. We would not wish to distinguish a trust by reason of a minor variation or additional administrative power or duties. But in the first situation which you mention the extension of the list of potential beneficiaries to brothers and sisters of the principal beneficiary could be a means of giving relief to a trust primarily intended to benefit them. Such a trust would be regarded as outside the scope of para 18 of Sched 5 to the Finance Act 1975 [*now IHTA 1984 s 88*].

On the other hand, it is clear from the existence of para 18(2)(b) that the insertion of a power to apply capital for the benefit of this primary beneficiary was contemplated as a possible feature of the settlement entitled to relief.

You wrote to us again about the special exemptions from capital transfer tax [*now IHT*] for protective trusts.

I appreciate that so long as the principal beneficiary has no spouse or issue the statutory trusts extend to the next of kin for the time being, who might well be brothers and sisters. But this is not all the same thing as including them in the primary class of beneficiaries *ab initio* on an equal footing with the spouse and issue. In that event the brothers and sisters could receive the income of settled property to the entire exclusion of the principal beneficiary, his spouse and issue. I confirm that trusts which could produce that result would not be regarded as 'to the like effect' as those specified in section 33(1) of the Trustee Act 1925.

HMRC Statement of Practice SP 10/79

Power for trustees to allow a beneficiary to occupy dwelling-house [15 August 1979]

Many wills and settlements contain a clause empowering the trustees to permit a beneficiary to occupy a dwelling-house, which forms part of trust property as they think fit. The Commissioners for Her Majesty's Revenue and Customs do not regard the existence of such a power as excluding any interest in possession in the property.

Whether is no interest in possession in the property in question, the Commissioners for Her Majesty's Revenue and Customs do not regard the exercise of the power as creating one if the effect is merely to allow non-exclusive occupation or to create a contractual tenancy for full consideration. The Commissioners for Her Majesty's Revenue and Customs also take the view that no interest in possession arises on the creation of a lease for a term or a periodic tenancy for less than full consideration, though this will normally give rise to a charge for tax under IHTA 1984 s 65(1)(b). On the other hand, if the power is drawn in terms wide enough to cover the creation of an exclusive or joint residence, albeit revocable, for a definite or indefinite period, and is exercised with the intention of providing a particular beneficiary with a permanent home, the Revenue will normally regard the exercise of the power as creating an interest in possession. And if the trustees in exercise of their powers grant a lease for life for less than full consideration, this will be regarded as creating an interest in possession, in view of IHTA 1984 s 43(3) and 50(6).

A similar view will be taken where the power is exercised over property in which another beneficiary had an interest in possession up to the time.

Appendix 3

Questions by STEP/CIoT and answers from HMRC relating to FA 2006 Sch 20 (Revised April 2007)

[The following is reproduced, with kind permission of the Society of Trust and Estate Practitioners, from a document originally published by them and the Chartered Institute of Taxation on their respective websites in November 2006, and later updated up to April 2007 to reflect additional material and HMRC responses]

Index of questions and answers

Section A	Questions 1–10	Transitional serial interests (TSI)
Section B	Questions 11–13	Administration of estates
Section C	Questions 14–18	Immediate post-death interests generally
Section D	Questions 19–32	Trusts for bereaved minors trusts; 18-to-25 trusts and modified section 71 trusts
Section E	Questions 33–35	Absolute interests; bare trusts; *Crowe v Appleby*
Section F	Question 36	Disabled trusts
Section G	Questions 37–39	General points: additions and annuities
Section H	Questions 40–43	Deeds of variation; section 54A

A Transitional serial interests (TSI)

Condition 1 contains the requirement that "immediately before 22 March 2006, the property then comprised in the settlement was property in which B, or some other person, was beneficially entitled to an interest in possession ('the prior interest')".

393

Can it be confirmed that this requirement will be satisfied where B, or some other person, has a beneficial interest in possession in some of the property then comprised in the settlement but not all the property so comprised.

Example 1

Under a trust there are two funds. In Fund A, Mr Smith has an interest in possession. In Fund B, Mr Jones has an interest in possession.

Question 1

Will Condition 1 be satisfied separately in relation to Fund A and/or Fund B?

HMRC Answer—We can confirm that condition 1 can be satisfied separately in relation to both funds.

The new s 49C starts from the point of the view of the "current interest" – a beneficial interest in settled property. Given the wide definition of that term in IHTA 1984 s 43, it seems that the beneficial IIP referred to in s 49C(1) can quite easily be in a fund or in property that was previously part of a larger disposition or settlement – and there is nothing to suggest that there must have been a single beneficiary.

Moreover, there is no requirement that the settlement must have been wholly IIP in nature (question 2 below) or that it must have come to an end in its entirety (question 3).

If one can then accept that the property referred to in s 49C(1) is also the property referred to in s 49C(2), and in which the "prior interest" (s 49C(2), (3)) existed, the concerns raised in questions 1 to 4 fall away.

Question 2

Can it be confirmed that Condition 1 will be satisfied in relation to Fund A where Fund B is held not on trusts giving Mr Jones an interest in possession but on discretionary trusts? There is nothing in the wording of s 49C to suggest that the pre-Budget interest in possession must subsist in the entire fund.

HMRC Answer—We agree. Section 49C(3) provides that Condition 2 requires the prior interest to come to an end at a time on or after 22 March 2006 but before 6 April 2008.

Question 3

Will Condition 2 be satisfied where the prior interest comes to an end in that period in part only of the settled property in which that interest subsists?

HMRC Answer—Yes, see the response to question 1 above.

Example 2

In the example given above, if Mr Smith's interest in possession in Fund A comes to an end in 60% of Fund A and is replaced by an interest in possession in favour of Mr Smith's daughter, but Mr Smith's interest in possession continues in relation to the remaining 40% of Fund A, can it be confirmed that the interest in possession in favour of the daughter will be a transitional serial interest?

HMRC Answer—We can confirm this – for the reasons given immediately below.

While it has been suggested that Condition 2 requires that the prior interest comes to an end in all the property in which the interest subsists, Condition 2 does not state this and given the definition of current interest it appears that Condition 2 must be construed as referring to the prior interest coming to an end in the settled property concerned in which B takes a current interest but not necessarily in all the settled property of a particular settlement. The "current interest" is merely defined as an interest in possession in settled property and does not in any way require all the settled property comprised in the settlement to be a current interest.

Question 4

Please also confirm that the remaining 40% of Fund A continues to satisfy Condition 1 so that a transitional serial interest could be created in that 40% prior to 6 April 2008.

HMRC Answer—We can confirm this.

Question 5(1)

Please also confirm that in the above example if 40% of Mr Smith's pre-Budget interest in possession is ended as to half for his daughter and half for his son, both son and daughter take transitional serial interests in their respective shares.

HMRC Answer—We can confirm this.

Question 5(2)

If later the trustees wished to appropriate assets between the two funds for son and daughter and the assets were of the same value as the assets previously contained in each fund, do HMRC accept that such appropriation does not represent the termination of any qualifying interest in possession and therefore does not result in an inheritance tax charge?

HMRC Answer—We agree.

We would be grateful for your views on the circumstances in which the prior interest would be considered to have come to an end and have been replaced by a current interest. This is relevant because if a prior interest is considered to have come to an end and have been replaced by a current interest (in favour of the same beneficiary) there will be no possibility of the interest being replaced by a transitional serial interest later and the point is particularly important in relation to spousal relief because spouse exemption will not be available if a spouse of a life tenant who already has a transitional serial interest takes an interest in possession on the death of that life tenant.

Example 3

Under a pre-Budget 2006 trust a beneficiary A is entitled to the capital contingently on attaining the age of 30 years. A was 21 on 22 March 2006 and had been entitled to an interest in possession under the Trustee Act 1925 s 31 from the age of 18. The interest is therefore an interest in possession which subsisted on 22 March 2006. Before 2008 the trustees exercise their [enlarged] powers of advancement under the Trustee Act 1925 s 32 to defer the vesting of the capital from the age of 30 to the age of 45 and A's interest in possession in the fund will therefore continue until age 45. Clearly A reaches 30 after 2008 in the above example.

Question 6

There are two possible interpretations of the above and we should be grateful if HMRC could confirm which view they take.

Option 1. The exercise of the trustees' powers in this way creates a new interest in possession for A immediately on exercise of the power of advancement which therefore takes effect as the "current interest" or "transitional serial interest". Any successive interest in possession after A's interest in possession has ended cannot then be a transitional serial interest. The property will be taxed as part of A's estate on his death if he dies with the transitional serial interest. He continues to have a transitional serial interest until termination at 45 or earlier death.

Option 2: A's new interest only arises when A attains the age of 30. Until then he has a pre-Budget qualifying interest in possession.

The new interest cannot take effect as a transitional serial interest at all since on the above facts it will arise after April 2008. Until 30 A will have a pre-Budget interest in possession on the basis that nothing has changed until he reaches 30. Only from 30 will he take a new non-qualifying interest so the settled property will then become relevant property. There will not be an entry charge for A at 30 of 20% due to IHTA 1984 s 53(2).

If A dies before reaching 30, then on this analysis his pre-Budget interest will not previously have ended and therefore if his spouse takes an interest in possession this is a transitional serial interest or if his children take interests in possession before 2008 these will be transitional serial interests.

Does the answer to whether option 1 or option 2 applies depend on whether the advancement is drafted in such a way that it extends the interest in possession from 30 without restating A's existing interest in possession until then? Or would any variation of A's interest in possession be regarded as a transitional serial interest from the date of the variation even if the variation only took effect in the future.

HMRC Answer—We consider that A's original IIP (until 30) will have "come to an end" when the trustees exercised their power of advancement and been replaced by a new IIP (until 45), which will therefore qualify as a TSI. A's interest is expressed as an entitlement to capital contingent on his attaining 30. It seems reasonable to regard the exercise of the Trustee Act 1925 s 32 power as immediately bringing this interest to an end and replacing it with a new one.

An interest in possession might also subsist as follows—

Example 4

Under a trust A has a life interest with remainder to his children. The trustees have a power of advancement and exercise such a power to provide that subject to A's existing life interest A's spouse takes a life interest on A's death with remainder to the children at the age of 25. A's interest in possession is not in any way altered.

Question 7

Can HMRC please confirm that the exercise of a power of advancement to create an interest in possession for the spouse, which is expressly made subject to A's existing life interest and does not in any way alter that interest but merely comes into effect on his death, will be a transitional serial interest. Similarly, if spouse predeceases A and the advancement on interest in possession trusts for A's children is made subject to A's interest and takes effect before 2008 (eg A surrenders his interest) presumably these trusts could also be transitional serial interests.

HMRC Answer—Assuming that A's present IIP existed before 22 March 2006, we can confirm that the spouse's IIP –whether or not it arises before or after 6 April 2008 – will qualify as a TSI provided that it arises on the death of A and that A is at the date of his death still entitled to a pre-Budget interest in possession. Any IIP taken by A's children on the death or earlier termination of A's IIP will also be a transitional serial interest provided that this occurs before 6 April 2008. If A's pre-Budget interest in possession terminates inter vivos in favour of the spouse then the spouse will only take a TSI if this termination occurs before 6 April 2008.

If, however, A's interest was in any way amended (eg the trustees exercised powers of revocation and reappointment restating A's interest in possession albeit in the same terms and then declaring interests in possession for A's spouse or for children if she has predeceased), presumably the interests for spouse and children could never be transitional serial interests because A's interest is a transitional serial interest?

HMRC Answer—We agree.

Can it be confirmed that an interest in possession can be a transitional serial interest where the interest arises under a different settlement to that in which the original interest subsisted?

Example 5

Under Trust A Mr Smith has an interest in possession and subject to that, the capital passes to Mr Jones absolutely. Mr Jones on 30 December 2006 assigns his reversionary interest into Trust B set up in December 2006 under which his children have interests in possession. Mr Smith's interest in possession then comes to an end on 30 November 2007 at which time the interests in possession of Mr Jones's children in Trust B fall into possession.

Question 8

Will the interest in possession that Mr Jones' children have following the termination of Mr Smith's interest in possession qualify as a transitional serial interest bearing in mind that the interests arise in relation to the same settled property even though not under the trusts of the original settlement? A similar situation could arise where there is technically a different settlement under which the successive life interest arises due to the exercise of the trustees' powers of appointment in the wider form (as referred to in *Bond v Pickford* [1983 (STC 517)]).

HMRC Answer—Taken with question 9 below.

Question 9

If the difficulty is that Condition 1 is not satisfied because the second settlement is "made" post Budget does it make any difference if the second settlement was made pre-Budget and the interests in the first settlement fall into the second settlement before 2008 to be held on interest in possession trusts. This is a very common situation where there are "trusts over" and there appears nothing in the conditions to prevent this.

HMRC Answer—We do not consider that the IIPs of Mr Jones's children will qualify as TSIs whether the second settlement was made before or after Budget 2006.

As we said earlier, s 49C begins from the point of view of the "current interest". Condition 1 requires that "the settlement" in which that interest subsists "commenced" before 22 March 2006.

It goes on to require that, immediately before that date, the property "then comprised" in the settlement – ie the same settlement – was subject to the "prior interest".

The IIPs of Mr Jones's children arise under a different settlement (albeit one which happens to hold, following Mr Smith's death, the property that comprised the earlier one) and will not, therefore, qualify as TSIs – and it will make no difference when the settlement was made.

For the same reasons, the exercise of powers of appointment in such a way that assets are removed from one settlement and subjected to the trusts of another will not give rise to TSIs.

Question 10

What is the position if the beneficiary holding the pre-Budget interest in possession assigns that interest in possession to another person? Does the assignee's interest qualify as a transitional serial interest? The concern here is that the original interest in possession is not "terminated" by virtue of the assignment, and so the precise terms of the legislation do not appear to have been met.

HMRC Answer—We consider that the assignee's interest can be a TSI in this case because the assignor's IIP will have "come to an end" for the purposes of s 49C(3). (The interest will be in the original settlement, so the problem outlined in our response to question 9 will not be an issue).

B Administration of estates

Question 11

Can it be confirmed that where a will provides that a beneficiary has an interest in possession in residue, that interest in possession will be treated as commencing on the date of death of the deceased and not only when the administration of the estate is completed. This appears to be the case by virtue of IHTA 1984 s 91.

HMRC Answer—We can confirm this.

Question 12

Can it be confirmed that the position will be the same as in Question 11 above where the interest in possession is in a settled legacy of specific assets not forming part of residue. It seems that this should be the case: *IRC v Hawley* [1929] 1 KB 578.

HMRC Answer—We agree. This is important for two reasons—

— in order for an interest in possession to satisfy Condition 2 in s 49A

for an immediate post-death interest (IPDI), L must have become beneficially entitled to the interest on the death of the testator or intestate;

— *in determining whether an interest in possession is one which subsisted prior to 22 March 2006 where the deceased died before 22 March 2006 but the completion of the administration of the estate was on or after 22 March 2006 there would be difficulties if the pre-Budget interest in possession was not regarded as commencing on the death of the deceased.*

Question 13

Many wills include a provision which provides that a beneficiary will only take if he survives the testator by a period of time. Please confirm that such a provision would not by itself prevent an IPDI arising.

HMRC Answer—We can confirm this. We consider that IHTA 1984 s 92 removes any doubt here.

C Immediate post-death interests generally

Question 14

Can it be confirmed that if on the death of X a discretionary trust set up in his will (eg a nil-rate band legacy trust) is funded by a share in property, and the trustees allow the surviving spouse L to occupy it on an exclusive basis albeit at their discretion along the lines that occurred in *Judge & anor (Representatives of Walden deceased)* SpC 506, this will not automatically be an IPDI but it will depend on the terms on which she occupies.

HMRC Answer—We agree.

There is a three month requirement for reading back under s 144 in respect of appointments of absolute interests but this does not apply to appointments of IPDIs. Therefore if the trustees immediately on the death of X or subsequently, conferred exclusive rights of occupation on L this could indeed be an IPDI.

HMRC Answer—We agree.

It appears to us unlikely that mere exclusivity of occupation could in itself be a problem because as Judge confirms a person can occupy exclusively but not have rights which constitute an interest in possession. Indeed if the surviving spouse merely continued in occupation on the same terms as before X's death without the trustees' doing anything positive either way to affect her occupation it would appear they have not exercised their powers so as to give her any IPDI anyway.

HMRC Answer—We agree. (Indeed it is doubtful that they have any ability under the Trusts of Land and Appointment of Trustees Act 1996 to disturb her occupation if she already owns a half share in the property personally and therefore the trustees have not exercised any power to confer her a present right to present enjoyment which could constitute an immediate post-death interest.)

It would be helpful (given how common this situation is) if HMRC could give some guidance on the various scenarios in which they would or would not regard the surviving spouse as taking an IPDI in a property left on nil-rate band discretionary trusts in the will if she is already in occupation.

HMRC Answer—This will depend on the precise terms of the testator's will or any deed of appointment exercised by the trustees after the testator's death, and we will continue to examine each case on its particular facts.

Question 15

Can it be confirmed that where a settlement (including a settlement created by will) includes a general power of appointment and that power is exercised by will giving an immediate interest in possession, the interest created over the trust property will qualify as an IPDI?

HMRC Answer—We can confirm this.

Question 16

Can it be confirmed that HMRC takes the view that if an individual (I) leaves by will a gift to a person's estate, when the assets in the estate are held on trusts which qualify as trusts for bereaved minors or age 18-to-25 trusts, the property added pursuant to I's will would also be treated as being held on trusts which qualify as trusts for bereaved minors or 18-to-25 trusts.

HMRC Answer—We have assumed that the scenario envisaged here is: I dies leaving a legacy in their will to P; P dies after I but before the legacy has been paid; P's estate is held on trusts that meet s 71A or s 71D. We agree that, in those circumstances, the legacy from I's estate would qualify under those provisions, also.

Example 6

I leaves his estate to his widow for life with remainder to his son S if alive at I's death. S survives I but predeceases the widow leaving a will under which his estate passes to his children on trusts which qualify as trusts for bereaved minors. The widow dies when the children are aged 10 and 12, so that I's estate falls to be held on the trusts of S's will. Will the property in I's estate benefit from trusts for bereaved minors status? I is the grandparent but the property is passing according to S's will.

HMRC Answer—We consider that the property added pursuant to I's will in this example would also fall within s 71A.

Question 17

If a property is left outright to someone by a will and they disclaim within two years of the deceased's death such that an interest in possession trust takes effect, can HMRC confirm that the trust will qualify as an IPDI?

HMRC Answer—We can confirm this.

Question 18

Can it be confirmed whether, when a will leaves property to an existing settlement (whether funded or unfunded) and under that settlement a beneficiary takes an immediate interest in possession, that interest will qualify as an IPDI. Such arrangements are common for US and other foreign domiciliaries in order to avoid complex probate issues. It might be argued that the interest in possession in the existing settlement does not arise under the will of the deceased. However, there are two arguments against this.

First, HMRC's own analysis is that additions by individuals to existing settlements should be treated as new settlements. Hence the addition by will to an existing settlement is a new settlement set up by virtue of the will.

Secondly, the wording in s 49A Condition 1 refers to "the settlement was effected by will or under the law of intestacy". The question though is what "the settlement" refers to. It would seem that it refers not as such to "the settlement" in the sense of a document but rather to the settlement into trust of the settled property which certainly is effected by will. The same wording is used on deeds of variation under IHTA 1984 s 142 and HMRC have always accepted that where property is added by will to a pre-existing settlement there is no reason why the beneficiary of that settlement cannot vary his entitlement.

HMRC Answer—We can confirm that the IIP in this scenario would qualify as an IPDI. We agree that "settlement" in this context relates to the contribution of property into the settlement rather than the document under which it will become held.

D Trusts for bereaved minors; 18-to-25 trusts and modified section 71 trusts: section 71A and section 71D

Question 19

Can it be confirmed that trusts otherwise satisfying the requirements of s 71A or s 71D will be regarded as satisfying those conditions where the trusts were appointed under powers contained in the will and were not provided in the will itself at the outset.

HMRC Answer—We can confirm this – where the trusts are set up as a result of the exercise of a special power of appointment. We consider the position is different with general powers, on the basis, broadly speaking, that having a general power of appointment is tantamount to owning the property.

Example 7

H dies in 2007. His will leaves an IPDI for his surviving spouse and subject thereto on discretionary trusts for issue of H. The trustees exercise their overriding powers of appointment to create s 71A trusts for the children of H. It would appear that the s 71A provisions do not need to be incorporated within the will trust from the start to qualify for relief but it would be helpful to have this confirmed. Presumably the presence of overriding powers of appointment over capital in favour of surviving spouse would not be treated as breaching the s 71A conditions while the s 71A interest was a remainder interest.

HMRC Answer—We agree (subject to our comments at question 19).

Question 20

Can it be further confirmed that the analysis in 16 above will apply both where the prior interest in possession is an IPDI and also where there is an interest in possession arising under the will of a person who died prior to 22 March 2006 where the interests will, by definition, not be an IPDI although in all other respects identical to an IPDI.

HMRC Answer—We can confirm this.

Question 21

Can it be confirmed that, where a will contains a gift "to such of my children as reach 18 and if more than one in equal shares" or "to such of my children as reach 25 and if more than one in equal shares" all the interests will qualify as trusts for bereaved minors (or as age 18-to-25 trusts) even though one or more of the children might die after the testator but before the capital vests (so that their shares are divided between their siblings).

HMRC Answer—We can confirm this. We consider that each child while alive and under 18/25 has a presumptive share that is held for his or her benefit, and one can apply s 71A or s 71D child by child and presumptive share by presumptive share.

Question 21A

On conversion of an existing pre-Budget A&M trust to s 71D status does the class need to close *ab initio* from the date the trust was converted or is it sufficient to say that until someone else is born, the trusts for "B" do qualify as s 71D trusts but not actually close the class?

HMRC answer—We consider that a trust in the position where anyone (whether unborn or not) who is not currently benefiting can nevertheless become entitled would not meet the requirements of s 71D(6), since it could not be said for certain that "B" will become absolutely entitled to the settled property etc. in due course or that no income will be applied for any other person in the meantime. So we take the view that it will be necessary to close the class of beneficiaries for s 71D to apply.

Question 22

Can it be confirmed that the answer to Question 21 is not affected by a gift over provision that substitutes the children (if any) of a deceased child who attain a certain age, so that the increase of the siblings' shares is dependent upon whether the child dies childless.

HMRC Answer—We can confirm this: the siblings' presumptive shares simply increase (or not) when one of their number dies, depending on whether or not the deceased child had any children of their own.

Question 23

Can it be confirmed that agricultural property relief (APR) and business property relief (BPR) will apply to charges arising under s 71E. It would appear that these reliefs should be applicable as the charges under s 71D (by reference to s 71E) are charges under IHTA 1984 Part 3 Ch 3 and the reliefs are expressly extended to events of charge under this Chapter (IHTA 1984 s 103(1) in relation to BPR and s 115(1) in relation to APR). Further, the formula for calculating the charge under s 71F is similar, in principle, to the charges as calculated under IHTA 1984 s 65 and s 68 in relation to exit charges for relevant property generally. Can HMRC confirm this analysis is agreed?

HMRC Answer—We agree for the reasons given.

Question 24

Section 71E(4) provides that there will be no event of charge where a transaction is entered into by trustees as a result of which the assets held subject to the 18-to-25 trusts are diminished in value, where the disposition by the trustees would not have been a transfer of value under IHTA 1984 s 10 or s 16 if they had been beneficially entitled to the trust assets. There is a further exemption in s 71E(3). There are no similar provisions in relation to actions by trustees concerning assets which are held on trusts qualifying under s 71A. Can it be confirmed that in practice HMRC would apply similar principles in relation to events of charge under s 71B for s 71A trusts?

HMRC Answer—The provisions in s 71E that the question refers to are not reproduced in s 71B because the charge there arises under s 70 – and s 70 already includes identical provisions at subsections (3) and (4). Section 71B(3) says—"Subsections (3) to (8) and (10) of section 70 apply for the purposes of this section as they apply for the purposes of that section ..."

Question 25

Can HMRC confirm that trusts which are held for beneficiaries as a class (eg on trust for such of my children as attain the age of 25 and if more than one in equal shares) will qualify as age 18-to-25 trusts under s 71D(3) and (4) notwithstanding that the class could be diminished by reason of the death of members of the class under the age of 25. While it might be said that the class gift does not fall within the strict wording of s 71D(6)(a) it might be said that nonetheless the assets are held on trust, for the time being, for each child being under the age of 25. HMRC are requested to confirm their view in relation to the continued application of s 71D to class gifts where a beneficiary (B) dies before reaching 25 and the assets pass to the other beneficiaries under 25 on s 71D trusts. (This is a separate point from the situation where in relation to existing *inter vivos* A&M trusts the class increases as a result of future beneficiaries being born before the eldest reaches 25.)

HMRC Answer—We can confirm this. [CIOT/STEP note: further queries are being raised with HMRC on the class closing rules and the application of s 71D generally and these will be posted on the websites shortly.]

Question 26

HMRC is asked to confirm that s 71A and s 71D will apply to trusts for a class of children whether or not the assets have been appropriated to each child's share.

HMRC Answer—We can confirm this.

Question 27

There will be a number of circumstances where different sets of beneficiaries under one accumulation and maintenance settlement may require to be treated differently (for example, a settlement for grandchildren where they differ widely in age). Can HMRC please confirm that trusts will qualify as age 18-to-25 trusts or modified s 71 trusts (capital vesting at age 18) if those trusts exist in only part of the settled property. Thus, a settlement might be divided into two sub-funds, one for A's children who are approaching adulthood and for whom an 18-to-25 trust is appropriate and another for B's children who are very young and where the trustees value retaining flexibility so that that sub-fund will be allowed to fall within the relevant property regime with effect from 6 April 2008 (or be converted into an 18 trust).

HMRC Answer—We can confirm this.

Question 28

There has been some confusion about the interaction of s 71D(3) and (4) with s 71D(1) and (2). Please confirm that existing A&M trusts set up before the Budget where the settlor may still be alive (and the beneficiary's parent has not died) can qualify for 18–25 status if converted before April 2008 if this occurs immediately after the funds cease to qualify under s 71.

HMRC Answer—We can confirm that s 71D can apply to existing A&M trusts if the conversion occurs before the funds cease to qualify under s 71 – for the reasons set out in example 8 below.

Further that there is no inheritance tax charge on conversion of an existing accumulation and maintenance trust to a s 71D trust. ie that FA 2006 Sch 20 para 3(3) protects all pre-Budget accumulation and maintenance trusts so that there is no inheritance tax entry charge either under s 71 or otherwise, at the point the trust starts to qualify for s 71D status (or indeed enters the relevant property regime).

HMRC Answer—We can confirm this.

Example 8

U sets up an accumulation and maintenance trust for his two nieces S and T in 1999. On 22 March 2006 neither has an interest in possession. Currently the nieces take capital at 30 and income at 21. S becomes 21 in January 2007. T becomes 21 in January 2011.

The trustees exercise their powers to ensure that the trusts qualify for 18–25 status in February 2007 ie after S has attained entitlement to income (albeit this is not a qualifying interest in possession post Budget). They provide that each child takes capital outright at 25 in a fixed half share. In these circumstances it would appear that S's share cannot qualify for 18–25 status because immediately after the property ceased to be subject to s 71 it did not then fall within s 71D. T's interest could however qualify under s 71D. There is no inheritance tax charge in February 2007 on S's part although there would be a ten year charge in 2009 on her share because this share is now within the relevant property regime and there would be an exit charge when she reaches 25. There are no ten year or entry or exit charges on T's interest until she reaches 25 at which point her share is subject to tax at 4·2%. (This assumes that she does not die before reaching 25).

It would be helpful if this could be spelt out in the guidance notes because trustees need to be aware of the requirement to act swiftly if beneficiaries are about to take entitlement to income. It would also be helpful if examples could be given as to how 18-to-25 trusts work in practice and their main advantages ie to avoid the ten year anniversary charge.

HMRC Answer—We agree with the consequences set out in the example and will incorporate them in guidance.

Question 29

It would appear that on the death of a child before 18 on a bereaved minor trust or on an 18-to-25 trust there is no inheritance tax charge even if they are entitled to income (albeit there is a base cost capital gains tax uplift if they are entitled to income).

HMRC Answer—We agree – by virtue of s 71B(2)(b) or s 71E(2)(b) and new s 5(1)(a)(i).

It would appear that after a child reaches 18 there is an exit charge on an 18-to-25 trust if the property ceases to be held on 18-to-25 trusts but no base cost uplift for capital gains tax purposes whether or not the child has a right to income. Please confirm.

HMRC Answer—We can confirm this.

Question 30

It would appear that, if a child reaches 18 and on his death his share of the trust fund remains on 18-to-25 trusts for his siblings under cross-accruer provisions, there will be no exit charge at that time. Please confirm.

HMRC Answer—We can confirm this.

Question 31

In the HMRC Customer Guide to Inheritance Tax recently published HMRC state under the heading of "What is an age 18 to 25 trust?"

"If the terms of the trust are not rewritten before 6 April 2008 and the trust has not come to an end then existing accumulation and maintenance trusts will automatically become relevant property trusts on the 18th birthday of the beneficiary."

What is the statutory justification for this view. First it is surely the case that an existing A&M trust can become subject to the relevant property regime before 6 April 2008 if a beneficiary takes a post–Budget interest in possession.

HMRC Answer—We agree and will amend the Customer Guide.

Second our understanding is that such trusts will become relevant property trusts on 6 April 2008 or the beneficiary becoming entitled to an interest in possession before that date unless the trust meets the requirements of a s 71D trust. If nothing has been done by April 2008 and a beneficiary is not entitled to an interest in possession then the trust falls within the relevant property regime from that date whether or not the beneficiary is a minor. This point needs to be clarified urgently and the information amended.

HMRC Answer—We agree. Section 71D(5)(b) provides that s 71D does not apply to property to which s 71 applies. A&M treatment will therefore continue up to an including 5 April 2008 if the trusts of the settlement meet s 71, and will fall away on 6 April 2008. If the trusts provide for absolute entitlement at 18 or 25, the settlement will then fall within s 71A or s 71D as appropriate; if they do not, the settlement will be "relevant property" from that date.

Question 32

Please also confirm whether or not holdover relief will be available if assets are distributed within three months of a beneficiary's 18th birthday under an 18-to-25 trust. There will be no inheritance tax charge as there will be no complete quarters since the 18th birthday. In these circumstances is holdover relief denied?

HMRC Answer—No. The distribution is still an occasion on which IHT is chargeable – it is just that the charge will be nil. There is no provision in s 71F along the lines of s 65(4).

E   Absolute interests; bare trusts; Crowe v Appleby

Where assets are held by a person on bare trusts for minor children the Trustee Act 1925 s 31 is implied in most cases without express reference and will apply unless expressly excluded.

It might be said that the application of the section will cause the property concerned to be settled property within s 43(2)(b) in view of the provisions for the accumulation of income under the Trustee Act 1925 s 31(2). However, the contrary argument is that the accumulations of income are held for the absolute benefit for the minor concerned and would pass to his estate if he died under 18 (the minor not being able to give a good receipt) and the assets are therefore not held in any real sense subject to any contingency or provision for the diversion of income from the minor. This latter view seems to be in line with the analysis in the IHT Manual which contemplates that s 43(2)(b) deals with the position where there is relevant property held on discretionary trusts (paragraph 4602). The statement in the Inland Revenue letter of 12 February 1976 where, in the last sentence of the second paragraph, it is stated that a provision to accumulate income will not prevent there being an interest in possession if the accumulations are held for the absolute benefit of the beneficiary, supports the view that the Trustee Act 1925 s 31 will not in these circumstances cause the relevant property regime to apply.

Question 33

Can HMRC confirm that the application of the Trustee Act 1925 s 31 to assets held on a bare trust for a minor will not result in the assets being settled property within the meaning of IHTA 1984 s 43?

HMRC Answer—We confirm that our view is that where assets are held on an absolute trust (ie a bare trust) for a minor the assets so held will not be settled property within the meaning of IHTA 1984 s 43 and that this will be the case whether or not the provisions of Trustee Act 1925 s 31 have been excluded.

There appear to be new and unforeseen capital gains tax problems now where Crowe v Appleby [1975 (STC 502)] applies on settled property. The position is complex albeit common and can best be illustrated by example.

Example 9

In February 2006 Andrew set up a trust for his children Charlotte and Luke. They each become entitled to one half of the income and capital on reaching 25. Charlotte becomes 25 in 2007 and Luke becomes 25 in 2009. They do not take interests in possession until reaching 25. The trust only holds one piece of land.

When Charlotte reaches 25 in 2007 she becomes absolutely entitled for inheritance tax purposes since *Crowe v Appleby* has no application for IHT purposes. The trusts over her share end for inheritance tax purposes before 6 April 2008 so there is no exit charge since she is within the transitional regime. She is treated from 2007 as entitled to the half share in the property and if she died after that date it would form part of her estate for inheritance tax purposes and hence be potentially taxable.

There is a further problem. For capital gains tax purposes Charlotte does not become absolutely entitled to one half of the land. Until the land is sold or Luke reaches 25 and becomes absolutely entitled (whichever is the earlier) there is no disposal made by the trustees.

There is no inheritance tax change on 6 April 2008 but from that date Luke's share is no longer within A&M trust protection but is taxed as an 18-to-25 trust. There is no ten year anniversary charge before Luke reaches 25 but if he dies before then there is an inheritance tax charge (likely to be less than 4·2%). As noted above, there is no basc cost uplift for capital gains tax purposes.

On Luke reaching 25 in 2009 there is an exit charge on Luke's share of 4·2%.

HMRC Answer—(Note: we do not consider this is quite right. We assume that the 4·2% is referred to on the basis of 7/10ths x 6%. However, the charge will not be based on the 7 years from Luke's 18th birthday. Section 71F(5)(a) provides that the starting date for calculating the relevant fraction is his 18th birthday "or, if later, the day on which the property became property to which section 71D above applies" – in this case, 6 April 2008).

If the land has not yet been sold there will at that point be a disposal of all the land by the trustees for capital gains tax purposes because both beneficiaries become absolutely entitled. Holdover relief is available on Luke's part under TCGA 1992 s 260 but not on Charlotte's part since there is no exit charge. In summary, the trustees will have to pay capital gains tax on any gain on Charlotte's share in 2009 and cannot hold over the gain on that share.

Question 34

Prior to the Finance Act 2006, Charlotte would have been treated as having a qualifying interest in possession in her share of the trust assets. If she died before Luke reached 25, there would have been a charge to inheritance tax on her death but because she had a qualifying interest in possession, for capital gains tax purposes, there would be an uplift in base cost on her share of the land under TCGA 1992 s 72(1).

Post the Finance Act 2006, if Charlotte dies before Luke reaches 25 there will be a charge to inheritance tax but TCGA 1992 s 72(1) does not seem to be applicable because Charlotte does not appear to have a qualifying interest in possession which qualifies her for the uplift. Hence she is subject to inheritance tax on her death with no uplift for capital gains tax.

Will HMRC regard her as having a qualifying interest in possession within TCGA 1992 s 72 for these purposes?

HMRC Answer—No, with the result, as stated, that there would be no CGT uplift under TCGA 1992 s 72(1).

Question 35

If Charlotte attained 25 in say June 2015 and Luke only reached 25 in 2017 there would be an exit charge on both Luke and Charlotte's shares when each becomes 25 (rate = 4·2%) but holdover relief is only available on Luke's share when the disposal of the land takes place for capital gains tax purposes.

Prior to the Finance Act 2006 there would have been no exit charge when Charlotte reached 25. However, the effect of the new rules is that on reaching 25 Charlotte will now suffer an exit charge but without any entitlement to hold over the gain which arises when the land is distributed to her when Luke reaches 25. Will HMRC in these circumstances allow holdover relief on both shares?

HMRC Answer—No, holdover relief will be due on Luke's share only.

F Disabled trusts

Section 89A(2) appears to conflict with s 89A(3). Condition 1 states that if any of the settled property is applied for A it is applied for the benefit of A but Condition 2 envisages that capital could be paid to A or another person on the termination of A's interest during his life provided that the other person became absolutely entitled.

Question 36

Is HMRC's view that capital can be appointed to someone else on the termination of the trust only if it can be demonstrated that it is for the benefit of A?

HMRC Answer—No, we do not consider that that condition is in point.

Otherwise why does s 89A(3) Condition 2 refer to other persons at all?

HMRC Answer—We do not agree with the proposition that there is a conflict between s 89A(2) and (3). Condition 1 refers to the application of "settled property" – ie to property that is held on the trusts referred to in s 89A(1)(c). Condition 2, however, is applying conditions that are effective in the event of such trusts being brought to an end.

G General points: additions and annuities

Question 37(1)

New ss 46A(4) and 46B(5) provide that additions (by way of payment of further premiums) to a pre-Budget interest in possession or A&M trust which holds an insurance policy would not result either in a chargeable transfer or in any part of the trust falling within the relevant property regime.

It is understood that HMRC believe that additions of cash or other property to existing pre-Budget interest in possession settlements are subject to the new rules in Schedule 20.

There are other payments which are often made by settlors or beneficiaries on behalf of a trust. For example, buildings insurance premiums and general maintenance costs, payments to cover trust, administration and taxation expenses.

It is noted that for the purposes of TCGA 1992 Sch 5 para 9(3) the payment of expenses relating to administration and taxation of a trust are not be treated as the addition of property to the trust. In SP 5/92 the costs of acquiring, enhancing and disposing of a trust asset are not regarded as expenses relating to administration but other property expenses appear to fall within the definition and therefore are not treated as the addition of property to the trust. Would HMRC maintain that the addition of cash or other property to a settlement which may be used either to enhance trust property (eg payment of costs relating to the building of an extension to property) or to purchase other property will be treated as additions but accept that the payment of other trustee expenses (eg trustee fees, buildings insurance premiums and general maintenance costs) will not be treated as chargeable additions?

HMRC Answer—TCGA 1992 Sch 5 is a statutory provision relating to certain, specific circumstances. There is no legal basis on which payments of "other trustee expenses" should not be treated as chargeable additions for IHT purposes.

Question 37(2)

If any of the additions do bring the trust within the new rules, what property within the trust will be caught and how will it be valued? For example, if an addition of cash was made which was then spent by the trustees and HMRC regard this addition as within the relevant property regime (eg an addition to pay expenses or improve properties), how would the proportion of the settled property subject to the new rules be calculated? Would a valuation be needed of the property before and after the improvement? In HMRC's view, do all subsequent post Budget additions need to be kept physically segregated?

HMRC Answer—If a payment of cash was made and then spent immediately on, say, a tax liability or another administration expense, then that short period will be the extent of its time as "relevant property" and there will be no question of having to consider what proportion of the existing settled property represents it going forward.

If a payment was made towards the improvement of a property, then this would appear to require "with" and "without" valuations when there is a chargeable event.

It is clearly up to trustees to decide whether to keep post-Budget additions separate from the rest of the trust fund. We think that it may be sensible to do so – or, at least, to keep good records of additions. (The trustees of discretionary trusts already need to do this, of course, in order for the ten year anniversary value of each addition to be identified correctly in light of the relief in IHTA 1984 s 66(2) for property that has not been "relevant property" for a full ten year period).

Question 38

It is understood that additions to a trust which fall within the normal expenditure out of income exemption will not need to be reported as and when they are made as, following the normal rules, it is not necessary to report exempt transactions? Please confirm.

HMRC Answer—We can confirm this.

Question 39

It is not unknown for wills to include a gift of an annuity. Some wills give the executors sufficient powers to enable them to choose how best to satisfy the annuity. In such a case there are typically four methods which executors may use to deal with an annuity.

— Pay the annuity out of residue. In such a case the executors delay the completion of the administration of the estate until the annuitant dies.

— Create an appropriated annuity fund. In such a case the executors appropriate a capital fund of sufficient size to pay the annuity.

— Purchase an annuity. The executors purchase an annuity from an insurance office or life company.

— Commute the annuity. The executors pay the annuitant a cash sum sufficient to allow him to purchase the annuity personally.

The first two options create settled property. Will HMRC confirm that a provision in a will conferring the payment of an annuity upon a person (eg to make a gift of an annuity of £x for life) which the executors satisfy by one of the first two options outlined above will be treated as the creation of an IPDI in favour of the annuitant?

HMRC Answer—We can confirm this. Under s 50(2), where a person is entitled to a specified amount (such as an annuity) for any period his interest is taken to subsist in that part of the property that produces that amount in that period. The property in which his interest subsists may therefore vary over time.

Example 10

Say A is entitled to an annuity of £1,000 and the executors set aside a fund of £40,000 to pay this annuity. In year 1 the income from the £40,000 is £2,000 and half is paid to the annuitant. In year 2 the income from the £40,000 is £1,000 and all the income is paid to A. In year 3 (the year in which the annuitant dies) the income from the £40,000 is £4,000 and a quarter is paid to A. Please could HMRC confirm what property would fall within A's estate on his death (assuming he is treated as having an IPDI) and the basis upon which this has been calculated?

HMRC Answer—We would follow the existing principles set out in IHTA 1984 s 50(2) to s 50(5) at the date of A's death. (As Dymond, at 16.611, points out, s 50(2) does not give any guidance as to the period over which the income of the settled property should be computed. But the learned authors suggest that looking at the income in the year immediately before the chargeable occasion would normally be a reasonable approach and we would agree.)

H   Deeds of variation; section 54A

Questions have arisen as to the effect of deeds of variation post-Budget.

Example 11

Testator dies pre-Budget leaving everything outright to X. His will is varied by X and an election made under s 142 to treat the variation as made by the will.

Question 40

Any trust established by the variation will be treated as having been established pre-Budget whether or not the variation is actually made pre- or post-Budget. If an interest in possession trust is established under such a variation by X, we assume it will be a qualifying interest in possession given it is deemed to be set up prior to the Budget by the deceased and not by X for inheritance tax purposes and further that it will be possible to create a transitional serial interest in relation to this trust before April 2008. Please confirm.

HMRC Answer—We can confirm this.

Example 12

Testator dies post-Budget leaving everything outright to Y. His will is varied to establish ongoing trusts and an election made under s 142 to read the variation back into the will.

Question 41

Assuming that the terms of the trusts are appropriate, it is possible to establish IPDIs, 18-to-25 trusts and BMTs by way of such a variation made by Y. Please confirm. As in question 40 it is assumed that for inheritance tax purposes the settlor is the deceased rather than Y.

HMRC Answer—We can confirm this.

Example 13

The testator is not domiciled in the UK at his death leaving everything outright to Z. His will dealing with property outside the UK is varied to establish trusts and an election made under s 142 to read the variation back into the will.

Question 42

Any trusts established by the variation holding non-UK property will be excluded property trusts whatever the domicile status of Z (the beneficiary making the variation) and whatever the terms of the new trusts. This will be the case whether or not the testator died pre- or post-Budget. Please confirm.

HMRC Answer—We can confirm this. Section 54A contains certain anti-avoidance provisions that arise where a settlor settles assets into a qualifying interest in possession trust by PET and then the life interest is terminated so that discretionary trusts arise within seven years. In effect the settlor rather than the life tenant can be treated as having made the chargeable transfer if this yields more tax. Section 54A(1A) states that where a person becomes beneficially entitled on or after 22 March 2006 to a disabled person's interest or a TSI, s 54(1)(b) applies. So if the disabled person or the holder of the TSI dies and relevant property trusts arise, the anti-avoidance provision potentially applies. Nothing is said though in respect of inter vivos terminations of the TSI or disabled person's interest when relevant property trusts arise and the termination occurs within seven years of the original PET made by the settlor.

Question 43

Is it intended that s 54A should only apply to interests in possession arising on or after 22 March 2006 if the disabled person's interest or TSI terminates on death rather than *inter vivos*?

HMRC Answer—Section 54A applies both to lifetime terminations of a TSI or disabled person's interest where the other conditions of s 54A are satisfied as well as a termination on the death of the life tenant. The fact that s 54A(1)(a) refers expressly to death and not to lifetime terminations does not mean that s 54A did not cover both scenarios because s 54A(1) covered lifetime terminations. We believe s 54A can apply to both inter vivos and terminations on death because s 54A(1)(a) refers back to s 52, where s 52(2A) already provides that, where the person becomes beneficially entitled to the interest in possession on or after 22 March 2006, there will only be a charge under s 52(1), and so s 54A will only potentially apply if the interest is—

— *an immediate post-death interest,*

— *a disabled person's interest, or*

— *a transitional serial interest.*

Submitted to HMRC by The Chartered Institute of Taxation and The Society of Trust and Estate Practitioners on 7 September 2006

Response by HMRC on 3 November 2006 (as amended on 12 December 2006, January 2007 and April 2007)

Note: answer to question 33 added on 4 April 2007 based on letter from HMRC dated 23 March 2007.

Appendix 4

FA 2006 Sch 20: pre-existing interests in possession and related matters

[The following is reproduced, with kind permission of the Society of Trust and Estate Practitioners, from a document published by them and the Chartered Institute of Taxation on their respective websites in June 2007]

8 May 2007

(Response received from HMRC on 29 May which they have agreed can be publicised and this exchange represents HMRC's further views on the transitional serial interest regime).

We are writing about a number of situations (set out in the questions below) where a person (A) was beneficially entitled to an interest in possession in settled property before 22 March 2006. Doubt has been expressed as to whether IHTA 1984 s 49(1) will continue to apply in the future, notwithstanding that A will throughout be entitled to the income of the settled property. We consider that, in all those situations, s 49(1) will continue to apply, notwithstanding s 49(1A) which (with exceptions) disapplies that sub-section where the interest in possession is one to which a person becomes beneficially entitled on or after 22 March 2006.

It has been suggested that A will, after that date, become entitled to a different proprietary interest in the settled property. As the Revenue argued in *Pearson v IRC* [1981] AC 753, and all the members of the House of Lords appear to have accepted, for inheritance tax purposes the expression "interest in possession" must be construed as a single phrase. Pearson decided that it means a present right to present enjoyment of the settled property, ie the right to the income from that property as it arises. And in each of the relevant situations, A became entitled to that right before 22 March 2006. Section 49(1A) does not, therefore, in our view, apply.

If we are right about this, then it means that the IHT treatment of the relevant situations will not depend on the accident of the particular drafting technique adopted, with settlements being treated differently notwithstanding that A's rights are the same and without any possible policy justification that we have been able to identify.

We would emphasise that, in each of the examples below, the trustees have not exercised any dispositive powers post-March 2006: the interest taken by A remains throughout merely an entitlement to income and, moreover, an entitlement which is defined under the terms of the settlement prior to March 2006.

We hope that you will be able to confirm that s 49(1) will continue to apply and, therefore, that the same pre-Budget interest in possession will continue to subsist in each of the following examples.

Example 1

(1) Settled property is held on trust to pay the income to A for life contingently on A attaining the age of 25. The trust carries the intermediate income.

(2) A attained the age of 18 on 1 January 2006 and thereupon became entitled to an interest in possession by virtue of the Trustee Act 1925 s 31. Section 49(1) applies.

In our view, it will continue to apply after age 25, when the express trust to pay income to him comes into effect. On any footing, A has only one interest, being the present right to present enjoyment, brought into possession earlier than would otherwise be the case by s 31.

Question 1

Do HMRC agree?

HMRC Answer—Yes.

Example 2

(1) Under a pre-Budget 2006 trust, A is entitled to capital contingently on attaining the age of 25 years. The clause goes on to provide that the trusts carry the intermediate income and the Trustee Act 1925 s 31 is to apply.

(2) The same clause provides that the capital should not vest absolutely on A attaining the age of 25 but should be retained on trust:

(a) to pay the income to A for life, and then

(b) for A's children after A's death,

(3) A attained the age of 18 on 1 January 2006. Section 49(1) applies.

In our view, it will continue to apply after A attains the age of 25 on 1 January 2013, when the "engrafted" trust to pay income to A comes into effect.

Question 2

Do HMRC agree?

HMRC Answer—Yes.

Example 3

The facts are the same as Example 2, except that the engrafted trusts are contained in a separate clause. In our view, the position is the same, and s 49(1) will continue to apply after A attains the age of 25.

Question 3

Do HMRC agree?

HMRC Answer—Yes.

Example 4

(1)   A became entitled to income at 25 in January 2006 and s 49(1) applies.

(2)   A is contingently entitled to capital at the age of 35, but the trustees retain overriding powers of appointment exercisable during his lifetime. He therefore attains only a defeasible interest in capital in 2016, and the capital remains settled property until his death.

(3)   In our view, s 49(1) will continue to apply after A attains the age of 35, notwithstanding that his contingent interest in capital is replaced by a vested but defeasible interest in capital.

Question 4

Do HMRC agree?

HMRC Answer—Yes.

Example 5

Presumably, where a transitional serial interest (TSI) arose after 21 March 2006 but before 6 April 2008 (eg a pre-22 March 2006 Budget life tenant's interest was ended in 2007 and A the new life tenant takes an immediate interest in possession and capital at 35 but that capital entitlement is defeasible being subject to any exercise of the overriding powers), HMRC would agree that s 49C continues to apply to A after he attains the age of 35 for the same reasons, ie that his transitional serial interest entitlement continues following his 35th birthday.

Question 5

Do HMRC agree?

HMRC Answer—Yes.

In all the above examples, A's interest arises under the terms of the settlement, and not from the exercise of the trustees' powers. We think these examples can be distinguished from the case where a beneficiary is absolutely entitled to capital on reaching a specified age and the trustees positively exercise their powers to defer that absolute entitlement and maintain the interest in possession, where we understand that different issues may arise as set out in the previous reply to queries on Sch 20 – see questions revised in April 2007 and in particular Question 6

HMRC Answer—Agreed

Interest in possession which continues after death of life tenant

In some circumstances, an interest in possession may continue after the death of the person entitled to the interest up until their death. HMRC have confirmed that a lifetime assignment of an interest in possession will qualify as a TSI (assuming the other requirements are satisfied – Question 10 of Sch 20 letter) on the basis that the interest in possession will have "come to an end" within the meaning of s 49C(3), presumably on the basis of IHTA 1984 s 51(1). There is no equivalent provision to IHTA 1984 s 51(1) in relation to transfers on death of an *autre vie*, but the entitlement of the prior beneficiary who is holding an interest *pur autre vie* will have come to an end, even though the interest itself will not have done so. This may arise, for example, where the will of the deceased life tenant leaves their residuary estate, which would include their remaining entitlement to the interest *pur autre vie*, to their surviving spouse.

Question 6

Do HMRC consider that, when a pre-Budget interest in possession beneficiary who holds the *pur autre vie* dies, any interest in possession in such property then taken by his spouse (or any other person if that occurs before 6 April 2008) will qualify as a transitional serial interest?

HMRC Answer to Question 6—Yes. In the circumstances outlined, it would seem that the death of the beneficiary holding a pur autre vie interest must bring "the prior interest" within the terms of IHTA 1984 s 49C to an end.

IHTA 1984 s 46B

We should be grateful if you would confirm your view in relation to pre-Budget 2006 settled life policies, where a policy is held on s 71 accumulation and maintenance trusts and the trusts are then converted into trusts within IHTA 1984 s 71D. Insurance premiums continue to be paid on the policy.

It is clear that the continued payment of the insurance premiums will be potentially exempt transfers under s 46B(5).

Question 7

Are the added rights arising from the payment of the premiums settled property within s 71D, or are they separate settled property which is within the relevant property regime?

There is no equivalent provision in relation to s 71D trusts to s 46B(2), which applies for s 71 trusts where premiums continue to be paid on or after 22 March 2006. Section 46B(2) provides that the rights arising by reference to the payment of the further premiums shall also be within s 71 if they would be but for s 71(1A).

The rights arising from the payment of premiums on policies held on trusts where the payments are made after such trust has been converted to s 71D status do not appear to be strictly within s 71D(3), which is necessary for those rights to be held on trusts within s 71D. Section 46B(1) in relation to s 71 trusts refers to s 46B(2), (5), but s 46B(3) in relation to s 71D trusts only refers to s 46B(5).

Do HMRC accept that the policy held on s 71D trusts is, in reality, the same asset as that previously held on s 71 trusts and that, in effect, no new rights become comprised in the settlement so that all the policy and its proceeds would be within s 71D?

We would be grateful for HMRC's views on this.

HMRC Answer to question 7—We do accept that any added rights from the payment of additional premiums would constitute settled property within s 71D. If a premium paid once the policy has become property to which s 71D applies gives rise to an addition to the settled property the addition will, in our view, automatically become property to which s 71D applies.

Section 200

Finally, we note that, under s 200(1)(c), a person with a non-qualifying interest in possession can become personally liable for the tax charged on death, with his liability limited only by reference to the value of the settled property (not the value of his actuarial interest). This seems a somewhat draconian provision, given that the beneficiary is no longer treated as beneficially entitled to the capital. Surely the liability should be limited to the property or income he actually receives? Similarly, in s 201(1)(b), the liability seems anomalous, given that most interests in possession will now be non-qualifying. Why should a beneficiary with a non-qualifying interest

in possession have a greater personal liability than a discretionary beneficiary? Can we press for these sections to be reviewed?

*HMRC Answer—We do not accept that there is an anomaly here.
Although an IIP holder whose interest arose before 22 March 2006 has
been regarded as owning the underlying property for inheritance tax
purposes, in reality he has only ever owned a limited interest. The FA
2006 changes do not alter the IIP owner's real position.*

Emma Chamberlain, Chairman CIOT Capital Taxes Sub-Committee

Judith Ingham, Chairman, STEP Technical

Appendix 5

Guidance on section 71a, section 71d and accumulation and maintenance trusts

[The following is reproduced, with kind permission of the Society of Trust and Estate Practitioners, from a document published by them and the Chartered Institute of Taxation on their respective websites in June/July 2007]

This guidance has been agreed with HMRC. It outlines the way in which HMRC interpret IHTA 1984 s 71 (as amended by FA 2006), s 71A and ss 71D–71H. **It should not be regarded as a comprehensive explanation covering all aspects of these sections.**

There are three particular areas of concern, namely—

1   the meaning of "B" in the legislation;

2   the class closing rules;

3   the scope of settled powers of advancement.

1   The meaning of "B" or "bereaved minor" in the legislation

Both s 71A and s 71D are drafted by reference to a single beneficiary (in s 71D called "B" and in s 71A called the bereaved minor). However, HMRC consider that it is possible to pluralise B or the bereaved minor to include all beneficiaries within the relevant class provided they are *alive* at the date the s 71A or s 71D trust takes effect and are under the specified age.

Accordingly a will trust in the following terms can qualify as a s 71A trust—"to such of my children alive at my death as attain the age of 18 years and if more than one in such shares as the trustees shall from time to time by deed or deeds revocable or irrevocable appoint and in default of such appointment in equal shares absolutely at 18 provided that no such appointment shall be made and no such appointment shall be revoked so as to either diminish or to increase the share (or the accumulations of income forming part of the share) of or give a new share (or new accumulations of income) to a child who at the date of such appointment or revocation has reached the age of 18 nor to benefit a child who has been excluded from benefit as a result of the exercise of the power."

Note the following—

1.1 It is not necessary to fix the shares in which each child takes income and capital while they are all under 18. Hence it is possible to pay out income and capital to the minor children in unequal shares.

1.2 The power of selection must not be capable of being exercised so as to vary the share of a child who has *already* reached 18. Assume three beneficiaries B1, B2 and B3. It is possible to specify at any time before the eldest (B1) reaches 18 the share he is to take but once he reaches 18 any further power of selection can only be exercised between B2 and B3. B1 ceases to be within the definition of "B" in these circumstances.

1.3 If the power of selection is exercised revocably then it is not possible by revoking that exercise to benefit someone who has been wholly excluded from benefit albeit revocably. If, for example, the whole relevant share is appointed revocably to B3 (but on terms that the appointment could be revoked to confer benefits on B1 or B2) then even though B1 and B2 are under 18 the trust ceases to qualify for s 71A status. HMRC consider that it is not possible under the s 71A regime for someone who is not currently benefiting to become entitled in the future. Practitioners will therefore need to be careful before exercising any power of appointment revocably.

1.4 HMRC do not consider that s 71A is breached merely because a power of appointment might be exercised in this way. Nor is it a problem if, in the above example, the power of appointment is exercised revocably so as to give B1 5%, B2 5% and B3 90%. Since B1 and B2 are not wholly excluded HMRC take the view that they can still benefit under a future exercise of the power since they remain within "B".

1.5 Nor is there a problem if a beneficiary dies under 18 leaving children in whose favour there will be incorporated substitutionary provisions. Hence if B1 dies before 18 leaving children and his presumptive or fixed share passes to those children under the terms of the will, it is only *from that point* that the presumptive share of B1 will cease to qualify under s 71A and fall within the relevant property regime. The mere possibility that B1 could die before 18 with children taking his share does not breach the s 71A conditions. Any power of selection though must not be capable of varying the presumptive share of the deceased B1 once he has died – because B1's children are not within the definition of B and their share must not be increased or deceased after B1 has died.

1.6 No overriding powers of appointment can be included so that "B's" absolute entitlement could be defeated at 18 although the legislation provides that the existence of an extended power of advancement (ie an express or statutory power of advancement that could be used to defer the beneficiary's capital entitlement by, for instance, providing that his share was to be held on life interest trusts beyond the age of 18) will not in itself cause the trust to fail to satisfy the s 71A conditions from the outset. However, if the settled power of advancement is exercised so as to defer vesting of capital at 18 (eg by the making of a settled advance) then although there is no charge under s 71A on the ending of the bereaved minor trust the relevant share from that point falls within the relevant property regime.

1.7   All the points above apply to s 71D trusts set up by will and to accumulation and maintenance ("A&M") trusts which are converted to fall within s 71D before 6 April 2008 (or before a beneficiary has attained an interest in possession if earlier). Hence it will be necessary to ensure that any powers of appointment that are retained do not permit a beneficiary's absolute share to be altered after he has reached 25 or defeated on reaching that age and if a power of appointment is exercised revocably it must not be capable of benefiting anyone who has been wholly excluded from benefit (even if under 25 and even if the exclusion was revocable).

2   The class closing rules

2.1   Difficult questions arise where an existing A&M trust is converted into a s 71D trust. Existing A&M trusts can become s 71D trusts provided this happens on the earlier of the beneficiary taking an entitlement to income or by 6 April 2008[1].

2.2   In the case of existing A&M trusts it is possible that the class of potential beneficiaries will not yet have closed. (This is different from s 71A and s 71D trusts set up by will where by definition the deceased parent cannot have any further children, apart from the case of a child *en ventre sa mère* whose father has died). In the same way that HMRC do not consider "B" can include a beneficiary who has been excluded from benefit (albeit revocably) HMRC do not consider that B can include any unborn beneficiary, again, apart from a child *en ventre sa mère*.

2.3   So if, for example, an existing A&M trust in favour of the settlor's grandchildren provides that the class closes only when the eldest becomes 25 and the trust currently benefits only B1 and B2 (say grandchildren of a settlor) being the sole living beneficiaries aged 8 and 9, in order to be s 71D compliant, the terms of the trust must be amended to exclude any future born beneficiaries. If B1 and B2's parent has a further child in 2009 that child *must not be capable of benefiting* from the trust fund (except in the event of the death of either B1 or B2 in which case the relevant portion of the trust will from that point fall within the relevant property regime).

2.4   Hence the power to appoint shares must only be exercisable between all or some of the beneficiaries under 25 *who are alive* at the date of conversion to s 71D status. HMRC consider this follows from the drafting in s 71D(1)(a), (3)(b)(i), (6)(a) when taken together.

2.5 This is not the case if an existing A&M trust continues to satisfy the conditions in s 71 beyond April 2008 because it falls within FA 2006 Sch 20 para 3. A trust which provides for all grandchildren to take outright at 18 will continue to have A&M status under s 71, as amended by Sch 20 para 3, beyond April 2008. It will be possible to pay income and capital between them in such shares as the trustees think fit and for future born children to benefit if the trust deed permits this flexibility provided that no child's share can be varied after reaching 18. The class should therefore generally be closed once the eldest child reaches 18.

3 The scope of settled powers of advancement

3.1 HMRC accept that the mere possibility of a power of advancement being used to defer entitlement to capital at 18 or 25 does not cause the trust to fail to satisfy the requirements of s 71A or s 71D given the terms of s 71A(4) or s 71D(7) respectively. If the power of advancement is exercised in favour of that person so as to create continuing trusts under which the beneficiary's capital entitlement will be deferred beyond the age of 18 or 25 as appropriate, those trusts will fall within the relevant property regime (with either no exit charge in the case of BMTs or with the usual exit charge under s 71E, computed according to the provisions in s 71F, assuming the proper exercise of the power causes property to be "paid or applied for the advancement or benefit of B"; otherwise, the computation would be under s 71G).

3.2 HMRC accept that in the case of A&M trusts (including trusts which are modified so that they satisfy the amended s 71 definition after 6 April 2008) the mere inclusion of a wide power of advancement is unobjectionable. The exercise of such a power will not trigger an inheritance tax charge if the beneficiary takes absolutely or an interest in possession (albeit not qualifying) on or before 18 (see IHTA 1984 s 71(4)) and his capital entitlement is deferred beyond 18, although in the latter event, the trust for the beneficiary will thenceforth be a relevant property trust unless it can come within s 71D.

Emma Chamberlain/Chris Whitehouse, 5 Stone Buildings, 29 June 2007

[1]It will not be possible to convert an A&M trust into a s 71D trust after the beneficiary has become entitled to income on or after 22 March 2006 because once a beneficiary takes entitlement to income it no longer qualifies as an A&M trust under s 71. Section 71D(3)(b) requires conversion of the trusts immediately before the property ceases to be property to which s 71 applies. Hence it will need to be s 71D-compliant by the time the beneficiary attains an interest in possession. Of course if

one beneficiary becomes entitled to income from part of the trust fund the remaining part will remain within the A&M regime and so may be converted subsequently (but before 6 April 2008).

Appendix 6

IHT and trusts: questions and anomalies

[The following is reproduced, with kind permission of The Law Society, from a document published on their website in October 2007]

Comments by the Tax Law Committee of the Law Society

In our "Tax Law Reform 2006/07" memorandum, we noted that we would be raising separately with HMRC a number of anomalies or areas of doubt which remain despite HMRC's helpful response on 3 November 2006 to certain issues submitted by STEP and the CIoT. This paper sets out a number of points requiring confirmation or clarification as to how the legislation introduced by Finance Act 2006 Schedule 20 will be interpreted or applied by HMRC. In some cases it is thought that changes to the legislation, or at the least formal concessions, ought to be considered, so as to rectify anomalies which we cannot think would have been intended.

Other more wide-ranging policy issues on the area covered by Schedule 20 are included in the memorandum referred to, and are omitted from this paper merely to avoid duplication.

Statutory references (other than to "Schedule 20") are to the Inheritance Tax Act 1984 as amended, unless otherwise stated.

Post-death rearrangements

Question 1

In the responses to questions 40, 41 raised by STEP/CIoT, HMRC confirmed that an IIP resulting from the variation of a will within s 142 will be an IPDI (and will be a pre-Budget IIP if the deceased died before Budget Day 2006); that BMTs and age 18-to-25 trusts can also be established by means of the variation of a will within s 142; and that in each case the settlor of the resultant settlement would be the deceased, not the original beneficiary. Do HMRC consider that the same will apply where the disposition being varied under s 142 was not itself made by the deceased's will or intestacy, but rather as a result of survivorship in respect of property of which the deceased was a beneficial joint tenant, or by nomination eg of National Savings investments (cf National Savings Bank

Regulations 1972 reg 33)? It is hard to see how the resultant settlement can be regarded as "effected by will or under the law relating to intestacy" (s 49A(2)) or "established under the will of [the beneficiary's] parent" (s 71A(2)(a) or s 71D(2)(a)), even if as a result of IHTA 1984 s 142(1) is to apply "as if the variation had been effected by the deceased".

HMRC reply—See comments on question 2 below.

Question 2

Where a court order is made under the Inheritance (Provision for Family & Dependants) Act 1975 s 2, the property concerned is treated for IHT purposes by s 146(1) "as if it had on [the deceased's] death devolved subject to the provisions of the order". If the order results in the property concerned being comprised in a settlement, do HMRC agree that the settlement cannot be within s 49A(2), s 71(2)(a) or s 71D(2)(a) (extracts just quoted in 1 above)?

HMRC reply—We agree that interests resulting from the operation of ss 142 or 146 will not come within ss 49A, 71A or 71D where the original disposition was not made under the deceased's will or law of intestacy. In the latter case, I(PFD)A 1975 s 19(1) will treat the will or intestacy rules as modified by the order.

Question 3

Where a testator died before Budget Day 2006 leaving a discretionary trust under his will, and an appointment on IIP trusts is made within two years after his death but after Budget Day 2006, s 144(4)(a) provides that the IHTA 1984 is to have effect "as if the will had provided that on the testator's death the property should be held as it is held after [the appointment]". Do HMRC agree that—

(a) the resultant IIP is therefore to be regarded as one to which the beneficiary in question was entitled immediately before Budget Day 2006, so that TSI status would then be available for a later IIP where the other conditions of s 49C or s 49D were met?

HMRC reply—We agree.

(b) the resultant IIP is also an IPDI (whether the appointment was made before or after Budget Day 2006), so that, if it is later terminated in the lifetime of the beneficiary in question in such a way that the property becomes subject to a BMT, PET treatment is available under s 3A(3B) (cf 5(c) below).

HMRC reply—We agree.

Transitional serial interests

Question 4

Condition 2 in each of sections 49C to 49E requires in each case that the prior interest, the previous interest or the earlier interest, as the case may be, should have come to an end, if TSI treatment is to be available for the current interest, the successor interest or the present interest as the case may be.

(a) Section 51 provides that the disposal of an IIP to which s 49 applies is to be treated for the purposes of Part 3 Chapter 2 as the coming to an end of the interest. Can it therefore be confirmed that where the current interest, the successor interest or the present interest as the case may be is assigned instead of coming to an end, this will meet Condition 2 in each of those sections, since they are all within that Chapter?

HMRC reply—We have taken it that you mean here that the assignor is the person with the prior, previous or earlier interest. And your question is therefore whether the assignee has a current, successor or present interest.

On that basis, we can confirm that they will because condition 2 in ss 49C, 49D or 49E will be met.

(b) Can it also be confirmed that, for the same reason, an IIP which does not in fact come to an end on the death of the beneficiary entitled to it will also be regarded as coming to an end, for the purpose of Condition 2 in each of those sections, at any rate if it passes under (and so was disposed of by) the will of the beneficiary rather than on his intestacy? Examples of such an IIP are an absolute interest in capital that is defeasible (eg by the exercise of a power of revocation), an interest *pur autre vie*, and an interest for a fixed term of years. It is noted by way of comparison that TCGA 1992 s 72(2) provides that the CGT treatment under subsection (1) of that section "shall apply where the persons entitled to an interest in possession in all or part of the settled property dies (although the interest does not then terminate) as it applies on the termination of such an interest".

HMRC reply—We can confirm this.

IPDIs and PETs under section 3A(3B)

Question 5

Assume that, under a will, the testator's surviving spouse has a life interest, subject to which the testator's only child (still a minor) is to inherit absolutely at age 18.

(a) If the trustees exercise a power conferred on them to terminate the surviving spouse's IIP and accelerate the bereaved minor's trust for the benefit of the minor child, s 3A(3B) provides for PET treatment except where the spouse was a disabled person at the date of death of the testator; in this instance the IIP (assuming the testator died after Budget Day 2006) is a DPI under s 89B(1)(c) and therefore cannot an IPDI (see s 49A(4)(b)). It is impossible to discern any policy reason for this distinction.

HMRC reply—We agree that PET treatment would not be available in the DPI example you give.

(b) If the surviving spouse instead assigns the IIP to the child, or to the trustees to hold for the child's benefit on the same terms as if the surviving spouse had died, the trust property will again be held on a bereaved minor's trust satisfying all the conditions of s 71A. (The child has two interests: a right to income for the rest of the spouse's life, and a right to capital at 18 or on the spouse's later death. If the child reaches 18 and the spouse is still living, these interests in combination amount to an absolute interest in capital and income then and there: no-one else has any possible interest in the fund, and he is in a position to demand that the capital be made over to him (*Saunders v Vautier*) just as much as if the spouse's interest had been terminated instead of assigned.) However, because the IIP has been assigned instead of brought to an end, do HMRC take the view that PET treatment is denied because s 3A(3B)(c) requires that the interest should have come to an end. Why should that distinction be made, especially having regard to 4(a) above?

HMRC reply—We can confirm that we take the view that PET treatment is not available where an IIP is assigned, for the reason you state.

(c) Can HMRC confirm that PET treatment under s 3A(3B) is available (subject to the above two anomalies) as much where the testator in the above example died before Budget Day 2006 as where he died on or after that date? There seems nothing in the definition of an IPDI in s 49A to confine it to deaths on or after Budget Day.

HMRC reply—We can confirm this.

Transitional provisions affecting pre-Budget life policy trusts

Question 6

Assume a pre-Budget life policy trust such as is contemplated in s 49E, under which A had an IIP immediately before Budget Day 2006.

— A dies on 1 January 2007 and B becomes entitled to an IIP in A's place.

— B then dies on 1 October 2008 and C becomes entitled to an IIP in B's place.

— In turn C dies on 1 June 2010 and D becomes entitled to an IIP in C's place.

The original policy still continues in force throughout, without variation, and the original settlor pays each annual premium under the policy as it falls due (assume that neither the annual exemption nor the normal income expenditure exemption applies). There seems no rational basis for the distinctions evident in the following paragraphs.

(a) Assume that B satisfied one or other of paragraphs (a) to (c) in s 89(4) at the date of A's death. B cannot however be a disabled person for the purpose of IHT, because status as such is tested once and for all at the date the property in question was originally settled. Do HMRC agree that—

    (i) B's IIP is a TSI under s 49C, and those of C and D are therefore TSIs under s 49E? and

HMRC reply—We agree.

    (ii) every premium payment by the settlor will constitute a PET under s 46A?

HMRC reply—We agree.

(b) Assume instead that B's condition was already such that he was a disabled person within s 89(4) at the date the life policy was originally settled. B's IIP cannot now be a TSI because it is a DPI under s 89B(1)(c) and therefore excluded by s 49C(5)(b). Do HMRC agree that—

    (i) neither C's interest, nor in turn D's interest, can therefore be TSIs, because s 49E(3)(b) requires that B's IIP must have been a TSI under s 49C? and

HMRC reply—We agree.

    (ii) each premium payment by the settlor starting with the first premium due after A's death will be a chargeable transfer? This seems to follow because s 46A(1)(d)(ii) requires that the policy should have been subject to a transitionally-protected interest continuously since Budget Day 2006, and B's IIP, being a DPI, was not within the definition of that expression in s 46A(5).

HMRC reply—We agree that s.46A would not apply. But it would seem that, because B, as the holder of an IIP which is a DPI, will be treated as beneficially entitled to the underlying property by virtue of ss.49 (1) and 49 (1A), we can regard each premium payment for the duration of B's IIP as a "gift to another individual" and therefore within s 3A(1A)(c)(i).

(c) Assume instead that B was not a disabled person, but C was living, and a disabled person within s 89(4), at the date the life policy was originally settled. B's IIP will therefore have been a TSI under s 49C, and C's IIP will be a DPI under s 89B(1)(c). Do HMRC agree that—

    (i) D's IIP is nevertheless a TSI under s 49E because once an initial

TSI has been established, s 49E does not require that the other successive IIPs after it should have been TSIs? but

HMRC reply—We agree.

    (ii) For the same reason as in 6(b)(ii) above, each premium payment by the settlor starting with the first premium due after B's death will be a chargeable transfer, by reference to C's IIP being a DPI not a TSI?

HMRC reply—See our answer to 6(b)(ii), as far as premiums paid during the duration of C's IIP are concerned.

Question 7

Assume another pre-Budget life policy, this time one which was held immediately before Budget Day 2006 on A&M trusts for X's benefit, on terms such that X will become entitled to an interest in possession at age 18 and will become absolutely entitled to capital at age 25. As in 6 above, the original settlor pays each annual premium under the policy as it falls due (assume again that neither the annual exemption nor the normal income expenditure exemption applies). X's 18th birthday falls on 1 February 2008.

(a) If X is not a disabled person, the trust leaves s 71, and enters s 71D, on 1 February 2008. Do HMRC agree that all premium payments by the settlor while the trust subsists are PETs, initially by virtue of s 46B(1), (5) and, after that date, by virtue of s 46B(3), (5).

HMRC reply—We agree that the continuing premium payments would be PETs.

(b) If however X was a disabled person at the date the policy was originally put in trust, the IIP to which he becomes entitled on reaching age 18 is a DPI within s 89B(1)(c), and as such the trust is excluded from s 71D by s 89B(3). Do HMRC therefore take the view that any premiums paid by the settlor after X's 18th birthday would appear to involve chargeable transfers since no provision in s 46A or 46B would appear to apply?

HMRC reply—We agree that ss 46A, 46B do not apply. But see our answer to 6(b)(ii).

Self-settled DPIs

Question 8

With reference to the deemed IIP under s 89A for a self-settled trust by a settlor suffering from a degenerative condition, condition 2 in s 89A(3) lays down requirements as to the position that must be achieved in the event of the exercise of a power to bring the trust to an end during the settlor's lifetime. The power must be such that either (a) or (b) below will be satisfied on its exercise.

(a) The property must vest absolutely in "A [the settlor] or another person". Can HMRC confirm that this provision would be satisfied if different parts of the trust property vested in different persons, whether the settlor or otherwise?

HMRC reply—We can confirm this.

(b) Alternatively a DPI within s 89B(1)(a) or s 89B(1)(c) must subsist in the settled property. Do HMRC agree that it is impossible for a DPI within either of those provisions to arise in favour of the settlor of the s 89A trust?

   (i) Such a settlor by definition was not in fact a disabled person at the date he formed the s 89A trust. As such, he can never have a DPI within either of those stated provisions of s 89B(1), in respect of property comprised in the trust in question, since both require that he should have been a disabled person at the date the property was originally settled (see s 89(4)–(6)).

HMRC reply—We agree.

   (ii) Even if the exercise of the power were to involve property being transferred to a separate settlement formed at a time when he was indeed a disabled person, s 81 would have the effect of treating the property as remaining within the original settlement, so that (i) above would continue to prevent a DPI within s 89B(1)(a) or (c). Sections 89–89B are comprised within Part 3 Chapter 3, for which s 81 operates.

HMRC reply—We agree.

BMTs and age 18-to-25 trusts

Question 9

Finance Act 2006 Sch 20 para 2(5) precludes an IHT charge under s 71(3) where property leaves s 71 "by the operation of the subsection (1B) inserted into [section 71] by [paragraph 2 of Schedule 20]". That protection is clear enough where, on a pre-Budget death, property became held on the statutory intestacy trusts for the deceased's minor children: s 71 applied until s 71(1B) was deemed to come into force on Budget Day, and from then on s 71A applied. However, assume instead that the deceased had left a will under which his minor children were to take capital at age 27 in equal shares, and that before 6 April 2008 – but while the children are all still under 18 – the trustees exercise their powers in such a way as to provide that the children will instead take capital at age 18 (with benefits in the meantime being suitably restricted so as to comply with s 71A(3)(c)). Do HMRC consider that the property leaves s 71 and enters s 71A "by the operation of" s 71(1B), or partly by the operation of that provision and partly as a result of the action of the trustees? If the latter, do HMRC consider that the protection of Sch 20 para 2(5) is unavailable as a result?

HMRC reply—We have taken it that the powers exercised by the trustees in this case are special powers, such as exercise of the statutory power of advancement. In that case, we can confirm that we take the view that, by virtue of paragraph 2(5) of Schedule 20, there is no charge to tax when s 71 ceases to apply because of the operation of s 71(1B).

Question 10

Do HMRC agree that a (current or future) protective trust under Trustee Act 1925 s 33 is incompatible with the trust falling within either s 71A or s 71D? It would seem that the discretionary trust of income (under Trustee Act 1925 s 33(1)(ii)) that would arise on forfeiture of the protected life interest itself would offend s 71A(3)(c)(ii) or s 71D(6)(c)(ii) as the case may be.

HMRC reply—We agree.

IIPs that are not within section 49

Question 11

Can it be confirmed that the purchaser of an IIP to which s 49 does not apply makes no transfer of value (even though neither the underlying settled property nor the IIP itself enters his estate, see s 5(1)(a)(ii)) provided the purchase is on fully arm's length terms, as a result of s 10?

HMRC reply—We can confirm this.

Question 12

It is clear from the amended s 5(1)(a)(ii) and 5(1A) that an assignment of an IIP will not involve a transfer of value on the part of the assignor if the IIP is not such as to bring the underlying capital within his estate.

(a) However, do HMRC consider that such an assignor, if making the assignment without consideration, nevertheless makes a gift such as to bring Finance Act 1986 s 102 into play in the event of his later receiving some benefit that is traceable to the IIP in the hands of the assignee? If so, the result would appear to be the possibility of an IHT charge in the assignor's estate on his death, when none would have arisen had he retained the IIP until then.

HMRC reply—We agree.

(b) If the assignment does involve a gift, and a benefit is found, is it agreed that the subject-matter of the gift was purely the IIP itself and not the underlying settled property, so that it is purely the value of the IIP immediately before the assignor's death that falls to be charged as part of his estate? It would appear that the termination of the IIP resulting from the assignor's death cannot be taken into account under s 171 (see the final sentence of s 171(2)); but is it agreed that the interest is likely to be of minimal value "immediately" before the death in all cases other than those of the most sudden and instantaneous death? Even if the assignor survives, say, a road accident or a sudden heart attack by no more than five minutes, it would be clear enough "immediately" before his death that his prospects of survival were slim.

HMRC reply—We agree that the subject matter of the gift is the IIP and, in many cases, the value of that will be minimal. But, as you say, there could be some cases of sudden death where that may not be the position, or cases where the IIP assigned is not on the assignor's life but a pur autre vie interest.

Section 71F and pre-1974 settlements

Question 13

Where a settlement within the relevant property regime commenced before the introduction of capital transfer tax in 1974, modifications to reflect this are built in to the formula for calculating the rate of IHT on ten year charges: see s 66(6), s 67(4) and the final words of s 66(5)(a). Similarly, in relation to an exit charge occurring within the first ten years of the settlement's existence, s 68(6) (now spent) set out a different approach to calculating the rate, in place of the standard provisions of sections 68(4), (5). The rate of charge on property in an age 18-to-25 trust, where calculated in accordance with s 71F, is in substance identical to the relevant property provisions in s 68, but makes no equivalent provision for cases where the settlement commenced before 1974, even though the issue was raised in representations during the passage of the Finance (No 2) Bill. Yet there are likely to be a number of settlements dating from before that time which were within s 71 immediately before Budget Day 2006. If a settlement of that type moves into the s 71D regime by the end of the transitional period, and a charge under s 71F subsequently falls to be computed,

(a) do HMRC consider that for the purpose of s 71F(8)(b), any disposition made by the settlor before 27 March 1974 was incapable of being a chargeable transfer, notwithstanding that the draftsman of the Finance Act 1982 saw it necessary to include what are now the final words of s 66(5)(a)?

HMRC reply—In our view, a disposition before 27 March 1974 is capable of being a chargeable transfer, hence the draftsman specified in s 66(5)(a) that transfers made before that date should be disregarded.

(b) will HMRC adopt a practice that, for the purpose of s 71F(9)(b), a settlement made before 27 March 1974 will not be considered to be a related settlement?

HMRC reply—Under the law as it now stands, we take the view that related settlements made before 27 March 1974 must be taken into account for the purposes of s 71F(9)(b).

(c) what account do HMRC consider should be taken, for the purpose of s 71F(9)(c), of property which had left the settlement before 27 March 1974?

HMRC reply—Under the law as it now stands, we consider that property which left the settlement before 27 March 1974 must be taken fully into account for the purposes of s 71F(9)(c).

Reporting under the relevant property and s 71F regimes

Question 14

The new rules will result in many long-standing settlements, which have always been in IIP or A&M form and were expected always to remain so and to which the relevant property rules were previously of no possible relevance, being brought, in time, into the charging regime for relevant property or (as a result of s 71F mirroring s 68, subject to 13 above) for age 18-to-25 trusts. Much of the information necessary for the purposes of working out the rate of charge under those regimes is historic information of which the trustees for the time being may – quite properly – have no records, and often very little prospect of finding out definitive (or any) details. Examples include—

— whether any other settlement was made by the settlor on the same day as the current settlement, and if so what property was comprised in it, or what were the terms on which it was made (eg initial IIP for the settlor or his spouse, such as to preclude related settlement treatment by virtue of s 80);

— what chargeable transfers had been made by the settlor (possibly since deceased) in the seven years prior to formation of the settlement, and where relevant also in the seven years prior to any later additions to the settlement (and in the latter case how far those chargeable transfers were attributable to property already taken into account in a separate component of the rate formula, cf s 67(5));

— sometimes even what property was comprised in the current settlement initially, and/or subsequently added to it (and when).

Those issues are likely to arise even more strongly where the present settlement was hived off out of an earlier settlement, or where a reversionary interest under an earlier settlement was placed in trust. In such cases s 81 will require the above matters to be established in relation to the "source" settlement.

How far will HMRC expect trustees to have to go in seeking information on these matters which is not readily to hand from the trust records? In relation to chargeable transfers made by the settlor (which would presumably have had in most cases to be reported at the time), will HMRC be able and willing to supply trustees on request with information on such matters which would never previously have had, or been expected to have, any relevance to the trust's position? If obvious lines of enquiry fail to yield definitive, or any, information on matters relevant to the calculation of a charge, what guidance can HMRC give to trustees who are concerned to submit an accurate IHT return? And what comfort can be offered to them in relation to the potential application of the penalty regime if something were to emerge which cast doubt on the accuracy of a return submitted?

HMRC reply—We are dealing here with the minority of people who have set up multiple lifetime settlements of a sort that might become chargeable under Sch 20, and on a scale where there is some prospect that IHT would be due. It is highly likely – if the need arises – that those responsible for such trusts will have perfectly adequate records for all of them, and will have no difficulty in meeting any requirements that may flow from Sch 20.

But trustees are not expected to do the impossible – if they truly do not know of any other settlements etc made by the same settlor, and have made reasonable enquiries without revealing any, then they are perfectly entitled to make their IHT returns on the basis of whatever information they do have, and to pay IHT accordingly.

We can also confirm that, where HMRC Inheritance Tax have information about the settlor's chargeable transfers, we will provide it on request.

Sections 71A and 71D: class gifts

Question 15

It is our understanding that, for a will trust in favour of the testator's children in defined shares to be within s 71A or s 71D, the class of beneficiaries must be closed. This follows from the very restrictive drafting of the conditions in s 71A(3) and s 71D(6), which focus on a single child (labelled "B" in s 71D(6)) and require in effect that no-one else must be able to benefit from the capital or income of his share of the fund (the settled property that is held for his benefit as mentioned in s 71A(1)(b) or s 71D(1)(a)) except in the event of his death under the requisite age.

HMRC reply—We agree. We consider that it is possible to pluralise B where there is already more than one existing beneficiary. We do not, however, consider that s 71A or s 71D will apply if someone other than "B" (plural or not) may benefit later.

Even if the will of the testator restricts the gift (as it frequently will) to his children "living at his death", it is well established that this expression will be construed to include a posthumous member of the relevant class if (but only if) this would serve to allow that member himself to take under the gift – which would of course be the case in the case we are discussing here.

It would seem to follow that a will trust for the deceased's children generically, whether at age 18 or age 25, could not initially be in either of those sections where the deceased's partner was expecting one or more further children of his at the time of his death, because in those circumstances the potential/prospective posthumous child would be a member of the class of beneficiaries in accordance with the principle just mentioned and the shares in which the children already living should take.

— Do HMRC agree that, in such a case, the trust would of necessity be a relevant property trust from the death (in whole or possibly just in part), and would move into s 71A or s 71D as the case may be once the further child was born (or the pregnancy was lost), as a result of s 144, given that this would have to occur within nine months after the death?

HMRC reply—We consider that such a trust would come within s 71A or s 71D from the outset. The unborn child would come within the existing beneficiaries, "B", and so there would be no question of someone other than B benefiting from the trusts later. For the sake of clarity, we confirm—

— *that we take this same view even if there are no children already born at the date of death, and*

— *that if in those circumstances the pregnancy is terminated or ends in a still-birth, the exemptions in ss 71B(2)(b) or 71E(2)(b) will apply on the basis that such event constitutes the "death" of the unborn child under the age of 18.*

The possibility of the fund being relevant property only in part would relate to the potential share of the child or children as yet unborn at the date of death – assuming that the pregnancy was actually known about at the death, which would not be guaranteed, and that it was also known precisely how many children might be capable of being born alive from the pregnancy. If that were the correct conclusion, what view would HMRC take in the case, for example of a pregnancy involving undiagnosed twins?

HMRC reply—Given our previous answer, this issue and the concerns immediately below seem to fall away.

— In that event, if in the meantime capital is applied for the benefit of a living child, or a living child passes the relevant birthday or dies,

— would s 71B (2) or s 71E (2) protect retrospectively from charge where the beneficiary in question was still under age 18?

Or—

— would applications of capital or absolute entitlements in the meantime be taxed under the relevant property regime, or (for age 18-to-25 trusts where the beneficiary in question had already reached age 18) s 71F (though not in substance different from the relevant property regime in this instance)?

The same point does not arise in respect of a trust for the deceased's issue under the intestacy rules, since the conditions in s 71(3) that lead to the "closed class" conclusion are not applicable in that case.

Section 144

Question 16

It is not entirely clear why it was necessary to refer to ss 71A and 71D in s 144(3)(c) and 144(6), since nothing in those sections appears to require that the conditions in s 71A(3) or s 71D(6) should have been satisfied with immediate effect after the death (in contrast to the IPDI requirement in s 49A(3)). (That there is no such requirement is borne out by s 3A(3B), which envisages that property can pass from an IPDI into a bereaved minor's trust within s 71A at any time while the minor is still under age 18.) That being so, and since property within s 71A or s 71D is not relevant property (section 58(1)(b)), an appointment for the testator's children on terms satisfying the conditions in s 71A(3) or s 71D(6) would result in the property in question leaving the relevant property regime, and would therefore have its effect backdated to the death under s 144(1), (2) in any event.

HMRC reply—While property can pass from an IPDI into a s 71A trust, it will only do so if it becomes "property to which s 71A below applies" – and PET treatment will only be available if it does (s 3A(3B)(e)(ii)).

This means that the trusts must have been established under the original testator's will.

So take the situation where the testator's surviving spouse has an IPDI and uses a power of appointment to appoint the settled property on trusts for the testator's minor child that would, if they had been provided in the testator's will, have satisfied the requirements of s 71A.

We consider that, if the power in question is a special power of appointment, s 71A will apply (and PET treatment will be available) because the trusts can be regarded as having been established under the testator's will.

We consider the position is likely to be different, though, if the trustees have wide powers, including the power to appoint property on new trusts.

Thus, s 144 (3) and 144 (6) need a reference to s 71A and s 71D because property appointed out of relevant property trusts on to supposed s 71A or s 71D trusts will not necessarily fall within those sections as having been established under the deceased's will. The property in question may not, therefore, leave the relevant property regime and s 144 would not operate.

However, the draftsman has chosen to include s 71A and 71D in the extended rules in subsections (3)–(6), in terms which give rise to something of an ambiguity, most particularly in the context of s 71D. The two competing interpretations can be illustrated by a scenario in which A, a single mother, dies leaving her estate to her three children B, C and D contingently on their reaching age 25, with income vesting at age 18 by virtue of Trustee Act 1925 s 31. B, C and D are aged 18, 16 and 14 at A's death.

Immediately after A's death, B's share is recognisably subject to an IPDI, and B's and C's shares are recognisably within s 71D. B's and D's shares will clearly retain that treatment until they vest at age 25, and D, but not B, will be visited with an IHT charge at that time (and will qualify for CGT holdover relief subject to UK residence). (Conversely, if they both die under age 25, B's share will be taxed as part of his estate but D's will not.)

The ambiguity relates to C's share. Within two years after A's death, C will attain age 18, and with it an interest in possession. In those circumstances, do HMRC consider that—

— section 144 operates at that time to backdate C's interest in possession to A's death, making it an IPDI, or

HMRC reply—No.

— the trust of C's share remains within s 71D until the capital vests in C at age 25?

HMRC reply—Yes. S 144 as a whole is predicated on the assumption that the property settled by a testator's will is relevant property – s 144(1). Such property cannot, it seems to us, be property to which either ss 71A or 71D applies.

Plainly the consequences of the two interpretations differ, as seen with B's and D's shares.

The arguments in favour of those respective interpretations seem to be—

— that no IPDI or DPI has subsisted in C's share prior to his 18th birthday, and that event (which occurs within two years after A's death) causes the property to be held on trusts which, had they been established by the will, would have resulted in the property being the subject of an IPDI;

— alternatively, that the results contemplated in sub-paragraphs (i) and (ii) of s 144(3) (sub-paragraphs (a) and (b) of s 144(6) if A had died before 22 March 2006) comprise a single "target group" – divided into two sub-paragraphs purely because of the different drafting approach adopted elsewhere in the Finance Act 2006 amendments for the different categories of trust – and an event occurring after the death can only "result in" the settled property in question falling within that target group if it did not fall within it immediately after the death. On this interpretation s 144(4) will only be invoked where the trust fitted none of the three types immediately after the death. That approach seems more in keeping with the purpose of the provisions as explained in the Explanatory Notes to Amendments 398–400, which refer in both paragraphs 1 and 5 to appointments out of a discretionary trust set up by will. (The debate in standing committee on these provisions was very short and the Minister made no reference to the actual intention beyond the fact that technical changes were required "to ensure that the arrangements continue to function as intended", though the Shadow Minister's remarks certainly suggest that both were envisaging a discretionary will – see Standing Committee A, 15 June 2006, column 705.)

Submitted to HMRC by The Law Society's Tax Law Committee on 12 January 2007 (questions 1 to 14) and 9 March 2007 (questions 15 and 16).

Responses by HMRC on 3 and 23 August 2007.

Appendix 7

Transferable nil-rate band: Draft legislation and initial guidance

1 Inheritance tax: transfer of unused nil-rate band etc

The Schedule contains provisions about the transfer of unused nil-rate band between spouses and civil partners and other matters for the purposes of the charge to inheritance tax.

Schedule

Inheritance Tax: Transfer of Nil-Rate Band etc

1 IHTA 1984 is amended as follows—

2 After section 8 insert—

"8A Transfer of unused nil-rate band between spouses and civil partners

(1) This section applies where—

  (a) immediately before the death of a person (a "deceased person"), the deceased person had a spouse or civil partner ("the survivor"), and
  (b) the deceased person had unused nil-rate band on death.

(2) For the purposes of this section a person has unused nil-rate band on death if M > VT

  where—

  M is the maximum that could be transferred by the chargeable transfer made (under section 4 above) on the person's death if it were to be wholly chargeable to tax at the rate of nil per cent; and
  VT is the value actually transferred by that chargeable transfer (or nil if there is no such chargeable transfer).

(3) Where a claim is made under this section, the nil-rate band maximum at the time of the survivor's death is to be treated for the purposes of

the charge to tax on the death of the survivor as increased by the percentage specified in subsection (4) below (but subject to subsection (5) and section 8C below).

(4) That percentage is—

$$\frac{E}{NRBMD} \times 100$$

where—

E is the amount by which M is greater than VT in the case of the deceased person; and

NRBMD is the nil-rate band maximum at the time of the deceased person's death.

(5) If (apart from this subsection) the amount of the increase in the nil-rate band maximum at the time of the survivor's death effected by this section would exceed the amount of that nil-rate band maximum, the amount of the increase is limited to the amount of that nil-rate band maximum.

(6) Subsection (5) above may apply either—

(a) because the percentage mentioned in subsection (4) above (as reduced under section 8C below where that section applies) is more than 100 because of the amount by which M is greater than VT in the case of one deceased person, or

(b) because this section applies in relation to the survivor by reference to the death of more than one person who had unused nil-rate band on death.

(7) In this Act "nil-rate band maximum" means the amount shown in the second column in the first row of the Table in Schedule 1 to this Act (upper limit of portion of value charged at rate of nil per cent.) and in the first column in the second row of that Table (lower limit of portion charged at next rate).

8B Claims under section 8A

(1) A claim under section 8A above may be made—

(a) by the personal representatives of the survivor within the permitted period, or

(b) (if no claim is so made) by any other person liable to the tax chargeable on the survivor's death within such later period as the Commissioners for Her Majesty's Revenue and Customs may specify.

(2) In subsection (1)(a) above "the permitted period" means—

(a) the period of two years from the end of the month in which the survivor dies or (if it ends later) the period of three months beginning with the date on which the personal representatives first act as such, or

(b) such longer period as the Commissioners for Her Majesty's Revenue and Customs may specify.

(3) A claim made within either of the periods mentioned in subsection (2)(a) above may be withdrawn no later than one month after the end of the period concerned.

8C Section 8A and subsequent charges

(1) This section applies where—

(a) the conditions in subsection (1)(a) and (b) of section 8A above are met, and

(b) after the death of the deceased person, tax is charged on an amount under section 32, 32A or 126 below, or Schedule 5 to this Act, by reference to the rate or rates that would have been applicable to the amount if it were included in the value transferred by the chargeable transfer made (under section 4 above) on the deceased person's death.

(2) If the tax is charged before the death of the survivor, the percentage referred to in subsection (3) of section 8A above is (instead of that specified in subsection (4) of that section)—

$$\left(\frac{E}{NRBMD} - \frac{TA}{NRBME}\right) \times 100$$

where—

E and NRBMD have the same meaning as in subsection (4) of that section;

TA is the amount on which tax is charged; and

NRBME is the nil-rate band maximum at the time of the event occasioning the charge.

(3) If this section has applied by reason of a previous event or events, the reference in subsection (2) to the fraction—

$$\frac{TA}{NRBME}$$

is to the aggregate of that fraction in respect of the current event and the previous event (or each of the previous events).

(4) If the tax is charged after the death of the survivor, it is charged as if the personal nil-rate band maximum of the deceased person were appropriately reduced.

(5) In subsection (4) above—

"the personal nil-rate band maximum of the deceased person" is the nil-rate band maximum which is treated by Schedule 2 to this Act as applying in relation to the deceased person's death, increased in accordance with section 8A above where that section effected an increase in that nil-rate band maximum in the case of the deceased person (as a survivor of another deceased person), and

"appropriately reduced" means reduced by the amount (if any) by which the amount on which tax was charged at the rate of nil per cent on the death of the survivor was increased by reason of the operation of section 8A above by virtue of the position of the deceased person."

3

(1) Section 151BA (rates of charge under section 151B) is amended as follows.

(2) In subsection (5), for "had been in force at the time of the member's death" substitute "("the applicable Table") had been in force at the time of the member's death, but subject to subsections (6) and (9) below."

(3) After that subsection insert—

"(6) The nil-rate band maximum in the applicable Table is to be treated for the purposes of this section as reduced by the used-up percentage of the difference between—
(a) that nil-rate band maximum, and
(b) the nil-rate band maximum which was actually in force at the time of the member's death.

(7) For the purposes of subsection (6) above "the used-up percentage" is—

$$100 - \frac{E}{NRBM} \times 100$$

where—
— E is the amount by which M is greater than VT under section 8A(2) above in the case of the member; and
— NRBM is the nil-rate band maximum at the time of the member's death."

(4) After subsection (7) insert—

"(8) The following provisions apply where—
(a) tax is charged under section 151B above, and
(b) immediately before the member's death, the member had a spouse or civil partner ("the survivor").

(9) If the survivor died before the event giving rise to the charge, tax is charged as if the personal nil-rate band maximum of the member were appropriately reduced.

(10) In subsection (9) above—

"the personal nil-rate band maximum of the member" is the nil-rate band maximum in the applicable Table, increased in accordance with section 8A above where that section effected an increase in that nil-rate band maximum in the case of the member (as a survivor of another deceased person), and

"appropriately reduced" means reduced by the amount (if any) by which the amount on which tax was charged at the rate of nil per cent on the death of the survivor was increased by reason of the operation of section 8A above by virtue of the position of the member.

(11) If the survivor did not die before the event giving rise to the charge, tax is to be charged on the death of the survivor as if the percentage referred to in section 8A(3) above in the case of the member were that specified in subsection (12) below.

(12) That percentage is—

$$\frac{AE}{ANRBM} \times 100$$

where—

AE is the adjusted excess, that is the amount by which M would be greater than VT under section 8A(2) above in the case of the member if—

(a) the taxable amount were included in the value transferred by the chargeable transfer made on the member's death, and

(b) the nil-rate band maximum at the time of the member's death were ANRBM; and

ANRBM is the adjusted nil-rate band maximum, that is the nil-rate band maximum in the applicable Table (as reduced under subsection (6) above where that subsection applies)."

4   In section 239(4) (certificates of discharge: cases where further tax not affected), after paragraph (a) (but before the "or") insert—

"(aa)—that may afterwards be shown to be payable by reason of too great an increase having been made under section 8A(3) above,".

5   In section 247(2) (tax-geared penalty), for "that person is liable" substitute "that or any other person is liable (in respect of any chargeable transfer whatsoever)".

6   In section 272 (general interpretation), insert at the appropriate place—"'nil-rate band maximum' has the meaning given by section 8A(7);".

7   (1)   The amendments made by paragraphs 2 and 3(4) have effect in relation to cases where the survivor's death occurs on or after 9 October 2007.

(2)   Section 8A of IHTA 1984 (as inserted by paragraph 2) has effect in relation to cases where the deceased person died before 18 March 1986 (and the survivor dies on or after 9 October 2007) subject to modifications prescribed by regulations made by the Treasury by

statutory instrument; and the regulations may make different modifications in relation to deceased persons dying at different times.

(3) The amendments made by paragraphs 3(2) and (3) have effect in relation to deaths, cases where scheme administrators become aware of deaths and cessation's of dependency occurring on or after 6 April 2008.

2 Transferable nil-rate bands—frequently asked questions

[The following was published on the HMRC website a few days after the Pre-Budget Report of 9 October 2007]

The Basics

What do you mean by a transferable nil-rate band?

A transferable nil-rate band arises when one party to a marriage or civil partnership dies and the amount of their estate that is chargeable to Inheritance Tax (IHT) does not use up all of the nil-rate band they are entitled to. Where this happens, the unused part can now be transferred to the surviving spouse or civil partner when they die.

How does that work then?

Everyone is entitled to a nil-rate band for IHT. Assets that pass from one spouse or civil partner to another are exempt from IHT. So if on death, someone leaves everything they own to their spouse or civil partner, it is exempt from IHT and they have not used any part of their nil-rate band. That unused nil-rate band can now be transferred to their surviving spouse or civil partner and used in working out the IHT liability on their estate when they die.

Does it matter when the deaths occurred?

Yes – this applies where the surviving spouse or civil partner died on or after 9th October 2007. But it does not matter how long before them their spouse or civil partner died. (Note: see paragraphs at the end of this Q&A about the impact for Capital Transfer Tax & Estate Duty).

How much is the nil-rate band?

For 2007/08 the nil-rate band is £300,000 – rising to £312,000 in 2008/09.

So you mean that if I inherited all the assets from my spouse or civil partner, my executors could add that nil-rate band to the nil-rate band that applies when I die?

Essentially yes – but it works by looking at proportion of the nil-rate band was unused when your spouse or civil partner died and uprating the nil-rate band available when you die by that same proportion.

What do you mean by uprating the nil-rate band available by the same proportion?

The amount to be transferred is worked out by taking the proportion of the nil-rate band that was unused on the first death and applying that to the nil-rate band available when you die. So if your spouse or civil partner left assets worth £150,000 to your children with everything else to you and the nil-rate band on the first death was £300,000; one-half of their nil-rate band is unused and is available for transfer. If, when you die, the nil-rate band had increased to £325,000, the amount available for transfer would be 50% of £325,000 or £162,500 giving your estate a nil-rate band of £325,000 + £162,500, or £487,500 in total.

What if my spouse of civil partner's estate was only worth £100,000, so that they did not need all of their nil-rate band. Is the amount that can be transferred tied to the amount that they actually left to me?

No – it doesn't matter what the size of first estate was, whatever proportion of the nil-rate band is unused may be transferred to you. If you spouse of civil partner's estate was worth only £100,000 and they left everything to you, they will not have used any part of their nil-rate band. So 100% of the nil-rate band is available for transfer when you die.

What about any gifts my spouse or civil partner may have made in the 7 years before they died; or any other assets that were chargeable when they died?

Gifts and any other assets that are chargeable on the first death (say assets in trust or assets owned jointly with a son or daughter) all eat into the nil-rate band in the normal way and so reduce the amount that may be available for transfer. (Note: see paragraphs at the end of this Q&A about in impact for Capital Transfer Tax & Estate Duty).

The process & recording keeping

How is the transfer made?

When the survivor dies, their personal representatives will make a claim to transfer the unused nil-rate band available from the first death. They will need to fill a claim form that will help them to work out how much of the nil-rate band is available for transfer. They will also need to provide certain documents to support their claim such as—

— the death certificate for the first person to die,

— the marriage certificate or civil partnership certificate for the couple,

— if the spouse or civil partner left a Will, a copy of it,

— a copy of the grant of probate/Confirmation, and

— if a Deed of Variation or other similar document was executed to change the people who inherited the estate of the spouse or civil partner, a copy of it.

The personal representatives should send the claim form and the supporting documents to HMRC when they send in the form IHT200 on the death of the survivor.

How long do the personal representatives have to make a claim?

The claim must be made within 24 months from the end of the month in which the survivor dies.

How will the personal representatives of the surviving spouse or civil partner know how much to claim?

When the estate of the first person to die is settled, their personal representatives will need to work out how much of the nil-rate band is transferable. They will then need to make sure the surviving spouse or civil partner knows what that amount is. They will need to let the surviving spouse or civil partner have sufficient documents and information so that when the surviving spouse or civil partner dies, their personal representatives can make a claim to transfer the unused nil-rate band. Where this happens people may want to consider keeping this information with their Will in a safe place.

What sort of documents and information do you have in mind?

So far as the person's own assets are concerned, the personal representatives for the first spouse or civil partner to die should let the surviving spouse or civil partner have—

— a copy of the HMRC return (form IHT205 or IHT200; in Scotland, forms C1 & C5)

— a copy of the deceased's Will (if any)

— a copy of any documents, such as a Deed of Variation, executed after the death of the first spouse or civil partner, that changes who benefits from their estate,

— any valuation(s) of assets that pass under Will or intestacy other than to the surviving spouse or civil partner,

— any evidence to support the availability of relief (such as agricultural or business relief) where the relievable assets pass to someone other than to the surviving spouse or civil partner.

But there can be other assets that are chargeable when someone dies such as—

— assets owned jointly with another person,

— assets held in trust from which the first to die was entitled to benefit and which are treated as forming part of their estate on death,

— any lifetime gifts made by the first to die in the 7 years before their death,

— any gifts made by the first to die where they did not give up possession and use of the assets, or where they retained a right to use the asset through an arrangement (a gift with reservation of benefit), and

— where the first to die was over 75, any alternatively secured pension fund from which they received a pension.

If any of these apply to the estate of the first person to die, the personal representatives will need to pass on information about these assets as well, for example—

— details of the assets concerned and evidence of their values,

— details about any exemptions and/or relief taken into account in arriving at the chargeable values.

We did not know about the need to keep records when the first person died and we do not have papers relating to that death – how can we make a claim?

The personal representatives will be able to obtain copies of some of the documents you need from—

— the Court Service (for England & Wales, www.hmcourts-service.gov.uk, for Scotland www.scotcourts.gov.uk, and for Northern Ireland www.courtsni.gov.uk), and

— the General Register Office (for England & Wales www.gro.gov.uk, for Scotland www.gro-scotland.gov.uk, and for Northern Ireland www.groni.gov.uk).

These will give you the value of the first estate that was declared for Probate/Confirmation and will also provide information about who inherited the assets that passed under the deceased's Will or intestacy. However, it will not provide any information about other assets that are chargeable when someone dies (list above). The personal representatives will need to make enquiries of those who inherited the first estate to see if they can recall whether or not there may have been other assets that were chargeable on the first death. If values are known, they should be included on the claim form; if values are not known, the personal representatives should complete the claim form to the best of their ability and explain the position to HMRC when they make they claim. If there is no evidence that any other assets were chargeable, the personal representatives can make their claim based on the information they have from the documents already mentioned.

What happens if the surviving spouse or civil partner loses the documents and information?

The information and documents about the claim could be very valuable to the second estate and it will be important to keep them safe. If the material is lost, the personal representatives will need to obtain copies of the documents required to substantiate the claim.

But suppose they are stolen, or destroyed in a fire?

Where something happens that is beyond the control of the surviving spouse or civil partner or their personal representatives, again the personal representatives will need to obtain copies of the documents required to substantiate the claim.

So there is nothing to do when the first person dies?

Not quite. It is important to work out what the transferable amount is and make sure that the surviving spouse or civil partner is given sufficient documents and information to support the claim their personal representatives will need to make. You should not contact HMRC to establish and agree the transferable amount when the first person dies.

What happens about agreeing values of assets like houses or household goods; and what about agreeing whether a relief such as agricultural or business relief applies?

It will only be necessary to agree values where such assets pass to chargeable beneficiaries on the first death (i.e. someone other than the surviving spouse or civil partner). This will be done when the surviving spouse or civil partner dies, but only where it is necessary to do so because the amount of the unused nil-rate band may affect the amount of IHT to pay on the second death. Similarly, if a farm is left to, say, a son and the personal representatives of the first death consider that agricultural relief is due against the whole property, the extent to which the relief is due will be established, if it is necessary, on the second death.

So what does this mean as far as information and documents left with the surviving spouse or civil partner is concerned?

The personal representatives of the estate of the first person to die will need to make sure that they take appropriate steps to value assets that pass to chargeable beneficiaries and to make sure that they give sufficient evidence to the surviving spouse or civil partner to support the values used and any relief that is considered due.

Isn't it easier to provide all this information and documents to HMRC on the first death and to agree values and the extent to which relief may be due at that time?

There is no telling how the circumstances of the surviving spouse or civil partner may change during the years before their death. It is possible that when they die, their estate is such that their personal representatives do not need to claim a transfer of unused nil-rate band (for example, it is covered by their own nil-rate band). In those circumstances, all the work done at the first death in agreeing the amount available for transfer will have been wasted. It is only sensible to defer this work until we know that it is actually relevant for IHT purposes on the second death.

Timing issues

Both parties to a marriage or civil partnership have died one shortly after the other. I want to apply for grants of probate, what should I do?

You should fill in the appropriate forms to apply for a grant in the estate of the first person to die in the normal way. This will allow you to establish how much of the nil-rate band is unused on the first death. You should then work out the size of the second estate by adding together the value of that person's own assets and any assets they inherited from the estate of the first spouse to die.

If this does not exceed single nil-rate band available to the estate of the second spouse or civil partner to die, there is no need to worry about transferring unused nil-rate band from the first death. Provided the other conditions are satisfied, you will be able to apply for a grant as an excepted estate.

If this does exceed the single nil-rate band, you will need to fill in form IHT200 for the estate of the second spouse or civil partner to die. You should also make a provisional claim to transfer the unused nil-rate band which should be based on the information available to you at the time you make your claim. You should indicate on the claim form that the value is an estimate and you should tell us what the final figure is once it is known. The estimated amount of the nil-rate band that can be transferred can be used to work out the tax payable on the second death.

Low value estates

How does the transferable nil-rate band affect whether the estate of the survivor qualifies as an excepted estate?

At present, the excepted estate rules remain as they are; so if the survivor's estate exceeds the single nil-rate band at their death (and assuming surviving spouse or civil partner exemption and charity exemption is not available), the estate cannot qualify as an excepted estate even though there may be no tax to pay because of transferred nil-rate band. So for the time being at least the survivor's personal representatives must deliver form IHT200 and make a claim to transfer the unused nil-rate band.

I'm going to leave all my estate to my spouse or civil partner; but between us our estates do not exceed one nil-rate band; what should I do?

You should still work out how much of your nil-rate band is available for transfer as the circumstances of your spouse or civil partner may change before they die. But if, when they die, their estate remains below a single nil-rate band and provided they have not remarried or entered into a new civil partnership, there is no need for their personal representatives to make a claim to transfer unused nil-rate band.

Miscellaneous

I want to change my Will in the light of these new rules, do I have to have the whole Will rewritten?

Not necessarily, it is possible to change parts of a Will by making a Codicil to the Will. This can revoke existing clauses and insert new ones. You may wish to speak to a solicitor about this.

What happens if my surviving spouse or civil partner remarries or enters into another civil partnership and they die before their new spouse or civil partner?

Where this happens, the nil-rate band available to your spouse or civil partner will be increased by any unused amount of your nil-rate band that their personal representatives wish to claim. If your surviving spouse or civil partner dies first and decides to leave all their assets to their new spouse or civil partner, then again, the full amount of the nil-rate band on their death is available for transfer to their new spouse or civil partner. But the maximum that can be added to anyone's own nil-rate band is 100% of the nil-rate band applicable to their death.

How does the idea of a transferable nil-rate band work where there is conditionally exempt property?

It all depends on whether the surviving spouse or civil partner dies before the conditional exemption ceases. Where the conditional exemption ceases before the survivor dies, the charge on cessation of the exemption will apply in the usual way – and if this exhausts the nil-rate, there will then be nothing left to transfer to the survivor. If, however, the survivor dies first and their personal representatives transfer the unused nil-rate band, the amount transferred will not be available for use when the conditional exemption ceases. Nevertheless, if this is some considerable time after the survivor dies, the charge on cessation of the exemption will still reflect any increase in the nil-rate band that has occurred between death and cessation.

I know that my spouse did not use up all their nil-rate band when they died and the unused portion is available for transfer to me. I want to make a lifetime gift that will give rise to an immediate liability to IHT, can I transfer the unused nil-rate band against this gift?

No, the unused nil-rate band can only be transferred to be used against your estate when you die. If you were to die within 7 years of making the immediately chargeable lifetime transfer, so that additional tax is payable on the gift as a result of your death, the transferred nil-rate band will be used in the normal way and may reduce any additional tax due as a result of your death – but you cannot transfer the unused nil-rate band against the tax due on a lifetime transfer at the time the transfer is made.

What's the position where my spouse or civil partner is domiciled outside the UK so relief for assets passing to them is restricted to £55,000?

This restriction may mean that bequests from you to your surviving spouse or civil partner will use up more of the nil-rate band available on the first death; but anything unused remains available for transfer and can be claimed by the personal representatives of the survivor when they die.

What do I do if all or most of the deceased's assets were jointly owned and so pass automatically to the surviving spouse or civil partner so that there is no need to take a grant of representation or Confirmation (in Scotland) on the first death?

Where the surviving spouse or civil partner is the other joint owner, it will be very important for them to keep information about any assets of the deceased that did not pass to them by survivorship, because the value of those assets will affect the proportion of nil-rate band that the personal representatives of the survivor will be able to claim. The same applies to any other assets that are chargeable to IHT on the deceased's death such as gifts made within 7 years that are not covered by one or other of the exemptions. Without all this information, it will be very difficult for the survivor's personal representatives to make a claim to transfer unused nil-rate band.

How does this work if the first death occurred during Capital Transfer Tax or Estate Duty?

The same basic principles apply, however, there will need to be some modifications to reflect the differences between IHT and Capital Transfer Tax (CTT)/Estate Duty. IHT was introduced on 18 March 1986, so points to bear in mind for deaths before that date are—

— Where the first spouse died between 13 March 1975 and 18 March 1986 then the estate would have been subject to CTT. Any transfers to the spouse would have been exempt from tax in the same way as for IHT and the transfer of nil-rate band provisions will operate in exactly the same way as it works for IHT.

— Before 13 March 1975 Estate Duty applied. Under Estate Duty there was no tax-free transfer permitted between spouses until 21 March 1972 when a tax-free transfer between spouses of up to £15,000 was introduced. This limit was removed for deaths after 12th November 1974.

— Where the first spouse died between 21 March 1972 and 13 March 1975 a claim to transfer the nil-rate band to the surviving spouse will be based on the amount of the tax free band that was unused on the death of the first spouse. For example, if a husband died in 1973 and left an estate valued at £10,000 that was all transferred to his wife, then as this is all within the spouse's exemption the husband's tax free band is unused. So if his widow dies in December 2007, her nil-rate band can be increased by 100% to £600,000. Where any part of the first spouse's individual tax free band was used then there will be a proportionate reduction in the amount by which the surviving spouse's IHT nil-rate band may be increased.

— Before 21 March 1972, there was no relief from Estate Duty for transfers between spouses so the amount by which the surviving spouse's IHT nil-rate band may be increased will be based on the proportion of the individual tax-free band that was unused on the death of the first spouse.

Were the rules about the assets that were chargeable on death any different for CTT & Estate Duty?

Again the basic principles remained the same, but there were some differences

— for CTT, initially, all the gifts made during an individual's lifetime were to be taken into account when they died, although this was limited to gifts within 7 years of the death during the first 7 years of CTT and this was subsequently cut from an unlimited cumulation to a period of 10 years in 1981.

— for Estate Duty, settled property in which the deceased had a life interest was not always aggregable with the estate on death.

If the first spouse died prior to 18 March 1986 and the question of other chargeable assets is relevant, and you are not sure what to include in your claims, please discuss the position with us first.

I am an Independent Financial Advisor with a range of products designed to make use of the nil-rate band, how will these be affected?

There will be no effect on these products, they will continue to work in exactly the same way as before.

I am divorced and my ex-husband has died without remarrying, can my personal representatives claim to transfer his unused nil-rate band to my estate when I die?

No, in order for your personal representatives to be able to make a claim to transfer unused nil-rate band, you must have still been married to your husband when he died.

Appendix 8

STEP Comment on Phizackerley

[The following is reproduced, with kind permission of the Society of Trust and Estate Practitioners, from a News Release originally published by them on their website in April 2007]

Phizackerley shows some advisors should be "more searching", couples should seek advice of experienced professionals

The case of *Phizackerley v CIR* has caused some concern amongst couples who have established a "debt or charge scheme" and amongst some trust and estate practitioners.

Tony Harris of STEP Technical Committee said: "The debt or charge scheme is complicated, both in its establishment and its management. *Phizackerley* tell us that the enquiries that professionals have to make should be more searching than some previously thought. Couples are advised to seek the advice of an experienced and qualified professional rather than rely on generalists."

Phizackerley v CIR reminds us that the fact that gifts between spouses are themselves exempt does not take those gifts outside the scope of section 103 of the Finance Act 1986. In practical terms, this will increase costs because of the extra enquiries to be made and, where it is appropriate for the residue of the estate to be left to the surviving spouse on an interest in possession trust rather than absolutely, extra time will be needed to explain how s103 works and how to avoid the trap that has caught the family of Mrs Phizackerley.

The English love houses and tend to tie up much of the family wealth in the family home with the result that few spouses are able, at death, to leave liquid assets equal to the nil-rate band to their children without unduly stretching the financial resources of the surviving spouse. The money is in the home.

The debt or charge scheme commonly operates by terms of the will under which the first spouse to die leaves the amount available to him or her of the nil-rate band at death to trustees for, usually, the immediate family, with residue to the surviving spouse. In the absence of sufficient liquidity, the gift of the nil-rate sum is satisfied in one of several ways, the commonest of which is effectively a promise of payment by the surviving spouse or a charge over the half share of the house owned by the first spouse to die.

The result is that the trustees of the nil-rate band have under their control only such liquidity as there may have been in the estate of the first spouse to die plus a loan document in respect of the balance of the nil-rate band. It is hoped that the value of the debt will in due course reduce the estate of the surviving spouse.

A full press briefing can be found at www.step.org/showarticle.pl?id=1837.

Table of Cases

This table is referenced to paragraph numbers in the work.

Table of Statutes

Table of Statutory Instruments

Index

GENERAL TERMS AND CONDITIONS
FOR USE OF THE COMPACT DISC GOODS
AND MATERIALS CONTAINED THEREIN

This Licence Agreement is between Reed Elsevier (UK) Limited trading as LexisNexis Butterworths ("we or us") and the individual or company ("you") to whom LexisNexis has agreed to supply the Compact Disc Goods ("the Goods") and the Materials and content contained therein ("the Materials"). The following terms and conditions govern your use of the Goods supplied by LexisNexis and the Materials available therein:

1. LICENCE; RESTRICTIONS ON USE

1.1   You are granted a non-exclusive, non-transferable, limited licence to access and use the Goods and the Materials from time to time made available to you for the purposes only of (i) research or study, (ii) providing professional services to your clients, and (iii) providing academic services to students. This licence is subject to the following limitations:

(a)   The right to electronically display the Materials retrieved from the Goods is limited to the display of such Materials primarily to one person at a time;

(b)   The right to obtain a printout of the Materials is limited to single printout of the Materials downloaded (collectively, "Authorised Printouts"). You are not permitted to sell these Authorised Printouts; and

(c)   The right to retrieve and store machine-readable copies of the Materials is limited to the retrieval of a single copy of the Materials included in the Goods and storage of that copy in machine readable form primarily for one person's exclusive use. You are not permitted to transfer the Goods or the Materials electronically or via any other medium for commercial profit or for resale.

1.2   To the extent expressly permitted by applicable copyright law, you may make copies of Authorised Printouts and distribute Authorised Printouts and copies.

1.3   Except as specifically provided in Sections 1.1 and 1.2, you are otherwise prohibited from downloading, storing, reproducing, transmitting, displaying, printing, copying, distributing, or using the Materials retrieved from the Goods.

1.4   All right, title, and interest (including all copyrights and other intellectual property rights) in the Goods and the Materials (in both print and machine-readable forms) belong to us or our third party suppliers. You acquire no ownership of copyright or other intellectual property rights or proprietary interest in the Goods, the Materials, or copies thereof.

1.5   Except as specifically provided herein, you may not use the Goods or the Materials retrieved from the Goods in any fashion that infringes the copyright or proprietary interests therein.

1.6   You may not remove or obscure the copyright notice or other notices contained in the Materials retrieved from the Goods.

2. ACCESS TO SERVICES

2.1   Only you shall be entitled to access and use the Goods and the Materials ("Authorised Users").

2.2   Except for use incidental to occasional, short-term travel, you may not access the Goods and the Materials from outside the country for which it was issued.

2.3   Materials and features may be added to or withdrawn from the Goods and the Goods otherwise changed without notice.

2.4   You must ensure that each person having access to the Goods and the Materials:
(a)   is an Authorised User; and
(b)   is using those Goods and the Materials only in accordance with these General Terms and Conditions.

3. LIMITED WARRANTY

3.1   We represent and warrant that we have the right and authority to make the Goods and the Materials available pursuant to these General Terms and Conditions.

3.2   EXCEPT AS OTHERWISE PROVIDED IN SECTION 3.1, THE GOODS AND THE MATERIALS ARE PROVIDED ON AN "AS IS", "AS AVAILABLE" BASIS AND WE MAKE NO EXPRESS WARRANTIES UNDER THIS AGREEMENT, INCLUDING WITHOUT LIMITATION THAT THE GOODS AND THE MATERIALS ARE OR WILL BE COMPLETE OR FREE FROM ERRORS OR THAT INFORMATION WILL CONTINUE TO BE AVAILABLE TO US TO ENABLE US TO KEEP THE GOODS AND THE MATERIALS UP-TO-DATE.

4. LIMITATION OF LIABILITY

4.1   To the maximum extent permitted by law, a Covered Party (as defined below) shall not be liable for any loss, injury, claim, liability, or damage of any kind resulting in any way from (a) any errors in or omissions from the Goods or any Materials available or not included therein, (b) the unavailability or interruption to the supply of the Goods or any features thereof or any Materials, (c) any Authorised Users use or misuse of the Goods or Materials (regardless of whether you received any assistance from a Covered Party in using or misusing the Goods), (d) your use of any equipment in connection with the Goods, (e) the content of Materials, (f) any delay or failure in performance of the Goods, or (g) any negligence of a Covered Party or its employees, contractors or agents in connection with the performance of our obligations under this agreement.

4.2   "Covered Party" means (a) us, our affiliates, and any officer, director, employee, subcontractor, agent, successor, or assign of us or our affiliates; and (b) each third party supplier of the Materials, their affiliates, and any officer, director, employee, subcontractor, agent, successor, or assign of any third party supplier of the Materials or any of their affiliates.

4.3   Our liability to you for breach of any condition or warranty implied under any law which cannot be lawfully modified or excluded by this agreement shall, to the extent permitted by law, be limited at our option to supplying the Goods or the Materials again or paying for their re-supply. Nothing in this Agreement is intended to exclude liability for death or personal injury resulting from any negligence by us.

4.4   Our liability to you for loss or damage of any kind (including loss or damage caused by negligence) is reduced to the extent that you caused or contributed to that loss or damage.

4.5   SUBJECT TO CLAUSE 4.3, THE AGGREGATE LIABILITY OF THE COVERED PARTIES IN CONNECTION WITH ANY OTHER CLAIM ARISING OUT OF OR RELATING TO THE GOODS OR THE MATERIALS SHALL NOT EXCEED THE AMOUNT OF YOUR ACTUAL DIRECT DAMAGES. YOUR RIGHT TO MONETARY DAMAGES IN THAT AMOUNT SHALL BE IN LIEU OF ALL OTHER REMEDIES WHICH YOU MAY HAVE AGAINST ANY COVERED PARTY.

4.6   SUBJECT TO CLAUSE 4.3, THE COVERED PARTIES SHALL NOT BE LIABLE FOR ANY SPECIAL, INDIRECT, INCIDENTAL, OR CONSEQUENTIAL DAMAGES OF ANY KIND WHATSOEVER (INCLUDING, WITHOUT LIMITATION, LEGAL FEES) IN ANY WAY DUE TO, RESULTING FROM, OR ARISING IN CONNECTION WITH THE GOODS, THE MATERIALS, OR THE FAILURE OF ANY COVERED PARTY TO PERFORM ITS OBLIGATIONS, REGARDLESS OF ANY NEGLIGENCE OF ANY COVERED PARTY.

4.7   The Materials are provided for reference purposes only and are not intended, nor should they be used, as a substitute for professional advice or judgement or to provide legal advice with respect to particular circumstances.

4.8   Whilst reasonable efforts are made to make sure the Materials are up to date, you should obtain independent verification or advice before relying upon any piece of information in circumstances where loss or damage may result.

5. MISCELLANEOUS

5.1   These General Terms and Conditions may be changed from time to time as described below or by written agreement.

5.2   The failure of us or any third party supplier of the Materials to enforce any provision hereof shall not constitute or be construed as a waiver of such provision or of the right to enforce it at a later time.

5.3   You may not assign your rights or delegate your duties under these General Terms and Conditions without our prior written consent.

5.4   These General Terms and Conditions shall be governed by and construed in accordance with the laws of England.

5.5   Each third party supplier of the Materials has the right to assert and enforce these provisions directly on its own behalf as a third party beneficiary.

5.6   We will use personal information collected about Authorised Users for the purposes of (a) providing access to and use of the Goods to Authorised Users, (b) providing customer support, billing and other similar activities related to the Goods, and (c) keeping Authorised Users informed about products, services, offers and upcoming events and to improve our services. We may also provide personal information about Authorised Users to third parties for the purpose of providing Authorised Users with direct marketing offers which we think may be of interest. If you do not wish to receive information about other products, services, offers and events, notify us in writing.

5.7   In accordance with the Data Protection Act 1998 we will provide and export personal information about Authorised Users to other members of our company group, including Reed Elsevier Inc. in the United States, for the purposes of (a) providing access to and use of the Goods to Authorised Users, and (b) providing customer support, billing and other similar activities related to the Goods.

5.8   Save for the owners of any intellectual property supplied by us, no third parties shall acquire any rights under this Agreement and the provisions of the Contracts (Rights of Third Parties) Act 1999 are excluded.

5.9   All Rights Reserved © Reed Elsevier.